The Legal
Answer Book for
Private Foundations

WILEY NONPROFIT LAW, FINANCE, AND MANAGEMENT SERIES

The Art of Planned Giving: Understanding Donors and the Culture of Giving by Douglas E. White

Beyond Fund Raising: New Strategies for Nonprofit Investment and Innovation by Kay Grace

Budgeting for Not-for-Profit Organizations by David Maddox

The Complete Guide to Fund Raising Management by Stanley Weinstein

The Complete Guide to Nonprofit Management by Smith, Bucklin & Associates

Critical Issues in Fund Raising edited by Dwight Burlingame

Faith-Based Management: Leading Organizations that Are Based on More than Just Mission by Peter Brinckerhoff

Financial and Accounting Guide for Not-for-Profit Organizations, Sixth Edition by Malvern J. Gross, Jr., Richard F. Larkin, John H. McCarthy, PricewaterhouseCoopers LLP

Financial Empowerment: More Money for More Mission by Peter Brinckerhoff

Financial Management for Nonprofit Organizations by Jo Ann Hankin, Alan Seidner, and John Zietlow

The First Legal Answer Book for Fund-Raisers by Bruce R. Hopkins

Fund-Raising Fundamentals: A Guide to Annual Giving for Professionals and Volunteers by James M. Greenfield

Fundraising Cost Effectiveness: A Self-Assessment Workbook by James M. Greenfield

Fund-Raising Regulation: A State-by-State Handbook of Registration Forms, Requirements, and Procedures by Seth Perlman and Betsy Hills Bush

Grantseeker's Budget Toolkit by James A. Quick and Cheryl S. New

Grantseeker's Toolkit: A Comprehensive Guide to Finding Funding by Cheryl S. New and James A. Quick

Grant Winner's Toolkit: Project Management and Evaluation by James A. Quick and Cheryl S. New

High Impact Philanthropy: How Donors, Boards, and Nonprofit Organizations Can Transform Nonprofit Communities by Kay Sprinkel Grace and Alan L. Wendroff

High Performance Nonprofit Organizations: Managing Upstream for Greater Impact by Christine W. Letts, William P. Ryan, and Allen Grossman

Improving the Economy, Efficiency, and Effectiveness of Nonprofits: Conducting Operational Reviews by Rob Reider

Intermediate Sanctions: Curbing Nonprofit Abuse by Bruce R. Hopkins and D. Benson Tesdahl

International Fund Raising for Nonprofits by Thomas Harris

International Guide to Nonprofit Law by Lester A. Salamon and Stefan Toepler & Associates

Joint Ventures Involving Tax-Exempt Organizations, Second Edition by Michael I. Sanders

The Law of Fund-Raising, Second Edition by Bruce R. Hopkins

The Law of Tax-Exempt Healthcare Organizations, Second Edition by Thomas K. Hyatt and Bruce R. Hopkins

The Law of Tax-Exempt Organizations, Seventh Edition by Bruce R. Hopkins

The Legal Answer Book for Nonprofit Organizations by Bruce R. Hopkins

A Legal Guide to Starting and Managing a Nonprofit Organization, Third Edition by Bruce R. Hopkins

The Legislative Labyrinth: A Map for Not-for-Profits, edited by Walter Pidgeon

Managing Affordable Housing: A Practical Guide to Creating Stable Communities by Bennett L. Hecht, Local Initiatives Support Corporation, and James Stockard

Mission-Based Management: Leading Your Not-for-Profit in the 21st Century, Second Edition by Peter Brinckerhoff

Mission-Based Management: Leading Your Not-for-Profit in the 21st Century, Second Edition, Workbook by Peter Brinckerhoff

Mission-Based Marketing: How Your Not-for-Profit Can Succeed in a More Competitive World by Peter Brinckerhoff

Nonprofit Boards: Roles, Responsibilities, and Performance by Diane J. Duca

Nonprofit Compensation and Benefits Practices by Applied Research and Development Institute International, Inc.

The Nonprofit Counsel by Bruce R. Hopkins

The Nonprofit Guide to the Internet, Second Edition by Michael Johnston

Nonprofit Investment Policies: A Practical Guide to Creation and Implementation by Robert Fry, Jr.

The Nonprofit Law Dictionary by Bruce R. Hopkins

Nonprofit Compensation, Benefits, and Employment Law by David G. Samuels and Howard Pianko

The Nonprofit Handbook, Third Edition: Management by Tracy Daniel Connors

The Nonprofit Handbook, Third Edition: Fund Raising by James M. Greenfield

The Nonprofit Manager's Resource Dictionary by Ronald A. Landskroner

Nonprofit Organizations' Business Forms: Disk Edition by John Wiley & Sons, Inc.

Planned Giving: Management, Marketing, and Law, Second Edition by Ronald R. Jordan and Katelyn L. Quynn

Private Foundations: Tax Law and Compliance by Bruce R. Hopkins and Jody Blazek

Program Related Investments: A Technical Manual for Foundations by Christie I Baxter

Reengineering Your Nonprofit Organization: A Guide to Strategic Transformation by Alceste T. Pappas

Reinventing the University: Managing and Financing Institutions of Higher Education by Sandra L. Johnson and Sean C. Rush, PricewaterhouseCoopers LLP

The Second Legal Answer Book for Nonprofit Organizations by Bruce R. Hopkins

The Second Legal Answer Book for Fund Raisers by Bruce R. Hopkins

Social Entrepreneurship: The Art of Mission-Based Venture Development by Peter Brinckerhoff

Special Events: Proven Strategies for Nonprofit Fund Raising by Alan Wendroff

Starting and Managing a Nonprofit Organization: A Legal Guide, Third Edition by Bruce R. Hopkins

Strategic Communications for Nonprofit Organizations: Seven Steps to Creating a Successful Plan by Janel Radtke

Strategic Planning for Nonprofit Organizations: A Practical Guide and Workbook by Michael Allison and Jude Kaye, Support Center for Nonprofit Management

Streetsmart Financial Basics for Nonprofit Managers by Thomas A. McLaughlin

A Streetsmart Guide to Nonprofit Mergers and Networks by Thomas A. McLaughlin

Successful Marketing Strategies for Nonprofit Organizations by Barry J. McLeish

Successful Corporate Fund Raising: Effective Strategies for Today's Nonprofits by Scott Sheldon

The Tax Law of Colleges and Universities by Bertrand M. Harding

Tax Planning and Compliance for Tax-Exempt Organizations: Forms, Checklists, Procedures, Third Edition by Jody Blazek

The Universal Benefits of Volunteering: A Practical Workbook for Nonprofit Organizations, Volunteers and Corporations by Walter P. Pidgeon, Jr.

Trade Secrets for Every Nonprofit Manager by Thomas A. McLaughlin

Values-Based Estate Planning: A Step-by-Step Approach to Wealth Transfers for Professional Advisors by Scott Fithian

The Legal
Answer Book for
Private Foundations

Bruce R. Hopkins
and
Jody Blazek

John Wiley & Sons, Inc.
New York • Chichester • Weinheim • Brisbane • Singapore • Toronto

Copyright © 2002 by John Wiley & Sons, Inc. All rights reserved.

Published simultaneously in Canada.

This publication is designed to provide accurate and authoritative information in regard to the subject matter covered. It is sold with the understanding that the publisher is not engaged in rendering legal, accounting, or other professional services. If legal advice or other expert assistance is required, the services of a competent professional person should be sought.

Library of Congress Cataloging-in-Publication Data:

Hopkins, Bruce R.
    The private foundation legal answer book / Bruce R. Hopkins and Jody Blazek.
      p.   cm. — (Wiley nonprofit law, finance, and management series)
    Includes index.
    ISBN 0-471-40579-5 (pbk. : alk. paper)
    1. Charitable uses, trusts, and foundations—United States—Miscellanea. 2. Charitable uses, trusts, and foundations—Taxation—United States—Miscellanea. I. Blazek, Jody.
    II. Title. III. Series
    KF1389.Z9 H67 2001
    346.73'064—dc21   2001045654

10 9 8 7 6 5 4 3 2 1

About the Authors

Bruce R. Hopkins is a lawyer in Kansas City, Missouri, having practiced law in Washington, D.C., for 26 years. He specializes in the representation of charitable and other nonprofit organizations, including private foundations. His practice ranges over the entirety of legal matters involving nonprofit organizations, with an emphasis on foundation law issues, charitable giving (including planned giving), the formation of nonprofit organizations, acquisition of recognition of tax-exempt and public charity status, unrelated business planning, application of intermediate sanctions, use of nonprofit and for-profit subsidiaries, and review of annual information returns.

Mr. Hopkins served as chair of the Committee on Exempt Organizations, Tax Section, American Bar Association; chair, Section of Taxation, National Association of College and University Attorneys; and president, Planned Giving Study Group of Greater Washington, D.C. He was accorded the Assistant Commissioner's (IRS) Award in 1984.

Mr. Hopkins is the series editor of Wiley's Nonprofit Law, Finance, and Management Series. In addition to co-authoring *The Legal Answerbook for Private Foundations,* he is the author of *The First Legal Answer Book for Fund-Raisers, The Second Legal Answer Book for Fund-Raisers, The Law of Fund-Raising, Second Edition; The Tax Law of Charitable Giving, Second Edition; The Legal Answer Book for Nonprofit Organizations; The Second Legal Answer Book for Nonprofit Organizations; The Law of Tax-Exempt Organizations, Seventh Edition; Charity, Advocacy, and the Law; The Nonprofit Law Dictionary; Starting and Managing a Nonprofit Organization: A Legal Guide, Third Edition;* and is co-author, with Jody Blazek, of *Private Foundations: Tax Law and Compliance;* with D. Benson Tesdahl, of *Intermediate Sanctions: Curbing Nonprofit Abuse;* and with Thomas K. Hyatt, of *The Law of Tax-Exempt Healthcare Organizations, Second Edition.* He also writes *The Nonprofit Counsel,* a monthly newsletter, published by John Wiley & Sons.

ABOUT THE AUTHORS

Mr. Hopkins earned his J.D. and LL.M. degrees at the George Washington University and his B.A. at the University of Michigan. He is a member of the bar of the District of Columbia and the state of Missouri.

Jody Blazek is a partner in Blazek & Vetterling LLP, a Houston CPA firm focusing on tax and financial planning for exempt organizations and the individuals who create, fund, and work with them. BV provides tax compliance, auditing, and planning services to over 200 nonprofit organizations.

Jody began her professional career at KPMG, then Peat, Marwick, Mitchell & Co. Her concentration on exempt organizations began in 1969 when she was assigned to study the Tax Reform Act that completely revamped the taxation of charities and created the law of private foundations. From 1972 to 1981, she gained nonprofit management experience as treasurer of the Menil Interests where she worked with John and Dominique de Menil to plan the Menil Collection, The Rothko Chapel, and other projects of the Menil Foundation. She reentered public practice in 1981 to found the firm she now serves.

She is the author of four books in the Wiley Nonprofit Series: 990 *HANDBOOK (2001) Tax Planning and Compliance for Tax-Exempt Organizations, 3rd Edition* (1999), *Financial Planning for Nonprofit Organizations* (1996), and *Private Foundations: Tax Law and Compliance* (1998) co-authored with Bruce R. Hopkins.

Jody is the chair of the Tax-Exempt Organizations Resource Panel and the Internet Services Task Force of the American Institute of Certified Public Accountants. She serves on the national editorial board of Tax Analysts' *The Exempt Organization Tax Review,* and the Community Service Committee of the Houston Chapter of Certified Public Accountants. She is a founding director of Texas Accountants and Lawyers for the Arts and a member of the board of the Gulf Coast Institute, the Anchorage Foundations, Houston Artists Fund, Main Street Coalition, and the River Pierce Foundation. She is a frequent speaker at nonprofit symposia, including those sponsored by Conference of Southwest Foundations, Association of Small Foundations, AICPA, New York and Texas Societies of CPAs, The University of Texas School of Law, United Way of the Texas Gulf Coast, and Nonprofit Resource Center, among others.

Blazek received her B.B.A. from University of Texas at Austin in 1964 and took selected tax courses at South Texas School of Law. She and her husband, David Crossley, nurture two sons, Austin and Jay Blazek Crossley.

The private foundation rules are really scary.

—Seminar Participant

Preface

Development of the Wiley Legal Answer Books series on subjects concerning federal and state law of interest to nonprofit organizations continues apace. This book is the fifth in the collection; more are in progress. The objective is the provision of information about this law in a direct and efficient manner, keeping technicalities to a minimum.

This objective notwithstanding, private foundations are a unique breed of nonprofit organization. Though relatively few in number, foundations are subject to a battery of complex, intricate, and tricky legal requirements that have become a significant component of nonprofit law. (Indeed, this body of law is slowly being imported to other fields, particularly those involving public charities.) In short, private foundations are heavily regulated. This mass of law, in other words, is a lawyer's or accountant's dream—and managers' and trustees' nightmare.

Foundations are restricted as to the extent of deductible giving to them and to their programs and other activities, forced to expend sums of money annually, limited as to their business holdings, restricted as to investments, taxable on their net investment income, required to file complex annual information returns—the list goes on. It is no wonder that alternatives to private foundations exist, and that the number of these options is increasing.

Private foundations have been favored, nonetheless, over the years by philanthropists as a way to create a family legacy. Families benefit from working together to support worthy causes. Many foundations today allow future generations to join the foundation board at an early age to foster their understanding of governance and financial affairs. It is hoped that this book can serve as a useful tool to all generations seeking guidance about the special rules pertaining to foundations.

Although the rules appear draconian at first glance, there are many useful exceptions, without which the overall scheme could not work. Once foundation representatives study and establish policies to comply with the rules, most find management of a private foundation to be a rewarding and personally ful-filling responsibility.

To assure foundation funds are not used to advance personal interests, Congress in 1969 imposed a complicated set of tax rules to constrain certain types of foundation activity. The names given to the rules connote their objec-tives—self-dealing, mandatory distributions, jeopardizing investments, excess business holdings, and taxable expenditures. Some advise against the crea-tion of a private foundation because the tax law levies penalties that can be imposed when the rules are violated. True enough: Intentional violations and disregard for the rules can result in severe sanctions. Except for self-dealing transactions, however, unintentional mistakes can be forgiven (technically, abated). We trust this book can provide an understandable matrix within which one can freely, and without fear of penalties, create and operate a private foundation.

Without doubt, careful attention must be paid in particular to the self-dealing rules because they generally mandate that a private foundation may have absolutely no financial transactions with those that control and fund it, nor their family members. A private foundation cannot make a grant to satisfy a binding pledge made by one of its directors or rent use of his or her airplane, for example. Readers will find, nonetheless, that more than a little leeway is allowed. Reasonable compensation, for example, can be paid for services actually rendered in serving the foundation, and expenses incurred by board members can be reimbursed. The foundation may not, on the other hand, buy a million-dollar piece of property from its founder for any price, regardless of the benefit the foundation might realize from the transaction.

The mandatory distribution rules say a private foundation must annually spend money to support its charitable mission. The minimum amount is equal to 5 percent of the value of the foundation's investment assets during the pre-ceding year. Assets that are devoted to charitable purposes, such as a historic building, student loan receivable, or an art collection, are not included in this calculation. If the foundation distributes more than it is required to for the year, the excess payout is carried over to offset distributions required during the next five years. The foundation's administrative expenses and the excise tax are counted as qualifying distributions.

A private foundations is prohibited from owning investments that jeop-ardize, or expose, its assets to substantial risk of loss. Its trustees or directors are expected to exercise fiduciary responsibility and adhere to the prudent investor rules. Diversification of its investment portfolios to protect its assets against market fluctuations of the various financial sectors is expected. A small portion of its assets, for example, might be held in a hedge fund to protect against market declines. Certain investment types, such as margined security purchases, uncovered puts and calls, working interests in oil properties, and others are said to require special scrutiny to prove they do not jeopardize the foundation's assets.

An impermissible excess business holding occurs when a private foun-dation's ownership combined with shares owned by its insiders exceeds more than 20 percent interest in a business enterprise. A foundation also may not itself own and operate a business. Although a foundation can receive a gift that creates an excess holding situation, it must dispose of the excess within five years of the time of its receipt. Due to the self-dealing rules, the foundation cannot sell its interests to a trustee or family member. Funding a private foundation with the family business requires careful attention to these rules.

In pursuing their mission, foundations are expected to sponsor programs that prompt charitable, religious, educational, or scientific purposes. Most foundations grant money to other charities in the United States and throughout the world. Some foundations hire staff to directly conduct charitable programs. The taxable expenditure rules require a private charity to maintain enhanced documentation and make special reports to the IRS if it grants money to another private charity or to a foreign organization. Though a foundation can study and publish information regarding public affairs, it is prohibited from making any attempts to influence the decisions of a legislative body. In contrast, a public charity can, within limits, seek to influence public affairs by lobbying to change the law. A foundation may make grants to individuals for study, travel, and the like, but must do so pursuant to a plan approved in advance by the IRS.

What to make of all this? One solution we arrived at was writing a book, intended to capture and discuss the basics of private foundation law—as well as every nuance of this panoply of law we could conjure up. *Private Foundations: Tax Law and Compliance* was published in 1997 and is regularly supplemented.

Still, this remains a tough area of the law to get a handle on, particularly for nonlawyers. While we don't want to discourage purchases of *Private Foundations: Tax Law and Compliance,* we think the format of *The Legal Answer Book for Private Foundations* lends itself nicely to grasping the massive amount of private foundation law. In preparing the book, we set about recalling the many questions we get in our practices and during seminars about the basics of private foundation law, and some of the subleties as well. They are all in this book, albeit with a few enhancements. (As noted in another Legal Answer Book, this can be a delightful position to be in: answering questions that the answerer posed.) Truth be told, there are also some questions in the book that weren't asked—but we wish they had been.

The book is intended to enable its users to promptly resolve a problem or answer a question before them. To facilitate its usefulness, all of the questions answered in this book are listed at the beginning. There is also an index. Endnotes have been kept to a minimum. (For more, see "How to Use This Book" on page xiii.) Those who need additional information on a private foundation law matter can—you guessed it—turn to *Private Foundations: Tax Law and Compliance* and its progeny.

We want to thank Louise Jacob at John Wiley & Sons, our managing editor on this book, for her fine work.

BRUCE R. HOPKINS
JODY BLAZEK

Contents

How to Use This Book

The Legal Answerbook for Private Foundations is designed for trustees and officers of private foundations, their lawyers and accountants, and others who need quick and authoritative answers concerning the law governing the structure and operation of foundations. It is designed to help the reader not only better understand this law, but, more important, to show how to work with it and within its boundaries while maintaining and enhancing the programs of private foundations. This book uses simple, straightforward language and avoids technical jargon when possible. This question-and-answer format offers a clear and useful guide to understanding the complex, but extremely important, area of the statutes, regulations, and other law governing private foundations. Citations are provided as research aids for those who need to pursue particular items in greater detail.

Numbering System: The question numbering system has been designed for ease of use. The questions are numbered consecutively within each chapter (e.g., 5:1, 5:2, 5:3).

List of Questions: The detailed List of Questions that follows the Contents in the front of this book helps the reader locate areas of immediate interest. This listing serves as a detailed table of contents.

Index: The index at the back of this book provides a further aid to locating specific information. All references in the index are to question numbers rather than page numbers.

List of Questions

CHAPTER 2   Disqualified Persons

LIST OF QUESTIONS

CHAPTER 3   Self-Dealing

CHAPTER 4 Mandatory Payout Requirements

CHAPTER 5   **Excess Business Holdings**

CHAPTER 6   Jeopardizing Investments

CHAPTER 7   Taxable Expenditures

LIST OF QUESTIONS

CHAPTER 10   Annual Information Return

CHAPTER 11   Disclosure and Substantiation Rules

CHAPTER 12   Public Charities

CHAPTER 13   **Termination of Private Foundation Status**

CHAPTER 16   Tax Exemption Recognition Process

CHAPTER 17   Charitable Contribution Deductions

LIST OF QUESTIONS

CHAPTER 1

Basic Legal Definitions

One of the most complex bodies of statutory law in the tax-exempt organizations setting is the battery of rules applicable to private foundations. Created over 30 years ago, the private foundation rules are the subject of hundreds of private determinations by the Internal Revenue Service (IRS) (and a few court opinions), and this process continues unabated. New issues constantly arise. This body of law can be onerous and, because of a myriad of penalty excise taxes, can be costly.

If a charitable organization can avoid being a private foundation, it is well advised to do so. If, however, private foundation status is unavoidable, the rules governing private foundations must be faced. Life as a private foundation is by no means impossible, but the organization's management and its advisors should proceed with caution.

Here are the questions most frequently asked (or those that should be asked) about the basic legal definitions in the private foundation rules—and the answers to them.

Q 1:1 What is a *private foundation*?

There is no affirmative definition of the term *private foundation*. The statutory definition basically states that a private foundation is a charitable organization[1] that is not a public charity (Q 1:2).

Generically, a private foundation has four characteristics:

1. It is a charitable organization.[2]
2. It is initially funded from one source (usually an individual, a married couple, a family, or a business).
3. Its ongoing income derives from investments (in the nature of an endowment fund).

4. It makes grants to other charitable organizations rather than operate its own program.

The nature of its funding and, sometimes, the nature of its governance (i.e., a closed, family-oriented board of trustees) are the characteristics that make this type of charitable organization *private*. This entity is sometimes referred to as the *standard* private foundation (Q 1:34).

NOTE: The Internal Revenue Code is misleading in this regard. The pertinent Code section is styled "Private foundation defined."[3] But, in fact, that section does not define the phrase *private foundation* at all. Rather, it defines what a private foundation *is not,* by listing the types of charitable organizations that are not private foundations.

Also, although technically this is not part of a *definition* of the term *private foundation,* there are some organizations that, for one or more purposes, are *treated as* private foundations, such as charitable remainder trusts (Q 17:28).

Q 1:2   What is a *public charity*?

There are several types of public charities (Chapter 12). One category includes churches, integrated auxiliaries of churches, associations and conventions of churches, universities, colleges, schools, hospitals, medical research organizations, and certain governmental entities. These are sometimes referred to as the *institutions* (Q 12:2).

Another category of public charity is the publicly supported charity. There are two basic types of publicly supported charity: the *donative* type (principally supported by gifts and grants) (Q 12:4) and the *service provider* type (principally supported by exempt function revenue, gifts, and/or grants) (Q 12:8).

The third category of public charity is the *supporting organization* (Q 12:15).

In applying these definitions of the term *public charity,* and in deciphering the private foundation rules, it is often critical that the charitable organization know which persons are disqualified persons (Q 1:3) with respect to it.

Q 1:3   What is a *disqualified person*?

A basic concept of the tax laws relating to private foundations is that of the *disqualified person* (Chapter 2). Essentially, a disqualified person is a person (including an individual, corporation, partnership, trust, or estate) that has a particular, usually intimate, relationship with respect to a private foundation.[4]

Thus, disqualified persons are commonly trustees, directors, officers, substantial contributors, members of their families, and controlling and controlled entities. The first three of these persons are collectively known as *foundation managers.* A controlling person is a *20 percent owner,* and controlled entities are corporations, partnerships, trusts, and estates.

In the public charity context, this definition generally is inapplicable. (It is used, however, in connection with the computation of public support in the case of service provider publicly supported entities (Q 12:8).) The term *disqualified person,* however, is used as part of the intermediate sanctions rules.[5] In that context, the term is broader in scope than that in the private foundation setting, in that the concept of *member of the family* there includes siblings (Q 2:15).

Also, in the public charity context, the *private inurement* doctrine applies.[6] There, the equivalent to the disqualified person is the *insider.* There is considerable controversy as to the sweep of this term. Clearly, the idea of the *insider* embraces trustees, directors, officers, and key employees. The controversy, however, is whether and to what extent it extends to vendors of goods and services, such as fund-raising companies.[7]

Q 1:4   Just what are the *private foundation rules*?

The federal tax law governing the operations of private foundations is a composite of rules pertaining to self-dealing (Chapter 3), mandatory payout requirements (Chapter 4), business holdings (Chapter 5), investment practices (Chapter 6), various types of expenditures (Chapter 7), and more.

Q 1:5   What are the sanctions for violation of these rules?

The sanctions for violation of these rules are five sets of excise taxes, with each set entailing three tiers of taxation. The three tiers are known as the *initial tax,*[8] the *additional tax,*[9] and the *involuntary termination tax.*[10]

In general, when there is a violation, the initial tax must be paid; the additional tax is levied only when the initial tax is not timely paid and the matter not timely corrected (Q 1:10). The termination tax (Chapter 13)—a third tax—is levied when the other two taxes have been imposed and there continues to be willful, flagrant, or repeated acts or failures to act giving rise to one or more of the initial or additional taxes.

Because of the stringency of these rules, the sanctions are far more than merely taxes; rather they are a system of absolute prohibitions.

Q 1:6   What are the rules concerning *self-dealing*?

In general, the federal tax law prohibits acts of self-dealing between a private foundation and a disqualified person (Chapter 3).[11] An act of self-dealing may be *direct* or *indirect.* The latter generally is a self-dealing transaction between a disqualified person and an organization controlled by a private foundation.[12]

The sale or exchange of property between a private foundation and a disqualified person generally constitutes an act of self-dealing.[13] The transfer of real or personal property by a disqualified person to a private foundation is treated as a sale or exchange if the property is subject to a mortgage or similar lien that the foundation assumes, or if it is subject to a mortgage or similar lien that a disqualified person placed on the property within the 10-year period ending on the date of transfer.[14]

The following generally constitute acts of self-dealing:

- The leasing of property between a private foundation and a disqualified person.[15]
- The lending of money or other extension of credit between a private foundation and a disqualified person.[16]
- The furnishing of goods, services, or facilities between a private foundation and a disqualified person.[17]
- The payment of compensation (or payment or reimbursement of expenses) by a private foundation to a disqualified person.[18]

The transfer to, or use by or for the benefit of, a disqualified person of the income or assets of a private foundation generally constitutes self-dealing.[19] Unlike the other sets of rules describing specific categories of acts of self-dealing, this one is a catch-all provision designed to sweep into the ambit of self-dealing a variety of transactions that might otherwise technically escape the discrete transactions defined to be those of self-dealing. Benefits to a disqualified person can occur when the foundation's assets are used by one or more parties that are not disqualified persons. There is no requirement that a disqualified person is intended to be benefited.

This is one of the most dangerous aspects of the self-dealing rules, in that self-dealing can occur without the parties realizing it. Part of the problem is that the *benefit* involved can be intangible, such as increased goodwill,[20] enhanced reputation,[21] and the provision of marketing advantages[22]—all with respect to nondisqualified persons.

TIP: This phraseology is also in the definition of the term *excess benefit transaction.*[23] As is the case with respect to much of the law defining self-dealing, developments in the private foundation arena can be used to interpret the intermediate sanctions rules. The reverse also is true.

An agreement by a private foundation to make a payment of money or other property to a government official generally constitutes self-dealing, unless the agreement is to employ the individual for a period after termination of his or her government service if the individual is terminating service within a 90-day period.[24]

Q 1:7   Are there any exceptions to the self-dealing rules?

There are many exceptions to the self-dealing rules. For example, in relation to the general prohibition on leasing transactions (Q 1:6), the leasing of property by a disqualified person to a private foundation without charge is not an act of self-dealing.[25] Likewise, in respect to the general prohibition on extensions of credit (Q 1:6), this rule does not apply to an extension of credit by a disqualified person to a private foundation if the transaction is without interest or other charge and the proceeds of the loan are used exclusively for charitable purposes.[26]

Concerning the general ban on furnishing of goods, services, or facilities (Q 1:6), the furnishing of goods, services, or facilities by a disqualified person to a private foundation is not an act of self-dealing if they are furnished without charge and used exclusively for charitable purposes.[27] Moreover, the furnishing of goods, services, or facilities by a private foundation to a disqualified person is not self-dealing if the furnishing is made on a basis no more favorable than that on which the goods, services, or facilities are made available to the general public.[28]

As to the rules in respect to compensation (Q 1:6), except in the case of a governmental official, the payment of compensation (or payment or reimbursement of expenses) by a private foundation to a disqualified person for the performance of personal services that are reasonable and necessary to carrying out the charitable purpose of the foundation is not self-dealing if the compensation (or payment or reimbursement) is not excessive.[29]

CAUTION: This exception is not necessarily as attractive as it might initially appear. A court held that the term *personal services* is confined to services that are "essentially professional and managerial" in nature.[30] In that case, the services involved were found not to qualify for the exception, being general maintenance, janitorial, and custodial services.

As to the catch-all provision (Q 1:6), the fact that a disqualified person receives an incidental or tenuous benefit from a private foundation's use of its income or assets will not, by itself, make the use an act of self-dealing.[31] In the case of a government official, the self-dealing rules do not apply to the receipt of certain prizes and awards, scholarship and fellowship grants, annuities, gifts, and traveling expenses.[32]

By reason of another exception, a transaction between a private foundation and a corporation that is a disqualified person with respect to the foundation is not an act of self-dealing if the transaction is engaged in pursuant to a liquidation, merger, redemption, recapitalization, or other corporate adjustment, organization, or reorganization.[33] For this exception to apply, all the securities of the same class as those held by the foundation prior to the transfer must be subject to the same terms, and these terms must provide for receipt by the foundation of no less than fair market value.[34]

Q 1:8   When does an act of self-dealing *occur*?

An act of self-dealing *occurs* on the date on which all of the terms and conditions of the transaction and the liabilities of the parties have been fixed.[35]

Q 1:9   What is the *amount involved*?

The *amount involved* generally is the greater of the amount of money and the fair market value of the other property given or the amount of money and the fair market value of the other property received.[36]

Q 1:10   What does *correction* mean?

Correction of an act of self-dealing means undoing the transaction that constituted the act to the extent possible, but in no case may the resulting financial position of the private foundation be worse than would be the case if the disqualified person was dealing under the highest fiduciary standards.[37] This means return to the private foundation of the amount involved (Q 1:9), plus another element (usually the payment of a suitable amount of interest), so as to place the parties in the position they were in before the transaction occurred.

NOTE: For example, in the case of excessive compensation (Q 1:6, Q 3:13), correction of the act of self-dealing includes return to the foundation of the excess portion of the compensation paid.

There are special rules in this regard in the context of the additional taxes (Q 1:5):

- In the case of the additional tax imposed in connection with the mandatory distribution rules (Q 1:15), the term *correct* means reducing the amount of undistributed income to zero.[38]
- In the case of the additional tax imposed in connection with the excess business holdings rules (Q 1:19), the term means reducing the amount of the excess business holdings to zero.[39]
- In the case of the additional tax imposed in connection with the jeopardizing investments rules (Q 1:22), the term means removing the investment from jeopardy.[40]

Q 1:11   What are the penalties for self-dealing?

An initial tax is imposed on each act of self-dealing between a disqualified person and a private foundation. The tax is imposed on the self-dealer at the rate of 5 percent of the amount involved (Q 1:9) with respect to the act for each year in the taxable period or part of a period.[41] Where this initial tax is imposed, a tax of 2½ percent of the amount involved is imposed on the participation of any foundation manager in the act of self-dealing, where the manager knowingly participated in the act.[43] This tax is not imposed, however, where the participation was not willful and was due to reasonable cause.[44] This tax, which must be paid by the foundation manager, may not exceed $10,000.[45]

CAUTION: The aspect of the self-dealing penalties rules represented by the words "for each year" requires emphasis. Each year with a set of self-dealing facts extant brings a new round of penalties. In one instance involving a loan to a disqualified person—remember, an extension of credit to a disqualified person can be self-dealing (Q 1:6, Q 3:8)—the matter concerned a 40-year mortgage. The IRS observed that there was a potential in these facts for 40 separate acts of self-dealing.[42]

Where an initial tax is imposed and the self-dealing act is not timely corrected (Q 1:10), an additional tax is imposed in an amount equal to 200 percent of the amount involved. This tax must be paid by the disqualified person (other than a foundation manager) who participated in the act of self-dealing.[46] An additional tax equal to 50 percent of the amount involved, up to $10,000,[47] is imposed on a foundation manager (where the additional tax is imposed on the self-dealer) who refuses to agree to all or part of the correction.[48]

In a case where more than one person is liable for any initial or additional tax with respect to any one act of self-dealing, all of the persons are jointly and severally liable for the tax or taxes.[49]

Willful repeated violations of these rules may result in involuntary termination of the private foundation's status and the imposition of additional taxes.[50] The involuntary termination tax thus serves as a third-tier tax.

Q 1:12   What are the mandatory distribution rules?

A private foundation is required to distribute, for each year, at least a minimum amount of money and/or property for charitable purposes (Chapter 4).[51] The amount that must be distributed by a private foundation, with respect to each year, is the *distributable amount*.[52] That amount must be in the form of *qualifying distributions,* which essentially are grants, outlays for administration, and payments made to acquire charitable assets.[53]

Generally, the distributable amount for a private foundation is an amount equal to 5 percent of the value of the noncharitable assets of the foundation.[54] This is the *minimum investment return.*[55] The distributable amount also includes amounts equal to repayments to a foundation of items previously treated as qualifying distributions (e.g., scholarship loans), amounts received on disposition of assets previously treated as qualifying distributions, and amounts previously set aside for a charitable project but not so used.[56]

Q 1:13   What are the *charitable assets* of a private foundation?

The *charitable assets* of a private foundation are of two categories. One is those actually used by the foundation in carrying out its charitable objectives. The other category is assets owned by the foundation where it has convinced the IRS that their immediate use for exempt purposes is not practical and that definite plans exist to commence a related use within a reasonable period of time.[57]

Thus, the assets that are in the minimum investment return base are those held for the production of income or for investment (e.g., stocks, bonds, interest-bearing notes, endowment funds, and leased real estate).[58] Where property is used for both exempt and other purposes, it is considered to be used exclusively for tax-exempt purposes where the exempt use represents at least 95 percent of the total use; otherwise, a reasonable allocation between the two uses is required.[59]

Q 1:14   Are there any exceptions to the mandatory distribution rules?

No, not as such. There is, however, an exception to the *timing* of distributions by a private foundation for mandatory payout purposes. This is the *set-aside,* whereby funds are credited for a charitable purpose rather than immediately granted; where the requirements are met, the set-aside is regarded as a qualifying distribution.[60]

One type of set-aside is that referenced in the *suitability test.* This requires a specific project, a payment period not to exceed 60 months, and a ruling from the IRS.[61] The other type of set-aside is the subject of the *cash distribution test.* This test entails set percentages of distributions over a multiyear period and does not require an IRS ruling.[62]

Q 1:15   What are the penalties for failure to meet the distribution rules?

An initial tax of 15 percent is imposed on the undistributed income of a private foundation that, for any year, has not been distributed on a timely basis in the form of qualifying distributions (Q 4:21).[63] In a case in which an initial tax is imposed on the undistributed income of a private foundation for a year, an additional tax is imposed on any portion of the income remaining undistributed at the close of the taxable period.[64] This tax is equal to 100 percent of the amount remaining undistributed at the close of the period.[65]

Payment of these taxes is required in addition to, rather than in lieu of, making the required distributions.[66]

The involuntary termination taxes[67] serve as third-tier taxes.

Q 1:16   What are the excess business holdings rules?

Private foundations are limited as to the extent to which they can own interests in commercial business enterprises (Chapter 5).[68] A private foundation and all disqualified persons with respect to it generally are permitted to hold no more than 20 percent of a corporation's voting stock or other interest in a business enterprise. These are *permitted holdings.*[69] If effective control of the business can be shown to be elsewhere, a 35 percent limit may be substituted for the 20 percent limit.[70] A private foundation must hold, directly or indirectly, more than 2 percent of the value of a business enterprise before these limitations become applicable.[71]

Q 1:17   Are there any exceptions to the excess business holdings rules?

There are three principal exceptions to these rules. One, the rules do not apply in the case of a business where at least 95 percent of its gross income is derived from passive sources.[72] These sources generally include dividends, interest, annuities, royalties, and capital gain.[73]

The second exception is for holdings in a *functionally related business.*[74] This is a business:

- That is substantially related to the achievement of the private foundation's exempt purposes (other than merely providing funds for the foundation's programs);
- In which substantially all the work is performed for the private foundation without compensation;
- Carried on by a private foundation primarily for the convenience of its employees;
- That consists of the selling of merchandise, substantially all of which was received by the foundation as contributions; or
- That is carried on within a larger aggregate of similar activities or within a larger complex of other endeavors that is related to the exempt purposes of the foundation.[75]

The third exception is for *program-related investments* (Q 1:21).[76]

Q 1:18   These excess business holdings rules seem strict; are there any relief provisions?

If a private foundation obtains holdings in a business enterprise, in a transaction that is not a purchase by the foundation or by disqualified persons with respect to it, and the additional holdings would result in the foundation's having an excess business holding, the foundation has five years to reduce the holdings to a permissible level without penalty.[77]

Moreover, the IRS has the authority to allow an additional five-year period for the disposition of excess business holdings in the case of an unusually large gift or bequest of diverse business holdings or holdings with complex corporate structures.[78] This latter rule entails several requirements, including a showing that diligent efforts were made to dispose of the holdings within the initial five-year period and that disposition within that five-year period was not possible (except at a price substantially below fair market value) by reason of the size and complexity or diversity of the holdings.

Q 1:19   What are the penalties for violation of the excess business holdings rules?

An initial excise tax is imposed on the excess business holdings of a private foundation in a business enterprise for each tax year that ends during the taxable period.[79] The amount of this tax is 5 percent of the total value of all of the private foundation's excess business holdings in each of its business enterprises.[80]

If the excess business holdings are not disposed of during the period, an additional tax is imposed on the private foundation. The amount of this tax is 200 percent of the value of the excess business holdings.[81]

The involuntary termination taxes[82] serve as third-tier taxes.

Q 1:20   What are the jeopardizing investments rules?

There are rules governing the type of investments that a private foundation is allowed to make (Chapter 6).[83] In general, a private foundation cannot invest any amount—income or principal—in a manner that would jeopardize the carrying out of any of its tax-exempt purposes.[84] An investment is considered to jeopardize the carrying out of the exempt purposes of a private foundation if it is determined that the foundation managers, in making the investment, failed to exercise ordinary business care and prudence, under the facts and circumstances prevailing at the time of the investment, in providing for the long-term and short-term financial needs of the foundation in carrying out its charitable activities.[85]

A determination as to whether the making of a particular investment jeopardizes the exempt purposes of a private foundation is made on an investment-by-investment basis, in each case taking into account the private foundation's portfolio in its entirety.[86] Although the IRS will not rule as to an investment procedure governing investments to be made in the future, it will rule as to a currently proposed investment.[87]

There is no category of investments that is treated as a per se violation of these rules. There are, however, types or methods of investment that are closely scrutinized to determine whether the foundation managers have met the requisite standard of care and prudence. These include trading in securities on margin, trading in commodity futures, investments in oil and gas syndications, the purchase of puts and calls (and straddles), the purchase of warrants, and selling short.[88]

Q 1:21   Are there any exceptions to these rules?

A *program-related investment* is not a jeopardizing investment. This is an investment the primary purpose of which is to accomplish one or more charitable purposes, and no significant purpose of which is the production of income or the appreciation of property.[89] A purpose of the investment may not be the furthering of substantial legislative or political campaign activities.[90]

Q 1:22   What are the penalties for violation of the jeopardizing investments rules?

If a private foundation invests in such a manner as to jeopardize the carrying out of any of its charitable purposes, an initial tax is imposed on the foundation on the making of the investment, at the rate of 5 percent of the amount so invested for each year or part of a year in the taxable period.[91]

In any case in which this initial tax is levied, a tax is imposed on the participation of any foundation manager in the making of the investment, knowing that it is jeopardizing the carrying out of any of the foundation's exempt purposes. This tax is equal to 5 percent of the amount so invested for each year of the foundation (or part of the year) in the period.[92] With respect to any one investment, the maximum amount of this tax is $5,000.[93] This tax, which must be paid by any participating foundation manager, is not imposed where the participation was not willful and was due to reasonable cause.[94]

An additional tax is imposed in any case in which this initial tax is imposed and the investment is not removed from jeopardy within the period. This tax, which is to be paid by the private foundation, is at the rate of 25 percent of the amount of the investment.[95] In any case in which this additional tax is imposed and a foundation manager has refused to agree to all or part of the removal of the investment from jeopardy, a tax is imposed at the rate of 5 percent of the amount of the investment.[96] With respect to any one investment, the maximum amount of this tax is $10,000.[97]

Where more than one foundation is liable for an initial tax or an additional tax with respect to a jeopardizing investment, all of the managers are jointly and severally liable for the taxes.[98]

The involuntary termination taxes[99] serve as third-tier taxes.

Q 1:23   What are the taxable expenditures rules?

The federal tax law provides restrictions, in addition to those discussed earlier, on the activities and purposes for which private foundations may expend their funds (Chapter 7).[100] These rules pertain to matters such as legislative activities, electioneering, grants to individuals, grants to noncharitable organizations, and grants for noncharitable purposes. Improper and, in effect, prohibited expenditures are termed *taxable expenditures.*

Q 1:24   What are the rules concerning lobbying?

One form of taxable expenditure is an amount paid or incurred by a private foundation to carry on propaganda or otherwise attempt to influence legislation.[101] Thus, the general rule by which charitable organizations can engage in a certain amount of legislative activity[102] is inapplicable to private foundations.

Attempts to influence legislation generally include certain communications with a member or employee of a legislative body or with an official or employee of an executive department of a government who may participate in formulating legislation, as well as efforts to affect the opinion of the general public or a segment of it.[103] An expenditure is an attempt to influence legislation if it is for a *direct lobbying communication* or a *grassroots communication.*[104]

Engaging in nonpartisan analysis, study, or research and making the results of this type of undertaking available to the general public (or a segment of it) or to governmental bodies or officials is not a prohibited form of legislative activity.[105] Likewise, amounts paid or incurred in connection with the provision of technical advice or assistance to a governmental body or committee (or subdivision of it) in response to a written request from the entity do not constitute taxable expenditures.[106]

Another exception is that the taxable expenditures rules do not apply to any amount paid or incurred in connection with an appearance before or communication to a legislative body with respect to a possible decision of that body that might affect the existence of the private foundation, its powers and duties, its tax-exempt status, or the deductibility of contributions to the foundation.[107]

NOTE: This is known as the *self-defense exception.*

Expenditures for examination and discussions of broad social, economic, and similar issues are not taxable even if the problems are of the types with which government would be expected to deal ultimately.[108]

Q 1:25   What are the rules concerning electioneering?

The term *taxable expenditure* encompasses an amount paid or incurred by a private foundation to influence the outcome of a specific public election or to carry on, directly or indirectly, a voter registration drive.[109] The first of these prohibitions generally parallels the prohibition on political campaign activities by all charitable organizations.[110]

A private foundation may, however, engage in electioneering activities (including voter registration drives) without making a taxable expenditure, where a variety of criteria are satisfied, such as not confining the activity to one election period and carrying it on in at least five states.[111]

Q 1:26   What are the rules concerning grants to individuals?

The term *taxable expenditure* also encompasses an amount paid or incurred by a private foundation as a grant to an individual for travel, study, or other similar purposes.[112] This type of grant is not prohibited, however, if it is awarded on an objective and nondiscriminatory basis pursuant to a procedure approved in advance by the IRS, and if the IRS is satisfied that the grant is one of three types. These are:

1. A scholarship or fellowship grant that is excludable from the recipient's gross income and used for study at an educational institution
2. A prize or award that is excludable from the recipient's gross income, where the recipient is selected from the general public

3. A grant for which the purpose is to achieve a specific objective, produce a report or similar product, or improve or enhance a literary, artistic, musical, scientific, teaching, or other similar capacity, skill, or talent of the grantee[113]

The requirement as to objectivity and nondiscrimination generally necessitates that the group from which grantees are selected be chosen on the basis of criteria reasonably related to the purposes of the grant. The group must be sufficiently broad so that the making of grants to members of the group would be considered to fulfill a charitable purpose.[114] The individual or group of individuals who select grant recipients should not be in a position to derive a private benefit as the result of the selection process.[115]

These rules as to individual grants generally require:

- The receipt by a private foundation of an annual report from the beneficiary of a scholarship or fellowship[116]
- That a foundation investigate situations indicating that all or a part of a grant is not being used in furtherance of its purposes[117]
- Recovery or restoration of any diverted funds, and withholding of further payments to a grantee in an instance of improper diversion of grant funds[118]

A private foundation must maintain certain records pertaining to grants to individuals.[119]

Q 1:27 What are the rules concerning grants to noncharitable organizations?

A private foundation may make grants to an organization that is not a public charity. When it does so, however, it must exercise *expenditure responsibility* with respect to the grant.[120] A private foundation is considered to be exercising expenditure responsibility in connection with a grant as long as it exerts all reasonable efforts and establishes adequate procedures to see that the grant is spent solely for the purpose for which it was made, obtains full and complete reports from the grantee on how the funds were spent, and makes full and detailed reports with respect to the expenditures to the IRS.[121]

Q 1:28 What are the rules concerning grants for noncharitable purposes?

The term *taxable expenditure* encompasses an amount paid or incurred by a private foundation for a *noncharitable* purpose.[122] Ordinarily, only an expenditure for an activity that was a substantial part of the organization's total activities, and that would cause loss of tax exemption, is a taxable expenditure.[123]

Expenditures ordinarily not treated as taxable expenditures are:

- Expenditures to acquire investments entered into for the purpose of obtaining income or funds to be used in furtherance of charitable purposes
- Reasonable expenses with respect to investments
- Payment of taxes
- Any expenses that qualify as deductions in the computation of the unrelated business income tax (see Chapter 9.)
- Any payment that constitutes a qualifying distribution (Q 4:10) or an allowable deduction pursuant to the investment income tax rules (Q 8:15)
- Reasonable expenditures to evaluate, acquire, modify, and dispose of program-related investments (Q 6:7)
- Business expenditures by the recipient of a program-related investment

Conversely, expenditures for unreasonable administrative expenses, including compensation, consultants' fees, and other fees for services rendered, are ordinarily taxable expenditures, unless the private foundation can demonstrate that the expenses were paid or incurred in the good-faith belief that they were reasonable and that the payment or incurrence of the expenses were in amounts consistent with ordinary care and prudence.[124]

Q 1:29   What are the penalties for violation of the taxable expenditures rules?

An excise tax is imposed on a taxable expenditure of a private foundation, which is to be paid by the foundation at the rate of 10 percent of the amount of the taxable expenditure.[125] An excise tax is imposed on the agreement of any foundation manager to the making of a taxable expenditure by a private foundation.[126] This latter initial tax is levied only where the private foundation initial tax is imposed, the manager knew that the expenditure to which he or she agreed was a taxable one, and the agreement was not willful and was due to reasonable cause. This initial tax, which is at the rate of 2½ percent of each taxable expenditure, must be paid by the foundation manager.[127]

An excise tax is imposed in any case in which an initial tax is imposed on a private foundation because of a taxable expenditure and the expenditure is not corrected (Q 1:10) within the taxable period. This additional tax is to be paid by the private foundation and is at the rate of 100 percent of the amount of the taxable expenditure.[128] An excise tax, in any case in which an initial tax has been levied, is imposed on a foundation manager if there has been a taxable expenditure and the foundation manager has refused to agree to part or all of the correction of the expenditure. This additional tax, which is at the rate of 50 percent of the amount of the taxable expenditure, is to be paid by the foundation manager.[129]

When more than one foundation manger is liable for an excise tax with respect to the making of a taxable expenditure, all the foundation managers are jointly and severally liable for the tax.[130] The maximum aggregate amount collectible as an initial tax from all foundation managers with respect to a taxable expenditure is $5,000; the maximum aggregate amount so collectible as an additional tax is $10,000.[131]

The second-tier excise taxes are imposed at the end of the taxable period. This period begins with the event giving rise to the expenditure tax and ends on the earlier of (1) the date a notice of deficiency with respect to the first-tier tax is mailed or (2) the date the first-tier tax is assessed if a deficiency notice is not mailed.[132]

The involuntary termination taxes[133] serve as third-tier taxes.

Q 1:30   Can these initial taxes be abated?

Generally, yes. Where the IRS is satisfied that (1) a *taxable event* was due to reasonable cause and not to willful neglect and (2) the event was corrected within the *correction period* for the event, then

- An initial tax imposed with respect to the event (including interest) will not be assessed.
- If the tax is assessed, the assessment will be abated.
- If the tax is collected, it will be credited or refunded as an overpayment.[134]

As noted (Q 1:5), these taxes are often referred to as the *initial taxes.* They are also sometimes referred to as the *first-tier taxes.*[135] In the abatement context, however, the taxes must be *qualified first-tier taxes.*[136]

CAUTION: The word *qualified* is a part of this terminology for a special reason: The IRS's abatement authority does not extend to the initial tax imposed in the self-dealing setting (Q 1:11).[137]

For these purposes, a *taxable event* is an act, or a failure to act, that gives rise to liability for tax under the various private foundation rules (Q 1:4).[138] The *correction period* is, with respect to a taxable event, the period beginning on the date the event *occurs* (Q 1:31) and ending 90 days after the date of mailing[139] of a notice of deficiency with respect to the additional tax imposed on the event.[140] This period may be extended by (1) a period in which a deficiency cannot be assessed[141] and (2) any other period that the IRS determines is reasonable and necessary to bring about correction of the taxable event.[142]

Q 1:31   When does a taxable event *occur*?

There are three rules for determining when a taxable event *occurs.* Two of these rules are unique to particular private foundation rules and one is general.

1. In the case of the mandatory distribution rules (Q 1:12), a taxable event is treated as occurring on the first day of the year for which there was a failure to distribute income.[143]
2. In the case of the excess business holdings rules (Q 1:16), the taxable event is treated as occurring on the first day on which there are excess business holdings.[144]
3. In all other instances, the taxable event is treated as occurring on the date the event actually occurred.[145]

Q 1:32   Can these additional taxes be abated?

Yes, under certain circumstances. As noted (Q 1:5), these taxes often are referred to as the *additional taxes.* They also are sometimes referred to as the *second-tier taxes.*[146]

The abatement rule in this context is this: If a taxable event (Q 1:31) is corrected (e.g., Q 1:10) during the applicable correction period (Q 1:30), then, as to any additional tax imposed with respect to the event (including interest, additions to the tax, and additional amounts):

- An additional tax imposed with respect to the event (including interest) will not be assessed.
- If the tax is assessed, the assessment will be abated.
- If the tax is collected, it will be credited or refunded as an overpayment.[147]

If there is a determination by a court that a person is liable for an additional tax, and that determination has become final, the court has jurisdiction to conduct any necessary supplemental proceedings to determine whether the taxable event was corrected during the correction period. There are rules as to when these and other proceedings must begin and when they must be suspended.[148]

Q 1:33   Are there other private foundation rules?

Yes, there are more. An excise tax of 2 percent is generally imposed on the net investment income of private foundations for each tax year (Chapter 8).[149] This tax must be estimated and paid quarterly, generally following the estimated tax rules for corporations.[150] Under certain circumstances, this tax rate is reduced to 1 percent in a year where the foundation's payout for charitable purposes (Q 1:12, Q 8:18) is increased by an equivalent amount.[151]

As to certain of the private foundation rules, nonexempt charitable trusts[152] and split-interest trusts[153] are treated as private foundations.[154]

A 4 percent tax is imposed on the gross investment income derived from sources within the United States by foreign organizations that constitute private foundations.[155]

Q 1:34   Is there more than one type of private foundation?

Yes. The entity that is normally thought of when the term *private foundation* is used is the *standard* private foundation. This is the typical grant-making private foundation. The standard private foundation essentially has, as noted (Q 1:1), four characteristics.

Private Operating Foundation

There is a hybrid entity—a blend of the characteristics of a public charity (Q 1:2) and a private foundation—known as the *private operating foundation.* These are organizations that, while not qualifying as public charities, devote most of their earnings and much of their assets directly to the conduct of their own tax-exempt purposes. That is, they make qualifying distributions (Q 1:12) directly for the active conduct of charitable activities.[156]

NOTE: The basic distinction, then, between a standard and an operating foundation is this matter of distributions. The private operating foundation makes its required charitable expenditures by sponsoring and managing its own programs. The standard private foundation makes grants to other organizations.

Typically, a private operating foundation is an entity that should be a public charity but cannot qualify as such because it is not one of the institutions (Q 1:2) and has a large endowment that precludes it from being a publicly supported organization (*id.*). Classic examples are museums and libraries.

To be considered as *operating,* the foundation must focus and spend a specified annual amount on one or more projects in which it is significantly involved in a continuing and sustainable fashion. The requisite involvement is, as a general rule, found to be present where the foundation's expenditures are made directly or used by it to purchase the goods and services that advance its purposes, rather than being paid to or indirectly through an intermediary organization.

A typical private operating foundation, being significantly involved in its programs, maintains a staff (which may be or include volunteers) of program specialists, researchers, teachers, administrators, or other comparable personnel needed to supervise, direct, and carry out its programs on a continuing basis. This type of foundation usually acquires and maintains assets used in its programs, such as buildings, collections of art objects or specimens, or research facilities. Qualifying direct expenditures also include the purchase of books and publications, supplies, computer programs, and project costs (i.e., food in the case of an organization feeding the poor and travel and equipment in the instance of an organization pursuing archeological studies).

To be a private operating foundation, the organization must satisfy an *income test.* Annually, it must expend directly, for the active conduct of its exempt activities, an amount equal to substantially all of the lesser of its adjusted net income or its minimum investment return.[157] In this setting, the phrase *substantially all* means at least 85 percent.[158] As noted, the minimum investment return is equal to 5 percent of the foundation's assets that are not used for charitable purposes (Q 1:12).

To qualify as a private operating foundation, an organization must satisfy at least one of three other tests:

1. The *assets test*: At least 65 percent of its assets must be devoted directly to the active conduct of its charitable activities.[159]
2. The *endowment test*: The organization must normally expend its funds directly for the active conduct of its charitable activities in an amount equal to at least two-thirds of its minimum investment return $(\frac{2}{3} \times 5 = 3\frac{1}{3})$.[160]
3. The *support test*: At least 85 percent of its support (other than investment income) must be normally received from the general public and/or at least five tax-exempt organizations (that are not disqualified persons); no more than 25 percent of its support can be derived from any one exempt organization; and no more than one-half of its support can be normally received in the form of gross investment income.[161]

Because of these rules, a private operating foundation is not subject to the minimum payout requirement imposed on standard private foundations (Q 1:12). Contributions to a private operating foundation are deductible to the full extent permitted for gifts to public charities. (See Chapter 12.) That is, the percentage limitations that restrict the deductibility of contributions to standard private foundations (Q 1:41) do not apply to gifts to private operating foundations.

Exempt Operating Foundation

Not content with the complexity introduced with the hybrid form of private foundation known as the private operating foundation, Congress created a hybrid of a hybrid. This entity is known as the *exempt operating foundation*.[162]

NOTE: The word *exempt* does not mean exempt from federal income taxes (which private foundations generally are in any case).

Exempt operating foundations are presumably otherwise private operating foundations, but they enjoy two characteristics that the others do not have:

1. Grants to an exempt operating foundation are exempt from the expenditure responsibility requirements otherwise imposed on grantor foundations (Q 7:24).
2. An exempt operating foundation does not have to pay the tax imposed on other private foundations' net investment income (Chapter 8).

NOTE: This, then, is the meaning of the word *exempt*: These operating foundations are exempt from these requirements and taxes.

To be an exempt operating foundation, an organization must (in addition to satisfying the requirements to be a private operating foundation) meet three tests:

1. It must have been publicly supported (Q 12:4, Q 12:8) for at least 10 years or have qualified as an operating foundation as of January 1, 1983.
2. It must have a board of directors that, during the year involved, consists of individuals at least 75 percent of whom are not *disqualified individuals* and was broadly representative of the general public (presumably using the facts and circumstances test (Q 12:5)).
3. It must not have an officer who is a disqualified individual at any time during the year involved.

These rules were written for the entities that are not really private foundations (the standard variety) but cannot meet the formal qualifications for public charity status—again, endowed entities such as museums. This approach is a compromise for them: They are treated as public charities in the sense that private foundation support for them does not trigger the expenditure responsibility requirements, and they do not have to pay the tax on net investment income.

COMMENT: Perhaps someday Congress will enact federal tax law provisions providing public charity status for entities such as museums, libraries, and like entities. The difficulty, of course, is the need to write these rules in sufficiently narrow fashion, if the original congressional intent in creating the private foundation rules is to be preserved.

NOTE: This area of the law, then, may be perceived as a spectrum, with standard private foundations on one end, followed by private operating foundations, followed by exempt operating foundations, followed by various forms of public charities. One of the anomalies of this law is that an organization that is able to qualify as an exempt operating foundation often is able to qualify under the facts and circumstances test (Q 12:5)—and thereby avoid all of the private foundation rules!

Q 1:35   Are private foundations subject to the unrelated business rules?

Yes. These rules do not often apply to private foundations, however, because foundations cannot actively engage in unrelated business undertakings; if they did, the activity would be an excess business holding, such as a sole propri-etorship (Q 1:16).

The federal tax law imposes a tax on organizations that derive net income from activities that do not further their exempt functions.[163] This income is called unrelated business income ("UBI"). Pursuant to the general rules, UBI is generated if (1) the activity constitutes a trade or business[164]; (2) the trade or business is regularly carried on[165]; and (3) the trade or business is not substantially related to the organization's exempt purposes.[166]

Private foundations, nonetheless, can derive unrelated business income from passive sources. Thus, the excess business holdings rules do not extend to a business where at least 95 percent of its income is passive, such as divi-dends, interest, annuities, royalties, and capital gains (Q 1:17).

A private foundation's primary UBI risk may well relate to the develop-ment of real property it acquired by gift. There may be several parcels of real property that should be further developed to maximize their respective values. The subdivision and development of certain parcels of real property may be viewed by the IRS as a trade or business resulting in recognition of UBI when the parcels are sold. If multiple sales and significant development occurs, the foundation may be viewed as a dealer in the real property rather than an investor. The foundation's sale of parcels that are treated as its inventory will be subject to the tax on UBI, whereas the sale of investment property would be exempt from UBI taxation by reason of the exclusion for capital gains.[167]

There is no bright-line test to determine when the real property shifts from investment property to inventory and, therefore, becomes subject to UBI taxation. The IRS and the courts utilize a facts and circumstances test to determine whether the tax-exempt organization in this circumstance is a dealer. Such factors as (1) the purpose of the acquisition, (2) the cost of prop-erty sold, (3) frequency, continuity, and size of sales, (4) sales activities, (5) improvements made, (6) the proximity of time of sale and time of purchase, (7) purpose for acquisition, and (8) market conditions will be analyzed in this regard. Many planning opportunities exist to maximize value while minimizing the tax paid, including the use of an installment sale approach and use of a for-profit subsidiary to develop the property. A for-profit subsidiary may not be utilized by a private foundation (because of the excess business holdings rules) but would be available were there a conversion of the foundation to public charity status (Q 1:2).

Q 1:36 Are private foundations required to file annual information returns with the IRS?

Yes. Every private foundation is required to file an annual information return with the IRS (Chapter 10).[168] This return is on Form 990-PF. Tax-exempt organizations generally have some exceptions in this area, such as for small organizations (i.e., those that normally receive more than $25,000 in revenues annually[169]). This is not the case with foundations; all foundations, including those without revenues or assets, are obligated to file.

This annual information return has several functions. It solicits the basic financial information—revenue, disbursements, assets, and liabilities—that is classified into meaningful categories to allow the IRS to statistically evaluate the scope and type of foundation activity, to measure the foundation's taxable investment income, and to tally the disbursements counted in connection with the foundation's minimum payout requirement.

The form has special parts containing questions designed to ferret out instances of noncompliance with the various federal tax law requirements, such as excessive compensation, other forms of self-dealing, inadequate payouts, excessive business holdings, jeopardizing investments, and taxable expenditures.

Q 1:37 Are private foundations subject to document disclosure and dissemination rules?

Yes. Private foundations are subject to the rules applicable to all tax-exempt organizations, by which their application for recognition of tax exemption and their three most recent annual information returns may be inspected at the foundation's office(s) during regular business hours (Chapter 11).[170] Foundations are also subject to relatively recent document dissemination rules, pursuant to which photocopies of these documents must be provided to those who request them (*id.*).

NOTE 1: The document dissemination rules do not apply where the organization makes them "widely available" (i.e., accessible on the Internet) or where the request is part of a "harassment campaign."

NOTE 2: The effective date for the document dissemination rules for tax-exempt organizations generally was June 8, 1999.[171] The effective date for these rules as applicable to private foundations was March 13, 2000.[172]

Q 1:38 Can a private foundation terminate its private foundation status?

Yes. A private foundation can voluntarily terminate its private foundation status (Chapter 13). There are essentially two ways to accomplish this type of termination:

1. The foundation can terminate its status as an entity. This is done by a distribution of all of its net assets to one or more qualified public charities, as long as each of them has been in existence (as a public charity) for a continuous period of at least 60 calendar months.[173]
2. The organization can convert to a public charity (Q 1:2). It must satisfy the rules of the public charity status it selected for an initial continuous period of 60 calendar months.[174]

NOTE: These options are not available to a private foundation where there have been either willful repeated acts (or failures to act) or a willful and flagrant act (or failure to act) giving rise to liability for tax under one or more of the private foundation rules (Q 1:4).[175]

Q 1:39   Are private foundations subject to the private inurement doctrine?

Yes, they most certainly are. All tax-exempt charitable organizations[176] are subject to the *private inurement doctrine.* This is the rule of law that prohibits charitable organizations from inappropriately distributing their net income and/or net assets to persons in their private capacity. A private foundation, being such a charitable organization, is bound by the private inurement doctrine. The sanction for violating the private inurement doctrine is revocation of tax-exempt status.

As a matter of practice, however, the IRS or a court is far more likely to impose one or more taxes for self-dealing (Q 1:6) in an instance of a private inurement transaction than adhere to the stricter dictates of the private inurement doctrine. At the same time, in an egregious set of circumstances, both the self-dealing rules and the private inurement doctrine may be invoked.

Q 1:40   Are private foundations subject to the private benefit doctrine?

Yes. There is, however, only one published instance of application of the doctrine in the private foundation setting. There, the IRS applied the *private benefit doctrine,* holding that even though a transaction did not amount to self-dealing, it would constitute an impermissible private benefit.[177]

An organization, to be a tax-exempt charitable one, must not offer private benefit, unless it is merely incidental. A single non-exempt purpose, if substantial, can lead to loss of tax-exempt status. There is no need of the presence of an *insider* (disqualified person). In the private benefit setting, impermissible non-incidental benefits can be conferred on disinterested persons where the benefits serve private interests.

In the facts of this case, a private foundation was the owner of a collection of original documents and other materials created by or related to an individual (G), and his wife and children. This collection was only partially catalogued and organized; access to these materials was generally limited. Portions of the collection were in fragile condition and conservation efforts had to be undertaken before any further public use of it could be considered. The foundation was planning on transferring the collection to a public charity.

Another individual (F) requested access to and copies of portions of the collection for the purpose of writing a book concerning G. F was an author who was writing a book about G. She requested access to the collection to research primary material for the book. Her book was not requested or authorized by the foundation. This book project was to be a commercial one. F was to hold the copyright on the book and all other proprietary rights. The private foundation was not to compensate for F's use of the collection.

A third individual (H) was the founder of and a substantial contributor to the foundation (and thus was a disqualified person with respect to it (Q 2:2)). F was a great niece of H. She also was a great granddaughter of G (who was not a substantial contributor to the foundation). F was not a trustee of the foundation, nor was she the child or grandchild of any trustees. She was the niece, sibling, or cousin of trustees. F was not the owner of more than 20 percent of the voting power, profit interest, or beneficial interest of any entity that was a substantial contributor to the foundation. Although F held positions on advisory committees of the private foundation, she did not have the power to vote on any action of the foundation.

F was not a disqualified person with respect to this private foundation. She was not a foundation manager, a substantial contributor, a 20 percent owner, or a family member. Basically, her relationship with the private foundation was too distant for her to be considered a disqualified person.

The IRS ruled that, in this case, the private foundation would confer impermissible private benefit to F by giving her preferential exclusive access to the collection. F's private interests would be served by allowing her to profit commercially in that the book about G would be enhanced by information found about G in the collection. Thus, the IRS held, the foundation would be jeopardizing its tax-exempt status if it acceded to F's request.

COMMENT: With some tinkering with the facts, the outcome in this case could be different. For example, if F paid the foundation fair value for access to the collection, there would not be private benefit. Or, if the book project was that of the foundation, rather than a commercial one, the outcome would be different. Far more important, however, is this fine example of how the private benefit doctrine applies in the private foundation setting. This is another of the traps to be found in the foundation context. Consider this: If a transaction is between a private foundation and a disqualified person, then, under the general rules at least, the transaction would be self-dealing (Chapter 3). If, however, a disqualified person is not in the picture, the transaction may nonetheless amount to self-dealing. This is because a self-dealing transaction includes a transaction that creates a use or benefit for a disqualified person (Q 3:20). This ruling illustrates that the analysis should not stop even if the facts show that there is no disqualified person or benefit created for the use of a disqualified person. That is, nonetheless, there may be impermissible private benefit. This shifts the sanction away from the disqualified person (an excise tax) and on the foundation (revocation of tax exemption). Thus, in this area, all three of these levels of analysis may have to be— carefully—made.

Q 1:41   Are contributions to private foundations deductible?

Absolutely. Private foundations are charitable organizations (Q 1:39) and thus are able to attract contributions that are deductible for federal income, estate, and gift tax purposes (Chapter 17).[178] Usually charitable deductions are also available under state law.

The difficulty in the income tax setting is the *extent* of gift deductibility. For the most part, the tax rules in this regard favor gifts to public charities (Q 1:2). The major determining factor in this context is the nature of the thing that is the subject of the gift. In the case of individuals, there are percentage limitations, annually applied to adjusted gross income, which can restrict the amount of charitable giving that is deductible in a year.

Thus, an individual can deduct an amount equal to as much as 50 percent of adjusted gross income in the case of one or more gifts of money to one or more public charities.[179] For example, if an individual has adjusted gross income of $100,000 in a year, he or she can make deductible gifts of money to public charities in that year up to $50,000. (Any excess can be carried forward and deducted in subsequent years, up to five.[180]) Contributions of money to private foundations, however, are subject to a 30 percent limitation.[181] (Again, carryovers are available.[182])

An individual can deduct an amount equal to as much as 30 percent of adjusted gross income in the case of one or more gifts of property to one or more public charities.[183] For example, if an individual has adjusted gross income of $100,000 in a year, he or she can make deductible gifts of property to public charities in that year up to $30,000.

NOTE: Where a special election is made, contributions of capital gain property may be subject to the 50 percent limitation rather than the 30 percent limitation.[184]

Contributions of this type to private foundations, however, are subject to a 20 percent limitation.[185] (Carryovers are available in both instances.[186])

Generally, contributions of property (including property that has appreciated in value) to public charities give rise to charitable deductions based on the fair market value of the property at the time of the gift.[187] At the same time, however, property gifts to private foundations generally yield a charitable deduction equal to only the donor's basis in the property.[188]

NOTE: There is a special rule, nonetheless, by which a contribution of most publicly traded securities to a private foundation gives rise to a charitable deduction based on the fair market value of the securities.[189]

Q 1:42   Is there any advantage to classification as a private foundation?

There certainly is no advantage *from the standpoint of the law* as to private foundation status. In every way, the federal tax law favors public charities (Q 1:22).

Nonetheless, there are advantages to classification as a private foundation. The principal one is *control.* An individual, couple, family, corporation, or the like can make one or more gifts to the foundation and retain control over the investment and distribution of funds. The individual or individuals who established the foundation can serve on its board of trustees (without limitation) and enjoy the personal benefits that flow to those who are philanthropists. A private foundation can be a source of employment for those who created it and for their children and subsequent generations.

NOTE: Of course, these advantages also can be obtained where the charitable organization involved is a public charity.

Q 1:43   Is there any disadvantage to classification as a private foundation?

Yes. From the standpoint of the law, there are eight disadvantages. The importance of any of them largely depends on the circumstances of the particular charitable organization.

1. Private foundations must comply with the private foundation rules or suffer penalties (Q 1:4).
2. Private foundations are required to pay a tax on their net investment income (Q 1:33).
3. Contributions to private foundations are likely to be less deductible than gifts to other types of charities (Q 1:41).
4. The charitable deduction for a gift of appreciated property to a private foundation generally is confined to its basis rather than the full fair market value of the property (*id.*), although this disadvantage is somewhat ameliorated by the special treatment accorded *qualified appreciated securities* (*id.*).
5. Private foundations have greater limitations on their ability to generate unrelated business income (Q 1:35).
6. Private foundations are required to file a more complex annual information return (Q 1:36).
7. More extensive record keeping requirements are involved.[190]
8. The organization probably cannot be funded by private foundations because of the requirement that grants of this nature be the subject of expenditure responsibility (Q 7:24).

Q 1:44   Are the private foundation rules generally understood?

Unfortunately, no. One would think that, by now—since these rules have been in existence for over 30 years—the private foundation rules would be mastered, both by the professional community and at least basically by the public, including the media. But matters have not worked out that way.

Two examples involving the media make the point. The *Kansas City Star,* in an article published in June 1998, summarized most of the criticisms leveled at private foundations these days. One of these complaints is that the annual mandatory payout (Q 1:12) is inadequate. In the process, the journalist attempted to state that rule; it came out this way: Private foundations must give away at least "5 percent of their total assets each year."[191] Were that true, a foundation would disappear after its first 20 years or so. (To reiterate, the rule essentially is that, for a year, grants must be made out of income in an amount *equal to* at least 5 percent of noncharitable assets.)

Another journalist fared far worse, however. The *Oregonian,* in an article published the same month, stated: "Self-sufficient and self-governing, the boards that govern foundations answer to no one."[192] The IRS and not a few courts, though, think otherwise. "And foundations don't pay a dime in taxes." Other than the tax on investment and unrelated income, that is (Q 1:30). "Their only requirement is to give away at least 5 percent of their assets each year to keep their nonprofit status." That is hardly the *only* requirement the law imposes on private foundations; their nonprofit status has nothing to do with this rule. As for the botching of the payout rule, see the preceding paragraph.

COMMENT: The law concerning private foundations is indeed complex. Nonetheless, although media scrutiny is to be applauded, journalists need to do a much better job in understanding the complicated and stringent legal environment in which foundations are forced to function.

Q 1:45   Do developments in the law concerning intermediate sanctions have an impact on the private foundation rules?

Very much so. The intermediate sanctions rules[193] are, in many ways, based on the private foundation rules. This is particularly the case with respect to the self-dealing rules. There are, however, other concepts that have been imported into the intermediate sanctions rules from the private foundation area. These include the principles of the tiers of taxation, the amount involved, and correction.

Thus, a development in the law in the intermediate sanctions context can have a meaningful impact on the comparable point of law in the private foundation setting.

CHAPTER 2

Disqualified Persons

The federal tax rules governing private foundations focus heavily on transactions between them and those who are, in the parlance of the private inurement rules, *insiders* with respect to them. Generally, transactions of this nature are prohibited, as being acts of self-dealing (Chapter 3). But disqualified persons can be involved in connection with other bodies of private foundation law as well, such as the payout rules (Chapter 4), the excess business holdings rules (Chapter 5), and the taxable expenditures rules (Chapter 7).

A publicly supported charity may need to worry about these rules also. In some instances, support from disqualified persons cannot be taken into account as *public support*—because it is not from a *permitted source*. (See Chapter 12.)

Thus, it is critical that every private foundation and certain public charities know, at all times, who their disqualified persons are.

Here are the questions that are most frequently asked (or that should be asked) about the rules defining disqualified persons—and the answers to them.

Q 2:1   In general, what is a *disqualified person*?

This question was generally answered earlier (Q 1:3). To reiterate in this context, however, there are several categories of persons who can be disqualified persons with respect to a private foundation:

- Substantial contributors (Q 2:2)
- Foundation managers (Q 2:6)
- 20 percent owners (Q 2:9)
- Members of the family (Q 2:15)
- Controlled corporations and partnerships (Q 2:16, Q 2:17)

- Controlled trusts and estates (Q 2:18, Q 2:19)
- Government officials (Q 2:23)
- Other private foundations (Q 2:20)

Q 2:2   What is a *substantial contributor*?

One category of disqualified person[1] is a *substantial contributor* to a private foundation.[2] A substantial contributor generally is any person who contributed or bequeathed an aggregate amount of more than $5,000 to the private foundation involved, where that amount was more than 2 percent of the total contributions and bequests received by the foundation before the close of its year in which the contribution or bequest was received by the foundation from that person.[3] In making this computation, all contributions and bequests to the private foundation, made since its establishment, are taken into account.[4]

Here is how this rule works. On January 1, 2001, individual A gave private foundation PF a gift of $3,000. PF's tax year is the calendar year. This was A's first gift to PF. As of that date, PF had cumulatively throughout its existence received gifts totaling $200,000. Inasmuch as A's gift was less than $5,000 and also was below the 2 percent floor (2 percent of $200,000 being $4,000), A did not become a substantial contributor because of this gift. A made an additional gift of $3,000 in 2003, when the cumulative total of gifts to PF equaled $250,000. A became a substantial contributor to PF as of the close of 2003, because A's total gifts were in excess of $5,000 and were higher than the 2 percent amount (2 percent of $250,000 being $5,000).

In the case of a trust, the term *substantial contributor* also means the creator of the trust.[5] The term *person* can include tax-exempt organizations[6] (Q 2:21, Q 2:22) but does not include governmental units.[7] The term *person* also includes a decedent, even at the point in time preceding the transfer of any property from the estate to the private foundation.[8]

Thus, any type of person can be a disqualified person. Disqualified persons include individuals, corporations, partnerships, limited liability companies, and tax-exempt organizations.

For certain purposes,[9] the term *substantial contributor* does not include most organizations that are not private foundations or an organization wholly owned by a public charity. Moreover, for purposes of the self-dealing rules (Chapter 3), the term does not include any charitable organization—because to require inclusion of charities for this purpose would preclude private foundations from making large grants to or otherwise interacting with other charitable organizations.[10]

Q 2:3   When does a person become a substantial contributor?

In determining whether a contributor is a substantial one, the total of the amounts received from the contributor and the total contributions and bequests received by the private foundation must be ascertained as of the last day of each year.[11] Each contribution and bequest is valued at its fair market value on the date received; an individual is treated as making all contributions and bequests made by his or her spouse.[12] Thus, a private foundation is expected to maintain a running tally of contributions and bequests, taking into account these attribution rules.

Thus, a donor becomes a substantial contributor as of the first date when the private foundation received from him, her, or it an amount sufficient to make him, her, or it a substantial contributor (Q 2:2). Therefore, as noted, a private foundation should tabulate accumulating totals, on an ongoing basis, as contributions and bequests are received, lest the foundation inadvertently commit an act of self-dealing (Chapter 3) or otherwise violate one or more of the other federal tax rules regulating the operations of private foundations.

A point here should be emphasized. As the above example (Q 2:2) reflects, the determination as to substantial contributor status is not made until the last day of a year. This means that contributions and bequests from others, made subsequent to the gifts of the contributor in question but within the same year, may operate to keep him, her, or it out of substantial contributor status—even though that status was "temporarily" obtained at an earlier point during that year.

Here is an example. On July 21, 2001, X corporation gave a private foundation PF $2,000. PF's fiscal year is the calendar year. As of December 31, 2002, PF had received $150,000 in contributions and bequests from all sources. On September 17, 2003, X gave PF $3,100. As of that date, PF had received a total of $245,000 in contributions and bequests from all sources. Between September 17, 2003, and December 31, 2003, PF received $50,000 in contributions and bequests from others. X was "temporarily" a substantial contributor to PF on September 17, 2003. At that time, X's gifts exceeded $5,000 (they totaled $5,100) and exceeded the 2 percent threshold (2 percent × $245,000 = $4,900). But X did not in fact become a substantial contributor with respect to PF as of 2003 because the additional $50,000 in contributions and bequests received in that year raised the threshold to an amount in excess of X's gifts (2 percent × $295,000 = $5,900).

Q 2:4 Must unusual grants be excluded from this calculation as to total contributions and bequests?

No. Although unusual grants (Q 12:7) can be excluded when an organization is computing its public support ratio (Q 12:4, Q 12:8), there is no comparable rule in this setting. This is just as well, since inclusion of larger contributions in the base of gifts used in determining the 2 percent figure (Q 2:2) reduces the likelihood of contributors becoming substantial contributors.

Q 2:5 Can a person cease being regarded as a substantial contributor?

With one exception, once a person becomes a substantial contributor to a private foundation, that person can never escape that status,[13] even though the person might not be so classified if the determination were first made at a later date.[14] That is, growth in a private foundation's level of giving cannot wash out a person's classification, once obtained, as a substantial contributor.

This exception enables a person's status as a substantial contributor to terminate in certain circumstances after 10 years with no connection with the private foundation.[15] For this disconnect in status to occur, during the 10-year period, three factors must be present:

1. The person (and any related persons) must not have made any contributions to the private foundation.
2. The person (and any related persons) was not a foundation manager of the foundation (Q 2:6).
3. The aggregate contributions made by the person (and any related persons) must be determined by the IRS to be insignificant in relation to the foundation's total contributions,[16] taking into account appreciation on contributions while held by the private foundation.

The term *related person* means related disqualified persons and, in the case of a corporate donor, includes the directors and officers of the corporation.[17]

Q 2:6   What is a *foundation manager*?

Another category of disqualified person[18] is the *foundation manager*. A foundation manager is an officer (Q 2:7), director, or trustee of a private foundation, or an individual having powers or responsibilities similar to one or more of those three positions.[19]

An organization can be a foundation manager, such as a bank, a similar financial institution, or an investment advisor.[20]

CAUTION: Even if an individual lacks the authority (i.e., that of an officer) to be classified as a foundation manager on an overall basis, he or she can be treated as a foundation manager with respect to a particular act (or failure to act) over which he or she does have authority.[21]

Q 2:7   Who is an *officer* of a private foundation?

An individual is considered an *officer* of a private foundation in two instances. One is obvious: An individual is an officer if the position held by the individual is specifically designated as such under the documents by which the foundation was formed. The other instance is where he or she regularly exercises general authority to make administrative or policy decisions on behalf of the foundation.[22] This second instance involves the *key employee*.

The term *key employee* includes the chief management and administrative officials of an organization (e.g., an executive director). It does not include the heads of separate departments or smaller units within the organization. A chief financial officer and the officer in charge of administration or programs operations are key employees if they have the authority to control the organization's activities, its finances, or both.[23]

An individual who has authority merely to make recommendations pertaining to administrative or policy decisions, but lacks the authority to implement them without approval of a superior, is not an officer and thus not a foundation manager.[24]

Employees of an organization that is a foundation manager (Q 2:6) can themselves be foundation managers because they are officers. In one such case, the IRS concluded that employees of a bank that was the trustee of a private foundation were officers. "[T]hey [were] free, on a day-to-day basis, to administer the trust and distribute the funds according to their best judgment."[25]

Q 2:8   Can an independent contractor be a foundation manager?

No. Independent contractors, acting in that capacity, are not officers.[26] Thus, they are not—for that reason—disqualified persons. This rule shields lawyers, accountants, and investment managers and advisors from consideration as officers.

Q 2:9   What is a *20 percent owner*?

An owner of more than 20 percent of the total *combined voting power* of a corporation (Q 2:11), the *profits interest* of a partnership (Q 2:12), or the *beneficial interest* of a trust or unincorporated enterprise (Q 2:13), any of which is (during the ownership) a substantial contributor to a private foundation (Q 2:2), is a disqualified person with respect to that foundation.[27]

Q 2:10   What does the term *voting power* mean?

Voting power generally means the ability of an owner of stock to vote the share or shares. It includes outstanding voting power but does not include voting power obtainable but not obtained. Here are three examples of what this means. One is voting power obtainable by converting securities or nonvoting stock into voting stock. Another is exercising warrants or options to obtain voting stock. The third is voting power that will vest in preferred stockholders only if and when the corporation has failed to pay preferred dividends for a specified period or has otherwise failed to meet specified requirements.[28]

Q 2:11   What does the term *combined voting power* mean?

Combined voting power[29] includes voting power represented by holdings of voting stock, actual or constructive,[30] but does not include voting rights held only as a director or trustee.[31]

For example, an employee stock ownership trust[32] that held 30 percent of the stock of a corporation that was a substantial contributor to a private foundation (Q 2:2) on behalf of the corporation's participating employees (who direct the manner in which the trust votes the shares) was held by the IRS to have merely the voting power of a trustee and not the ownership of the stock, and thus not to be a disqualified person with respect to the private foundation.[33]

Q 2:12   What does the term *profits interest* mean?

The profits interest[34] of a partner is that equal to his, her, or its distributive share of income of the partnership as determined under special federal tax rules.[35] The term includes any interest that is outstanding but not any interest that is obtainable but has not been obtained.[36]

Q 2:13   What does the term *beneficial interest* mean?

The beneficial interest in an unincorporated enterprise (other than a trust (Q 2:18) or an estate (Q 2:19)) includes any right to receive a portion of distributions from profits of the enterprise or, in the absence of a profit-sharing agreement, any right to receive a portion of the assets (if any) upon liquidation of the enterprise, except as a creditor or employee.[37] A right to receive distribution of profits includes a right to receive any amount from the profits other than as a creditor or employee, whether as a sum certain or as a portion of profits realized by the enterprise. Where there is no agreement fixing the rights of the participants in an enterprise, the fraction of the respective interest of each participant is determined by dividing the amount of all investments or contributions to the capital of the enterprise, made or obligated to be made by the participant, by the amount of all investments or contributions to capital made or obligated to be made by all of the participants.[38]

A person's beneficial interest in a trust is determined in proportion to the actuarial interest of the person in the trust.[39] The term *beneficial interest* includes any interest that is outstanding but not any interest that is obtainable but has not been obtained.[40]

Q 2:14   Are there attribution rules in this context?

Yes. For the purpose of determining the combined voting power (Q 2:11), profits interest (Q 2:12), or beneficial interest (Q 2:13) of an individual, there are some complex attribution rules in this context.

With respect to combined voting power, stock (or profits or beneficial interests) owned directly or indirectly by or for a corporation, partnership, estate, or trust is considered as being owned proportionately by or for its shareholders, partners, or beneficiaries.[41] (An individual is considered as owning the stock owned by members of his or her family, as discussed (Q 2:15).)

Any stockholders that have been counted once (whether by reason of actual or constructive ownership) in applying these rules[42] are not counted a second time.[43] Essentially, the attribution rules are the same as the federal tax rules generally,[44] and there is a special rule for constructive ownership of stock.[45]

With respect to profits interests or beneficial interests, ownership of these interests is similarly taken into account in determining whether an individual is a disqualified person.[46]

There has not been much interpretation of these rules, but an IRS ruling offers an illustration of them. The matter involved three national trade associations that elect the directors of a private foundation. There were 30 local association members of one of the three national associations (which thus is a federation of associations). There was another national association controlled by these three associations. The IRS held that the private foundation could make grants to the local associations without committing acts of self-dealing (Chapter 3), even though the controlled national association was a substantial contributor and the federation of associations held more than 20 percent of the combined voting power of the controlled association. The reason: The federation of associations did not have an ownership interest in its local association members, and they were not otherwise disqualified persons with respect to the private foundation.[47]

Q 2:15   When is an individual a *member of the family*?

Another category of disqualified person is a member of the family of an individual who is a substantial contributor (Q 2:2), a foundation manager (Q 2:6), or a 20 percent owner (Q 2:9).[48] The term *member of the family* is defined to include an individual's spouse, ancestors, children, grandchildren, great-grandchildren, and the spouses of children, grandchildren, and great-grandchildren.[49] Thus, these family members are themselves disqualified persons.

A legally adopted child of an individual is treated for these purposes as a child of the individual by blood.[50] A brother or sister of an individual is not, for these purposes, a member of the family.[51]

CAUTION: When applying the excess benefit transactions rules,[52] remember that brothers and sisters are disqualified persons in that setting.[53]

The spouse of a grandchild of an individual is a member of his or her family for these purposes.[54]

Q 2:16   Can a corporation be a disqualified person?

Yes. A corporation is a disqualified person if more than 35 percent of the total combined voting power (Q 2:11) in the corporation (including constructive holdings[55]) is owned by substantial contributors (Q 2:2), foundation managers

(Q 2:6), 20 percent owners (Q 2:9), or members of the family of any of these persons (Q 2:15).[56]

Q 2:17   Can a partnership be a disqualified person?

Yes. A partnership is a disqualified person if more than 35 percent of the profits interest (Q 2:12) in the partnership (including constructive holdings[57]) is owned by substantial contributors (Q 2:2), foundation managers (Q 2:6), 20 percent owners (Q 2:9), or members of the family of any of these persons (Q 2:15).[58]

Q 2:18   Can a trust be a disqualified person?

Yes. A trust is a disqualified person if more than 35 percent of the beneficial interest (Q 2:13) in the trust (including constructive holdings[59]) is owned by substantial contributors (Q 2:2), foundation managers (Q 2:6), 20 percent owners (Q 2:9), or members of the family of any of these persons (Q 2:15).[60]

Q 2:19   Can an estate be a disqualified person?

Yes. An estate is a disqualified person if more than 35 percent of the beneficial interest (Q 2:13) in the estate (including constructive holdings[61]) is owned by substantial contributors (Q 2:2), foundation managers (Q 2:6), 20 percent owners (Q 2:9), or members of the family of any of these persons (Q 2:15).[62]

According to the IRS, an estate is not a disqualified person with respect to a trust funded by the estate solely because the estate is a continuation of the decedent who was a disqualified person. Where the disqualified person/decedent's children and grandchildren (also disqualified persons (Q 2:15)) are beneficiaries of trusts funded by the estate and these beneficial interests are more than 35 percent of the beneficial interest in the estate, however, the estate is a disqualified person.[63]

Q 2:20   Can a private foundation be a disqualified person?

Yes, to a limited extent. A private foundation may be a disqualified person with respect to another private foundation—but only for purposes of the excess business holdings rules (Chapter 5).[64] The disqualified person private foundation must be effectively controlled,[65] directly or indirectly, by the same person or persons (other than a bank, trust company, or similar organization acting only as a foundation manager) who control the private foundation in question, or must be the recipient of contributions substantially all of which were made, directly or indirectly, by substantial contributors (Q 2:2), foundation managers (Q 2:6), 20 percent owners (Q 2:9), or members of their families (Q 2:15) who made, directly or indirectly, substantially all of the contributions to the private foundation in question.[66]

One or more persons are considered to have made *substantially all* of the contributions to a private foundation for these purposes if the persons have contributed or bequeathed at least 85 percent of the total contributions and bequests that have been received by the private foundation during its entire existence, where each person has contributed or bequeathed at least 2 percent of the total.[67]

Here is an example of this rule. Private foundation PF1 has received contributions totaling $100,000 throughout its existence. These funds came from X, in the amount of $35,000, $51,000 from Y (X's father), and $14,000 from an unrelated person. During its existence, private foundation PF2 received $100,000 in contributions, as follows: $50,000 from X and $50,000 from Z (X's spouse). For excess business holdings purposes, PF1 is a disqualified person with respect to PF2 and PF2 is a disqualified person with respect to PF1.

Q 2:21   Can a public charity be a disqualified person?

For certain purposes,[68] the term *substantial contributor* does not include most organizations that are not private foundations[69] or an organization wholly owned by a public charity. Moreover, for purposes of the self-dealing rules (Chapter 3), the term does not include any charitable organization[70] because to require inclusion of charities for this purpose would preclude private foundations from making large grants to or otherwise interacting with other charitable organizations.[71]

NOTE: In computing the support fraction in the case of a service provider publicly supported organization (Q 12:8), the term *substantial contributor* includes public charities where the $5,000/2 percent test (Q 2:2) is exceeded. In this circumstance, nonetheless, this support may qualify as an unusual grant (Q 12:7).

Q 2:22   Can any other type of tax-exempt organization be a disqualified person?

Certainly, although it is not likely to happen often. There is no exclusion in the law from the definition of the term *disqualified person* for tax-exempt organizations other than charitable ones. Thus, if an exempt organization meets one (or more) of the definitions of a disqualified person (Q 2:1), it is one. Most likely, when this occurs, the exempt organization is a substantial contributor. For example, a previous discussion included an example involving tax-exempt trade associations (Q 2:14).

Q 2:23   Can a government official be a disqualified person?

Yes, but again only to a limited extent. A government official can be a disqualified person with respect to a private foundation—but only for purposes of the self-dealing rules (Chapter 3).[72]

The term *government official* means:

1. An elected public official in the U.S. Congress or executive branch
2. Presidential appointees to the U.S. executive or judicial branches
3. Certain higher compensated or ranking employees in one of these three branches
4. House of Representatives or Senate employees earning at least $15,000 annually
5. Elected or appointed public officials in the U.S. or District of Columbia governments (including governments of U.S. possessions or political subdivisions or areas of the United States) earning at least $20,000 annually, or
6. The personal and executive assistant or secretary to any of the foregoing[73]

In defining the term *public office* for purposes of the fifth category of governmental officials, this term must be distinguished from mere employment. Although holding a public office is a form of public employment, not every position in the employ of a state or other governmental subdivision constitutes a public office. Although a determination as to whether a public employee holds a public office depends on the facts and circumstances of the case, the essential element is whether a significant part of the activities of a public employee is the independent performance of policy-making functions.

Several factors may be considered as indications that a position in the executive, legislative, or judicial branch of the government of a state, possession of the United States, or political subdivision or other area of any of the foregoing, or of the District of Columbia, constitutes a public office. Among these factors—in addition to the element of policy-making authority—are that the office is created by Congress, a state constitution, or a state legislature, or by a municipality or other governmental body pursuant to authority conferred by Congress, a state constitution, or a state legislature, and that the powers conferred on the office and the duties to be discharged by the official are defined either directly or indirectly by Congress, a state constitution, or a state legislature, or through legislative authority.[74]

NOTE: In one instance, a lawyer appointed by the attorney general of a state to perform collection services on a part-time basis for the attorney general's office was held by the IRS to not be a governmental official.[75] Likewise, the IRS ruled that the holder of the office of county attorney is not a governmental official for these purposes.[76]

Further, in applying the rules concerning the above fifth category of governmental officials, the monetary amounts pertain to the individual's *gross compensation.*[77] This term refers to all receipts attributable to public office that are includible in gross income for federal income tax purposes. Thus, an elected member of a state legislature may receive an annual salary that is less than $20,000, but also receive an expense allowance that, when added to the salary, results in a total amount of more than $20,000 per year. Where the expense allowance is a fixed amount given to each legislator regardless of actual expenses, there is no restriction on its use, and there is no requirement that an accounting for its use be made to the state, the allowance is part of the legislator's gross compensation, making the legislator a disqualified person (for self-dealing purposes).[78]

NOTE: In another instance, a lawyer in private practice, who had been a director of a private foundation for more than 10 years and compensated in that capacity, was appointed by the president of the United States to be chair of a government entity. Reviewing this individual's status, the IRS concluded that the individual was not a governmental official, in that the individual was a special government employee because the employment would not be for more than 30 days over any 365-day period.[79]

Q 2:24   Can an individual ever jettison disqualified person status?

Yes, an individual can, under certain circumstances, cease being a disqualified person with respect to a private foundation. It is, however, difficult to do this. (As discussed, there are separate rules in this regard for those who become substantial contributors (Q 2:5).) Moreover there is very little law or other IRS guidance on this point.

There is, nonetheless, an IRS ruling that illustrates how an individual can jettison disqualified person status. In that ruling, the IRS held that an individual, formerly a director of a private foundation, could purchase assets from a private foundation without engaging in acts of self-dealing (Q 3:1), by reason of the fact that he resigned as foundation manager (Q 2:6) the day before submitting his bid and through other facts showing that he would not unduly influence the sale of the assets.[80] Here is what happened.

Under the will of the founder of this foundation, the residue of the estate was bequeathed to the foundation. Included in these assets was all of the stock of an investment company. This company and its subsidiaries owned various businesses, including all of the stock of another business enterprise. In the will, the founder expressed his intention that the executors of his estate convert these businesses into money, to be distributed to the foundation.

The decedent was the sole "member" of the foundation. The will appointed eight individuals as successor members; these individuals have the power to appoint or remove directors. At the present, the board of directors of the foundation consists of 11 individuals, six of whom are also members. Several of these members and directors are officers or key employees of these businesses. The executors are members of the foundation and key employees of the businesses.

About one year after the death of the founder, the investment company's businesses were restructured. This was done to maximize the proceeds to be received by the foundation. The restructuring also was done to place the businesses in a logical and manageable structure from an operational and managerial perspective. The assets of the businesses are now owned by wholly owned corporate subsidiaries of a holding company that is wholly owned by the foundation. The managers of the holding company are the executors.

Until his retirement from one of these businesses in 1996, X was an employee of the business and its predecessor for about 25 years. He was the chief operating officer for many of those years. Following his retirement, X was retained as a consultant to advise the predecessor of the holding company on business matters. X was appointed to the board of directors of the foundation by the founder, because of his knowledge and expertise concerning the businesses; he has never been a member of the foundation. After the founder's death, X did not attend any foundation board meetings. Neither X nor any member of his family or any entity in which X or his family has a 20 percent or greater interest has made any contributions to the foundation. Similarly, no member of X's family is a foundation manager with respect to the foundation.

Following the death of the founder, the individual who succeeded X as chief operating officer of the business became seriously ill. X was persuaded to return as CEO on an emergency basis to oversee the operation of the businesses during the administration of the estate and the expected disposition of certain of the businesses.

Prior to the formation of the holding company, a bank was retained to assist and advise the executors in the selling of all or a portion of the businesses. During the period prior to X's resignation from the foundation's board of directors, X participated in the auction process acting in his capacity as the CEO of the business. He compiled information on the businesses as requested by the bank, assisted the bank in the preparation of a memorandum describing the assets and operation of the businesses, participated in the discussions as to which potential bidders to contact, reviewed the bids submitted in the first round of the auction process, and met with and otherwise assisted bidders as they conducted their due diligence reviews.

In the late stages of the first round of the bidding process, the foundation retained a prominent investment firm to work with the bank and provide advice to the foundation in connection with the sale of all of a portion of the businesses. This investment bank reviewed the sales process to date and conducted its own review of the businesses. Subsequently, the bank and the investment firm reviewed the bidding process and resolved to commence another round of bidding.

Five days after the investment firm was retained, X resigned as a director of the foundation. The next day he submitted a bid on his own behalf for one of the businesses and other assets of the foundation. X recused himself from representing any of the businesses during the bidding process and discontinued any contact with other bidders or potential bidders. All bidders involved in the original and new bidding round were advised of X's bidder status and recusal from the sales process.

Old and new bidders were, at the time of this ruling, in the process of revisiting the relevant company facilities, conducting additional due diligence, and meeting with company officials (other than X), under the supervision of the bank and the investment firm. These advisors have distributed additional material to all bidders, including X. He will participate in the bidding process on the same terms as the other bidders.

Each set of bids will be evaluated by the holding company and the private foundation, with the assistance of the bank and investment firm. The sales of all or a portion of the businesses will be subject to the approval of the court that has jurisdiction over the estate. Any sale of the assets will require approval of the state attorney general.

The issue before the IRS was whether X was a disqualified person, as a foundation manager. This was critical to the determination of self-dealing, as obviously if his bid prevailed, there would be a sale of foundation assets to him and perhaps an extension of credit (Q 3:8). The only precedent the IRS unearthed was a 1980 revenue ruling,[81] holding that an individual was not a disqualified person with respect to a foundation because of a resignation five years before the transaction at issue.

Here the circumstances were dramatically different. While X resigned as a director of the private foundation, thus no longer being a disqualified person, he did so the day before submitting his bid. He was an active participant in the planning of the sale of the businesses. As the chief operating officer of one of these businesses, he is in a position of authority with respect to the employee/directors and the employee/members.

Nonetheless, the IRS found several factors that prevented X from exercising any undue influence over the sale of the assets by the foundation. There was an open bidding process designed to obtain fair market value for the assets. There was a solicitation of additional bidders. X has recused himself from the bidding process, other than as a bidder. The bank and investment firm evaluated the bids. The sale of the assets was under the supervision of a court and subject to the approval of the state attorney general.

The IRS noted that the sale of the businesses by the foundation was a direct result of the founder's intentions as expressed in his will. This was seen as insulating X from any suggestion or inference that, while a disqualified person, he may have instigated or otherwise set in motion the chain of events that eventually led to sale of the businesses and other assets.

Because of these facts, and representations that the compensation, including bonuses, of the employee/directors was reasonable and that X did not participate in setting them, and that X was not being accorded any preference in the transaction, the IRS ruled that X was no longer a disqualified person with respect to the foundation. Thus, any sale of foundation assets to him did not amount to self-dealing.

This is one of the most generous rulings the IRS has issued in the private foundation setting. It is a fair and reasoned determination. The private foundation rules, however, can be quite rigid, and often fairness and reason are beside the point. Thus, caution should be exercised when someone is trying to escape disqualified person status; it likely will not always be this easy.

Can it truly be said that X no longer was in a position to have influence over the remaining managers of the foundation? He was an employee of the company he was bidding for for 25 years and was CEO of the company for many of those years. He had been a consultant to the holding company. He was overseeing the process of selling the businesses until he decided to become a bidder. His personal relationships with the management of the businesses and the foundation must have been extensive.

In the 1980 ruling, the IRS observed that all aspects of the transaction occurred after the foundation manager resigned. It was noted that this individual was not connected with the proposed transaction while he was a disqualified person.

Q 2:25   Can a corporation ever jettison its classification as a disqualified person?

Yes. Here is an example. A corporation made an exchange offer to a private foundation concerning certain shares of the corporation's nonvoting stock. The corporation was once a disqualified person with respect to the private foundation solely because an individual who was a manager of the foundation owned more than 35 percent of the total combined voting power (Q 2:11) of the corporation. Five years before the exchange took place, the foundation manager resigned that position. The IRS ruled that the resignation of the foundation manager terminated the status of the corporation as a disqualified person with respect to the private foundation, noting that all aspects of the exchange occurred after the separation of the foundation manager and that he was not connected with the proposed exchange while serving in that capacity.[82]

CHAPTER 3

Self-Dealing

Of all the rules private foundations are forced to contend with, those concerning the sweeping subject of self-dealing are the most complex and treacherous. These rules embody tough standards—rules that are far more strict than any comparable ones imposed on any other type of tax-exempt organization and related persons. They can even bar transactions where the foundation's economic circumstances would be enhanced.

The intricacy of these rules lies not only in the details of the statute but in the many pages of tax regulations. Here can be found grand generalizations, followed by exceptions that sometimes are nearly as hefty as the general rule, followed by exceptions to the exceptions. The dictates of case law layered on all of this only add to the complexity.

Traps abound here. It is common for disqualified persons (Chapter 2) to act in accordance with notions of reasonableness, only to find nonetheless that they have stumbled into a self-dealing transaction. Sometimes, in trying to extricate themselves, they commit another one (and/or violate one or more other private foundation rules). Even when it wants to, the IRS is forbidden to abate the self-dealing taxes.

Private foundations and their disqualified persons are well advised to tread cautiously when in the realm of potential self-dealing. The going can be perilous and extrication can be costly.

Here are the questions most frequently asked (or should be asked) about the self-dealing rules—and the answers to them.

Q 3:1   What are the general self-dealing rules concerning the sale of property?

The sale of property between a private foundation and a disqualified person with respect to the foundation generally constitutes self-dealing.[1] That is to say, for all practical purposes, this type of transaction is prohibited.

This rule applies in connection with all types of property: tangible personal property, intangible personal property, and real property. For example, the sale of incidental supplies by a disqualified person to a private foundation is an act of self-dealing, irrespective of the amount paid to the disqualified person for the supplies. Likewise, the sale of securities by a disqualified person to a private foundation in a bargain sale (Q 17:26) is an act of self-dealing, regardless of the amount paid for the securities.[2]

CAUTION: A transaction can constitute an act of self-dealing in more than one way. Thus, an installment sale can violate this rule—and also constitute self-dealing by being a prohibited extension of credit (Q 3:8).[3]

The transfer of real or personal property by a disqualified person to a private foundation is treated as a sale for these purposes if the foundation assumes a mortgage or similar lien that was placed on the property prior to the transfer or takes the property subject to a mortgage or similar lien that a disqualified person placed on the property within the 10-year period ending on the date of transfer.[4] The term *similar lien* includes deeds of trust and vendors' liens but not any other lien if the lien is insignificant in relation to the fair market value of the property transferred.

By the way, these rules cannot be circumvented successfully by interposing an agent or some other like intermediary. That is, self-dealing occurs when a disqualified person buys private foundation property from an agent of the foundation. For example, in an instance involving an art object consigned to a commercial art auction house, the purchase of the object by a disqualified person constituted self-dealing.[5] Similarly, the leasing of property to a disqualified person by a management company resulted in self-dealing inasmuch as the foundation controlled the manager's actions through a retained veto power.[6]

It was mentioned above that a transaction can be self-dealing even if it would be financially advantageous to the private foundation. Thus, in this setting, a purchase of a mortgage by a foundation held by its bank trustee (and therefore a disqualified person) was ruled to be self-dealing, even though the rate was more favorable than would otherwise have been available.[7]

NOTE: There are outer limits to all of this. A *contribution* to a private foundation by a disqualified person with respect to it is not an act of self-dealing.[8]

Q 3:2   What are the general self-dealing rules concerning the exchange of property?

An exchange of property between a private foundation and a disqualified person is an act of self-dealing.[9] The above-noted rule as to mortgaged property (Q 3:1) encompasses exchanges of property.[10]

Thus, as an illustration, these rules apply in the case of the transfer of shares of stock in payment of a loan.[11] Similarly, a transfer of real estate equal to the amount of the disqualified person's loan (undertaken in an effort to correct an act of self-dealing) was ruled to be a second act of self-dealing.[12] Conversely, a transfer of real estate in satisfaction of a pledge to pay cash or readily marketable securities was held not to be an exchange because the pledge was not legally enforceable and because a pledge is not considered a debt; essentially, the transaction was a gift.[13]

Q 3:3   Are there any exceptions to these rules?

Yes. One is that an exchange of a private foundation's securities in a reorganization or merger of a corporation that is a disqualified person is not necessarily an act of self-dealing. That is, if all of the securities of the same class as those held by the foundation, prior to the transaction, are subject to the same or uniform terms and the foundation receives full fair market value for its securities, prohibited self-dealing does not occur.[14]

The partition of property held as tenants-in-common with a disqualified person did not produce reportable gain nor constitute self-dealing for a private foundation.[15] Without directly saying as much, the IRS deems a partition as a transaction that is not a prohibited exchange (or sale). The foundation had received the undivided interest in the unproductive property as a gift from the disqualified person. Local law barred a nonprofit corporation from holding unproductive property; the foundation wanted to make the property marketable by creating a divided interest.

Q 3:4   What are the general self-dealing rules concerning the leasing of property?

The leasing of property between a private foundation and a disqualified person generally constitutes self-dealing.[16] For example, a foundation's rental of an aircraft from a charter aircraft company that is a disqualified person was held to be an act of self-dealing.[17]

Q 3:5   Are there any exceptions to these rules?

Yes. One of some consequence is that the leasing of property *by* a disqualified person to a private foundation is not an act of self-dealing if the lease is without charge. A lease is considered to be *without charge* even though the private foundation pays for janitorial services, utilities, or other maintenance costs it incurs for the use of the property, as long as the payment is not made directly or indirectly to a disqualified person.[18]

This exception can be used in connection with the display of a work of art. A private foundation can borrow (lease) an art object, without cost, from a disqualified person for the purpose of displaying it in a museum operated by the foundation. The foundation may permissibly pay the maintenance and insurance costs connected with display of the art directly to the vendors. The law thus permits the foundation to pay costs that the disqualified person might have to incur while the object is being displayed.

CAUTION: This use of a disqualified person's art works only where there is a public benefit. Placement of a foundation's art in the home of a disqualified person, away from public view, is not allowed.[19] Occasionally, displaying art on the property of a disqualified person is permitted, such as where the foundation's collection was displayed throughout the community, primarily on public lands, as part of a comprehensive outdoor museum program.[20]

The IRS usually tries to make the best of these strict rules. In one instance, a private foundation desired to dispose of ranch land it had owned for over 30 years to acquire other income-producing property to carry out its programs. The foundation was advised by an engineer that the foundation would maximize the ranch's value by developing the property—a process expected to take considerable time and requiring someone to live on the ranch during its development. The IRS approved a plan by which the foundation leased to its executive vice president, for a nominal sum, 1 percent of the ranch acreage, on which he, at his expense, constructed a residence. The lease provided for the foundation to pay the officer the then fair market value of any improvements upon termination of the lease. The primary purpose of the transaction was to "ensure the foundation's interests in the ranch were safeguarded." The IRS concluded that, although the officer and his wife were disqualified persons, the duties were reasonable and necessary to the accomplishment of the foundation's exempt purposes and thus that the lease and subsequent payments to the officer would not result in self-dealing.[21]

Q 3:6   What are the general rules concerning the lending of money?

The lending of money between a private foundation and a disqualified person generally constitutes an act of self-dealing.[22]

Thus, for example, an act of self-dealing occurs where a third party purchases property and assumes a mortgage, the mortgagee of which is a private foundation, and subsequently the third party transfers the property to a disqualified person who either assumes liability under the mortgage or takes the property subject to the mortgage. Likewise, generally, an act of self-dealing occurs where a note, the obligor of which is a disqualified person, is transferred by a third party to a private foundation that becomes the creditor under the note.[23]

COMMENT: As is so often the case in the world of self-dealing law, circuitousness does not erase the self-dealing taint.

A loan by a private foundation to an individual, before he or she becomes a foundation manager (Q 2:6)—and thus a disqualified person—may not be an act of self-dealing, because the self-dealing rules may not apply, in that the disqualified person status arose only following completion of the negotiation of the compensation package. Where, however, the loan principal remains outstanding once the individual becomes a disqualified person, an act of self-dealing takes place. Indeed, an act of self-dealing takes place in each year in which there is an uncorrected extension of credit.[24]

These rules are accorded broad interpretation. One example of this is the determination by the IRS that the contribution by a disqualified person to a private foundation of a life insurance policy subject to a policy loan is an act of self-dealing. This conclusion rested on the analysis that a life insurance policy loan is sometimes characterized as an advance of the proceeds of the policy, rather than amounts that must be paid to the insurer. The IRS concluded that the effect of the transfer is essentially the same as the transfer of property subject to a lien, in that the transfer of the policy relieves the donor of the obligation to repay the loan, pay interest on the loan as it accrues, or suffer continued diminution in the value of the policy. Application of the self-dealing rules to this type of transaction was completed by a finding that the amount of the loan is not insignificant in relation to the value of the policy.[25]

NOTE: The fact that, pursuant to a loan arrangement, a private foundation may obtain a better rate of interest than the foundation could otherwise receive does not eliminate the fact that it is nonetheless impermissible self-dealing.[26]

Q 3:7   Are there any exceptions to these rules?

Yes, there are two. One is that the self-dealing rules do not apply to the lending of money by a disqualified person to a private foundation where the loan is without interest or other charge.[27] For this exception to be available, however, the proceeds of the loan must be used exclusively for charitable purposes.[28]

This exception is effectively voided where a private foundation repays or cancels the debt by transferring property other than cash (such as securities) to repay the loan. This type of a transaction, when viewed in connection with the making of the loan, is tantamount to a sale or exchange of property between the foundation and the disqualified person—and thus constitutes an act of self-dealing (Q 3:1, Q 3:2).

The payment of expenses incurred on behalf of a private foundation by a disqualified person can be considered an interest-free loan to the foundation. If expense advances are treated as loans without charge and are paid in connection with its exempt activities, a foundation can repay the loan, in the nature of a reimbursement. Limited advances and reimbursements of expenses are permitted for foundation managers (Q 3:15). The tax regulations explaining the facility-sharing exception, however, prohibit a foundation's payment of costs it incurs in using the property directly or indirectly to a disqualified person.[29] Despite this conflict, the IRS has taken a practical approach by permitting reimbursement in certain circumstances where the transaction clearly allows the foundation to better accomplish its exempt purposes (Q 3:15).

The other exception is for general banking functions. The performance by a bank or trust company, which is a disqualified person, of certain general banking services and trust functions for a private foundation is not an act of self-dealing where the services are reasonable and necessary to the carrying out of the foundation's charitable purposes. Also, the compensation paid to the bank or trust company, taking into account the fair interest rate for the use of the funds by the institution, for the services may not be excessive. The general banking services that are permitted are:

- Checking accounts, as long as the bank does not charge interest on any overwithdrawals
- Savings accounts, as long as the foundation may withdraw its funds on no more than 30 days' notice without subjecting itself to a loss of interest on its money for the time during which the money was on deposit
- Safekeeping activities[30]

NOTE: This exception is based on the broader one concerning the payment of reasonable compensation for personal services (Q 3:14).

Q 3:8   What are the general rules concerning extensions of credit?

An extension of credit between a private foundation and a disqualified person generally constitutes an act of self-dealing.[31] There is not, however, much law on this point. Most of the law that exists concerns loans (Q 3:7).

As noted, the transfer of property by a disqualified person to a private foundation is self-dealing if the property is subject to a lien that a disqualified person placed on the property within the 10-year period ending on the date of the transfer (Q 3:1). The date on which the loan is made, not when the loan or line of credit was approved, is the date from which this exception is measured. It is normally the date a lien is actually placed on the property, even though the loan is part of a multiphase financing plan commenced more than 10 years before the gift.[32]

In one instance, a disqualified person transferred to a private foundation a parcel of real property that was subject to a lien placed on the property by the disqualified person within the 10-year period ending on the transfer date. When the property was originally acquired, a lien created by the deed of trust executed in conjunction with the purchase of the property was placed on the property prior to the 10-year period. Within that period, however, the disqualified person obtained another loan; the lien created by the deed of trust executed in conjunction with this loan was placed on the land within the 10-year period.

The IRS said that, for purposes of the self-dealing rules, "it [did] not matter that the taxpayer placed the second lien on the property as part of a multi-phased financing program begun more than ten years before the date of transfer."[33]

Q 3:9   Are there any exceptions to these rules?

There are two "exceptions," although that word is placed in quotes because the first of them is not much of a true exception. The making of a promise, pledge, or similar arrangement to a private foundation by a disqualified person, whether evidenced by an oral or a written agreement, a promissory note, or other instrument of indebtedness, to the extent motivated by charitable intent and unsupported by consideration, is not an extension of credit, for these purposes, before the date of maturity.[34]

As discussed above, the self-dealing rules do not apply to the lending of money by a disqualified person to a private foundation where the loan is without interest or other charge (Q 3:7). That is the rule as stated in the statute. The tax regulations, however, extend that exception to extensions of credit other than loans.[35]

Q 3:10   What are the general rules concerning the furnishing of goods, services, or facilities?

The general rule is that the furnishing of goods, services, or facilities between a private foundation and a disqualified person is self-dealing.[36] This rule applies, for example, to the furnishing of goods, services, or facilities such as office space, automobiles, auditoriums, secretarial help, meals, libraries, publications, laboratories, or parking lots. As an illustration, if a foundation furnishes personal living quarters to a disqualified person, other than a foundation manager (Q 2:6) or employee, without charge, the furnishing is an act of self-dealing.[37]

This, of course, is a rather expansive rule, and it is considerably tempered by three exceptions, as discussed next (Q 3:11).

Q 3:11   What are the exceptions to these rules?

The furnishing of goods, services, or facilities by a private foundation to a foundation manager (Q 2:6) in recognition of his or her services as a foundation manager, or to another employee in recognition of his or her services in that capacity, is not an act of self-dealing if

- The value of the furnishing (whether or includible in the recipient's gross income) is reasonable and necessary to the performance of his or her tasks in carrying out the exempt purposes of the foundation, and
- Taken in conjunction with any other payment of compensation or payment or reimbursement of expenses to him or her by the foundation, the value of the furnishing is not excessive.[38]

> **NOTE:** This rule is also available to an individual who would be an employee but for the fact that he or she does not receive any compensation for the services provided.

For example, if a private foundation furnishes meals and lodging that are reasonable and necessary, and are not excessive, to a foundation manager by reason of his or her being a manager, the furnishing is not an act of self-dealing.[39]

> **OBSERVATION:** Meals and lodging furnished in this context may be excludable from the gross income of the recipient as being furnished for the convenience of the employer.[40]

In an application of this rule, the IRS found that the furnishing of living quarters in a historical district to a disqualified person, who worked 25 to 35 hours a week overseeing the complex and managing the foundation's financial affairs, was not self-dealing—because the value of the personal living quarters, when combined with other compensation, was reasonable.[41]

Another exception is that the furnishing of goods, services, or facilities by a disqualified person to a private foundation is not self-dealing if the furnishing is without charge and if the goods, services, or facilities furnished are used exclusively for charitable purposes.[42] For example, the furnishing of goods such as pencils, stationery, or other incidental supplies, or the furnishing of facilities such as a building, by a disqualified person to a private foundation is allowed if the supplies or facilities are furnished without charge. Similarly, the furnishing of services (even though the services are not personal services (Q 3:14)) is permitted if the furnishing is without charge.[43]

> **NOTE:** The term *without charge* means, of course, that the furnishing is free (no cost). Also, however, a furnishing of goods is considered to be without charge even though the private foundation pays for transportation, insurance, or maintenance costs it incurs in obtaining or using the property, as long as the payment is not made directly or indirectly to the disqualified person.[44]

The IRS has, as reflected in private letter rulings, provided somewhat relaxed interpretations of this rule (Q 3:12).

As to the third exception, the furnishing of goods, services, or facilities by a private foundation to a disqualified person is not an act of self-dealing if the furnishing is made on a basis that is no more favorable than that on which the goods, services, or facilities are made available to the general public.[45] The tax regulations, however, narrow the scope of this exception, mandating that the goods, services, or facilities be functionally related (Q 5:3) to the exercise or performance by the foundation of its charitable purpose or functions.[46] This exception is testimony to the breadth of the self-dealing rules. Without it, for example, a private foundation operating a museum would become entangled in the self-dealing rules if one of its directors paid the normal admission price to view an exhibition or purchase a book in the museum bookstore.

In this context, the term *general public* is accorded particular attention. The term includes those individuals who, because of the particular nature of the activities of the private foundation, would be reasonably expected to utilize the goods, facilities, or services involved. Having said that, however, there must be a substantial number of persons, other than disqualified persons, who are actually utilizing the goods, facilities, or services. Thus, a private foundation that furnishes recreational or park facilities to the general public may furnish the facilities to a disqualified person, as long as they are furnished to him or her on a basis which is not more favorable than that on which they are furnished to the general public. Likewise, the sale of a book or magazine by a foundation to disqualified persons is not an act of self-dealing if the publication of the book or magazine is functionally related to a charitable activity of the foundation and the publication is made available to the disqualified persons and the general public at the same price.[47]

NOTE: If the terms of this type of sale require, for example, payment within 60 days from the date of delivery of the book or magazine, the terms are consistent with normal commercial practices, and payment is made within the 60-day period, the transaction is not treated as a loan or other extension of credit (Q 3:7, Q 3:9).

For example, the IRS ruled that the use of a private foundation's meeting room by a disqualified person was not an act of self-dealing, inasmuch as the room was made available to the disqualified person on the same basis that it was made available to the general public and was functionally related to the performance of a tax-exempt purpose of the foundation.[48] Similarly, the IRS held that it was not an act of self-dealing for a museum, which was a private foundation, to allow a disqualified person corporation to use its private road for access to the corporation's headquarters. The road was made available to the general public on a comparable basis, a substantial number of nondisqualified persons used the road, and the use of the road as an entrance to the museum was functionally related to the foundation's exempt purpose. The corporation had agreed to maintain the road, although that obligation did not entitle it to any special privileges with respect to the use of the road.[49] In another instance, however, because the rental of office space to disqualified persons did not contribute importantly to a private foundation's exempt purpose of conducting agricultural research and experimentation, the rental was held to be self-dealing, even though the disqualified persons conducted business activities in the same subject field of the foundation's research.[50]

Q 3:12   What about co-ownership of property?

Mere co-ownership of an item of property by a private foundation and one or more of its disqualified persons does not, in and of itself, amount to self-dealing.[51] Thus, for example, a private foundation can receive and hold a gift or bequest of an undivided interest in property from a disqualified person. The catch is that only the foundation can *use* the property, in that the law prohibits the use of foundation income or assets by a disqualified person (Q 3:19).

A number of private letter rulings illustrate why limited-use or shared ownership can be of some advantage to persons holding this type of an interest. In one instance, an individual and his spouse owned an extensive art collection that they planned to bequeath to a museum, a private foundation, they were creating. On the husband's death, the foundation museum and the spouse became joint tenants holding an undivided interest in each object in the art collection. Although the IRS would not permit the spouse to display a small portion of the co-owned objects in her home and strictly applied the statute to prohibit her use of the art, the museum was permitted to pay the insurance on all of the artworks.[52]

A gift of an undivided interest in property the donor planned to subsequently sell was sanctioned by the IRS. The donor relinquished all rights to use the improved real estate and retained only the right to inspect the property. The expenses were to be shared proportionately between the donor and the foundation. On subsequent sale of the co-owned property, the proceeds were divided proportionately. Self-dealing did not result from the gift, holding the property jointly, or the eventual sale of the property by the foundation to an independent party.[53]

The restrictions on use have also been found to include the making of improvements to an item of property. In one case, a private foundation jointly held property bequeathed to it by the co-owner's spouse prior to 1969, so she was permitted to receive income on her undivided share due to a transitional rule. The co-owners wanted to make substantial improvements to the property to enhance its income-producing potential. Despite the fact that the foundation and the spouse were to carefully divide the income and costs on a strict proportional basis, the IRS ruled that the improvement of the co-owned property would result in self-dealing (and that the transitional rule could no longer apply).[54]

An alternative to holding property as co-owners—a partnership—has been approved by the IRS. A limited partnership interest given to a private foundation is different from the "jointly owned property" contemplated by the tax regulations. In the IRS's opinion, the "holding and use of separate interests in a limited partnership is not the use of jointly owned property." In one instance, instead of donating an undivided interest in a shopping center, the donors transferred the property to and became general partners in a limited partnership. Then they gave a freely transferable limited partnership interest to an independent corporate trustee to hold in a charitable remainder trust (Q 17:28) (which is treated as a private foundation). Self-dealing did not arise.[55]

CAUTION: When planning these arrangements, it is essential to ensure that the terms of the partnership agreement permit each partner to have exclusive control, or use, of its respective interests and not create any common or shared interests.

Q 3:13 Can a private foundation pay compensation to a disqualified person?

Believe it or not, the general rule is: no. By statute, the payment of compensation—and even the payment or reimbursement of expenses—by a private foundation to a disqualified person is self-dealing.[56]

Sensibly, however, there is an exception—albeit not a capacious one—to this rule (Q 3:14).

Q 3:14 What Is the exception to this rule?

The payment of compensation (and the payment or reimbursement of expenses) by a private foundation to a disqualified person for personal services that are reasonable and necessary to carrying out the exempt purpose of the foundation is not self-dealing, as long as the compensation (or reimbursement) is not excessive.[57] The tax regulations expand on this exception a bit, to embrace "reasonable advances for expenses anticipated in the immediate future."[58]

NOTE: This exception does not extend to services provided by a government official (Q 2:23).

Q 3:15 Can a private foundation advance expenses to a disqualified person?

The making of a cash advance to a foundation manager or employee for expenses on behalf of the foundation is not an act of self-dealing, as long as the amount of the advance is reasonable in relation to the duties and expense requirements of the foundation manager. Except where reasonably allowable, these advances may not ordinarily exceed $500. For example, if a foundation makes an advance to a foundation manager to cover anticipated out-of-pocket current expenses for a reasonable period (i.e., a month) and the manager accounts to the foundation under a periodic reimbursement program for actual expenses incurred, the foundation is not regarded as having engaged in an act of self-dealing

- When it makes the advance,
- When it replenishes the funds upon receipt of supporting vouchers from the foundation manager, or

• If it temporarily adds to the advance to cover extraordinary expenses anticipated to be incurred in fulfillment of a special assignment (such as long distance travel).[59]

Q 3:16   What does the term *compensation* mean?

The term *compensation*, in this setting, means far more than an individual's salary or wage. It includes that but also encompasses bonuses, commissions, fringe benefits, retirement benefits, and the like.

Occasionally, however, other economic benefits are treated as compensation for purposes of application of the self-dealing rules. For example, under certain circumstances, the value of an indemnification by a private foundation of a foundation manager, or the payment by a foundation of the premiums for an insurance policy for a foundation manager, must be treated as compensation to avoid self-dealing (Q 3:30).

The portion of a payment that represents payment for property is not treated as payment of compensation (or payment or reimbursement of expenses) for the performance of personal services.[60]

Q 3:17   What does the term *reasonable* mean?

The term *reasonable* is not defined in this context. The tax regulations offer a cross-reference on this point to the law developed in the business expense deduction setting.[61]

This is a fact, rather than law, issue. It essentially is an exercise in the marshaling of comparable data. For example, to prove that compensation (Q 3:16) is reasonable, a private foundation must show that the pay and other benefits are equal to "such amount as would ordinarily be paid for like services by like enterprises under like circumstances."[62]

Factors to be taken into account include:

• Compensation paid to individuals in similar positions, preferably in the same community
• The individual's training, expertise, and responsibilities
• The size and complexity of the organization
• The amount of time devoted to the job
• Whether the compensation amount was the result of arm's-length bargaining
• The individual's actual job performance
• The scale of compensation for other employees

Q 3:18   What does the term *personal services* mean?

Neither the Internal Revenue Code nor the tax regulations define the term *personal services.* The regulations, however, offer a few examples: the services of a broker serving as agent for the private foundation (but not the services of a dealer who buys from the foundation as principal and resells to third parties); the services of lawyers and investment counselors; and certain banking services.[63]

The IRS is not particularly generous with the personal services exception. This rule is being narrowly interpreted—with, so far, the support of the courts. Thus, the agency is of the view that the personal services exception "is a special rule that should be strictly construed" because otherwise the "fabric woven by Congress to generally prohibit insider transactions would unravel."[64]

COMMENT: This once again highlights the difference between the rules for private foundations and public charities on this sensitive matter of insider compensation. In the public charity context, the fundamental requirement is not prohibition; it is reasonableness. In the private foundation setting, self-dealing generally is prohibited. Therefore, the IRS utilizes the personal services exception as a regulator: to minimize the range of instances where private foundations can permissibly compensate disqualified persons, even where the compensation is reasonable (Q 3:17).

In one instance, the IRS considered a variety of real estate services, such as management services, maintenance services, brokerage of sales and leasing transactions, construction services, and certain marketing and advertising services. The services were held to not be "personal" but akin to the selling of goods. These services were said to be "in a commercial business context and are not engaged in to directly carry out the exempt purposes of the foundation."[65]

In two instances, the IRS concluded that real estate management activity fit within the personal services exception. In the first case, the foundation's executive vice president lived on a ranch owned by the foundation so that he could oversee the real estate development activities conducted on the ranch. His duties included protecting and safeguarding the ranch, dealing with potential developers, and otherwise fulfilling his responsibilities as executive vice president. The compensation paid to the executive vice president for these services, including nominal rent for a house on the ranch in which he lived, was not considered self-dealing. Although the ruling does not discuss the personal services exception, it appears the IRS viewed the services as personal services because they were managerial in nature.[66]

In the second case, a parcel of real estate was being developed as a religious retreat to be used in a foundation's exempt activities. The president and secretary of the foundation (husband and wife) lived on the property to oversee the development. They used their best efforts to resolve zoning, utilization, access, and other property issues. Their responsibilities included management and oversight of maintenance, security, finances, and successful completion of the feasibility study phase. The rent-free accommodations and the payment of other compensation was considered payment for personal services. Again, although it was not discussed in the ruling, the rationale for the allowance of personal services exception appears to be that the services were managerial in nature.[67]

In the only court opinion to date on this point, it was held that the exception extends only to services that are "essentially professional and managerial in nature."[68] In the case, the exception was said to not embrace "general maintenance, janitorial, and custodial functions."[69] Thus, the payment by a private foundation for janitorial services to a company wholly owned by a disqualified person was held to be self-dealing, even though the fees paid were reasonable.

NOTE: Despite the terminology, this exception applies without regard to whether the person who receives the compensation is an individual.[70]

Q 3:19   What are the rules concerning the use of money or assets of a private foundation by or for the benefit of a disqualified person?

The general rule is that a transfer to, or use by or for the benefit of, a disqualified person of the income or assets of a private foundation is self-dealing.[71]

Thus, the purchase or sale of securities by a private foundation is self-dealing if the purchase or sale is made in an attempt to manipulate the price of the securities to the advantage of a disqualified person. Similarly, the indemnification (of a lender) or guarantee (of repayment) by a private foundation with respect to a loan to a disqualified person is treated as a use for the benefit of a disqualified person of the income or assets of the foundation. In addition, if a private foundation makes a grant or other payment that satisfies the legal obligation of a disqualified person, the payment ordinarily constitutes an act of self-dealing.[72]

This rule may be seen as a catchall provision, designed to apply to acts of self-dealing that may not be addressed by the foregoing rules. It encompasses three categories of transactions: a transfer to a disqualified person, a use by a disqualified person, and a use for the benefit of a disqualified person. This latter type of transaction lurks as a trap for the unwary, as discussed next (Q 3:20).

Q 3:20   What is a transaction *for the benefit of* a disqualified person?

One of the mistakes that can be made in this setting is to analyze a set of facts and conclude that the self-dealing rules are not implicated because the party to the transaction with a private foundation is not a disqualified person. The analyst should press on, to determine if the transaction nonetheless throws off a tangible or intangible economic benefit to a disqualified person.

Thus, where a lawyer was the sole trustee of a private foundation (and thus a disqualified person), the IRS ruled that the benefit to the lawyer from a loan by the foundation to an individual (not a disqualified person) who had substantial business dealings with the lawyer and his law firm was self-dealing because the placing of the loan enhanced the lawyer's reputation in the eyes of his client and provided an economic benefit to him.[73]

Likewise, the IRS found that a bank, a disqualified person, in extending credit to large corporations and tax-exempt organizations, where the notes were to be purchased by private foundations for which the bank acted as trustee, was engaging in an activity that enhanced the bank's reputation and significantly increased its goodwill, so that the transactions were (or would be) acts of self-dealing.[74]

Q 3:21 Are there any exceptions to these rules?

Yes, there is a significant exception, although it is usually narrowly construed by the IRS. This exception is for *incidental* benefits. Thus, the fact that a disqualified person receives an *incidental or tenuous* benefit from the use by a private foundation of its income or assets will not, by itself, make the use an act of self-dealing.[75]

For example, the public recognition a person may receive, arising from the charitable activities of a private foundation to which that person is a substantial contributor (Q 2:2), does not in itself result in an act of self-dealing—the benefit is incidental and tenuous. Thus, a grant by a private foundation to a public charity (Q 1:2) is not an act of self-dealing merely because the grantee is located in the same area as a corporation that is a substantial contributor to the foundation or merely because one of the public charity's trustees, directors, or officers is also a manager of or a substantial contributor to the foundation.[76]

An incidental or tenuous benefit occurs when the general reputation or prestige of a disqualified person is enhanced by public acknowledgment of a specific contribution by the person, when a disqualified person receives some other relatively minor benefit of an indirect nature, or when a disqualified person merely participates to a wholly incidental degree in the fruits of a charitable program that is of broad public interest in the community.[77]

Here are some examples of application of this exception:

- A private foundation grant to a tax-exempt hospital for modernization, replacement, and extension was not an act of self-dealing, even though two of the trustees of the foundation served on the board of trustees of the hospital.[78]
- A grant by a private foundation to a public charity did not constitute an act of self-dealing, despite the fact that the grant was conditioned on the agreement of the charity to change its name to that of a substantial contributor to the foundation.[79]
- A grant by a private foundation to a university to establish an educational program providing instruction in manufacturing engineering was not an act of self-dealing, where a disqualified person corporation intended to hire graduates of the program and encouraged its employees to enroll in the program, as long as the corporation did not

receive preferential treatment in recruiting graduates or enrolling its employees.[80]

- The loan program of a private foundation that provided financing to public charities for construction projects in disadvantaged areas did not result in acts of self-dealing merely because some contractors and subcontractors involved in the construction projects, their suppliers, and employees of those involved may have had ordinary banking and business relationships with a bank that was a disqualified person with respect to the foundation.[81]
- A private foundation was able to assume and operate a charitable program previously conducted by a for-profit company, which was a disqualified person with respect to the foundation, as a public service, without engaging in self-dealing, because the benefit to the company was incidental.[82]

A scholarship or fellowship grant to a person other than a disqualified person, which is paid or incurred by a private foundation in accordance with a program that is consistent with

- The requirements of the foundation's tax-exempt, charitable status,
- The requirements for the allowance of charitable contribution deductions for contributions made to the foundation (Chapter 17), and
- The taxable expenditures rules (Chapter 7)

will not be an act of self-dealing (Q 3:3) merely because a disqualified person indirectly receives an incidental benefit from the grant. Thus, a scholarship or fellowship grant made by a private foundation in accordance with a program to award grants of this nature to the children of employees of a substantial contributor will not constitute an act of self-dealing if these three requirements are satisfied.[83]

Q 3:22   Can a private foundation make a grant in satisfaction of a charitable pledge made by a disqualified person?

Generally, no; that would be self-dealing. Self-dealing in the form of use of a private foundation's assets for the benefit of a disqualified person (Q 3:20) occurs if the foundation makes a grant that satisfies the disqualified person's legally enforceable pledge to pay the amount. Where this type of a pledge qualifies as a debt (under local law), payment of the pledge by the foundation relieves the disqualified person of its obligation and constitutes self-dealing.[84]

Payment by a private foundation of church membership dues for an individual, a disqualified person with respect to the foundation, was found, for example, to be self-dealing inasmuch as the membership provided a personal benefit to the individual.[85] Similarly, the IRS ruled that the payment of pledges by a private foundation, which were legally binding before the foundation was created, was self-dealing. The foundation was established by several corporations to serve as a conduit for their contributions. Part of the foundation's initial funding was received on the condition that the foundation use the funds to pay certain charitable pledges that the corporations had previously made.[86]

COMMENT: As to this latter ruling, it is, of course, a harsh and even silly outcome. The foundation was established and funded to satisfy the sponsoring corporations' charitable pledges; the funds, after all, came from the corporations, which could have paid the pledges directly. But this is the nature of the self-dealing rules: Once the assets were transferred to the foundation, they became the foundation's property, which cannot be used for the benefit of disqualified persons.[87]

The making of a pledge or promise obligating a disqualified person to make a gift *to* a private foundation in the future is not an act of self-dealing, as long as it is motivated by charitable intent and unsupported by consideration. This is the case even though the arrangement is evidenced by a promissory note or other evidence of indebtedness.[88] This is not a form of extension of credit (Q 3:8).

Q 3:23   What about the purchase by a private foundation of tickets to a benefit event?

This is a tricky area. Self-dealing can arise because of the economic benefit provided to a disqualified person who attends an event, with the ticket purchased by the private foundation. Self-dealing was found when a joint purchase of benefit tickets was made by sharing the cost of tickets. The private foundation paid the deductible, or charitable contribution, portion of the ticket; the disqualified person paid the part of the ticket price allocable to the fair market value of the dinner, entertainment, and other benefits provided to contributors in connection with the fund-raising event.[89]

In this case, to be able to attend the benefit, foundation representatives would have been required to individually pay the full ticket price. Thus, they were held to have reaped a direct economic benefit—which was not incidental (Q 3:21)—to the extent the foundation paid its portion of the ticket; self-dealing occurred.

COMMENT: There are those in the private foundation community who contend that it is appropriate for their foundation managers to attend fund-raising events as representatives of the foundation who are participating for the benefit of the community. The IRS disagrees. This essentially comes down to the following: If the foundation manager *wants* to attend the event, foundation purchase of the ticket is self-dealing; if the manager doesn't want, but is forced, to go, it is not self-dealing.

Q 3:24   Can a private foundation share space, individuals, and/or expenses with a disqualified person?

This is a difficult problem. As a practical matter, many private foundations are operated in tandem with those who created them, such as a family or a corporation. For many of them, rental of a separate office and engagement of separate staff is beyond reasonable economic capability. Yet the law prohibits the furnishing of goods, services, or facilities between (to or from) a private foundation and a disqualified person (Q 3:10).

The IRS has been sympathetic in this area. Here are some examples:

- Self-dealing did not occur when a private foundation rented contiguous office space with a common reception area (constituting sharing); its offices were separate from those of the disqualified person. There were separate leases. The disqualified persons did not receive any benefit, such as reduced rent, because of the foundation's rental of the related space.[90]
- A private foundation and a disqualified person together purchased a duplicating machine and hired a shared employee. Time records were maintained to determine each entity's share of the cost of the machine and the allocable time of the employee. Because "nothing was paid directly or indirectly to" the disqualified person, and there was "independent use" by the foundation that was measurable and specifically paid to outside parties, there was no self-dealing.[91]
- A "time-sharing arrangement" of a disqualified person management company's employees was condoned by the IRS.[92] This favorable ruling was rested on the law that permits a foundation to pay reasonable compensation to a disqualified person for the performance of personal services necessary to carry out its tax-exempt purposes (Q 3:14).

The key to success in this area is separateness. Payments should be made directly to independent vendors of services (particularly landlords) whenever possible. Payments may be calculated on a proportional basis. If there are shared employees, there should be separate contracts. If there is a shared telephone system, there should be separate maintenance agreements.[93]

Q 3:25   Do these rules apply to securities transactions?

Yes. Indeed, there has been reference to securities transactions in various contexts previously (Q 3:1, Q 3:2).

Also, a transaction between a private foundation and a corporation that is a disqualified person, pursuant to a liquidation, merger, redemption, recapitalization, or other corporate adjustment, organization, or reorganization, is not an act of self-dealing if

- All of the securities of the same class as that held by the foundation are subject to the same terms, and

- The terms provide for receipt by the foundation of no less than fair market value.[94]

All of the securities are not subject to the same terms unless, pursuant to the transaction, the corporation makes a bona fide offer on a uniform basis to the foundation and every other person who holds the securities. The fact that a private foundation receives property, such as debentures, while all other persons holding securities of the same class receive cash for their interests is evidence that the offer was *not* made on a uniform basis.[95]

NOTE: This rule can apply even if no other person holds any securities of the class held by the foundation. In that event, however, the consideration received by holders of other classes of securities, or the interests retained by holders of the other classes, when considered in relation to the consideration received by the foundation, must indicate that the foundation received at least as favorable treatment in relation to its interests as the holders of any other class of securities.[96]

An issue on which the IRS has not directly ruled concerns the sale of securities by a private foundation in a secondary public offering, where the offering would not take place but for the involvement of the foundation, where one or more disqualified persons desire to also participate in the securities transaction. To allow the disqualified persons to participate in the transaction would be an act of self-dealing, as an attempt either to manipulate the price of the securities to the advantage of the disqualified persons (Q 3:19) or to otherwise use the assets of the foundation for the benefit of the disqualified persons. In one instance, a public offering of stock made to enable a private foundation to sell its shares was ruled to not entail self-dealing—but the disqualified persons were excluded from the transaction.[97]

Q 3:26   Can a private foundation make a payment to a government official?

Basically, the law prohibits a payment by a private foundation to a government official, but there are a number of exceptions to that rule. An agreement by a foundation to make any payment of money or other property to a government official generally constitutes self-dealing, unless the agreement is to employ a government official for a period after termination of his or her government service and he or she is terminating his or her service within a 90-day period.[98] An individual who otherwise meets the definition of a government official is treated as a government official while on leave of absence from the government without pay.[99]

Certain payments to government officials are permitted:[100]

- A prize or award that is not includible in gross income,[101] if the government official receiving the prize or award is selected from the general public. The prize or award must be paid over to a charitable organization.

- A scholarship or fellowship grant that is excludable from gross income[102] and that is to be utilized for study at a qualified educational institution.[103] This type of grant can only be for tuition, fees, and books.
- Certain types of pension plans and annuity payments.
- Any contribution (other than of money) to, or services or facilities made available to, a government official, if the aggregate value of the contribution, services, and facilities provided total no more than $25 in a year.
- Government employee training program payments.
- Reimbursement of the actual cost of travel, including meals and lodging, solely within the United States for attendance at a charitable function, not to exceed 125 percent of the prevailing per diem rate.

NOTE: Thus, for example, as to this last item, reimbursement by a private foundation for travel expenses incurred by a member of Congress it selected to participate in a conference it cosponsored in a foreign country constituted an act of self-dealing.[104]

Q 3:27   What is *indirect* self-dealing?

Self-dealing transactions can be *direct* or *indirect.* Most self-dealing transactions—certainly the ones discussed to this point—are of the direct variety. Indirect self-dealing can arise when a disqualified person engages in a transaction with an entity controlled by a private foundation.[105] This type of self-dealing also can arise when such a transaction is with respect to a private foundation's interest or expectancy in property, held by an estate or a revocable trust, including a trust that has become irrevocable on a grantor's death (Q 3:28).

Q 3:28   How do these rules apply to property held in an estate or trust?

The rules as to indirect self-dealing (Q 3:27) can be triggered in the estate and trust context in two instances: where a private foundation has a deemed ownership interest in property held in an estate or trust or where a foundation controls an estate or trust.

Foundation as "Owner" of Estate and Trust Assets

As a general principle, where a private foundation is the prospective distributee of income or assets in an estate or trust, for purposes of the self-dealing rules, the private foundation has a vested beneficial interest in the property held by the estate or trust. Thus, transactions with the estate or trust are generally considered as the functional equivalent of transactions with the foundation. This is a form of indirect self-dealing.

Specifically, a transaction involving property held in an estate or trust, where the property is destined for a private foundation, can be considered an act of indirect self-dealing if the transaction is with a disqualified person with respect to the foundation and the foundation is considered to own an interest or expectancy in the property in the estate or trust. The same is the case where the private foundation has an interest or expectancy in property held by an estate or revocable trust that, on the grantor's death, became irrevocable.

Under certain circumstances, transactions during administration of an estate, with a disqualified person, regarding a private foundation's interest or expectancy in property held by an estate (or trust) are not self-dealing.[106] These circumstances generally concern the sale of property by the estate or trust.

The following conditions must be met for this exception to the self-dealing rules to arise:

1. The executor or trustee has the authority to either sell the property or reallocate it to another beneficiary, or is required to sell the property by the terms of the trust or will.
2. A probate court having jurisdiction over the estate approves the terms of the transaction.
3. The transaction occurs before the estate or trust is terminated.
4. The estate or trust receives an amount equal to or in excess of the fair market value of its interest or expectancy in the property at the time of the transaction, taking into account the terms of any option subject to which the property is acquired by the estate or trust.
5. The foundation receives
   a. an interest at least as liquid as the one given up,
   b. an exempt function asset, or
   c. an amount of money equal to that required under an option binding on the estate or trust.

Generally, then, where these circumstances are not involved, a prohibited transaction involving an estate or trust, holding property destined for a private foundation, almost always constitutes indirect self-dealing. In one case, an individual, a disqualified person with respect to a charitable trust, purchased property from the estate of the decedent who created the trust. The property was destined to be a substantial part of the trust corpus. The disqualified person argued reliance on the above exception. The IRS concluded, however, that the purchase was an act of self-dealing because the disqualified person had not paid the estate the fair market value of the property. The matter was litigated, with the district court and the court of appeals concluding that the IRS was correct and that the above regulation was constitutional.[107]

Subsequently, the U.S. Tax Court discussed this carve-out rule. It wrote that, "in the absence of those exceptions, such transactions would have been covered by section 4941." The court added that "it is clear that transactions affecting the assets of an estate generally are treated as also affecting the assets of any private foundation which, as a beneficiary of the estate, has an expectancy interest in the assets of the estate.[108] (The principal issue in the case, not resolved in this opinion, was whether executors of the estate of an artist engaged in acts of self-dealing when they purchased paintings from the estate.)

This exception is available only with respect to transactions during administration of an estate, with a disqualified person, regarding a private foundation's "interest or expectancy in property" held by an estate (or trust). It seems to be confined to the sale or other disposition of property by the estate or trust.[109] It does not apply to transactions involving compensation for services.

Q 3:29 Does indirect self-dealing occur in control situations?

There is another potentially applicable exception. The term *indirect self-dealing* does not include a transaction between a disqualified person and an organization "controlled" by a private foundation if

1. The transaction results from a business relationship that was established before the transaction constituted an act of self-dealing,
2. The transaction was at least as favorable to the organization controlled by the private foundation as an arm's-length transaction with an unrelated person, and
3. Either
   a. the organization controlled by the private foundation could have engaged in the transaction with someone other than a disqualified person only at a severe economic hardship to the organization, or
   b. because of the unique nature of the product or services provided by the organization controlled by the foundation, the disqualified person could not have engaged in the transaction with anyone else, or could have done so only by incurring severe economic hardship.[110]

An organization is controlled by a private foundation if the foundation or one or more of its foundation managers may, by aggregating their votes or positions of authority, require the organization to engage in a transaction that, if engaged in with the private foundation, would constitute self-dealing.[111]

Also, an organization is controlled by a private foundation in the case of such a transaction between the organization and a disqualified person, if the disqualified person, together with one or more persons who are disqualified persons by reason of such person's relationship (e.g., a member of the family) to the disqualified person, may, by aggregating their votes or positions of authority with that of the foundation, require the organization to engage in such a transaction.[112]

As to this second rule, an organization is considered to be controlled by a private foundation, or by a private foundation and disqualified persons, if such persons are able, in fact, to control the organization (even if their aggregate voting power is less than 50 percent of the total voting power of the organization's governing body) or if one or more of such persons has the right to exercise veto power over the actions of the organization relevant to any potential acts of self-dealing.[113]

Generally, then, where these three circumstances are not involved, this type of a transaction almost always constitutes indirect self-dealing. Two other exceptions may be available:

1. The benefit to a disqualified person is incidental or tenuous (Q 3:21) or
2. The benefit is compensation for personal services where the compensation is reasonable (Q 3:17) and in furtherance of charitable activities.

Q 3:30   Can a private foundation indemnify and insure its disqualified persons?

It is common for a private foundation to provide officers' and directors' liability insurance to, or to indemnify, foundation managers in connection with civil proceedings arising from the foundation managers' performance of services for the foundation. The general rule is that indemnification by a private foundation or the provision of insurance, for the purpose of covering the liabilities of an individual in his or her capacity as manager of the foundation, is not self-dealing. Moreover, the amounts expended by a foundation for insurance or indemnification generally are not included in the compensation of the disqualified person for purposes of determining whether the disqualified person's compensation is reasonable (Q 3:17).

This body of law is a component of the general regulatory scheme by which transfers to, or use by or for the benefit of, a disqualified person of the income or assets of a private foundation generally constitute self-dealing (Q 3:19). Indemnification payments and insurance coverage in this area are divided into noncompensatory and compensatory categories.

Noncompensatory Indemnification and Insurance

Self-dealing does not occur, as a general rule, when a private foundation indemnifies a foundation manager with respect to the manager's defense in any civil judicial or civil administrative proceeding arising out of the manager's performance of services (or failure to perform services) on behalf of the foundation. This indemnification may be against all expenses (other than taxes, including any of the private foundation taxes, penalties, or expenses of correction) and can include payment of lawyers' fees, judgments, and settlement expenditures.

The following conditions must exist, however, for the indemnification to not be considered self-dealing:

- The expenses must be reasonably incurred by the manager in connection with the proceeding, and
- The manager must not have acted willfully or without reasonable cause with respect to the act or failure to act that led to the proceeding or liability for a private foundation tax.[114]

Likewise, the self-dealing rules do not apply to premiums of insurance to make or to reimburse a foundation for this type of indemnification payment.[115]

These payments are viewed as expenses for the foundation's administration and operation rather than as compensation for the manager's services. An indemnification or payment of insurance of this nature is not regarded as part of the compensation paid to the manager for purposes of determining whether the compensation is reasonable for purposes of the private foundation rules.[116]

Compensatory Indemnification and Insurance

The indemnification of a foundation manager against payment of a penalty tax, and the associated defense, is considered part of the manager's compensation. This type of payment by a private foundation is an act of self-dealing unless, when the payment is added to other compensation paid to the manager, the total compensation is reasonable.

A *compensatory expense* of this nature includes payment of any of the following:

- Any penalty, tax (including a private foundation tax), or expense of correction that is owed by the foundation manager
- Any expense not reasonably incurred by the manager in connection with a civil judicial or civil administrative proceeding arising out of the manager's performance of services on behalf of the foundation, or
- Any expense resulting from an act or failure to act with respect to which the manager has acted willfully and without reasonable cause.[117]

Likewise, the payment by a private foundation of the premiums for an insurance policy providing liability insurance for a foundation manager for any of these three categories of expenses is self-dealing, unless when the premiums are added to other compensation paid to the manager the total compensation is reasonable for purposes of the private foundation rules.[118] If the total compensation is not reasonable, the foundation will have engaged in an act of self-dealing. These payments are viewed as being exclusively for the benefit of the managers, not the private foundation.

Allocation of Premiums

A private foundation is not engaged in an act of self-dealing if the foundation purchases a single insurance policy to provide its managers both noncompensatory and compensatory coverage, as long as the total insurance premium is allocated and each manager's portion of the premium attributable to the compensatory coverage is included in that manager's compensation for purposes of determining reasonable compensation.[119]

The term *indemnification* includes not only reimbursement by the foundation for expenses that a foundation manager has already incurred or anticipates incurring but also the direct payment by the foundation of these expenses as they arise.[120]

Q 3:31 How do these rules apply with respect to volunteers?

The determination of whether any amount of indemnification or insurance premiums is included in a manager's gross income for individual income tax purposes is made on the basis of general federal tax law principles and without regard to the treatment of the amount for purposes of ascertaining whether the manager's compensation is reasonable for self-dealing purposes (Q 3:17).[121] Any property or service that is excluded from income under the *de minimis* fringe benefit rules[122] may be disregarded for purposes of determining whether the recipient's compensation is reasonable.[123]

The IRS promulgated regulations relating to the exclusion from gross income of benefits known as *working condition fringe benefits.*[124] This type of benefit is any property or service provided to an employee of an employer to the extent that, if the employee paid for the property or service, the amount paid would be allowable as a business deduction[125] or a depreciation deduction.[126] These regulations clarified the treatment, in this regard, of bona fide volunteers who perform services for private foundations and other tax-exempt organizations. These regulations, which do not directly address the self-dealing aspects of this matter, apply to volunteers (including trustees and directors) who provide services to exempt organizations and who receive directors' and officers' liability insurance and/or indemnification protection from these organizations.

The federal tax law excludes certain fringe benefits from an individual's gross income.[127] Generally, these fringe benefits are excludable by those who are employees, whether these individuals are compensated or serving as volunteers (where the tax-exempt organization has the right to direct or control the volunteers' services). For certain purposes, the term *employee*[128] includes independent contractors. For other purposes,[129] however, independent contractors are not treated as employees. Thus, bona fide volunteers, like their paid counterparts, could not (prior to the adoption of these regulations) exclude the value of no-additional-cost services from their gross income (unless there was an employer-employee relationship, which was unlikely). That is, although volunteers who were employees could exclude these fringe benefits from gross income, and all volunteers (including independent contractors) could exclude *de minimis* fringe benefits, the language of the regulations relating to working condition fringe benefits did not encompass bona fide volunteers.

The difficulty in this connection pertained to the business expense deduction rules.[130] An individual engaged in carrying on a trade or business has the requisite profit motive for business expense deduction purposes. An individual who performs services as a bona fide volunteer, by contrast, lacks a profit motive and thus cannot claim an expense deduction for amounts incurred in connection with the volunteer work. For example, the value of directors' and officers' insurance provided to a volunteer was not excludable from gross income as a working condition fringe benefit, even though the same insurance coverage is excludable from the income of a paid employee or director (who has the requisite profit motive). These regulations are designed to eliminate this distinction.

The regulations provide that, solely for these purposes, a bona fide volunteer (including a director or an officer) who performs services for a tax-exempt organization is *deemed* to have a profit motive for purposes of the business expense deduction.[131] An individual is a *bona fide volunteer* only if the total value of the benefits provided with respect to the volunteer services is substantially less than the total value of the volunteer services the individual provides to the organization.[132] The value of liability insurance coverage (or indemnification for liability) is deemed to be substantially less than the value of an individual's volunteer services to the organization, provided that the insurance coverage is limited to acts performed in the discharge of official duties or the performance of services on behalf of the exempt organization employer.[133]

As noted, these regulations do not directly address the self-dealing aspects of this issue. The explanation accompanying these regulations, however, states that, "like other tax-exempt organizations, private foundations need not allocate portions of D & O [directors' and officers'] insurance premiums to individual directors or officers or include any such allocable amounts" as reportable compensation, "provided such amounts are excludable from gross income under the[se] final regulations" and that "whether or not such allocable amounts need to be treated as compensation for the limited purpose" of the self-dealing rules, "no employer should issue [compensation tax form] 1099 or W-2 for any such amount that is excludable from gross income as a working condition fringe benefit."

Consequently, while a private foundation manager still must (to avoid the self-dealing rules) be certain that this form of compensation is reasonable, the amount involved is excludable from the gross income of the manager.

Q 3:32   What should be done when an act of self-dealing occurs?

Once it has been determined that an act of self-dealing has occurred, the self-dealing transaction should be corrected (Q 3:33), an excise tax return (Form 4720) should be prepared and filed, and the tax due should be paid. The steps involved in this regard include undoing the transaction, assigning an amount attributable to the self-dealing, termed the *amount involved* (Q 3:34), deciding who has to pay an excise tax, and advancing any claim of reasonable cause to reduce or avoid any additional tax.

Q 3:33   How is an act of self-dealing *corrected*?

To undo an act of self-dealing, the transaction must be corrected and rescinded. The term *correction* means, as noted, undoing the transaction to the extent possible, but, in any case, placing the private foundation in a financial position that is not worse than that in which it would be if the disqualified person were dealing under the highest fiduciary standards.[134]

If the matter involves a sale to the private foundation, rescission of the sale is required. The property must be returned to the disqualified person/seller, and the seller must return to the foundation the proceeds of the sale, plus the appropriate amount of interest to take into account the time value of the money.[135]

Q 3:34   What is the *amount involved*?

The penalties for entering into a self-dealing transaction are based on the *amount involved,* which is defined as the "greater of the amount of money and the fair market value of the other property given or the amount of money and the fair market value of the other property received."[136]

Where a transaction entails the use of money or other property, the amount involved is the greater of the amount paid for the use or the fair market value of the use for the period for which the money or other property is used.[137] If a private foundation lends a trustee money at a below-market interest rate (Q 3:6), the amount involved equals the principal of the loan plus the interest that would have been charged at the prevailing market rate at the time the loan was made.[138]

In the case of compensation paid for personal services to persons other than governmental officials (Q 3:18), the amount involved is the portion of the total compensation in excess of the amount that would have been reasonable.[139]

To calculate the first-tier tax initially imposed in connection with a transaction, the amount involved is determined as of the date on which the self-dealing occurred.[140] An act of self-dealing *occurs* on the date on which all the terms and conditions of the transaction and the liabilities of the parties have been fixed.[141] If the self-dealing goes uncorrected and the additional tax is calculated, the valuation is equal to the highest value during the period of time the self-dealing continued uncorrected.

Q 3:35   Who pays the self-dealing first-tier tax?

Generally, this tax is paid by the self-dealer, namely, the disqualified person (Chapter 2) who participated (Q 3:37) in the act of self-dealing for each year (or part of a year) in the taxable period (Q 3:42). The self-dealer is taxed even if he or she was unaware that a rule was being violated.

Foundation managers (Q 2:6) who participate in an act of self-dealing are also potentially taxable. This tax may be imposed, however, only where:

- The initial (first-tier) tax on the self-dealer is imposed,
- The foundation manager knows (Q 3:40) that the act is an act of self-dealing, and
- The participation by the foundation manager is willful and not due to reasonable cause.[142]

CAUTION: A self-dealer also acting as a foundation manager can be subject to both taxes.[143]

Q 3:36   How is the self-dealing first-tier tax computed?

The disqualified person self-dealer (other than a foundation manager acting only in that capacity) who participates is liable for a 5 percent tax on the amount involved.[144] A foundation manager who participates in an act of self-dealing is subject to a tax at the rate of 2½ percent of the amount involved.[145]

Q 3:37   What does the term *participation* mean?

For purposes of the initial tax (Q 3:36), a manager is treated as *participating* in an act of self-dealing in any case in which the person engages or takes part in the transaction by himself, herself, or itself, or directs any person to do so.[146] The term includes silence or inaction on the part of a foundation manager where he or she is under a duty to speak or act as well as any affirmative action by the manager. A foundation manager, however, is not considered to have participated in an act of self-dealing where he or she has opposed the act in a manner consistent with the fulfillment of his or her responsibilities to the private foundation.[147]

Q 3:38   What does the term *willful* mean?

Participation (Q 3:37) by a foundation manager is deemed *willful* if it is voluntary, conscious, and intentional. A motive to avoid the restrictions of the law or the incurrence of any tax is not necessary to make the participation willful. Participation by a foundation manager is not willful, however, if he or she does not know (Q 3:40) that the transaction in which he or she is participating is an act of self-dealing.[148]

Q 3:39   What does the term *reasonable cause* mean?

A foundation manager's participation is due to *reasonable cause* if he or she has exercised his or her responsibility on behalf of the private foundation with ordinary business skill and prudence.[149] A manager having reasonable cause would be one found to be attentive to the affairs of the foundation, to be aware of the private foundation sanctions, and to remain sufficiently informed of the foundation's activities to prevent any violation of the sanctions.

Q 3:40 What does the term *knowing* mean?

The term *knowing* does not mean "having reason to know." Evidence tending to show that an individual has reason to know of a particular fact or particular rule, however, is relevant in determining whether he or she had actual knowledge of that fact or rule. For example, evidence tending to show that an individual has reason to know of sufficient facts so that, based solely on those facts, a transaction would be an act of self-dealing is relevant in determining whether he or she has actual knowledge of those facts.[150]

An individual is considered to have participated (Q 3:37) in a transaction knowing that it is an act of self-dealing only if he or she

- Has actual knowledge of sufficient facts so that, based solely on those facts, the transaction would be an act of self-dealing.
- Is aware that the act under these circumstances may violate the self-dealing rules.
- Negligently fails to make reasonable attempts to ascertain whether the transaction is an act of self-dealing, or is in fact aware that it is this type of act.[151]

In the case of a governmental official (Q 2:23), the self-dealing tax can be imposed only if the official, as a disqualified person, participated in the act of self-dealing knowing that it was such an act.[152]

NOTE: Otherwise, the tax is imposed on a disqualified person even though the person did not have any knowledge, at the time of the act, that it constituted self-dealing.[153]

Q 3:41 What about reliance on the advice of a lawyer?

If an individual, after full disclosure of the facts to a lawyer (including house counsel), relies on the advice of that lawyer, expressed in a reasoned written legal opinion, that an act is not an act of self-dealing—even though that act is subsequently held to be self-dealing—the individual's participation (Q 3:37) in the act will ordinarily not be considered knowing (Q 3:40) or willful (Q 3:38) and will ordinarily be considered due to reasonable cause (Q 3:39).

A written legal opinion is considered *reasoned,* even if it reaches a conclusion that is subsequently determined to be incorrect, as long as the opinion addresses itself to the facts and applicable law. A written opinion is not considered reasoned, however, if it does nothing more than recite the facts and express a conclusion.[154]

NOTE: The absence of advice from a lawyer with respect to a self-dealing act does not, by itself, give rise to any inference that a person participated in the act knowingly, willfully, or in the absence of reasonable cause.

Q 3:42   What does the term *taxable period* mean?

The term *taxable period* is, with respect to an act of self-dealing, the period beginning with the date on which the act of self-dealing occurred and ending on the earliest of the date:

- Of mailing of a notice of deficiency with respect to the initial tax,
- On which the tax is assessed, or
- On which correction (Q 3:33) of the act of self-dealing is completed.[155]

If a transaction between a private foundation and a disqualified person concerns the leasing of property (Q 3:4), the lending of money (Q 3:6) or other extension of credit (Q 3:8), other use of money or property (Q 3:19), or payment of compensation (Q 3:13), the transaction will generally be treated as giving rise to an act of self-dealing on the day the transaction occurs, plus an act of self-dealing on the first day of each applicable tax year after that date.[156]

Q 3:43   Who pays the self-dealing second-tier tax?

Where the initial tax (Q 3:35) is imposed and the self-dealing is not corrected (Q 3:33) within a timely manner (Q 3:42), an additional tax of 200 percent of the amount involved (Q 3:34) is imposed on the self-dealer.[157] A foundation manager who refuses to agree to the correction faces a penalty of 50 percent of the amount involved.[158]

Q 3:44   Can more than one person be liable for a self-dealing tax?

If more than one self-dealer is liable for an initial tax (Q 3:35) or an additional tax (Q 3:43), all of them are jointly and severally liable for the tax with respect to the act of self-dealing involved.[159]

If joint participation in a transaction by two or more disqualified persons constitutes self-dealing (e.g., a joint sale of property to a private foundation), the transaction generally is treated as a separate act of self-dealing with respect to each disqualified person.[160]

Joint and several liability also applies with respect to the tax on foundation managers, although there is a maximum on the tax imposed, which is $10,000.[161]

Q 3:45   Can the IRS abate a self-dealing tax?

The IRS generally has the authority to abate the private foundation first-tier taxes where reasonable cause is shown, as well as in the absence of willful neglect.[162] This authority does not extend, however, to the self-dealing taxes.[163]

COMMENT: Nonetheless, in one instance, the IRS found acts of self-dealing on audit of a private foundation, yet worked with foundation management to revise the organization's operations so as to correct the activities that gave rise to the transgression. The IRS used its general authority to grant relief[164] to do so retroactively for the benefit of the foundation (because tax-exempt status was also at issue) and its management on the self-dealing issues.[165] While this relief was not formal abatement, it was virtual abatement.

CHAPTER 4

Mandatory Payout Requirements

The Treasury Department concluded, back in 1964, that some private chari-ties were making few, if any, disbursements for charitable purposes. Reportedly, foundations were formed with the shares of family companies that paid no dividends, so that the foundation had no income to support charitable activ-ities. Congress responded by designing the mandatory payout rules imposed without regard to the actual current income.

Here are the questions that are most frequently asked (or that should be asked) about the mandatory payout rules—and the answers to them.

Q 4:1   What are the mandatory distribution rules?

Stated most simply, a private foundation must annually spend, or pay out cash and other property, a minimum amount for charitable and administrative pur-poses. The payout amount equals at least 5 percent of the average fair market value of a private foundation's investment assets (less any debt incurred to acquire the property) for the preceding year (Q 4:5). This mandatory payout is also referred to as the *distributable amount* and the *minimum distribution requirement* (Q 4:3, Q 4:4). To illustrate the rule, a foundation with investments averaging $10,000,000 in value in the prior year must distribute $500,000 for charitable purposes before the end of the current year. The rationale behind the payout requirement is twofold.

Q 4:2   Why is the rule imposed on private foundations?

Investigations of private charities during the 1960s revealed instances of foun-dations funded with closely held company shares that paid modest, if any, dividends, resulting in foundations that made few, if any, charitable grants. Congress felt it was unfair to allow a charitable deduction to offset what at that time was a 70 percent top individual tax rate when no money went to charity.

Concurrently, an excess business holdings rule (Chapter 5) and a jeopardizing investment rule (Chapter 6) were imposed to limit the type of investments a foundation can hold. It was thought the rules would impel foundations to make investments that yielded interest and dividends with which to make disbursements for charitable purposes. Ironically, most foundations today follow a *total return* style of investing, with most of the income produced from gains in the underlying value of the security with little or no dividends. Thus, many foundations today either sell or distribute shares to meet the requirement that they support charitable causes.

Q 4:3   How is the mandatory payout amount calculated?

The federal tax law terms the mandatory payout amount the *distributable amount* and calculates it by means of the following formula:

$$A + B - C = \text{Minimum Distributable Amount (MDR)}$$

A = Minimum investment return (Q 4:4)
B = Add back any amounts previously included as a qualifying distribution, but now not qualifying, such as:

- Grant, student loan, or program-related investment repaid or returned to the foundation (Q 4:10).
- Set-aside amounts not used or completed during allowable time period.
- An asset previously used in conducting program activity that is either sold during the year or converted into an investment asset.[1] The acquisition or conversion of assets to be used in program, or exempt function, is counted as a qualifying distribution in the year acquired. Thus, if an asset ceases to be used for charitable programs, either the sales proceeds or fair market value on the date of conversion is the amount added back, or essentially must be distributed.

C = Excise tax on investment income and any unrelated business income tax.

Q 4:4   How is the minimum investment return calculated?

The formula for calculating the minimum investment return (MIR) follows[2]:

$$\begin{array}{c} \text{Average value of investment assets} - \text{debt} \\ - \text{cash reserve} \times 5\% = \text{MIR} \end{array}$$

The 5 percent applicable percentage is reduced for a foundation with a short taxable year.[3] Say a foundation receives its first assets on October 1 and chooses to report on a calendar year basis. Its first Form 990-PF would be due for the three months ending on December 31. Its payout percentage would be 1.25 percent calculated as follows:

$$92 \text{ days in its year} \div 365 \text{ days} = 25\% \times 5\% = 1.25\%$$

Q 4:5 What assets are involved in the calculation of the minimum investment return?

Assets owned by a private foundation for the purpose of producing investment income form the basis for calculating the minimum investment return. These assets are included whether acquired by purchase, gift, devise, or any other means. All types of assets, including stocks, bonds, rental property, mineral interests, and the like, are included in the calculation of minimum investment return. Even if the foundation intends to dispose of such a property, it is counted while it is owned.

By contrast, those assets used by the foundation in actually conducting its charitable activities—called *exempt function assets*—are not counted in the averaging formula. Examples of these assets include a collection of art, a public library building, and a low-income apartment project.[4] Those assets acquired and held to accomplish a charitable purpose, rather with the intention of producing income, are not included in the payout calculation. Investments made to accomplish a charitable purpose, such as a venture capital fund for minority business enterprises or a student loan fund, are called *program-related investments* (Q 5:4), and are also excluded from the calculation even though they may produce some income.

An asset used dually for investment and program purposes, such as the foundation's office building, is allocated between its respective functions.[5] For assets that are used 95 percent or more for one purpose, the remaining 5 percent is ignored. In allocating a building, the actual usage of the space is the factor customarily used. In one instance, the IRS ruled that fair rental value should be used when the building is partly rented to commercial tenants.

Future interests or expectancies in property are not included. The value of a remainder or income interest in a trust, a pledge to make a donation in the future, and the right to receive the residuary interest in an estate are not counted as foundation assets until the foundation actually receives the underlying property.

An investment-type asset, such as a building rented to commercial tenants, can be excluded from the payout calculation for a limited period of time after its acquisition if the foundation acquired it to be used as an exempt function asset. If the conversion will take more than a year, IRS permission for doing what is referred to as *setting aside* the property can be requested (Q 4:17).

Q 4:6 When are assets valued for purposes of calculating the minimum investment return?

Four valuation types are prescribed for different kinds of assets, essentially acknowledging the ease with which suitable market information is available:

1. Cash and cash equivalents are valued at actual balances at the beginning and end of each month in the year.

2. Readily marketable securities are valued on any day of each month so long as the method is consistent and reasonable.
3. Real estate must be revalued every five years, except it can be revalued more often if the value declines.
4. All other assets, such as collectibles, office equipment, partnership interests, nonmarketable securities, and all other assets are valued once a year.[6]

Q 4:7   How are assets valued for purposes of calculating the minimum investment return?

Most assets can be valued by using the prices published for the market in which the property is customarily sold. The definition of *fair market value* for this purpose is the price a willing buyer would pay a willing seller in the normal marketplace in which the item is sold, neither one being under any unusual compulsion to buy or sell. Valuations made in accordance with the methods prescribed for estate tax valuations are acceptable. Pertaining to marketable securities for which share prices are quoted on a daily basis, any consistently used valuation pattern of the sort suggested below can be used.

- The closing quotation for each security owned by the foundation on the last trading day of each month
- The monthly portfolio value reported by an investment management company or financial institution
- The quoted value on the fifth, tenth, or any other day of each month

The value of real property, including land, buildings, and mineral properties, must be determined by an independent appraiser once every five years.

COMMENT: The date on which a newly acquired property must be valued is not specified by the regulations. Thus, the foundation can choose any valuation date, but subsequently should use approximately the same date on a consistent basis.

Q 4:8   How is the average value of the assets calculated?

To arrive at the average fair value of all assets, one must first calculate the average for each of the four types of assets (Q 4:6) and then add the four averages together.

- For cash (type 1), the balance on the end of each month and the first day of the year is added and divided by 12 to arrive at an average.
- For marketable securities (type 2), a monthly value (can be any day of the month, but is usually the month-end value) of the assets is added and divided by 12 to arrive at a simple annual average.

- For assets valued annually (type 3) and real property (type 4) held for an entire year, the value for the year from each is added together. Assets held less than one year are subject to special rules (Q 4:9).

Q 4:9   What about an asset held for less than one year?

A prorated value based on the number of days in the year the asset was held is included in the minimum investment return formula. First, the value of the property must be determined under the general rules (Q 4:6); then that value is prorated. If, for example, a private foundation bought a rental office building on July 1, half of its value would be included applying the following formula:

$$\frac{\text{Days in year the asset was held}}{\text{Days in tax year}} \times \text{Value} = \text{Includible value}$$

COMMENT: Although a private foundation is technically required to prorate the daily value of any asset held for less than a year, it may be burdensome to make this calculation for an actively managed portfolio of marketable securities. As a practical matter, each time a security is sold, it is immediately reinvested in another security, making the holding period immaterial. Thus, many foundations consider the required proration as accomplished for such securities without a separate calculation.

Q 4:10   What is a *qualifying distribution*?

A *qualifying distribution* is an expenditure made to accomplish a charitable purpose. A pledge to make a payment in the future is not counted; only actual cash disbursements and distributions of property are qualifying distributions. The federal tax law defines *qualifying distributions* to include:

- Any amount, including reasonable and necessary administrative expenses, paid to accomplish one or more tax-exempt purposes. Contributions to an organization controlled by the distributing foundation, to one or more disqualified persons with respect to the foundation, or to another private foundation that is not an operating foundation are not includable.
- Any amount paid to acquire an asset used or held for use specifically for carrying out one or more tax-exempt purposes, and
- Qualified set-asides (Q 4:17) and program-related investments (Q 6:7).[7]

Direct grants made to nonprofit organizations recognized as public charities (Chapter 12) comprise the bulk of qualifying distributions made by private foundations. Direct expenditures made to accomplish a charitable purpose, such as purchasing food to distribute to the homeless or hiring a scientist to research a cure for disease, are also counted as qualifying distributions. Foundations that regularly conduct active programs may choose to be subject to different distribution requirements as private operating foundations (Q 14:2). Conversion of an investment asset into an exempt function asset is treated as a qualifying distribution. Payments made to individual students under a scholarship program count.

Q 4:11 Are distributions from a charitable lead trust included in a foundation's distributable amount?

No, not according to the statute that was revised in 1982. Contrary to the tax law, Form 990-PF and its instructions direct a private foundation to add the amount received as distributions from split-interest trusts to its mandatory payout requirement. The Ann Jackson Family Foundation's successful challenge to this IRS position in a 1991 Tax Court decision was affirmed by the U.S. Court of Appeals for the 9th Circuit in 1994.[8] The confusion arose because, before 1982, all foundations were required to distribute either their actual net income or the minimum amount, whichever was higher. In an effort to preserve foundations' principal, Congress changed the tax law to only require the minimum amount without regard to the foundation's actual income. Thus, trust distributions became irrelevant in calculating the mandatory distribution table amount. The ongoing confusion about the trust income add-back is compounded by the fact that it continues to apply to private operating foundations. A foundation that chooses to comply with the IRS position should pay careful attention to the dates trust assets were dedicated to its benefit. Additions to a trust prior to May 26, 1969, can be excluded.

Q 4:12 Can a foundation count in-kind qualifying distributions?

The issue is whether the lending of its property by a private foundation or some forbearance of income yields an amount that can be considered a qualifying distribution. A private foundation may, for example, provide office space to a public charity without charging rent. Other illustrations include a foundation lending a work of art to a museum or a no-interest loan for charitable purposes. These *in-kind* distributions arguably are qualifying distributions.

NOTE: There is no law as such on this subject. What follows is an extrapolation from old law in the charitable giving context.

There is some charitable giving law on the subject of a gift of the *right to use* real property. Thus, for example, a private foundation may make a grant of a leasehold estate to a public charity of the right to use the foundation's real property. This type of leasehold has a fair market value. It certainly is of value to the grantee.

A court opinion issued in 1964 pertains to this matter. (The date is significant because the law, as noted below, was changed in 1969.) In the case, an individual was allowed an income tax charitable contribution deduction for a gift of the right to use real estate.[9] The IRS contended that permission to occupy and use property granted to a charitable organization does not constitute a gift of property but instead is merely the granting of a privilege.[10] The court rejected this view of the IRS and, as noted, allowed the deduction.

In so doing, the court wrote the following: "'Property' is more than just the physical thing—the land, the bricks, the mortar—it is also the sum of all the rights and powers incident to ownership of the physical thing. It is the tangible and intangible. Property is composed of constituent elements and of these elements *the right to use the physical thing to the exclusion of others is the most essential and beneficial.* Without this right all others would be of little value, for if the owner is deprived of the use of the tangible thing, little more than a barren title is left in his hands "[11]

The private foundation mandatory distribution rules do not necessarily parallel the rules as to deductible charitable gifts. For example, pursuant to a law that was enacted in 1969, an individual is not entitled to an income tax charitable contribution deduction for a gift of the right to use property because it is a gift of less than the donor's entire interest in the property.[12] Nonetheless, this type of transfer is still a gift and thus akin to a grant for private foundation law purposes.

A private foundation may make a grant of an interest-free loan to a public charity for charitable purposes and receive a qualifying distribution for the amount of the loan principal and a separate qualifying distribution for the fair market value of the interest foresworn.[13]

NOTE: In the year or years when the loan is repaid, the principal amount must be added to the foundation's minimum payout obligation for that year (Q 4:3).

Based on this scant law, the better view is that the fair market value of a free leasing or rental of property constitutes a qualifying distribution. This would be a grant of, in the language of the above court opinion, the "right to use the physical thing to the exclusion of others." The grant of this intangible aspect of the property is, in this context, comparable to the value of interest foresworn when a private foundation makes an interest-free loan to a public charity.

Admittedly, there is a problem with this approach. Another way to analyze this situation is to see what the tax consequences would be if a foundation were to lend property, such as a work of art, to a public charity for a fee and then grant the money back to the public charity. The rent amount would be taxed as unrelated business income (Chapter 9) and the grant amount would be a qualifying distribution in full. Thus, there is the possibility that the IRS would assert the presence of some "phantom" unrelated business income when personal property is leased without charge to a public charity and a qualifying distribution is claimed for the fair market value of the leasehold.

NOTE: This would not be the result in the case of an interest-free loan because the interest income is shielded from normal income taxation by statute (Q 9:23).

It is known that the IRS probably would not rule favorably on this issue. As is often the case in this context, the IRS is troubled because of difficulties in valuing the interest granted.

COMMENT: The fact that there may be some difficulty associated with placing a value on this type of an interest has no bearing as to whether something of economic substance is being transferred and thus constitutes a qualifying distribution.

Therefore, the state of what little law there is on the point appears to indicate that a private foundation may make this type of in-kind grant and be entitled to a qualifying distribution for the fair market value of the interest transferred. Nonetheless, there is the possibility, as noted, of triggering unrelated business income. Also, the intransigence of the IRS on this point cannot be ignored.

TIP: A private foundation in this situation has one of two approaches. It can make the grant, claim a qualifying distribution, and assume the risk as a matter of business judgment. Or (and this is certainly the more prudent course of action), it can seek a ruling on the matter from the IRS.

Q 4:13   What is the deadline for satisfying the payout requirement?

A private foundation must make qualifying distributions (Q 4:10) equaling the minimum amount at the close of the year immediately following the year for which the amount was determined. The calculated amount for a foundation's fiscal year ending on June 30, 2001, must be paid out by June 30, 2002. A foundation that changes its fiscal year accelerates this payment deadline. A foundation with a June 30 fiscal year changing its year end to December 31 would have only six months to make its required distributions.

Q 4:14   What is the consequence of a foundation making a grant distribution to a controlled organization, either private or public?

A grant paid to a controlled organization is permitted, but the payment is not counted as a qualifying distribution unless three factors are present:

1. The controlled grantee is a charitable organization that no later than the close of its first fiscal year following the year in which it receives the grant regrants an equal amount.
2. A private foundation grantee cannot count the redistribution of the grant toward satisfying its distribution requirements.
3. The granting foundation must obtain and maintain evidence that the redistribution was accomplished and a statement verifying the recipient treated their payments as being out of corpus and not as a qualifying distribution.[14]

Q 4:15   When is another organization deemed to be controlled by the foundation?

A recipient organization is treated as controlled by the foundation when one or more of its disqualified persons (Chapter 2) can, by aggregating their votes or positions of authority, require or prevent the recipient organization from making an expenditure. Conditions can, however, be placed on the recipient organization. The foundation can designate the specific charitable purpose for which its grant is to be spent, such as improving child care conditions in the community. Requiring that the recipient engage certified child care specialists to conduct the program does not constitute control. Requiring an audit of the recipient's financial statements is not controlling the organization.

Q 4:16   Can a qualifying distribution of property, rather than cash, be made?

Yes, a distribution of property, such as a work of art or a piece of property, can count as a qualifying distribution. The current fair market value of the property is counted. Any appreciation in the value of the property over the amount originally paid by the foundation or its donees is not subject to the excise tax. This tax savings can be valuable to a foundation with a substantially appreciated portfolio of marketable securities (Q 8:10).

Q 4:17   Can a foundation treat money saved for a future project as a qualifying distribution?

Set-aside rules allow a foundation to delay the distribution of money or property for a project that can be better accomplished by saving, or accumulating, the money and property rather than spending it. To treat a set-aside as a qualifying distribution, the foundation must seek IRS approval for its long-term plans. The types of specific projects deemed to qualify for set-aside include:

- Plan to construct a building to house the foundation's art collection
- Plan to acquire a group of paintings offered for sale as a unit that require an expenditure or more than one year's income
- Plan to fund a specific research program that is of such magnitude as to require an accumulation prior to commencement of the program

The foundation reflects the amount set-aside as a qualifying distribution for the year the plans are made and records a liability. The eventual expenditures would be treated as being made out of corpus.

A newly created foundation can, without prior IRS approval, apply an alternative cash distribution test during its first four years of existence. If the foundation has a genuine plan to implement a long-term program similar to those described above, it may delay payout of the cost of the program. During those four years, the foundation must only spend the following portion of the normal minimum distribution requirement: first year (20 percent), second year (40 percent), third year (60 percent), and fourth year (80 percent). If the amounts set aside are not ultimately spent on the project, they must be added back to the pay-out requirement.[15] Although the statute, the regulations, court decisions, and IRS rulings contain no mention of the question, the amount reserved, or set aside, by the new foundation must ultimately be spent on the project. The tax form does not reflect any means by which to report this type of set-aside.

Q 4:18   Does a disbursement made for programs in a foreign country constitute a qualifying distribution?

Yes. A grant payment to a foreign organization, the purchase of an asset located in a foreign country, and hiring a person outside the United States to conduct a program all constitute qualifying distributions as long as the purpose for making the payments is charitable. The taxable expenditure rules require that the private foundation take additional steps to document these grants (Q 7:22).

Q 4:19   How does a foundation calculate satisfaction of the payout requirements?

The foundation compares its distributable amount for the current year (equal to the calculated amount for the past year as illustrated in Q 4:3) to its qualifying distributions for the year. Next, it offsets any deficit for this year with excess distributions from past years. Part XIII of Form 990-PF displays a cumulative report of the required annual distribution amounts compared to actual distributions for a standard private foundation. Distributions in excess of the minimum distribution requirement result in a carryover that can be applied to a succeeding year as reflected below. In this example, the 2001 excess of $20 can be carried to 2006.

Distribution Application and Carryovers

	1997	1998	1999	2000	2001	2002	Cumulative Excess Distributions
Qualifying distributions for year	0	250	70	40	160	100	
Distributable amount for year	100	100	100	100	100	100	
Net distributions for year	−100	+150	−30	−60	+60	0	
Application of annual amounts:							
Apply '98 to '97	+100	−100					+50
Apply '98 to '99		−30	+30				+20
Apply '98 to '00		−20		+20			0
Apply '01 to '00				+40	−40		+20
Balance	0	0	0	0	+20	0	

Q 4:20 What types of foundation expenditures are not counted in tallying up its qualifying distributions?

Examples of disbursements of foundation funds that do not count as qualifying distributions to offset its minimum distribution requirements are as follows:

- Purchases of investments
- Purchase of assets used to conduct and manage investment activity, such as a new computer to track investments or office space for staff monitoring the investments to occupy
- Grants paid to an organization controlled by the foundation's disqualified persons
- Expenditures made to correct a deficiency in a prior year minimum distribution requirement
- Redistribution of an amount equal to the contribution of noncash and nonmarketable security property to the foundation in order to allow donor maximum value deduction

Q 4:21 What happens when a foundation fails to meet its minimum distribution requirement?

A foundation that fails to make sufficient qualifying distributions (Q 4:10) to meet its mandatory distribution requirement must first correct the mistake.[16] Sufficient funds must be expended to make up the deficit. Next, the foundation is subject to an excise tax equal to 15 percent of the undistributed amount for each year or partial year during which the deficiency was outstanding. For example, a foundation that discovers in 2002 that it made a mistake in reporting its qualifying distributions for the year 1999 faces a potential penalty of 45 percent of the deficit. Form 4720 must be filed by the foundation to report the problem and present its case. An explanation of why the mistake occurred and how it has been corrected is presented in attachments to the form. The statute excuses the penalty in the following cases[17]:

- A failure to value the assets properly was not willful and was due to reasonable cause.
- The deficiency is distributed as a qualifying distribution by the foundation within 90 days after receipts of IRS notice of deficiency.
- The foundation notifies the IRS of the mistake by submitting information on its Form 990-PF and recalculating its qualifying distributions.
- The extra distribution made to correct the deficiency is treated as being distributed in the deficiency year.

Q 4:22   On what basis can the penalty be abated?

The penalty can be abated, or forgiven, if the foundation can show that the mistake was based on reasonable cause and not due to willful neglect. A foundation can develop systems and maintain its financial records in a fashion intended to make correct and accurate calculations of its payout requirement. In good faith, a foundation is expected to value it assets correctly and be able to show how it did so. For example, a foundation holding a portfolio of marketable securities should retain a copy of each month-end report reflecting the security investments and their month-end valuation. A foundation that holds partnership interests wants to be able to show the financial history on which it based its evaluation of its annual market value. In the unlikely event an independent appraisal is found to be in error, the foundation needs to document the due diligence it exercised in finding a qualified appraiser. A foundation can be forgiven if it can show that it relied in good faith upon an outside advisor that incorrectly advised it. Certainly the foundation that engages accountants and lawyers to make the calculations and monitor its compliance has an enhanced chance of avoiding penalties if a mistake is made.

Q: 4:23   Are additional penalties applied if the foundation fails to correct a deficit in its minimum distribution requirement?

An additional penalty of 100 percent of the deficit can be assessed if the problem is not corrected within 90 days of the foundation's receipt of a notice of deficiency. Attention to the notice date is critical to avoid this tax. It is obviously preferable that a foundation discover and self-report its mistakes. The IRS has been known to be cooperative when the underdistribution is due to some problem beyond the foundation's control. Say a foundation holds nonmarketable assets, such as real estate or a partnership interest, that produce no income and cannot be divided into property suitable for paying out to charitable grantees. Such a foundation should notify the IRS of its problem and seek an extension of time to make its qualifying distributions. A private foundation wants to avoid an IRS notice resulting from the deficiency in distributions being reflected on its Form 990-PF.

CHAPTER 5

Excess Business Holdings

As discussed in Chapter 1, private foundations are limited as to the extent to which they, and disqualified persons with respect to them, can own interests in commercial business enterprises. This primarily pertains to ownership of stock in a business corporation. These rules, however, also apply to other forms of interests in businesses. A holding by a private foundation in a business enterprise that is greater than the federal tax law permits is an *excess business holding.*

Of the many private foundation rules, the rules as to excess business holdings are among those that are not applied very often. Congress provided generous phase-in periods for these rules; those periods have expired.[1] Nearly all private foundations that were adversely affected by these rules have disposed of their excess business holdings. Few private foundations these days become entangled in the excess business holdings rules, although problems can arise because of situations such as changes in the holdings of disqualified persons, holdings obtained by contribution or bequest, or holdings acquired by a private foundation inadvertently.

Here are the questions that are most frequently asked (or that should be asked) about the excess business holdings rules—and the answers to them.

Q 5:1 What is a *business enterprise*?

This certainly is a good question with which to start. The activity involved must be a business enterprise before these rules can begin to apply. The definition of the term *business enterprise* is based on the definition of the term *business* in the unrelated business income setting (Chapter 9).

Thus, the term *business enterprise* includes the active conduct of a trade or business, including any activity that is regularly carried on for the production of income from the sale of goods or the performance of services, and that constitutes an unrelated trade or business.[2] Where an activity carried on for profit is an unrelated business, no part of it may be excluded from classification as a business enterprise merely because it does not result in a profit.[3]

A bond or other evidence of indebtedness is not a holding in a business enterprise unless it is otherwise determined to be an equitable interest in the enterprise.[4] Thus, an ostensible indebtedness will be regarded as a business holding if it is essentially an equity holding in disguise. A leasehold interest in real property is not an interest in a business enterprise, even if the rent is based on profits, unless the leasehold interest is an interest in the income or profits of an unrelated trade or business.[5]

Q 5:2   Are there any exceptions to this definition of a *business enterprise*?

Yes. There are three significant exceptions to this definition. That is, the term *business enterprise* does not include a functionally related business (Q 5:3), a program-related investment (Q 5:4), or a trade or business that is a passive investment business (Q 5:5).[6]

NOTE: A program-related investment is excluded from the definition of a business enterprise by the tax regulations, even though the exception is not provided by statute.

Q 5:3   What is a *functionally related business*?

The taxes on excess business holdings (Q 5:22, Q 5:26) do not apply with respect to holdings in a *functionally related business.*[7] That is, this type of business is not considered a *business enterprise.*[8]

A functionally related business is a business or activity that is not an unrelated business.[9] Thus, it is a business that has at least one of the following features:

- The conduct of the business is substantially related (aside from the mere provision of funds for the tax-exempt purpose) to the exercise or performance by the private foundation of its charitable, educational, or other exempt purpose (Q 9:19).
- Substantially all of the work in connection with the activity is performed for the foundation without compensation (Q 9:22).
- The activity is carried on by the foundation primarily for the convenience of its employees, members, patients, visitors, or students (*id.*).
- The activity consists of the selling of merchandise, substantially all of which has been received by the foundation by means of contributions (*id.*).

A functionally related business also is an activity that is carried on within a larger aggregate of similar activities or within a larger complex of other endeavors that is related to the tax-exempt purposes of the foundation (other than the need to simply provide funds for these purposes).[10]

Here are examples of a functionally related business operated by a private foundation.

- A private foundation maintains a community of historic value that is open to the general public. For the convenience of the public, the foundation, through a wholly owned taxable corporation, maintains a restaurant and hotel in the community. These facilities are within the larger aggregate of activities that makes available for public enjoyment the various buildings of historic interest and which is related to the foundation's purpose. The operation of the restaurant and hotel constitutes a functionally related business.[11]
- A private foundation, as part of its exempt medical research program, publishes a medical journal in carrying out its exempt purpose. Space in the journal is sold for commercial advertising. Notwithstanding the fact that the advertising activity may be subject to unrelated business income taxation, the activity is within a larger complex of endeavors that makes available to the scientific community and the general public developments with respect to medical research. It is, therefore, a functionally related business.[12]
- A music publishing company that concentrated on classical music was held to be related to the purposes of a private foundation that promotes music education and selection of music as a career. Thus, it was found to be a functionally related business.[13]

Q 5:4   What is a *program-related investment*?

A *program-related investment* is an investment, the primary purpose of which is to accomplish one or more charitable purposes, and no significant purpose of which is the production of income or the appreciation of property.[14] This type of investment activity is discussed in greater detail elsewhere (Q 6:7).

Q 5:5   What is a *passive investment business*?

A *passive investment business* is a trade or business where at least 95 percent of its gross income is derived from passive sources.[15]

An alternative to this passive-source gross income rule is a multiyear averaging mechanism.[16] Thus, stock in a passive holding company is not considered a holding in a business enterprise even if the company is controlled by a private foundation; the foundation is treated as owning its proportionate share of any interests in a business enterprise held by the company.[17]

The concept of *passive source income* is derived from the unrelated business income rules (Chapter 9). Thus, passive income embraces items of income considered passive in nature for purposes of these rules,[18] including the following:

- Dividends
- Interest
- Annuities
- Royalties, including overriding royalties, whether measured by production or by gross or taxable income from the property

---

NOTE: By contrast, working interests in mineral properties are active businesses.

- Rental income from real property and from personal property leased with real property, if the rent attributable to the personal property is incidental (less than 50 percent of the total rent)
- Gains or losses from sales, exchanges, or other dispositions of property, other than stock in trade held for regular sale to customers
- Income from the sale of goods, if the seller does not manufacture, produce, physically receive or deliver, negotiate sales of, or keep inventories in the goods[19]

A tax-exempt title-holding company[20] can be utilized to house passive business operations.[21]

NOTE: The fact that the unrelated debt-financed income rules (see Chapter 9) may apply to an item of passive income does not alter the character of the income as passive.[22]

Q 5:6   Can an interest in a business not be a business enterprise under any other rationale?

Yes. According to the IRS, the term *business enterprise* "may not encompass certain partnerships that engage solely in investment activities," even though less than 95 percent of the partnership's income may be derived from passive sources (Q 5:5).[23] The matter involved the formation and operation of an investment partnership by 15 private foundations, each of which is a disqualified person with respect to the others (Q 2:17). The partnership agreement prohibits the admission of partners that are not private foundations; one of the foundations will serve at the managing general partner. An investment management company that provides services to the manager foundation is to provide investment management and administrative services to this investment partnership without charge. Each foundation's investment in and capital commitment to the investment partnership will not exceed 20 percent of the value of its investment portfolio (Q 5:7).

The purpose of this investment partnership is to enable each of these private foundations to invest in equity interests in private businesses and private equity funds not otherwise available to them and to achieve greater diversification in investments. The investments generally will be made in other (lower-tier) limited partnerships, to which this investment partnership will subscribe as a limited partner. The investment partnership's gross income from nonpassive sources (e.g., income from partnerships engaged in an active business) may exceed 5 percent a year.

NOTE: A foundation in this instance treats its proportionate share of income of this nature as unrelated business income and may have to pay the resulting tax if the underlying property is debt-financed (Q 9:30).

The partnership agreement prohibits this investment partnership from making any investments that would cause any of the foundations to be involved in jeopardy investments (Chapter 6). The partnership may not directly engage in an operating business. The agreement forbids the partnership from making any investment that would cause the combined interests of any partner and all disqualified persons with respect to that partner in any business enterprise to exceed the permitted business holdings of the partner (Q 5:7). The investment partnership will not purchase property from, sell property to, exchange property with, or lease property to or from a disqualified person with respect to any of the foundation partners (Q 3:1–3:5). The partnership will not receive credit from or extend credit to a disqualified person with respect to any of the foundation partners (Q 3:8). The partnership will not purchase or sell investments in an attempt to manipulate the price of the investments to the advantage of a disqualified person (Q 3:20).

If this investment partnership were a business enterprise, then the investment of each of the participating foundations would be an excess business holding, since the combined profits interests of each foundation and its disqualified persons would be in excess of 20 percent and the 2 percent *de minimis* rule would be inapplicable (Q 5:7). The IRS conceded that a "strict reading" of the tax regulations would limit the concept of the passive business to organizations receiving at least 95 percent of their gross income from passive sources. Nonetheless, because the partnership's activities will consist of investing in private business, mostly as a limited partner in other limited partnerships, and because limited partnership interests "may represent passive investments," the IRS ruled that the investment partnership will not be treated as a business enterprise for purposes of the excess business holdings rules.

In a buttressing of its position, the IRS reviewed the legislative history of the excess benefit rules.[24] It said that Congress "only sought to prevent private foundations from engaging in active businesses." The IRS observed that a contrary conclusion would prevent a participating private foundation from indirectly investing in limited partnership interests, through the partnership, even though it could invest in such interests directly. There was, as noted, a representation that a foundation would not acquire more than a 20 percent interest in any limited partnership. Said the IRS: The "mere interposition" of this investment partnership "should not produce a different result."

The IRS wrote that "this is a situation that calls for the application of the constructive ownership rule." Under this rule (Q 5:9), the investment partnership will not hold an impermissible interest in any business enterprise that would result in an indirect excess business holding for any of its private foundation partners. The IRS concluded that, given that the private foundation partners could directly hold these interests in business enterprises, and given that the investment partnership is formed for "valid business reasons," the foundations should be allowed to form and hold interests in the partnership to achieve the same result indirectly.

COMMENT: This type of investment partnership has been the subject of proposed legislation, by which its tax exemption and terms and conditions of operation would be prescribed by statute, somewhat along the lines of the exemption provision for investment pools for schools, colleges, and universities.[25] The most recent manifestation of this legislative proposal was in the Revenue Reconciliation Act of 1995, which was vetoed.

Q 5:7   What are *permitted holdings*?

The excess business holdings rules generally limit to 20 percent the permitted ownership of a corporation's voting stock or other interest in a business enterprise that may be held by a private foundation and all disqualified persons with respect to it combined.[26] These, then, are *permitted holdings*. Thus, as a general rule, a private foundation and its substantial contributors, managers, their family members, and the like cannot collectively own more than 20 percent of a corporation or other business enterprise.

Usually ownership of a corporation is accomplished by means of voting stock. For these purposes, the percentage of voting stock held by a person in a corporation is normally determined by reference to the power of stockholders to vote for the election of directors, with treasury stock and stock that is authorized but unissued disregarded.[27]

Where all disqualified persons with respect to a private foundation together do not own more than 20 percent of the voting stock of an incorporated business enterprise, the foundation can own any amount of nonvoting stock.[28] Equity interests that do not have voting power attributable to them are classified as nonvoting stock. Evidences of indebtedness (including convertible indebtedness) and warrants and other options or rights to acquire stock are not equity interests.[29]

Stock carrying voting rights that will vest only when conditions, the occurrence of which are indeterminate, have been met (known as stock with contingent voting rights) is treated as nonvoting stock until the conditions have occurred that cause the voting rights to vest. When the rights vest, the stock is treated as voting stock that was acquired other than by purchase, but only if the private foundation or disqualified persons lacked control over whether the conditions would occur.[30]

NOTE: An illustration of this latter point is preferred stock that can be voted only if dividends are not paid; these shares are considered nonvoting until the voting power is exercisable. Thus, the intrinsic character of stock, and not any side agreements, determines whether a stock is voting stock. For example, entering into a binding agreement (scripted on the shares and transferable to any purchaser of the shares) not to vote a private foundation's stock does not reduce excess business holdings.[31]

Similarly, nonvoting stock that may be converted into voting stock is not treated as voting stock until the conversion occurs.[32]

These rules for nonvoting stock do not apply with respect to partnerships or other unincorporated business enterprises.[33]

If effective control of a business enterprise can be shown, to the satisfaction of the IRS, to be elsewhere—that is, other than by the private foundation and its disqualified persons—a 35 percent limit may be substituted for the 20 percent limit.[34]

The term *effective control* means possession of the power, whether direct or indirect, and whether actually exercised or not, to direct or cause the direction of the management and policies of a business enterprise. Effective control can be achieved through ownership of voting stock, the use of voting trusts, contractual arrangements, or otherwise. For example, where a minority interest held by individuals, who are not disqualified persons, historically has elected the majority of a corporation's directors, effective control is in the hands of those individuals.[35]

It is the reality of control that is decisive, rather than its form or the means by which it is exercisable. For this 35 percent rule to apply, a private foundation must demonstrate by affirmative proof that an unrelated party, or group of parties, does in fact exercise control over the business enterprise involved.[36]

A private foundation must, however, hold, directly or indirectly, more than 2 percent of the voting stock or other value of a business enterprise before either of these limitations becomes applicable.[37] The holdings of related foundations are aggregated for the purpose of computing this 2 percent amount,[38] so as to preclude the use of multiple private foundations as a means of converting this *de minimis* rule into a method of evading the excess business holdings rules.

Therefore, the *permitted holdings* of a private foundation are those business holdings that are within these 20 percent or 35 percent limitations.

NOTE: Thus, *excess business holdings* constitute the amount of stock or other interest in a business enterprise that a private foundation would have to dispose of by transferring it to a person (other than a disqualified person) in order for the remaining holdings of the foundation in the enterprise to constitute permitted holdings.[39]

If a private foundation is required to dispose of certain shares of a class of stock in a particular period of time and other shares of the same class of stock over a shorter period of time, any stock disposed of will be charged first against those dispositions that must be made in the shorter period.[40]

Q 5:8   Are these rules as to business holdings confined to interests in corporations?

By no means. It is true that the excess business holdings rules often focus on holdings in the form of stock in incorporated businesses. These rules also apply, however, with respect to holdings in unincorporated business entities, such as partnerships, joint ventures, and trusts.[41] In these contexts, the terms identifying the nature of the ownership are different.

In the case of a partnership (limited or general) or a joint venture, the terms *profit interest* and *capital interest* are substituted for *voting stock* and *nonvoting stock*.[42] The interest of a private foundation and its disqualified persons in a partnership is determined using the distributive share concepts that are part of the federal tax law.[43] In the absence of a provision in the partnership agreement, the capital interest of the foundation (or the disqualified person) in a partnership is determined on the basis of its interest in the assets of the partnership that would be distributable to the foundation (or disqualified person) on its withdrawal from the partnership or on liquidation of the partnership, whichever is greater.[44]

For trusts or any other form of unincorporated business enterprise—other than a partnership (see above) or sole proprietorship (see below)—the term *beneficial interest* is used to define ownership.[45]

CAUTION: A private foundation may not operate a business enterprise as a *sole proprietorship* (unless it is one of the exempted enterprises (Q 5:2)).[46] The reason: This type of business undertaking, by definition, entails a 100 percent ownership.

NOTE: If a private foundation owns a sole proprietorship and subsequently divests itself of a portion of the interest in it (so that the foundation has less than a 100 percent interest in the equity of the business enterprise), the resulting business arrangement is treated as a partnership.[47]

The beneficial interest of a private foundation or any disqualified person in an unincorporated business enterprise (other than a partnership, other joint venture, or sole proprietorship) includes any right to receive a portion of distributions of profits of the enterprise and, if the portion of distributions is not fixed by an agreement among the participants, any right to receive a portion of the assets (if any) on liquidation of the enterprise.

NOTE: This rule does not apply, however, where the right to receive profits or assets is as a creditor or employee.

A right to receive distributions of profits includes a right to receive any amount from the profits (other than as a creditor or employee), whether as a sum certain or as a portion of profits realized by the enterprise. Where there is not an agreement fixing the rights of the participants in an enterprise, the interest of the foundation (or the disqualified person) in the enterprise is determined by dividing the amount of all equity investments or contributions to the capital of the enterprise made or obligated to be made by the foundation (or disqualified person) by the amount of all equity investments or contributions to capital made or obligated to be made by all participants in the enterprise.[48]

Q 5:9   Are there constructive ownership rules in this area?

Yes. In computing the holdings of a private foundation, or a disqualified person with respect to a private foundation, in a business enterprise, any stock or other interest owned, directly or indirectly, by or for a corporation, partnership, estate, or trust is considered as being owned proportionately by or for its shareholders, partners, or beneficiaries.[49]

An interest in a business enterprise actually or constructively owned by a shareholder of a corporation, a partner of a partnership, or a beneficiary of an estate or trust is not considered as constructively held by the corporation, partnership, trust, or estate.[50] If a corporation, partnership, estate, or trust has a warrant or other option to acquire an interest in a business enterprise, the interest is not deemed to be constructively owned by the entity until the option is exercised.[51]

NOTE: As discussed, options are not equity interests for purposes of determining excess business holdings (Q 5:7).

Any interest in a business enterprise over which a private foundation or a disqualified person has a power of appointment, exercisable in favor of the foundation or disqualified person, is treated as if it were owned by the foundation or disqualified person holding the power of appointment.[52]

If an interest in a business enterprise owned by a corporation is constructively owned by a shareholder, each shareholder's proportion of ownership is generally computed on the basis of the voting stock each shareholder has in the corporation. In determining permitted holdings (Q 5:7), each shareholder's proportion of ownership in the business enterprise must also be computed on the basis of value, taking into account both voting and non-voting stock.[53]

If a private foundation, its disqualified persons, or both own, directly or constructively, nonvoting stock of a parent corporation, the holdings of which are treated as constructively owned by its shareholders, the nonvoting stock is regarded as nonvoting stock of any corporation in which the parent corporation holds an interest for purposes of the limitation on the holding of nonvoting stock (Q 5:7).[54]

In the case of an entity that is a disqualified person (other than a controlled private foundation (Q 2:20)), the holdings of which are treated as constructively owned by its shareholders, partners, or beneficiaries, for purposes of determining the total holdings of disqualified persons, the holdings of the entity are considered held by a disqualified person only to the extent the holdings are treated as constructively owned by disqualified persons who are shareholders, partners, or beneficiaries of the entity. In the case of a controlled foundation or an entity, the holdings of which are not treated as constructively owned by its shareholders, partners, or beneficiaries, all holdings of the entity are treated as held by a disqualified person only if the entity itself is a disqualified person.[55]

An interest in a business enterprise owned by a trust underlying a pension or profit-sharing plan is not considered as owned by its beneficiaries, unless disqualified persons control the investment of the trust assets.[56]

An interest in a business enterprise owned by a revocable trust is treated as owned by the grantor of the trust.[57]

An interest actually or constructively owned by an estate or trust is generally deemed constructively owned, in the case of an estate, by its beneficiaries or, in the case of a trust, by its remainder beneficiaries.[58] An interest in a business enterprise held by a split-interest trust[59] is not considered constructively owned by a private foundation where the sole relationship that the foundation has with the trust is that it is an income or remainder interest beneficiary of the trust.[60]

In the contexts of estates, the term *beneficiary* includes any person (including a private foundation) entitled to receive property of a decedent pursuant to a will or to laws of descent and distribution. A person is no longer considered a beneficiary of an estate when all the property to which he, she, or it is entitled has been received by that person, when he, she, or it no longer has a claim against the estate, and when there is only a remote possibility that it will be necessary for the estate to seek the return of property or to seek payment from the person by contribution or otherwise to satisfy claims against the estate or expenses of administration. When a person (including a private foundation) ceases to be a beneficiary, stock or another interest in a business enterprise owned by the estate is not thereafter considered owned by that person. If any person is the constructive owner of an interest in a business enterprise actually held by an estate, the date of death of the testator or decedent intestate is the first day on which the person is considered a constructive owner of the interest.[61]

Exempted from this constructive ownership rule (subject to certain exceptions) are holdings of corporations that are engaged in an active trade or business.[62] This is known as the *myopia rule.* A passive parent of an affiliated group of active business is treated as an active business for these purposes.[63]

Q 5:10   What happens if a private foundation acquires excess business holdings without realizing it?

The answer depends on how the excess business holdings were acquired. The law differentiates between acquisitions by purchase and acquisitions other than a result of a purchase by a private foundation. (As to the latter, see Q 5:14.)

A private foundation is not subject to taxation for having excess business holdings, where the holdings were acquired *by purchase,* where it did not know it was acquiring excess holdings, or did not have reason to know of prior acquisitions by disqualified persons with respect to it, *but only* under certain circumstances. These protective circumstances arise only where the private foundation disposes of the excess holdings within 90 days from the date on which it knows, or has reason to know, of the event that caused it to have the excess business holdings.[64] Moreover, for this 90-day rule to be available, the purchase must have created an excess business holding only because of the prior acquisition(s) by one or more disqualified persons. In determining compliance by a private foundation with this 90-day rule, any disposition of holdings by a disqualified person during the period is disregarded.[65]

Q 5:11   Is there any way to extend this 90-day period?

Generally, no. There is this one exception: The period can be extended to include the period during which the private foundation is prevented, by federal or state law, from disposing of those excess business holdings.[66]

Q 5:12   Can a private foundation impose any restriction on the interest that is being disposed of to eliminate excess business holdings?

Basically, no, because that would mean that the interest in the business enterprise was not effectively transferred. If the restriction were considered *immaterial,* its presence probably would not pose a problem.

By contrast, if a private foundation disposes of an interest in a business enterprise and imposes a *material* restriction or condition that prevents the recipient person from freely and effectively using or disposing of the transferred interest, the transferor private foundation is treated as continuing to own the interest until all material restrictions or limitations are eliminated.[67]

COMMENT: The term *material restriction* is not defined in this context. A good place to begin, when seeking to interpret this rule, would be the definition of the term as found in the private foundation termination rules.[68]

NOTE: A restriction or limitation that is imposed in compliance with federal or state securities laws, or in accordance with the terms or conditions of the gift or bequest through which the interest was acquired by the foundation, is not considered a material restriction or condition imposed by a private foundation.[69]

Q 5:13   How is a private foundation to *know* about the acquisition of business holdings by a disqualified person?

Whether a private foundation is treated as *knowing,* or having reason to know, of the acquisition of holdings by a disqualified person is dependent on the facts and circumstances of each case. Here are the factors that will be considered:

- The fact that the foundation did not discover acquisitions made by disqualified persons even though it utilized procedures reasonably calculated to discover such excess business holdings
- The diversity of the foundation's holdings
- The existence of large numbers of disqualified persons who have little or no contact with the foundation or its managers[70]

Q 5:14   What about excess business holdings that come into being by reason of a gift or the like?

If a private foundation obtains holdings in a business enterprise, *other than by purchase* by the foundation or by disqualified persons with respect to it, and the additional holdings would result in the foundation's having excess business holdings, the foundation has five years to reduce these holdings to permissible levels.[71] This is because the excess holdings (or an increase in excess holdings) resulting from the transaction are treated as being held by a disqualified person—rather than by the foundation—during the five-year period beginning on the date the foundation obtained the holdings.

Acquisitions by gift, devise, bequest, legacy, or intestate succession are the subject of this five-year rule,[72] as are certain increases in holdings in a business enterprise that are the result of a readjustment of the enterprise.[73]

NOTE: A *readjustment* may be a merger or consolidation, a recapitalization, an acquisition of stock or assets, a transfer of assets, a change in identity, form, or place of organization, a redemption, or a liquidating distribution.[74]

CAUTION: Holdings that are attributable to holdings owned by a private foundation that would have been excess business holdings except for the fact that the holdings were treated as held by a disqualified person prior to the readjustment cannot be treated as held by a disqualified person after the date on which the holdings to which the change is attributable would have ceased to be treated as held by a disqualified person.[75]

This five-year rule is not applicable to any transfer of holdings in a business enterprise by a private foundation to another private foundation, where the two foundations are related.[76]

Also, this rule does not apply to an increase in the holdings of a private foundation in a business enterprise that is part of a plan by which disqualified persons will purchase additional holdings in the same enterprise during the five-year period beginning on the date of the change (e.g., for the purpose of maintaining control of the enterprise).[77] This is because the increase in the holdings is treated as caused in part by the purchase of the additional holdings.

The purchase of holdings by an entity whose holdings are treated as constructively owned by a private foundation, its disqualified persons, or both (Q 5:9) is treated as a purchase by a disqualified person if the foundation, its disqualified persons, or both have effective control of the entity or otherwise can control the purchase.[78]

If a private foundation, its disqualified persons, or both hold an interest in specific property under the terms of a will or trust, and if the foundation and/or its disqualified persons agree to the substitution of holdings in a business enterprise for the property, the holdings are regarded as a purchase by a disqualified person.[79]

When a private foundation has a program-related investment (Q 5:4, Q 6:7)—and thus does not have an interest in a business enterprise—and subsequently the investment fails to qualify as a program-related one—so that the holding becomes an interest in a business enterprise—for purposes of this five-year rule the interest becomes one acquired other than by purchase as of the date of nonqualification.[80] A similar rule applies with respect to passive holdings[81] and to other circumstances in which an interest not originally a business enterprise becomes a business enterprise.[82]

Q 5:15   What about a stock redemption by a disqualified person corporation?

Generally, a stock redemption by a corporation that is a disqualified person with respect to a private foundation is protected by this exception—that is, the transaction is not regarded as a purchase.

Specifically, if a private foundation holds an interest in a corporation that is a disqualified person, an increase in the holdings of the foundation, its disqualified persons, or both, as a result of a redemption or a purchase of stock of the disqualified person corporation by the corporation is not treated as acquired by purchase by a disqualified person based solely on the status of the corporation as a disqualified person.[83]

If the holdings of a private foundation, its disqualified persons, or both, in a business enterprise are increased as a consequence of one or more redemptions during a year, then—unless the aggregate of these increases equals or exceeds 1 percent of the outstanding stock or 1 percent of the value of all outstanding shares of all classes of stock—the determination of whether the increases cause the foundation to have excess business holdings is made only at the close of the foundation's year.[84]

NOTE: The five-year period (Q 5:14) or the 90-day period (Q 5:10) in this instance begins on the last day of that year.[85]

If, however, the aggregate of the increases equals or exceeds 1 percent of the outstanding voting stock or 1 percent of the value of all outstanding shares of all classes of stock, the determination of whether the increases cause the private foundation to have excess business holdings is made as of the date the increases, in the aggregate, equal or exceed 1 percent.[86]

NOTE: The five-year period (Q 5:14) or the 90-day period (Q 5:10) in this instance begins on the date of the increases.[87]

Q 5:16   What happens if a corporation stops active business operations?

A change in holdings in a business enterprise that occurs because a corporation ceases to be actively engaged in a trade or business, thus causing its holdings to be constructively owned by its shareholders, is treated as acquired other than by purchase.[88]

Q 5:17   What does a private foundation do when it acquires a holding in a business enterprise pursuant to the terms of a will or trust?

In the case of an acquisition of holdings in a business enterprise by a private foundation pursuant to the terms of a will or trust, the five-year period (Q 5:14) does not commence until the date on which the distribution of the holdings from the trust occurs.[89] There are rules for determining this date of distribution.[90]

Holdings in a business enterprise are not treated as acquired by a private foundation pursuant to the terms of a will where the decedent did not hold the holdings in the business enterprise. Thus, in the case of after-acquired property, the five-year period commences on the date of acquisition of the holdings by the estate. This period may expire prior to the date of distribution of the holdings from the estate.[91]

Q 5:18   Isn't that rule inconsistent with the constructive ownership rules?

Excellent question, and the answer would be yes, were it not for a sentence in the tax regulations. On one hand, in computing the holdings of a private foundation, or a disqualified person with respect to a private foundation, in a business enterprise, any stock or other interest owned, directly or indirectly, by or for an estate or trust is considered as being owned proportionately by or for its beneficiaries (Q 5:9). For example, if an irrevocable testamentary trust provides that all of its assets are destined for a private foundation, the foundation is deemed to own all of those assets.

On the other hand, for purposes of the five-year exception, the five-year period does not start to run until the date on which there is the distribution of the assets from the trust (Q 5:17). Thus, in the example of the testamentary trust, the foundation is considered to have owned the assets all along, yet the five-year period does not commence until the foundation actually obtains the assets.

These rules are reconciled by treating the five-year rule as a special carve-out exception. For all other purposes (e.g., computing the foundation's business holdings and ascertaining the conduct of unrelated business activities), then, the foundation is considered the owner of the trust assets. Still, the question remains: What is the status of the ownership during the period between the time the trust acquires the property, which is destined for the private foundation, and the time of the distribution? The answer: The property, prior to the date of distribution, is treated as held by a disqualified person prior to that date.[92]

Q 5:19   What happens if the terms of this exception as to gift holdings cannot be satisfied?

In some instances, the holding would then become an excess business holding (Q 5:7). The IRS has the authority, however, to allow an additional five-year period for the disposition of excess business holdings in the case of an "unusually large gift or bequest of diverse business holdings or holdings with complex corporate structures" if:

- The private foundation establishes that diligent efforts to dispose of the holdings were made within the initial five-year period (Q 5:14) and that

disposition within that initial period was not possible (except at a price substantially below fair market value) by reason of the size and complexity or diversity of the holdings,
- Before the close of the initial five-year period, the private foundation submits to the IRS a plan for disposition of all of the excess business holdings involved in the extension, submits the plan to the appropriate state attorney general or similar official, and submits to the IRS any response received by the foundation from the state official to the plan during the initial period, and
- The IRS determines that the plan can reasonably be expected to be carried out before the close of the extension period.[93]

Private letter rulings illustrate situations in which the IRS has granted extensions of this nature for private foundations that have demonstrated the requisite diligence. For example, a plan developed by an independent financial consultant to assist a private foundation in selling its holdings, in conjunction with the substantial contributor's family members who owned interests in the same business, was approved by the IRS.[94] By contrast, the IRS concluded that a private foundation was not adequately diligent in this regard and thus denied a request for an extension.[95]

Q 5:20   What happens when a private foundation has an excess business holding?

Unless the excess business holding is one of the exempted ones (Q 5:2, Q 5:6), a tax penalty system comes into play. This initially involves a first-tier—or initial—tax (Q 5:21, Q 5:22) and a correction requirement (Q 5:23), and can involve a second-tier—or additional—tax (Q 5:25, Q 5:26). In egregious circumstances, the involuntary termination tax (Q 5:29) can be imposed.

Q 5:21   Who pays the first-tier tax?

An initial excise tax is imposed on a private foundation in an instance of excess business holdings (Q 5:7) in a business enterprise (Q 5:1) for each tax year that ends during the taxable period (Q 5:24).[96] This tax is imposed on the last day of the tax year.[97]

Q 5:22   How is the first-tier tax calculated?

The amount of the first-tier tax is 5 percent of the total value of all of the foundation's excess business holdings in each of its business enterprises.[98] This tax is determined using the greatest value of the foundation's excess holdings in the enterprise during the year involved.[99]

The IRS has promulgated a return that is used to calculate and report the tax due (Form 4720). The valuation is determined by means of the estate tax rules.[100]

Q 5:23   How is a *correction* accomplished?

A *correction* of an excess business holding situation is a matter of the facts and circumstances of the case. There is very little law on the point. Essentially, a correction is a complete elimination of the excess business holdings.[101]

Correction is considered as made when no interest in the business enterprise held by the private foundation is classified as an excess business holding (Q 5:7). In a case where a private foundation has excess business holdings that are constructively held for it (Q 5:9), correction is considered made when either a corporation, partnership, estate, or trust, in which holdings in the enterprise are constructively held for the foundation or a disqualified person, the foundation itself, or a disqualified person with respect to it, disposes of a sufficient interest in the enterprise so that no interest in the enterprise held by the foundation is classified as excess business holdings.[102]

Q 5:24   What is the *taxable period*?

The *taxable period* is the period of time beginning with the first day on which there are excess business holdings and ending on the earliest of the following dates:

- The date on which the IRS mails a notice of deficiency with respect to the initial tax in respect of the excess business holdings,
- The date on which the excess business holding is eliminated (Q 5:23), or
- The date on which the initial tax in respect of the excess business holdings is assessed.[103]

If the deficiency is self-admitted by the filing of the return (Q 5:22), the taxable period ends when the return is filed.

Q 5:25   Who pays the second-tier tax?

If the initial tax (Q 5:21) is imposed and the excess business holdings are not disposed of (Q 5:23) by the close of the taxable period (Q 5:24), an additional tax is imposed on the private foundation involved.[104]

Q 5:26   How is the second-tier tax calculated?

The amount of the second-tier tax is 200 percent of the value of the excess business holdings.[105] This additional tax is imposed at the end of the taxable period (Q 5:24).

Where the act or failure to act that gave rise to the additional tax is corrected (Q 5:23) within the correction period (Q 5:27), the tax will not be assessed, or if assessed will be abated (Q 5:31), or if collected will be credited or refunded.[106]

Q 5:27   What is the *correction period*?

The *correction period* is the period of time beginning on the date on which the taxable event (Q 5:28) occurs and ending 90 days after the date of mailing of a notice of deficiency with respect to the additional tax imposed on the event, extended by any period in which a deficiency cannot be assessed and any other period that the IRS determines is reasonable and necessary to bring about correction of the taxable event.[107]

Q 5:28   What is a *taxable event*?

In this setting, a *taxable event* is an act or failure to act giving rise to liability for tax under the excess business holdings rules.[108] This event occurs on the first day on which there are excess business holdings.[109]

Q 5:29   When is the involuntary termination tax imposed?

As noted (Q 5:20), the involuntary termination tax can be imposed in egregious circumstances. Technically, this tax can be imposed where there have been either willful repeated acts (or failures to act) or a willful and flagrant act (or failure to act) that gives rise to liability for one or more of the excess business holdings taxes (or other violation of the private foundation rules).[110] Also, the IRS must give adequate notice to the private foundation of its liability for the tax.[111]

This tax is hefty; it essentially amounts to a confiscation by the IRS of the net assets of the private foundation. It is an amount equal to the lower of

- The amount that the private foundation substantiates by adequate records or other corroborating evidence as the *aggregate tax benefit* (Q 5:30) resulting from the tax-exempt status of the foundation, or
- The value of the net assets of the foundation.[112]

Q 5:30   What does the term *aggregate tax benefit* mean?

The aggregate tax benefit essentially is the total of all the benefits that accrued to a private foundation because of its tax-exempt status. There basically are two components to this: The aggregate increases in tax that would have been imposed on all substantial contributors (Q 2:2) were the charitable

---

NOTE: In computing these two types of aggregate tax increases, one must go all the way back to when these two tax benefits were created. Thus, in the case of tax exemption, the computation period commences with tax years beginning after December 31, 1912. In the case of charitable deductions, the period starts with contributions to the foundation made after February 28, 1913.

---

contribution deduction for the gifts disallowed and the aggregate increases in tax that would have been imposed had the entity not been exempt from federal taxation.[113] Also, interest must be paid on these two tax increases.[114]

Q 5:31   Can these taxes be abated?

Yes. The IRS has the discretionary authority to abate the initial tax on excess business holdings (Q 5:21) where the private foundation is able to establish that the violation was due to reasonable cause and not to willful neglect, and timely corrects (Q 5:23) the violation.[115]

In one instance, the IRS declined to abate the initial taxes imposed on a private foundation, in an amount in excess of $200,000, for excess business holdings because of a lack of showing of reasonable cause.[116]

CHAPTER 6

Jeopardizing Investments

A private foundation, as are all charitable organizations exempt from income tax, is expected to permanently dedicate its assets to charitable purposes. Tax exemption is based on the fact that the assets will be used to accomplish charitable purposes and that the assets will be invested in a fashion intended to maximize resources available to support charitable causes. Federal tax law parallels state law in requiring that officers and directors of private foundations exercise fiduciary responsibility to safeguard the foundation's assets on behalf of its charitable constituents by following the prudent investor standards. In a similar spirit, the tax code says that a private foundation should not "invest any amount in such a manner as to jeopardize the carrying out of any of its exempt purposes." An imprudent investment is one that fails to follow the standards.

Here are the questions that are most frequently asked (or that should be asked) about the jeopardizing investment rules—and the answers to them.

Q 6:1   What is a *jeopardizing investment*?

To deter a private foundation from making investments that might imperil its assets, an excise tax is imposed on the foundation and on any of its managers that approve of the making of a jeopardizing investment.[1] The rule is designed to shield private foundation assets from risk, so as to maximize both capital and income available for charitable purposes. An investment that exposes the foundation's assets to excessive risk of loss is considered a jeopardizing investment. Managers are expected to use a high degree of fiduciary responsibility in investing foundation funds, and to follow the *prudent investor rules* (Q 6:2).

Q 6:2   What are the prudent investor rules that a foundation must follow?

The prudent investor rules have been developed in accordance with common law principles and are compiled in the American Law Institute's *Restatement of the Law, Trusts—Prudent Investor Rule* volume.[2] The *prudent investor rule* recognizes that return on investment is related to risk, that risk includes the risk of deterioration of real return owing to inflation, and that the risk/return relationship must be taken into account in managing trust assets. In essence, the rule recommends that a foundation diversify its investment following the *business judgment rules.* Foundation investment managers are expected to ask what a cautious businessperson would do, under the conditions existing at the time the investment is made, after taking all of the facts and circumstances of the foundation's property and income needs into account.

Q 6:3   What types of investments are considered to be jeopardizing investments?

A jeopardizing investment is one that fails to take into consideration the long- and short-term financial needs of the foundation to carry out its exempt purposes. Certain types of investments are deemed to possess a higher degree of risk. Their attributes within the context of the foundation's overall investment plan base must be closely scrutinized to determine whether they present jeopardy. After conceding that no category of investment will be treated as jeopardizing per se, the Treasury regulations list the following types as investments requiring close scrutiny:

- Trading in securities purchased on margin
- Trading in commodity futures
- Working interests in oil and gas
- Puts, calls, and straddles
- Purchases of warrants
- Selling shares short

In 1998, the IRS expanded the list of investments that require close scrutiny to include what it calls *recent investment strategies* (that by reference are not necessarily prohibited) to include:

- Investment in "junk" bonds
- Risk arbitrage
- Hedge funds
- Derivatives
- Distressed real estate
- International equities in third world countries[3]

NOTE: The IRS expansion of the list reflects the reality of financial markets in the 1990s, which were not anticipated when the regulations were written in 1972. Foundations can be guided by the investment concepts and practices set out under the prudent investor rules apparently now recognized by the IRS. Based on these rules, maintaining all of a foundation's assets in certificates of deposit or other fixed money obligations, a policy thought by many to be secure, could theoretically be treated as a jeopardizing situation.[4]

Q 6:4   Are investments the foundation receives as gifts subject to the jeopardizing investment penalties?

No. The jeopardizing investment sanctions are not applied to penalize a foundation upon receipt of a donated investment property that is imprudent. Unless the foundation pays some consideration in connection with the gift, such as a bargain sale, it is not treated as having purchased the investment and is not required to dispose of it.[5] Similarly, stock received in a corporate reorganization is not jeopardizing.

Q 6:5   When is an investment evaluated to determine if it is jeopardizing?

The identification of jeopardy is based on facts available to the foundation managers at the time the investment is made and not subsequently on the basis of hindsight. The existence of jeopardy is made on an investment-by-investment basis, in each case taking into account the foundation's portfolio as a whole. The expected return, including current dividends, rents, and interest as well as future appreciation reasonably expected to occur, are among the factors to be considered. Managers must consider possible rising and falling price levels and the need for diversification in the foundation's assets. Foundation managers must also consider the type of security involved, the type of industry, the maturity of the company, the degree of risk, and the potential for return.

Once it is ascertained that an investment is prudent, the investment is not considered to be a jeopardizing one, even if the foundation ultimately loses money. A change in the form or terms of an investment is considered to be a new investment as of the date of the change, and a new determination is to be made at that time by the IRS.

Q 6:6   What are some examples of jeopardizing investments?

There is little guidance on this subject. The regulations, unchanged since issuance in 1972, contain three examples. The examples describe three stocks and compare factors that indicate jeopardy with those that do not:

1. Corporation X has been in business a considerable time, its record of earnings is good, and there is no reason to anticipate a diminution of its earnings (not jeopardizing).
2. Corporation Y has a promising product. It has had earnings in some years and substantial losses in others, has never paid a dividend, and is widely reported in investment advisory services as seriously undercapitalized (is jeopardizing unless Y's shares are purchased in a new offering of an amount intended to satisfy Y's capital needs).
3. Corporation Z has been in business a short period of time and manufactures a product that is new, is not sold by others, and must compete with a well-established alternative product that services the

same purpose (is jeopardizing unless the management has a demonstrated capacity for getting new businesses started successfully and Z has received substantial orders for its new products).

Another example finds a foundation's purchase of unimproved real estate not to be jeopardizing where it was purchased following the advice of a professional manager. The foundation sought recommendations on how best to diversify its investments to provide for its long-term financial needs and protect against inflation. Its short-term financial needs could be satisfied with its other assets.

The only published ruling on jeopardizing investments concerns an indebted whole-life insurance policy. The private foundation received a gift of an indebted policy covering an insured with a 10-year life expectancy. Based on the scheduled death benefit, the private foundation could expect to pay more in premiums and loan interest than it would receive. Each payment on the policy was found to be a jeopardizing investment.[6] In the only court case, placement of the entire foundation corpus in a Bahamian bank without inquiring as to the integrity of the bank was found to be jeopardizing since the bank at the time had lost its license to do business.[7]

In private rulings, the IRS has approved investments of the type that it says require close scrutiny. In one ruling, gold stocks purchased as a hedge against inflation were not jeopardizing despite a net loss of $7,000 on a $14,500 investment. The private foundation bought the shares over three years, made money on one block, and lost on two others. The ruling noted that the private foundation had realized $31,000 in gains and $23,000 in dividends during the same period on its whole portfolio. Importantly, the portfolio performance as a whole was found to enable the private foundation to carry out its purposes.[8]

A "managed commodity trading program" was found to give diversity to a private foundation's marketable security portfolio and not to be a jeopardizing investment. Since commodity futures have little or no correlation to the stock market, the added diversity may provide less risk for the private foundation's overall investment. The foundation invested 10 percent of its portfolio.[9]

NOTE: Due to the significant losses that would have occurred, it will be interesting to see whether the IRS takes the position that a foundation fully invested in technology company stocks during the year 2000 had jeopardized its investments.

Q 6:7   What is a *program-related investment*?

Investments made to advance a charitable purpose are called *program-related investments* and are not subject to the same standards of risk/reward applicable to other investments, even if they bear no interest or dividend and possess a high degree of risk of loss. The primary purpose of a program-related investment is to accomplish one or more charitable purposes, rather than to produce income.[10] Such investments "would not have been made" but for the relationship between the investment and the accomplishment of the foundation's exempt purposes. In evaluating the foundation's motivation, it is "relevant whether investors solely engaged in investment for profit would be likely to make the investment on the same terms as the foundation." The following examples illustrate the concept:

- A small business enterprise, X, is located in a deteriorated urban area and is owned by members of an economically disadvantaged minority group. Conventional sources of funds are unwilling or unable to provide funds to the enterprise. A foundation's below-market interest rate loan to encourage economic development would be program-related.
- The private foundation described above allows an extension of X's loan in order to permit X to achieve greater financial stability before it is required to repay the loan. Since the change is not motivated by attempts to enhance yield, but by an effort to encourage success of an exempt project, the altered loan is also considered to be program-related.
- Assume instead that a commercial bank will loan X money if it increases the amount of its equity capital. A private foundation's purchase of X's common stock to accomplish the same purposes as the loan described above is again considered to be program-related.
- Assume instead that substantial citizens own X, but continued operation of X is important for the economic well-being of the low-income persons in the area. To save X, a private foundation loans X money at below-market rates to pay for specific projects benefiting the community. The loan is program-related.
- A private foundation wants to encourage the building of a plant to provide jobs in a low-income neighborhood. The foundation loans the building funds at below-market rates to a successful commercial company that is unwilling to build the plant without such inducement. Again, the loan is program-related.
- A private foundation loans a socially and economically disadvantaged individual funds to attend college interest-free. Once more, the grant is considered to be program-related.
- Land purchased for land conservation, wildlife preservation, and the protection of open and scenic spaces is program-related.[11]

A change in the terms of a program-related investment will not create jeopardy if the change continues to advance the exempt purposes for which the investment was originally made and is not made to produce income or appreciation.[12] A program-related investment is treated as a qualifying distribution by the foundation at the time the investment is made. This type of investment must be monitored and reported to the IRS throughout its life under the expenditure responsibility rules.

Q 6:8   What excise taxes are imposed when a jeopardizing investment is made?

An initial, or first-tier, tax of 5 percent is imposed on the amount invested in a jeopardizing fashion on both the private foundation and its responsible managers. The tax is due for each year the investment is held, beginning on the date the investment is made and ending on the earliest of the following dates:

- Date of mailing of a notice of deficiency with respect to the tax;
- Date on which the tax is assessed; or
- Date on which the amount so invested is removed from jeopardy—when it is sold or otherwise disposed of and the proceeds are not reinvested in a jeopardizing fashion.

NOTE: Correction may be difficult or impossible if the asset is not marketable. Evidence that the foundation is making every effort to maximize available funds from the investment may help to avoid the additional tax.

If the jeopardy is not removed within the time frame requested by the IRS, the foundation must pay an additional 25 percent tax. Managers who refuse to agree to remove part or all of the investment from jeopardy must pay an additional tax of 5 percent. The tax imposed on managers who knowingly participate in the decision to purchase the investment is a joint and severe liability with a maximum of $5,000 of first-tier tax and $10,000 of second-tier tax assessed for all parties involved.

Q 6:9   Are all foundation officials subject to the penalty tax?

Foundation managers who participate in making a decision to purchase an investment knowing that it is a jeopardizing one are taxed unless their participation is not willful and is due to reasonable cause. A manager is treated as *knowing* only if three factors are present:

1. He or she has actual knowledge of sufficient facts so that he or she knew, based solely on such facts, that the investment would be a jeopardizing one;
2. He or she is aware that the investment under such circumstances may violate the jeopardizing investment rules; and
3. He or she negligently fails to make reasonable attempts to ascertain whether the investment is a jeopardizing investment, or he or she is in fact aware that it is such an investment.[13]

> **NOTE:**   *Knowing* does not mean having reason to know. The question is whether the manager actually did know based on the actual facts and circumstances. To be excused, the manager has to be essentially ignorant of the facts. Assume that a foundation's board has 10 members, with a three-member finance committee. The written investment policy of the foundation provides that the board approves investment actions proposed by the finance committee, based on the advice of independent counselors. Nonfinance committee board members are not expected to be aware of details discussed in finance committee meetings.

A manager's participation is willful if he or she voluntarily, consciously, and intentionally ignores the facts pointing to jeopardy. A manager is excused if he or she has a good reason for not knowing and exercises good business judgment with ordinary business care and prudence in participating in the decision.

> **NOTE:**   Any manifestation of a manager's approval of the investment in question is considered to be participation in the decision to make the investment. Clearly, a vote as a board member to approve a purchase is participation. Board members who do not attend meetings but sanction investment decisions may be derelict in their fiduciary responsibility, but their inability to participate in the decision and resulting lack of knowledge may shield them from the tax. If they receive a board information packet revealing the questionable investment they have knowledge; but the tax only applies if they participate in the approval.

Q 6:10   Can foundation managers escape penalties by delegating their responsibility for managing investments to others?

A manager fails to exercise the appropriate level of responsibility if he or she fails to exercise "[o]rdinary business care and prudence, under the facts and circumstances prevailing at the time the investment is made, in providing for the long and short-term needs of the foundation to carry out its exempt purposes."[14] A basic standard in exercising fiduciary responsibility is a duty to delegate the task to those whose qualifications make them most capable of performing the task. Managers are not expected necessarily to personally make the investment decisions. Managers hire persons with the knowledge and experience to make the best choices. They are responsible for evaluating and monitoring those persons to whom it delegates the jobs on a reasonably regular basis, but not to question each decision they make.

A manager who relies on outside advisors will not be treated as *knowingly* and *willfully* participating in a jeopardizing investment and may be excused from the tax. The factual situation existing when the investment was made must be fully disclosed to the outside advisor. The fact that a manager failed to seek advice is one of the factors pointing to willful participation.[15] The types of reliance permitted may be different for different types of investments:

- For *program-related investments,* a manager may rely on a "reasoned" written legal opinion that a particular investment would not jeopardize the carrying out of any of the foundation's exempt purposes. The opinion must state that, as a matter of law, the investment is a program-related one not classified as a jeopardizing investment.
- For *financial investments* from which the private foundation derives its operating income, qualified investment counselors are customarily relied on. Again, all facts must be disclosed to the advisor. Advisors must render advice "in a manner consistent with generally accepted practices" of persons in their business. The written advice must recommend investments that provide for the foundation's long- and short-term financial needs.

Q 6:11   Are any other sanctions placed on jeopardizing investments?

Yes. An imprudent investment can conceivably cause several excise taxes to be imposed simultaneously.[16] A foundation that buys its founder's 40 percent share of an insolvent computer software development company, for example, has committed the following impermissible acts:

- Self-dealing (Chapter 3) occurs because the purchase takes place between the private foundation and a disqualified person.
- Excess business holdings (Chapter 5) are created because the combined ownership of the foundation and its insider own more than 20 percent of the company.
- A jeopardizing investment occurs unless the foundation is focused on scientific development of software and the company can be considered a functionally related business.
- Last, the money paid could be considered a taxable expenditure (Chapter 7) because the purchase did not serve a charitable purpose.

CHAPTER 7

Taxable Expenditures

A private foundation may spend its money for only two purposes: to accomplish a charitable purpose and to manage and conserve its assets. Expenditures to promote the election of a candidate for public office and efforts to influence their votes once they are elected (lobbying) are not charitable activities. The law also imposes enhanced record-keeping requirements to prove the charitable nature of expenditures when a private foundation makes grants to individuals or to entities that are not considered public charities. This chapter explores the breath of the constraints on foundation grant-making, but also gives suggestions for reducing the burdens when a foundation chooses to support another foundation, an international program, public policy research, and the like.

Here are the questions that are most frequently asked (or that should be asked) about the taxable expenditures rules—and the answers to them.

Q 7:1 Are there special rules governing the way in which a private foundation spends its money?

Yes. A private foundation must first meet what are called organizational and operational tests[1] that require it operate *exclusively*—meaning its major focus not necessarily 100 percent—for charitable purposes. The taxable expenditure rules add an absolute and subject a private foundation to higher standards than those applicable to public charities.[2] A private foundation is prohibited from spending its money in support of an electoral candidate or in an attempt to influence legislation and special requirements apply to grants to individuals or nonpublic charities.

NOTE: Foundation creators and managers need not be discouraged by the taxable expenditure rules. The rules are actually broader than many realize. Once the rules are understood and procedures are in place to review compliance, a private foundation has a fairly high degree of latitude in developing its grant and program activity. Some foundations have needlessly forgone efforts directed at improving matters of broad social and economic impact, such as healthcare or the environment. Educational and scientific efforts involving such subjects are not necessarily legislative efforts, even if the problems are of a type that government ultimately would be expected to deal with.

Q 7:2   What types of expenditures are treated as taxable?

The private foundation and its disqualified persons will incur a penalty tax, and possible loss of its tax-exempt status, if any amount is paid or incurred for the following purposes:

- To carry on propaganda or otherwise to attempt to influence legislation
- To influence the outcome of any specific election, or to carry on any voter registration drive, except efforts involving at least five states
- As a grant to an individual for travel, study, or other similar purpose, except according to a preapproved plan
- As a grant to an organization unless it is one of the following:
  - A public charity (Chapter 12)
  - Exempt operating foundation (Chapter 14)
  - The private foundation making the grant exercises expenditure responsibility
- For any purpose that is not religious, charitable, scientific, literary, educational, to foster national or international amateur sports competition, or to prevent cruelty to children or animals

Q 7:3   What is meant by "carry on propaganda or attempt to influence legislation"?

Lobbying is the common term used to describe activities intended to influence legislation, such as information published in newsletters or posted on a Web site, placement of advertisements, holding of meetings, or similar efforts to communicate a position on legislation. A private foundation is strictly prohibited from carrying out propaganda or otherwise attempting to influence legislation—defined to *include any attempt to influence any legislation* through:

- An attempt to affect the opinion of the general public or any segment thereof (called *grassroots lobbying*); or

---

- An attempt to influence legislation through communication with any member or employee of a legislative body, or with any other government official or employee who may participate in the formulation of the legislation (except technical advice or assistance provided to a governmental body or to a committee or other subdivision thereof in response to a written request by such body or subdivision, as the case may be), other than through making available the results of nonpartisan analysis, study, or research (*direct lobbying*).[3]

NOTE: Confusingly, the tax law contains several different limitations on and definitions of lobbying activities conducted by charitable organizations. The definition of lobbying for private foundation purposes is cross-referenced to the regulations applicable to those public charities that elect to lobby. While there was some uncertainty before these regulations were finalized, private foundations can participate in educational activity involving public issues that eventually may be the subject of legislation.

Q 7:4   Can a private foundation lobby for issues that impact its mission?

Unfortunately, the answer is no. Despite the fact that proposed law changes would protect or authorize funding for the environment, children, the sick, and so on, a private foundation is prohibited from urging passage of specific legislation. It is important to note, however, that a foundation can support public charities that do, so long as its grants are not earmarked specifically for lobbying. The foundation, however, can work to influence regulations or other administrative rules clarifying and interpreting existing laws.

Q 7:5   Is there any type of lobbying activity that a private foundation can conduct?

Yes. Germane, or self-defense, lobbying on decisions of legislative bodies that might affect the existence of the private foundation, its powers and duties, its tax-exempt status, or the deduction of contributions to it may be conducted. A foundation can spend its money to make an appearance before, or communicate to, any legislative body with respect to a possible decision that would impact its being. Note that existence for this purpose does not include funding. Its being is not impacted, in the IRS's view, by a possible loss of economic support.[4] Lobbying in favor of an appropriations bill that funds a program under which the private foundation has received support in the past is not self-defense. Similarly, a private foundation that provides care for the elderly is lobbying when its executive director appears before the state legislature to favor or oppose a bill authorizing the state to provide nursing care for the aged. Likewise, a private foundation receiving governmental grants to support its research programs is lobbying when it testifies about the advisability of continuing the program unless foundation representatives are asked to testify. It is the economic condition and the resulting scope of the private foundation's operation, not its underlying existence, at issue in these examples. On the other hand, an effort to influence a state's reformation of its charitable corporation statutes to include provisions not now present in a private foundation's charter would be self-defense and therefore permissible legislative activity.

NOTE: Foundation managers are free, however, to lobby on their own behalf, despite the fact that they are identified publicly for their affiliation with the foundation.

Q 7:6   How can a foundation involve itself in solutions to broad social, economic, and similar problems?

The foundation and its representatives can give technical assistance or expert testimony in regard to legislation under consideration if it does so in response to a request. A foundation also can sponsor discussions or conferences, conduct research, and publish educational materials about matters of broad social and economic subjects, such as human rights or war and peace. Since topics of this nature are often the subject matter of legislation, involve public controversy, and raise the possibility of the foundation being treated as conducting prohibited legislative activity, a foundation doing so must carefully document a disconnection from the legislative aspect of the issue. As a rule, a foundation can sponsor such discussions and examine such issues when three specific factors are *not* present. The private foundation's written communications, either directly with members of the general public or with the legislators themselves, may not:

1. Mention or refer in any way to specific legislation;
2. Take a position on any legislation; or
3. Recommend that the reader take any steps to contact legislators, employees of legislators, or government officials or employees involved in legislation, or contain a call to action.

Q 7:7   Can a foundation study and publish results of social issues pertaining to proposed legislation?

A private foundation can conduct independent and objective examinations and studies of social policy matters and make the information or results of its work available to the general public and to governmental bodies, officials, or employees. When a communiqué distributing the results presents a particular viewpoint or position—for example, that oil tankers should have double hulls to lessen the possibility of oil spills—the materials must be educational in content. Mere opinion, unsupported by pertinent facts enabling individuals to form their own opinions, is not nonpartisan. The regulations contain 12 examples that can be studied for more illustrations of these activities.[5]

A broadcast or publication series must meet the same standards as printed matter. One of the presentations can contain biased information if another part of the series (broadcast within six months of the initial viewing) contains contrary information or the other side of the argument. If the private foundation selects the time for presentation of information to coincide with a specific legislative proposal, the expenses of preparing and distributing that part of the study may be treated as lobbying and result in a taxable expenditure. A display on the foundation's Web site should have the same balanced approach.

Q 7:8   Can a private foundation make a grant to a public charity that conducts lobbying activity?

As a general rule, a private foundation can make a grant to a public charity that conducts legislative lobbying, whether the grant recipient has elected the expenditure test or not.[6] The foundation's money cannot be earmarked for lobbying. There must be no agreement, oral or written, that the granting private foundation can direct the manner in which the funds are expended.[7] Also, the private foundation's grant cannot be more than the amount needed to fund the recipient organization's budget for nonlobbying projects. If, after a grant satisfying these rules is paid, the grant recipient loses its exempt status due to excessive lobbying, the money paid is not a taxable expenditures only if:

- The grant was not earmarked for lobbying (Q 7:3);
- The recipient had a valid determination of its public status (Q 7:20);
- Notice of the revocation was not published when the grant was made; and
- The private foundation does not control the public charity (Q 4:15).[8]

Q 7:9   Can a private foundation participate in elections in any fashion?

All charitable organizations, including private foundations, are prohibited from participating or intervening in elections of public officials with the intent to influence the outcome. Certain educational efforts in connection with the electoral process may, however, be permitted. What a foundation is specifically forbidden to do *is to attempt to influence the outcome of any specific public election, or to carry on, directly or indirectly, any voter registration drive.*[9] In the South during the early 1960s, certain foundations financed voter drives aimed specifically at registering blacks to vote, in connection with the foundations' effort to eliminate discrimination. Partly as a result, very specific rules govern a private foundation's participation in such efforts. A foundation is permitted to make a grant to another organization, including another private foundation, that itself conducts a voter registration drive if the recipient organization meets the following requirements:

- The organization is a charitable one;
- Activities of the organization are nonpartisan, are not confined to one specific election period, and are carried on in five or more states;
- At least 85 percent of the organization's income is spent directly on the active conduct of its charitable purposes;
- At least 85 percent of its support (other than gross investment income) comes from other tax-exempts, the general public, and governmental units, and not more than 25 percent comes from a single organization; and
- Contributions for voter registration drives cannot be earmarked for particular states or political subdivisions.

Q 7:10   Can a private foundation make grants to individuals?

A private foundation may make grants, that serve a charitable purpose, to individuals. The terms for payment of individual grants for travel, study, or other similar purposes must be preapproved by the IRS; otherwise such grants are taxable expenditures. Individual grants also cannot be earmarked to be used for political, legislative, or other noncharitable activities the foundation itself cannot not otherwise conduct.[10] Travel, study, or similar-purpose grants, payable only by means of a preapproved plan, must also be one of the following[11]:

- A grant constituting a scholarship or fellowship grant[12]
- A prize or award paid to a recipient selected from the general public.[13]
- A grant to achieve a specific objective, produce a report or other similar product, or improve or enhance a literary, artistic, musical, scientific, teaching, or other similar capacity, skill, or talent of the grantee.

Q 7:11   What is a grant for "travel, study or other purposes"?

Only grants paid to individuals for the three specified purposes (Q 7:10) are subject to the prior plan approval rules. The concepts are best illustrated in three scenarios.[14] In the first, the grant is not subject to IRS approval, but in the second and third, approval is required.

1. A private foundation organized to promote the art of journalism makes awards to persons whose work represent the best example of investigative reporting on matters concerning the government. Potential recipients are nominated; they do not apply for the award. The awards are granted in recognition of past achievement and are not intended to finance any specific activities of the recipients nor to impose any conditions on the manner in which the award is expended by the recipient. Therefore, since the payments are not to

finance study, travel, or a similar purpose, the awards project was not subject to prior approval.

2. Assume instead that the annual award recipients are required to take a three-month summer tour to study government at educational institutions. These awards are subject to prior approval because the payment is required to be used for study and travel.

3. The facts are the same as in Scenario 1, except that the award is a scholarship that must be used to pursue study at an educational institution. Again, prior approval is required. A similar conclusion was reached in a ruling concerning grants to science fair winners that required them to use the prizes for their education. The program was a scholarship plan requiring approval.[15]

The meaning of grants for *other similar purposes* is elusive. Student loans and program-related investments constitute such grants,[16] If the payment is given with the expectation or requirement that the recipient perform specific activities not directly of benefit to the foundation, a grant occurs. Research grants, and payments to allow recipients to compose music or to choreograph a ballet, are examples of awards for *similar purposes* when the recipient must perform to earn the award. Grants and interest-free loans made to persons that incur extraordinary medical expenses, funeral or burial costs, or suffer financial hardship due to medical emergencies, natural disasters, or violent crimes are not grants for *other purposes.* Therefore, a corporate foundation that established a hardship grant and loan program was not technically required to obtain advance approval for its program to avoid the payments being classified as taxable expenditures.[17]

Q 7:12   What kind of payments to individuals are not treated as grants?

Payments that have no strings attached, or do not require the recipient to perform specific tasks, are not grants for this purpose. A payment to an indigent individual for the purchase of food or clothing is a good example of an amount not paid for travel, study, or other purpose and, therefore, not subject to these rules. Awards paid to winners of a craft school competition on an unconditional and unrestricted basis are also deemed not to be grants for this purpose.[18] Grants in recognition of literary achievement not given to finance future activity and not imposing any future condition on the recipient are not grants subject to preapproval.[19]

Compensatory payments for personal services, such as salaries, consultant fees, and reimbursement of travel and other expenses incurred on behalf of the foundation, require no preapproval. A foundation can freely hire persons to assist it in planning, evaluating, and developing projects and program activity by consulting, advising, and participating in conferences organized by the foundation. Persons hired to develop model curricula and educational materials, for example, are not grant recipients.[20]

NOTE: Since 1986, the traditional award system is less advantageous since only that portion spent on tuition and books is tax-free to the recipients. Certain scholarships and, particularly, teaching fellowships are taxable for another reason—the fact that the recipient is expected to render services in return for receiving the grant. Rather than fund research under a grant program, a foundation might choose to avoid the approval process by establishing internal research projects. Nonperformance, nonstudy grants in recognition of achievement also can be made without preapproval. Such awards should still be made on a nondiscriminatory basis to ensure they are awarded to members of a charitable class.

Q 7:13   What standards are applied for scholarship plan approval?

Once a foundation chooses to make grants subject to the approval process (Q 7:11), it must adopt a suitable plan. The primary criterion for approval of a plan for making individual grants is that the grants must be awarded on an "objective and nondiscriminatory basis." The plan must contain the following provisions:

- An "objective and nondiscriminatory" method of choice, consistent with the private foundation's exempt status and the purpose of the grant, is used.
- The group from which grantees are selected is sufficiently broad so as to constitute a charitable class. The size of the group may be small if the purpose of the grant so warrants, such as research fellows in a specialized field.
- Criteria used in selecting the recipients include academic performance, recommendations from instructors, financial need, and/or motivation and personal character.
- Selection committee members are not in a position to derive a private benefit, directly or indirectly, if one person or another is chosen.
- Grants are awarded for study at an academic institution, fellowships, prizes or awards, or study or research involving a literary, artistic, musical, scientific, or teaching purpose.
- Plans to obtain reports are provided for scholarships, fellowships, and research or study grants.[21]

Examples

A group including all students in a city or all valedictorians in a state is a sufficiently large class. A plan to pay 20 annual scholarships to members of a certain ethnic minority living within a state was approved. However, a group of girls and boys with at least one-quarter Finnish blood living in two particular towns was found to be a discriminatory group and not sufficiently broad. Likewise, a plan that gave priority to family members and relatives of the trust's creator, if their qualifications were substantially the same as an unrelated party, was found to be discriminatory.[22]

Q 7:14   How must a foundation supervise its scholarship recipients?

The standards of supervision a foundation must perform vary according to the type of grant.

Scholarships and Fellowships

A report of the grantee's courses taken and grades earned in each academic period must be collected at least once annually and verified by the educational institution. For grantees whose work does not involve classes but only the preparation of research papers or projects, such as a doctoral thesis, the foundation should receive an annual report approved by the faculty members supervising the grantee or other school official. Upon completion of a grantee's study, a final report also must be obtained.

Research or Study Grants

At least annually, a report of progress and use of funds is due. A final report describing the grantee's accomplishments and funds expended with respect to the grant also must be made.

Investigation of Diversions

When the foundation notes a grantee has not complied with the reporting standards or when reports indicate a failure to maintain qualification, the foundation is expected to investigate. Procedures that alert the foundation to failures in academic work or any diversion of money from the purpose for which it was granted must be established. The private foundation is not held responsible for such programs and is not treated as making a taxable expenditure, if the recipient had not previously misused funds and if the private foundation takes the following steps during its investigation:

- During the investigation, the private foundation withholds additional payments until it receives the grantee's assurances that future diversions will not occur, and requires the grantee to take extraordinary precautions to prevent future diversions from occurring.
- The private foundation takes reasonable steps to recover the funds.
- If a grantee was reprieved after an initial investigation and the private foundation reinstituted the grant only to have the funds diverted for a second time, a taxable expenditure will not occur if the same steps are repeated and the diverted funds are recovered.

Recordkeeping

A foundation making individual grants must maintain and keep available for IRS examination documentation that the recipients are chosen in a nondiscriminatory manner and that proper follow-up is accomplished. The following records must be kept:

- Information used to evaluate the qualification of potential grantees.
- Reports of any grantee/director relationships.
- Specification of amount and purpose of each grant.
- Grade reports or other progress reports approved by a faculty member must be received annually.

Q 7:15   How do these rules apply to employer-related grant programs?

A company foundation may establish a scholarship plan or education loan program for children of the company employees and seek approval under the same rules described above (Q 7:10). Tests designed to measure whether the plan discriminates in favor of the corporate executives or shareholders or represent a means of paying additional compensation also apply. The primary criteria are:

- The scholarship plan is not used by the private foundation on behalf of the employer to recruit employees or to induce continued employment.
- The selection committee is made up of totally independent persons, not including former employees, and preferably including persons knowledgeable about education.
- Identifiable minimum requirements for grant eligibility are established. Eligibility does not depend on employment-related performance, although up to three years of service for the parent can be required.
- Selection criteria is based on substantial objective standards, prior academic performance, tests, recommendations, financial need, and personal interviews.
- A grant may not be terminated because the recipient or parent terminates employment.
- The courses of study for which grants are available are not limited to those of particular benefit to the employer.
- The terms of the grant and course of study allow recipients to obtain an education in their individual capacities solely for their personal benefit and do not include any commitments, understandings, or obligations of future employment.
- A mathematical test is applied to prove a sufficiently large class of applicants. No more than 10 percent of the eligible persons, and no more than 25 percent of the eligible persons who submitted applications and were considered by the selection committee, can be awarded grants. A fraction of one-half or greater can be rounded up to determine plan qualification in calculating the allowable percentage of children of employees permitted to receive scholarships.[23]

NOTE: Due to the self-dealing rules, no grants can be paid to children of disqualified persons. The plan must avoid a disproportionate amount of grants to executives' children. The application for approval is the same as for other scholarship plans, although satisfaction of the eight tests listed above must be outlined.

Q 7:16   How does a foundation seek approval for its individual grant program?

A letter describing the foundation's plan and its proposed procedures for awarding grants, including the methods of meeting the selection process requirements described above (Q 7:13), is submitted to the IRS Service Center in Cincinnati, Ohio. The approval process reviews the foundation's standards, procedures, and follow-up designed to meet the law's requirements for all of the private foundation's individual grant programs. If, within 45 days after submission of the plan, no notification is received that the procedures are unacceptable, the private foundation can consider the plan approved. Silence signifies approval. Written approval is customarily sent by the IRS to successful applicants, but many months and, in past years, a year or so later. Although authorized to do so, the IRS has not imposed a user fee for seeking approval of an individual grant program in recent years. Newly created foundations can seek approval for their plans in connection with filing the application for recognition of tax exemption to avoid the need to make a separate application.

Q 7:17   Can a foundation create a scholarship program within a public charity?

Yes. A foundation wishing to avoid the administrative burden and cost of applying for approval and disbursing scholarships directly can instead fund a grant program at an independent public charity. As long as the foundation has no control over the choice of recipients, it is not considered to have made the grants directly to the individuals. There must be no agreement, oral or written, that the private foundation can cause the selection of particular individuals. No earmarking is permitted.

The parameters of the grant, such as the study discipline—medicine or law, for example—or qualifications, such as grades or civic achievement, can be stipulated by the foundation. Actually suggesting the individual grantee is permitted, as long as there is an objective manifestation of the public charity's control over the selection process. Maintaining the right to veto a potential recipient *is de facto control*. Likewise, a research grant to a college contingent on supervision by the professor designated by the private foundation is treated as an individual grant from the foundation. The regulations contain useful examples for further study.[24]

Q 7:18   Can a private foundation make grants to public charities?

Private foundations mostly make grants to public charities (Chapter 12) or those grant recipients specifically excluded from the taxable expenditure list (Q 7:2).[25] This is partly true because so much charitable work is performed by those organizations and private foundations have traditionally used their endowments to fund these institutions. A private foundation can make a grant to a public charity without exercising expenditure responsibility.

A foundation is, however, permitted to make a grant to any type of entity, exempt or nonexempt, if it properly documents its purposes in making the grant and insures the transaction with *expenditure responsibility* agreements (Q 7:24). The purpose of these rules is to see that private foundation funds are used to benefit the public, not the private interests of their creators. Grants to public charities are preferred simply because they require less documentation. Public charities serve a broad constituency that monitors their responsiveness to public needs and use of their funds for charitable purposes.

Q 7:19   What is a *public charity*?

Public and private charities must first qualify as tax-exempt charitable organizations. Next, public charities—that is, nonprivate foundations—are one of three types (Chapter 12):

- 509(a)(1): Institutions that serve a large number of constituents, such as churches, universities, schools, hospitals, medical research organizations, and governmental unites and agencies.
- 509(a)(2): Publicly supported organizations that receive more than one-third percent of their revenues from modest donors and/or fees and sales of services and goods performed in conducting their charitable activities for a large number of persons.
- 509(a)(3): A charity created to support and benefit one or more other public charities.

NOTE: The definition is a bit convoluted. Some organizations can qualify under more than one category. Nonetheless, it is very useful for foundation officials to learn the definitions for ease in evaluating grantees. Exempt operating foundations are treated as public for this purpose. A grant to an instrumentality of a foreign government is also considered to be a grant to a public charity, as long as it is made for charitable purposes.[26]

Q 7:20   How does a private foundation satisfy itself that a grantee is a public charity?

The effort to document tax status begins for most foundations when they request that a copy of the IRS determination letter accompany grant requests.

A private foundation can rely on the grantee organization's proof—the IRS determination letter stating that it is a public charity—until a notice of its revocation is published in the weekly *Internal Revenue Bulletin* or is otherwise made public.[27] The letter itself, however, does not prove current status, and too many times an outdated letter is furnished. The IRS eased this burden by placing its master list of charitable organizations, and their public or private status, on the Internet. Prudent foundations go to *www.irs.ustreas.gov* and click on *Tax Information for Business* to view the list. The list is updated on an ongoing basis. The information is also published on paper in Publication 78 with updates three times a year.[28]

Sometimes the amount of funding a foundation wants to provide to an existing public charity may cause the recipient to fail the one-third public support test. If the grantee organization is not controlled by the foundation— that is, the private foundation cannot cause it to act or prevent its acts—the private foundation need not investigate the effect of its grant on the recipient public charity status.[29] When the foundation has a relationship with the grantee organization, and certainly if the private foundation controls it (Q 4:15), the foundation also has a responsibility to determine whether its grant will cause the recipient organization to lose its public status. When a public entity undergoes a "substantial and material change," the private foundation has three choices if it chooses to make a grant:

1. The private foundation can satisfy itself that it was not responsible for the change by reviewing financial information from the grantee's officers. The grantor is not responsible if its gift in a year is less than 25 percent of the recipient's total gifts for the immediately preceding four years.
2. The private foundation can ascertain that the grant is an unusual one (Q 12:7) that will not cause the grantee to lose public status.
3. The private foundation can exercise expenditure responsibility.[30]

NOTE: A grant-making private foundation should establish a system for documenting the tax character of its grant recipients.[31] Additionally, the charitable nature of each grant should be documented with a grant request or other information and evidence the funds will not be used for a prohibited purpose. The Council on Foundations and the Association for Small Foundations provide guidance in this regard, and computerized grant tracking systems are available.

Q 7:21   Can a private foundation retain control over its grant funds?

An earmarked grant to a public charity to do something the private foundation itself is not permitted to do results in a taxable expenditure. Public charities are free to make grants to individuals, to support a newly created but yet-unrecognized organization, to finance lobbying efforts, and to conduct a host of other projects that might not be permissible for a private foundation. There is sometimes a temptation for a private foundation to funnel or pass money through a public charity for a project that the private foundation itself cannot undertake or for which it does not wish to exercise expenditure responsibility.

A foundation grant to an intermediary organization—sometimes called a fiscal agent—may be treated as a grant by the private foundation to the ultimate grantee if the foundation retains control over the ultimate spending of the funds.[32] The rules are similar to the rules applicable to designating scholarship recipients (Q 7:17). A *look-through rule* applies when the private foundation earmarks its grant in an oral or written manner. If the regrant is to another public charity, there is no problem (unless the grant is earmarked for lobbying or for a particular individual). If the regrant is made to another private foundation or for some impermissible purpose (Q 7:2), a taxable expenditure may occur. When a foundation grants funds to an organization or fiscal agent in this fashion, the grant should be carefully documented.[33]

Q 7:22   Can a private foundation make a grant to a foreign organization?

A foreign government and any agency or instrumentality thereof is treated as a public organization for this purpose. Certain international organizations also qualify as public charities, such as the World Health Organization, the United Nations, the International Bank for Reconstruction and Development, the International Monetary Fund, and others designated by the president.[34]

A foreign charitable organization that does not have an IRS determination letter, but that is equivalent to and would in fact qualify as a public charity if it sought approval, also may be treated as a public entity. The private foundation is allowed to make a good-faith determination of the foreign organization's status. An affidavit from the foreign entity or an opinion of counsel that contains sufficient facts about the operations and type of financial support is required. The information should indicate the grantee would qualify as a public charity.[35] The equivalency method of proving public status does not necessarily apply to a foreign organization that receives over 15 percent of its support from U.S. sources.[36]

Documentation

Seeking the appropriate information from a foreign organization is often troublesome due to language, currency, and legal differences. Because of these difficulties, private foundations usually find it more comfortable to treat such foreign grants as expenditure responsibility grants (Q 7:24) to avoid unexpected results. The paperwork may be simpler and the possibility for a taxable expenditure is less.[37]

NOTE: Nonetheless, some foundations find translating foreign currency, non-U.S. accounting methodology, and foreign language invoices and expense vouchers a very difficult task. Retrieving grant funds that lack proper documentation is not always possible (Q 7:22). To avoid such uncertainty, many private foundations support public charities that conduct programs in foreign countries.

Charitable Deduction Connection

Among the reasons why a private foundation would involve itself in foreign projects is the charitable deduction rules[38] disallow deductions for gifts to foreign charities. When the U.S. charity's board (private or public) has control and discretion as to the use of the funds raised, the fact that the funds are contributed to the private foundation specifically for projects outside the United States does not render contributions nondeductible.

Mexican Organizations

The tax treaty between Mexico and the United States establishes a protocol under which Mexican charitable organizations can be recognized as public charities for private foundation purposes. The treaty also provides for an income tax deduction against a U.S. resident's Mexican-source income reportable in the United States and vice versa. Private foundations that are interested in supporting charitable activities in Mexico and other foreign countries should be alert for similar provisions in income tax treaties impacting the status of such organizations.[39]

Q 7:23 Can a private foundation conduct programs outside the United States?

A private foundation (and public charities) can directly conduct programs anywhere in the world. The only requirement is that the activity be charitable. Foundations feed the poor, conduct agricultural research, restore historic sites, preserve animals, conduct archeological digs, and operate a wide range of pursuits in foreign countries.

Example

Gifts to a pair of organizations established to build a basketball stadium and to sponsor and operate the games in the foreign country were allowed in one private ruling and by reference sanctioned the exempt status for the AA. Interestingly, only one organization was designed to qualify for U.S. charitable deductions. Organization 1 raised funds to regrant to organization 2 and to build and own the stadium in which organization 2 would operate. The ruling continues the tax policy that recognizes the exempt nature of the activity, regardless of its location.[40]

Q 7:24 What is an *expenditure responsibility grant*?

A private foundation is allowed to make a grant to any type of entity so long a charitable purpose is served. Enhanced recordkeeping is, however, required unless the grantee is classified as a public charity. Expenditure responsibility must be exercised to assure accountability for grants and program-related investments made by private foundations to:

- Another private foundation or a private operating foundation (see Chapter 14)
- A tax-exempt organization other than a charitable one
- A nonexempt business for a direct charitable program or a program-related investment

A foundation is not the "insurer of the activities of the grantee."[41] The private foundation can make such grants "as long as it exerts all reasonable efforts and establishes adequate procedures" to:

- See that the grant is spent solely for the purpose for which it is made; and
- Obtain required reports with respect to the expenditures and submit information on its annual information return.

To exercise expenditure responsibility, a foundation must take seven steps:

1. Conduct a pregrant inquiry (Q 7:25).
2. Establish proper terms for the grant or program-related investment.
3. Enter into a written agreement requiring the terms to be followed and establishing a reporting system for the grantee.
4. Follow up by receiving and reviewing grantee reports.
5. Investigate any diversions of funds.
6. Annually disclose proper information on its annual information return evidencing compliance with the steps.
7. Keep documentation of these steps for IRS inspection.

Examples

A foundation can grant funding to a social club if the funding is suitably dedicated for charitable purposes. A grant to a social fraternity's title-holding organization[42] to build a study room in the chapter house was sanctioned. The facility was to contain exclusively educational equipment and furniture, along with computers linked to the university's mainframe. The university certified in writing that the room benefited the school by supplementing its resources, alleviating overcrowding in its library and study areas, and providing additional computer terminals. The fraternity agreed to return any grant funds not used for construction of the study space. There was no time period stipulated for this guarantee, but the foundation required that it be able to inspect the room annually.[43] Another example was "urban enterprise association" established to operate a recycling facility to provide jobs for a city's unemployed.[44] The private foundation's grant, alongside commercial loans, provided startup funds for the project. The project's purpose was to train workers and find them permanent employment. A public charity partner planned to turn the facility into a "viable self-sustaining business" (presumably related), the net income of which would go to the public charity. Note that the regulations permit such a grant to be made to a nonexempt business as long as the charitable purposes of the activity are clearly evident.

Q 7:25 What is a *pregrant inquiry*?

The first step in exercising expenditure responsibility is to investigate the grantee organization and its proposed project. A pregrant inquiry is a limited investigation directed at obtaining enough information to "give a reasonable man assurance that the grantee will use the grant for the proper purposes."[45] The inquiry should concern itself with matters such as:

- The identity, prior history, and experience (if any) of the grantee organization and its managers. Is the other organization capable of accomplishing the grant purposes?
- Information about the management, activities, and practices of the grantee organization, obtained either through the private foundation's prior experience and association with the grantee or from other readily available sources.

The scope of the inquiry is expected to be tailored to the particular grantee's situation, the period over which the grant is to be paid, the nature of the project, and the private foundation's prior experience with the grantee. The regulation examples present the following profiles of successful inquiries:

- A private foundation is considering a grant to a newly created drug rehabilitation center located in a neighborhood clinic and classified as a tax-exempt social welfare organization because it is an "action" organization. One of its directors, they are informed, is an ex-convict. The private foundation determines that he is fully rehabilitated and that the board as a whole is well qualified to conduct the program, since they are members of the community and more likely to be trusted by drug offenders.
- A grant recipient provides medical research fellowships. It has conducted the program for years and receives a large number of other private foundation grants. Another private foundation that supports this recipient informs the private foundation that it is satisfied that its grants have been used for the purposes for which they were made.

If the grantee has received prior expenditure responsibility grants from the private foundation and has satisfied all of the reporting requirements, a pregrant inquiry is not necessary. Likewise for a grant to a split-interest trust that is required by its instrument to make payments to a specified public charity, a less extensive inquiry would be necessary.

Q 7:26   What type of information must be contained in an expenditure responsibility agreement?

An officer, director, or trustee of the grant recipient must sign a written commitment that, in addition to stating the charitable purposes to be accomplished, obligates the grantee to do the following:

- Repay any portion of the amount granted that is not used for the purposes of the grant.
- Submit full and complete annual reports on the manner in which the funds are spent and the progress made in accomplishing the purposes of the grant.
- Maintain records of the receipts and expenditures, and make its records available to the grantor at reasonable times.
- Not to use any of the funds for electioneering, lobbying, or other purposes that result in taxable expenditures.

When making a grant to an organization that is not a charitable one, the private foundation must require the grantee to establish, and maintain as long as grant funds remain, a separate fund dedicated to the charitable purposes for which the grant is made.

Program-Related Investments

In addition to the information required above, the recipient of program-related investment funds must also agree to:

- Repay the funds not invested in accordance with the agreement, but only to the extent permitted by applicable law concerning distributions to holders of equity interests.
- Submit financial reports of a type ordinarily required by commercial investors under similar circumstances, and a statement that it has complied with the terms of the investment.
- Maintain books and records of a type normally required by commercial investors.

Foreign Grants

An agreement with a foreign entity (Q 7:22) should phrase the restrictions in appropriate terms under foreign law or custom. While not specifically required, an affidavit or opinion of counsel stating that the agreement is valid under the foreign laws is "sufficient." Transaction of the agreement into applicable languages may be appropriate.

Q 7:27   Are follow-up reports required by recipients of expenditure responsibility grants?

Each year, details must be provided for each expenditure responsibility grant upon which "any amount or any report is outstanding at any time during the taxable year." The grantor private foundation must receive a report on the use of the grant funds reflecting the nature of the expenditures—salaries, travel, supplies, and so on. For a general support grant, an annual financial report or annual information return may be sufficient. In addition to financial information, the report should state the grantee is in compliance with the terms of the grant and describe the progress made by the grantee toward achieving the purposes for which the grant was made. The reports are to be made at the end of the grantee's fiscal year for each year the grant is outstanding, and should be received within a reasonable time after the close of the year. For multiyear grants, a final report summarizing all expenditures should be submitted.[46]

Endowment Grants

A grant of endowment funds or funds for the purchase of capital equipment or other capital purposes must be monitored for the year of the grant and for the two following years. The use of the principal and income (if any) from the grant funds is to be reported. Such grants are outstanding for 990-PF purposes for three years. If it is reasonably apparent before the end of the second succeeding year that the funds have been used for the purpose granted, the reports can be suspended.

Program-Related Investments

A grantee report must be received for each year during which the investment is in existence. One private foundation found out the hard way that program-related investments must be reported for the life of the loan or as long as the investment is held (in its case, 12 years).[47] This foundation had relied on the three-year endowment reporting requirement.

Private Foundation Successor Organizations

A private foundation that distributes part of its assets to another private foundation in a termination distribution (Q 13:6) has a duty to exercise expenditures responsibility indefinitely.[48]

Grantee Accounting Records

The recipient grantee need not maintain separate bank accounts or books for the grant unless the private foundation requires it or the grantee is a non-charitable entity. Records of the manner in which the funds are expended must, however, be maintained for at least four years after completion of the use of the funds. The grantor private foundation is entitled to rely on information submitted by its grantees.

Q 7:28   Is there enhanced IRS reporting of expenditure responsibility grants?

Yes. Each year a foundation must provide information about each outstanding expenditure responsibility grant as an attachment to its annual information return. No special form is provided but the regulations specify submission of the following data:

- Name and address of grantee
- Date and amount of the grant
- Purpose of the grant
- Amounts expended by grantee based upon the most recent report
- Whether (to the knowledge of the grantor) the grantee has diverted any portion of the funds, or income therefrom in the case of an endowment, from the intended purpose
- Dates of any reports received from the grantee
- Dates and results of any verification of grantee reports undertaken because the private foundation doubted their accuracy or reliability

Q 7:29   What if there is a diversion of an expenditure responsibility grant?

Rules similar to those governing scholarship fund diversions (Q 7:14) apply to expenditure responsibility grant diversions. The grant is not considered to be a taxable expenditure even though the grantor private foundation finds that any or all of the funds were used for improper purposes, if the grantor private foundation:

- Takes all reasonable and appropriate steps either to get the funds back or to cause the grantee to use other funds to satisfy the grant terms; and
- Withholds, as soon as it discovers the problem, any further payments to the grantee until it receives the grantee's assurance that future diversions will not occur, and requires the grantee to take extraordinary precautions to prevent future diversion from occurring.
- If a grantee fails to make reports, a taxable expenditure will result unless the private foundation:
  - Originally made the grant following the appropriate pregrant inquiry;
  - Complied with all reporting requirements;

- Makes a reasonable effort to obtain the required report; and
- Withholds any future payments on the specific grant and on any other grants to the same grantee.

Q 7:30 What kind of expenditures, other than grants, is a private foundation permitted to make?

The term *taxable expenditure* includes any amount paid or incurred for a noncharitable purpose.[49] The following expenditures are not considered to be noncharitable, even though they are neither grants nor project expenditures:

- Payments to acquire investments entered into for the purpose of obtaining income or funds to be used in furtherance of charitable pursuits (Chapter 6)
- Payment of taxes
- Expenses deductible against unrelated business income
- Payments constituting a qualifying distribution (Chapter 4) or a deduction against investment income (Chapter 8)
- Reasonable expenses to evaluate, acquire, notify, and dispose of a program-related investment
- Business expenses by the recipient of a program-related investment
- Return of contingent contributions[50]

Conversely, the following expenses are taxable expenditures:

- Unreasonable administrative costs, including consulting fees
- Payment of unreasonable compensation (Q 3:17)[51]
- Payment of legal costs and settlement amounts to defend officers and directors in an unsuccessful state mismanagement action[52]
- Payments to a cemetery company eligible to receive charitable contributions[53]

Q 7:31 What is the penalty for making a taxable expenditure?

A penalty, or excise tax, of 10 percent of the amount of any taxable expenditure is imposed on the private foundation making such an expenditure. A 2½ percent tax is payable by any foundation manager who willfully agreed to the expenditure knowing that it was such an expenditure, up to a maximum of $5,000.

To be subject to the tax, the manager must intentionally agree to the expenditure knowing that it is taxable. *Knowing* does not necessarily mean having reason to know. Such manager must have agreed to make the expenditure willfully and without reasonable causes, such as reliance on the written advice of outside or inside counsel. Only those managers in a position to decide what expenditures are paid and approve such disbursements are subject to the tax.[54] The rules for excusing the managers and the possible abatement of the tax are the same as those outlined elsewhere (Q 6:8, Q 6:9).

Q 7:32   Can the penalty be abated?

The IRS has the discretionary authority to abate the initial tax whether the private foundation itself discovers and reports the error or the IRS discovers it upon examination. To be allowed abatement, the private foundation must prove the violation was due to reasonable cause, not due to willful neglect, and that a timely correction has been made. Form 4720 is filed to inform the IRS that a potential taxable expenditure occurred and to explain the foundation has taken steps to make the required corrections.

If the taxable expenditure is not "corrected" before the date of mailing a notice of deficiency or the date on which the initial tax is assessed, known as the *taxable period,* an additional tax of 100 percent of the expenditure is imposed upon the foundation.[55] The knowing managers are jointly and severally liable for an additional tax of 50 percent, up to a maximum of $10,000.

CAUTION: Despite the fact that penalties can be abated, the IRS has strictly enforced the expenditure responsibility reporting requirement. Before 1984, reporting the information on an amended return did not correct the taxable expenditure. Stiff penalties were upheld against a group of three commonly controlled organizations in one case. Their annual information return did not contain a report. The foundation argued unsuccessfully that all of its internal documents, meeting transcriptions, and actual observations of the activities amounted to the exercise of expenditure responsibility. Even though the foundation argued its failure to report was due to an oversight, the penalty assessment was upheld.[56]

Q 7:33   How does a private foundation correct a taxable expenditure?

Correcting the taxable expenditure is accomplished when the private foundation takes whatever corrective steps the IRS recommends, including the following:

- Requiring that any unpaid funds due the grantee be withheld
- Requiring that no further grants be made to the grantee
- Requiring additional, possibly quarterly, reports to be made
- Improving methods of exercising expenditure responsibility
- Improving methods of selecting recipients of individual grants[57]

If the taxable expenditure was caused by inadequate reporting by grantees, receipt of the appropriate reports is a correction. For failure to obtain advance approval for a scholarship or fellowship grant program, obtaining such advance approval for grant-making procedures is a correction.

CHAPTER 8

Excise Tax on Investment Income

A private foundation joins social clubs, political organizations, and home-owners' associations as one of only a few types of tax-exempt organizations that pay tax on investment income. To preserve the concept that private foundations are tax-exempt entities, this tax is titled an *excise* tax rather than an *income* tax.

Here are the questions that are most frequently asked (or that should be asked) about the private foundation tax on investment income—and the answers to them.

Q 8:1 Why are private foundations subjected to a tax on their investment income?

When Congress established the special sanctions to constrain the activities of private foundations in 1969, it included a taxing provision to raise funds to enforce the new rules. The tax was referred to as an *audit tax* because its percentage level was established to collect sufficient funds to pay for IRS audits of foundations. The initial rate was set at 4 percent, but the receipts from the tax far exceeded the actual costs of the government enforcement efforts. Thus, in 1978, the tax was reduced to 2 percent. The tax rate was again reduced in 1984 to 1 percent for those years in which a private foundation's charitable distributions exceed a hypothetical historic rate (Q 8:18).

Q 8:2 How is the tax calculated?

A private foundation's tax is equal to either 1 or 2 percent of its net investment income for the year. A foundation reports its income following the accounting method it uses for financial statement purposes, either the cash or the accrual method. Because the foundation must report its qualifying charitable distributions for minimum payout purposes on a cash basis (see Chapter 4), many foundations retain their financial records on a cash basis. Once chosen, the accounting method must be used consistently from year to year. The attributes of the formula are as follows:

$$\text{Gross investment income} + \text{capital gains} - \text{allocable expenses} = \text{Net investment income}$$

Q 8:3   What is meant by *investment income*?

Only four specific types of income—dividends, interest, rent, royalties, and any capital gains that result from selling the assets that produce that type of income—are treated as gross investment income for a foundation.[1] Even though an asset, such as common stock, does not actually pay out a dividend, any gain on its sale is treated as investment income because a marketable security is capable of producing a dividend. Similarly, gain on the sale of raw land that never produced rental income is taxed unless it can be proven that the land was not capable of producing rent.

Properties the foundation receives by gift or bequest, including retirement accounts, are not taxed. Assets that do not normally produce one of the four specified types of income, such as timber on a foundation's land or a work of art or other collectible, are also not taxed.

NOTE: The IRS has issued conflicting rulings on the taxability of retirement accounts during the 1990s and, although it has promised to do so, has not issued clear guidance on this subject. Certainly, the principal amount of a retirement account on the date of gift should not be taxable to the foundation. Any interest or other income earned from the date of the gift until the actual transfer might be considered taxable.

Income that is taxed as unrelated business income, such as distributions from a small business corporation, is not taxed another time as investment income. A foundation's share of items of partnership income flows through to it as either one of the four specified types of income (taxed as investment income) or as unrelated business income subject to normal income tax.

Q 8:4   Is a foundation taxed on money it earns on program-related investments and other charitable programs?

Yes, if the income is in the form of the four specified types of income—dividend, interest, rent, or royalty. Thus, the interest received on student, minority-business, or other loans made to accomplish a charitable purpose, are included in investment income and subject to tax.[2] Similarly, the net rental income for use of a historic home or a space in an artists' loft (maintained to provide low-cost studios to local artists) is considered to be investment income. The gain on the sale of such assets is not taxed, despite the fact that current income derived from the property is taxed. Conversely, a foundation that operates a museum and an art school would not include admission fees, tuition, or sales of art books in its investment income.

Q 8:5   Are all types of interest income taxable?

Interest income is taxed if it is earned on the following types of obligations and investments:

- Bank savings or money market accounts, certificates of deposit, commercial paper, and other temporary cash investment accounts
- Commercial paper, U.S. Treasury bills, notes, bonds and other interest-bearing government obligations, and corporate bonds
- Interest on program-related loans like student loans receivable, mortgage loans to purchasers in low-income housing projects, and loans to minority business owners as a program-related investment
- Payments on collateral security loans

A foundation is not taxed on the following items:

- Municipal bond interest paid by state and local government is excluded and is not taxed, and any expenses allocable to the non-taxable interest are not allowable as deductions. Municipal interest is included in "adjusted net income" for a private operating foundation.
- Interest income earned on a retirement account while it was held on behalf of the donor, although the IRS has rules that Series E bond interest, not previously reported by a decedent or by the estate, is taxable to the foundation.[3]
- Distributions attributable to interest income earned by an estate do not retain their character as interest, but instead are treated as contributions when distributed to a foundation.

Q 8:6   Are all dividends treated as investment income?

Dividends that are taxable include the following:

- Dividends paid on all types of securities, whether listed and marketable or privately held and unmarketable
- Mutual fund dividends (the capital gain portion is taxed as capital gain)
- For-profit subsidiary dividends
- Corporate liquidating distributions classified as dividends[4]

Stock distributions received in connection with a business reorganization generally are not taxed, although any gain on complete redemption of shares would be classified as investment income. The redemption of a foundation's stock, to the extent necessary to avoid the excess business holdings tax, is treated as a sale or exchange not equivalent to a dividend, so that neither the payment nor the gain are taxed as investment income.[5] Similarly a conversion of the foundation's shares in a tax-free reorganization is not considered as taxable investment income.[6]

Q 8:7   Are all types of rental income taxed?

Yes, and rents are defined as amounts paid in return for the use of real or personal property—whether the reason for renting the property is an investment purpose or is related to the foundation's exempt activities.[7] Any rental income that is taxed as unrelated income due to debt financing[8] or because is it paid out to the foundation as a small business corporation shareholder is excluded.

Q 8:8   Are all types of royalties taxed?

Payments received in return for assignments of mineral interests owned by the foundation, including overriding royalties, are taxed. Only cost depletion, not percentage, is permitted as an offset. Royalty payments received in return for use of a foundation's intangible property, such as the foundation's name or a publication containing a literary work commissioned by the foundation, are also taxable though gain on sale may not (Q 8:10).

Q 8:9   Are distributions from an estate or trust taxable?

Payments to the foundation from an estate or trust do not generally "retain their character in the hands" of the foundation. In other words, such payments do not pass through to the foundation as taxable income.[9] Part of the reason for this rule lies in the fact that the wholly charitable trust pays its own 2 percent investment income tax, and its distributions are not taxed again to the foundation upon their receipt. Income earned during administration of an estate and set aside for the foundation is not taxable to either the estate or the foundation, unless administration is unreasonably continued.[10]

Payments from a split-interest trust created after May 26, 1969, do pass through to the foundation as taxable income if they are attributable to trust income from interest, dividends, or the other specific types of taxable investment income. Capital gains distributed from a split-interest trust do not, however, retain their character as capital gains.[11]

Q 8:10   Are all types of capital gains taxed?

Net short- and long-term capital gains from the sale of property used for the production of the specific types of income subject to the investment income tax—interest, dividends, royalties, rents, and security loan payments—are also taxed.[12] Mutual fund capital gain dividends are classified as investment income.[13] Gains or losses from sales of assets used directly by the foundation in conducting its exempt activities are not taxed, and this includes program-related investments as well.[14] The investment-use portion of a dually used property is taxed. The gain from property used in an unrelated trade or business is not taxed if it is subject to the normal income tax. Certain capital gains are not taxed:

- Gain from the sale of exempt function assets, including program-related investments, unless the income earned from such property is incidental. Property used for both exempt and income-producing purposes (e.g., an office building partly used for administrative offices and partly rented to paying tenants), however, will produce pro rata nontaxable and taxable gain or loss.[15]
- Distribution of property for charitable purposes is not considered a sale or other disposition for purposes of this tax. Thus, the gain inherent in appreciated property distributed as a grant to another charity is not taxed (Q 8:19).
- Gain from disposition of excess business holdings (Chapter 5) held on December 31, 1969 (or received as a bequest under a trust irrevocable on May 26, 1969) and sold to or redeemed by a disqualified person to reduce the holdings.[16]
- Gain realized in a merger or corporate reorganization ruled to be tax free.[17]
- Appreciation on warrants or options to purchase securities.[18]
- Capital gains distributed by a split-interest trust.

Q 8:11 Can a net capital loss offset other investment income or be carried over to the next year?

No. Capital losses only offset capital gains. Losses may not offset other investment income, and a net capital loss for a year cannot be used to offset gains in a succeeding or preceding year. Year-end tax planning to avoid a net capital loss for the year is very important to avoid a net loss situation. A foundation that has net capital losses might have appreciated assets it could dispose of to offset the loss and thereby increase its tax base with no tax consequence.

Q 8:12 What is the foundation's tax basis of assets for purposes of calculating gain?

The tax basis for calculating gain or loss is equal to the amount paid by the private foundation for the assets it purchases or builds, less any allowable depreciation or depletion. Assets acquired by gift, on the other hand, retain the donor's, or a so-called carryover, basis.[19] Under accounting principles, a foundation records donated property at its value on the date the property is given. For tax purposes, however, it may not "step-up" the tax basis on such property to such value. Essentially, the private foundation pays the tax unpaid by the donor. A foundation holding low-basis securities should make every effort to use the tax-planning steps outlined below (Q 8:17) to reduce this tax burden. If reasonable from a market standpoint, the shares can be sold in years in which its tax rate is reduced to 1 percent or distributed in satisfaction of pledges, to totally avoid the tax.

The basis of property inherited by the foundation upon someone's death is equal to its Form 706 value, which is ordinarily its value on the date of the decedent's death. For property held by a foundation on December 31, 1969 (the date when the tax became effective), the tax basis is equal to the value on that day, unless a loss is realized on the sale using such a value.

Q 8:13   What expenses can be deducted against investment income?

Gross investment income is reduced by "all the ordinary and necessary expenses paid or incurred for the production and collection of investment income or for the management, conservation, or maintenance of property held for the production of such income."[20] In other words, to be deductible, expenses must have a connection or nexus to taxable income. Two examples of deductible and nondeductible expenses follow:

1. A termination fee paid by a foundation upon reccipt of the remainder interest in a trust was deemed not deductible because the value of the property received was not taxable.[21]
2. Interest expense paid on debt attributable to bonds to be used for construction of an exempt facility was deductible against income from temporary investment of the bond proceeds (and against any taxable income produced by the facility), but would not be deductible against other investment income.[22]

Examples of the expenses directly related to investment income that a typical foundation pays are many, including the following:

- Investment management fees
- Financial journals for monitoring of investments
- Rental property insurance, utilities, maintenance, property taxes, and the rent collector
- Depreciation, calculated on a straight-line basis, for the cost of computers, office furniture, buildings, and other capital costs of assets used in income-producing activity
- Cost, but not percentage, depletion on mineral properties
- Expenses paid incident to a charitable program that produces investment income is deductible to the extent of the income earned

Many foundations incur expenses that are attributable to both investment and charitable activities. A reasonable method for measuring those costs allocable to the respective activities must be developed, as described in the next answer. The types of expenses most commonly requiring allocations include:

- Officer and staff salaries and associated costs, office supplies, equipment costs, travel, and other costs associated with personnel
- Officer, director, and trustee fees

- Legal and accounting fees
- Investment management and counseling fees paid by a foundation that earns tax-exempt income
- Taxes, insurance, maintenance, rent, mortgage interest, and other costs of providing foundation office spaces

Q 8:14 How does a foundation allocate its costs when they are attributable to both investment income and charitable activities?

First, a foundation identifies expenses that are 100 percent allocable to, or made specifically to, produce its investment income. Investment management, trustee, rental agent, legal, and other types of professional fees are good examples of expenses that may be totally attributable to investment income and need not be allocated. Next, the foundation allocates, or apportions, the cost of its personnel and advisors who spend their time on both functions. Additionally, the foundation's overall administrative expenses, such as the cost of office spaces, accounting and bookkeeping, and computer costs, must be apportioned between the functions.

A foundation is expected to establish a reasonable basis to be used consistently to apportion costs associated with both the management of income-producing properties and its charitable programs. The customary method used to allocate costs is a record of time devoted to the respective activities. Staff persons can keep a diary of time devoted to managing and maintaining different aspects of the foundation's activities during the year. At a minimum, time records might be kept for a typical month or perhaps a week each month throughout the year. If specific time records are not maintained, a good-faith allocation can be made. Independent advisors can be asked to render billings specifically identifying the portion of the fee attributable to charitable versus investment activities based on time actually spent. Documentation should be maintained as evidence of the manner in which the allocations are made.

Q 8:15 What type of expenses are not deductible against investment income?

As a general rule, no deduction against investment income is permitted for costs associated with a foundation's charitable programs, or what are called *exempt functions*. When a project or asset produces interest, rent, royalty, or dividends subject to tax, the expenses allocable to the charitable program are deductible only to the extent of the revenue.[23] With such joint-purpose activities, the primary motivation for undertaking the project (investment or program) can be a factor. An investment project conceivably could result in a loss deductible against other investment income. The typical historic restoration project is not expected to produce net income. Since the admission charges for visiting such buildings are normally incidental to the overall cost of the project, it would be hard to prove that the building loss is deductible.

The following items are examples of nondeductible expenses for investment income purposes:

- Charitable distributions and administrative expenses associated with grant-making program costs are not deductible. Similarly, expenses in excess of revenues from programs directly conducted by the foundation are not deductible.
- Purchase of exempt function assets, depreciation of their cost, and cost of their maintenance, repair, or conservation are not deductible.
- Capital losses in excess of capital gains are not deductible, nor is a carryover permitted to the succeeding year. This is a potentially costly rule to a foundation that does not properly time its asset dispositions (Q 8:11).
- A net loss incurred in investment activity in a preceding year does not carry forward from year to year.
- The allocable portion of expenses of an exempt function income-producing property or activity, in excess of the income produced by the property, is not deductible. (It is treated as a charitable distribution.)
- Expenses allocable to taxable unrelated business income. (The income is also not includable.)
- Interest paid on borrowing to acquire exempt function assets is not deductible. For example, interest paid on a bond issued to finance the building of a retirement community is not paid on behalf of an investment. If the building is a rental property, however, the interest and other property maintenance and operational expenses are deductible to the extent of the income.[24]
- Interest paid on borrowing funds, which a foundation relends to another charitable organization (presumably interest-free), has been deemed not deductible. Such interest expense should be deductible only to the extent of any interest income collected from the relending or temporary income earned on the funds.[25]
- The special corporation deductions including the dividends received deduction are not allowed.

Q 8:16   When must a foundation pay the excise tax?

A foundation must pay its annual investment income tax in advance when the amount exceeds $500, or a penalty will be assessed. Following the estimated tax system used to pay normal income tax, quarterly payments are deposited on the fifteenth of the fifth, sixth, ninth, and twelfth month of the foundation's fiscal year. Normally, a foundation will deposit a safe harbor amount equal to one-quarter of its prior year tax quarterly. A foundation whose net investment income exceeded $1 million in any of the past three years must calculate its payment based on current annualized income rather than the prior year tax.

Q 8:17   What can a foundation do to reduce its investment income tax?

A foundation has several opportunities to reduce its tax burden:

- Qualify for the 1 percent tax rate because current year distributions exceed its historic average grant payout (Q 8:18).
- Distribute appreciated property, rather than cash from selling such property, for two different reasons as explained below.

NOTE: As the rate fell over the past 25 years, private foundation excise tax has become an accepted cost of retaining private control over donated funds. Perhaps because of the modest tax rate, very little is written on the subject. Its immaterial annual amount mitigates the need to hire skilled professional advisors to perform year-end tax planning. Nevertheless, substantial savings can result from taking advantage of relatively simple tax-planning methods systematically over a period of years.

Q 8:18   How can a foundation qualify for the reduced 1 percent rate?

The excise tax rate on a private foundation's net investment income is reduced to 1 percent for each year during which the foundation's qualifying distributions[26] equal a hypothetical distribution amount plus 1 percent of net investment income.[27] (Some say a foundation can essentially choose to distribute 1 percent of its investment income to charitable recipients rather than the U.S. Treasury.) Basically, a reduction is permitted for a foundation whose current year distributions (Q 4:10) exceed its historic payout percentage times the average value of its current year investment assets, plus half of the normal 2 percent tax it is excused from paying.

The qualifying formula recalculates a historic payout rate using the qualifying distributions for the past five years and calculating the percentage relationship to the value of the assets in each year. This result differs from the minimum distribution requirement payout calculation that instead uses the prior year asset value (Chapter 4). In the following example, the private foundation qualifies for a 1 percent rate:

Multiply the current year average monthly FMV	$2,000,000
times a 5-year historic payout rate	× 5.2%
	104,000
Add 1 percent of private foundation's current net investment income	1,000
Baseline to compare to current year distributions	$ 105,000
Qualifying distributions for the year	$ 110,000

Since the qualifying distributions made by the private foundation illustrated above during the current year equal or exceed $105,000, the foundation's tax rate is reduced to 1 percent. Since the calculation is based on the average monthly value of the foundation's investment assets (including the last day of its year), planning for this savings is not always easy. Since this tax reduction opportunity came into effect in 1985, foundations that realize the reduction often do so accidentally, rather than with specific planning.

Except and unless the value of the foundation's assets fluctuate widely, it is possible to deliberately time grant payments to reduce the tax to 1 percent in alternate years. For a foundation normally paying about $20,000 in tax, a $10,000 biannual savings may be worth the trouble.

Q 8:19   How does a foundation save tax by distributing, rather than selling, property?

Reducing the tax rate from 1 percent to 2 percent is just the first way a private foundation can reduce the excise tax on investment income. There are also opportunities embodied in the interaction between the excise tax on investment income, the minimum distribution requirements (Chapter 4), and the charitable deduction for contributions of appreciated property. For two very different—but interacting—reasons, a foundation might sell assets that result in recognized capital gains subject to tax.

Tax Reduction Possibility # 2

A typical foundation, according to the Council on Foundations,[28] invests its assets for *total return.* Under this investment philosophy, a security portfolio, on average, is often comprised of securities with low current income payments and an expectation for underlying appreciation in the value of the securities, typified by common stocks. The aim is a combined income from current dividends, interest, and enhancement in the capital values. It is expected that capital gains will be regularly earned as portfolio holdings are sold in response to market changes. When the desired result—capital gain— occurs, tax is due.

A foundation with a 2 percent current dividend and interest yield on its total return portfolio needs to raise additional cash to meets its 5 percent annual charitable distribution amount. A foundation with such a portfolio essentially distributes a portion of its capital gains to meet the requirement. Thus, tax occurs for the second reason—securities are sold to raise the cash to make qualifying distributions. Herein also lies the possibility for tax savings. If instead the securities themselves (rather than cash from their sale) are distributed to grantees, the capital gain earned on the security is not taxed. A distribution of property by a foundation to a grantee is not treated as a sale or other distribution subject to the excise tax.[29]

For example, suppose that one-half, or $500,000, of a foundation's $1 million of income is capital gains on highly appreciated securities. Assume also the foundation makes grants of $100,000 each to five charitable grantees. As much as $10,000 in tax is saved if the grants are paid with the securities themselves ($500,000 × 2 percent tax). The higher the untaxed gain in a foundation's portfolio, the greater the possibility for savings. The tax basis for calculating the gain for donated securities is equal to the donor's basis—giving many foundations a good chance to realize this savings. Readily marketable securities are most suitable for delivery to grantees due to the ease with which they can be converted to cash. However, any investment property producing dividends, rents, and royalties is subject to this special tax exception; such property might include a partnership interest or a rental building.

Implementing the savings requires some advanced planning and cooperative grantees. Grants are normally pledged and paid in round numbers ($5,000 or $50,000). Securities do not usually sell for round numbers, and the price changes constantly. The grantee, rather than the granting foundation, will have to pay the sales commission. The foundation may want to gross up the number of shares to be delivered to assure the grantee receives the intended funding. The potential savings can be compared to the costs before such noncash grants are made. The size of the grant and the likelihood the grantee may retain the securities in their own portfolio can enhance the attractiveness of this medium for grant funding.

Consider an example. A foundation is funded with zero-basis shares donated by a now-publicly traded company's founding family. The foundation keeps a supply of stock certificates in a variety of share numbers. When a grant is due to be paid, one or more certificates for the number of shares approximating the amount pledged are delivered to the grantee in satisfaction of its pledge. If the shares are selling for $60 and a $100,000 grant is due; approximately 1,670 shares would be delivered. (The few extra shares cover the commission.) The full fair market value of the shares on the delivery date is treated as a qualifying distribution, and the difference between the value and the foundation's basis ($100,000 of capital gain in this example) is not taxed, saving the foundation $2,000.

Tax Reduction Possibility # 3

A donation to a standard, or nonoperating, private foundation (Chapter 14) is not necessarily fully deductible under the charitable donation rules. The fair market value of noncash gifts, other than qualified appreciated stock,[30] to normal private foundations is not fully deductible. For a contributor to claim an income tax deduction, the foundation must give away the full value of the gift, or the gift itself, within 2½ months after the end of its year in which the donation is received.[31] Thus, a noncash donation retained by the foundation and essentially added to its endowment may be limited in its deductibility to the donor's tax basis for calculating gain or loss for federal income tax purposes.[32]

A foundation that receives a property donation subject to a redistribution requirement has several alternatives. The types of choices include:

1. Redistribute the property itself
2. Distribute cash (possibly from sale of the property itself)
3. Allocate accumulated excess distributions, if any

A type 1 redistribution normally saves excise tax because it is not treated as a sale. To achieve this treatment, the foundation must grant the property in a manner that is considered a *qualifying distribution.*[33] The grant must be made for a charitable purpose to an unrelated and uncontrolled public charity and cannot be counted as a current year distribution in calculating whether the private foundation meets is current payout requirement.

A type 2 distribution may mean the foundation may incur taxable gain dependent on the type of property it sells, if any, to raise the cash to make the redistribution. Choosing to redistribute the property itself allows the private foundation to avoid tax on the gain inherent in the property.

Last, a type 3 distribution creates no excise tax because no sale of property is necessary.[34] This tax savings opportunity is only available for those foundations that have distributed more than the minimum distribution requirement in the past. When this situation exists, this unique rule can be highly beneficial for certain foundations and their funders, particularly those that would like to give their highly appreciated real estate or closely held business to the foundation.

Q 8:20 Are all private foundations subject to this tax?

An exempt operating foundation is not subject to this tax. Such a foundation meets a three-prong test (Chapter 14). It actively conducts its own programs, such as operating a museum or publishing literary works. It, at some time in the past, was publicly supported (Chapter 12) for at least 10 years. Last, it must be controlled by a broad public board made up of persons who are not its creators, funders, their relatives, or other disqualified persons (Chapter 2).

Q 8:21 Are foreign foundations subject to this tax?

A foreign foundation pays a 4 percent tax on its gross investment income received from U.S. sources.[35] The United States enters into tax treaties that may excuse certain foreign foundations from this tax.

CHAPTER 9

Unrelated Business Activities

The taxability of income derived by an organization that is otherwise exempt from federal income taxation, from the conduct of *unrelated business,* is an important feature of the federal tax law applicable to tax-exempt organizations. It is often overlooked in the context of private foundations. This aspect of the law of tax-exempt organizations looms large these days as the IRS intensifies its searches for opportunities to ferret out unrelated business income. The concept of the unrelated business rules is crisp and clear; application of it, however, is often very difficult because the specifics of these rules can be vague and varying.

It is often thought that the unrelated business income rules do not, or cannot, apply to private foundations because they generally are not permitted to own or operate a business in any event (Chapter 5). As will be seen, however, this is not always the case.

Here are the questions that are most frequently asked (or that should be asked) about the applicability of the unrelated business law (including the availability of exceptions) to private foundations—and the answers to them.

Q 9:1 How do the unrelated business rules mesh with the concept of tax exemption?

An organization that is a tax-exempt entity must be operated *primarily* for its exempt purposes. This is the case even though the statute for charitable organizations uses the term *exclusively.*[1] Most tax-exempt organizations, then, are able to engage in some activities that are *unrelated* to the organization's tax-exempt purposes without fear of loss of tax exemption. (See, however, Q 9:33.)

Private foundations, however, generally do not enjoy the liberality afforded by this regime. This is because the excess business holdings rules largely prohibit foundations from actively engaging in business enterprises or from owning significant interests in business (Chapter 5). Thus, for the most part, unrelated business income that is allowable for private foundations must be *passive* in nature (Q 9:28). Income from permitted Subchapter S and partnership interests do produce unrelated income.

Q 9:2   How does an organization measure what is primary?

This question can be answered with the caveat that, as noted (Q 9:1), the concept is not likely to be directly applicable to private foundations. It is applicable, however, to grantees of private foundations.

Measuring what is *primary* often is not easy to do; there is no mechanical formula for doing this. The measurement is done on the basis of what the law likes to term the *facts and circumstances.* The IRS heartily rejects the thought of applying any particular percentage in measuring primary activities and invokes this principle of law on a case-by-case basis. As to this stance, the IRS is uniformly supported by the courts.[2]

TIP: Often, in practice, however, percentages are used in this and comparable contexts as a guide. The term *primary* has been assigned percentages in other settings; for unrelated business income purposes, it can mean at least 65 percent. By comparison, *substantial* is sometimes defined as at least 85 percent; *substantially all* is sometimes set at 90 percent. *Incidental* is sometimes defined as up to 15 percent.

   If these percentages have any validity—and, to a limited extent, they do for evaluation purposes—then a tax-exempt organization could have as much as one-third of its activities or income be unrelated. There are IRS private letter rulings upholding tax-exempt status where unrelated income was in excess of 40 percent; however, in these cases, the amount of *time* actually devoted to the unrelated business was considerably less. Indeed, in one instance, the IRS tolerated unrelated income as high as 98 percent of total income; this income was, however, passive in nature.[3]

A prudent assessment or review would cause a tax-exempt organization to seriously evaluate its situation, if its unrelated income annually exceeds 20 or 25 percent of total revenue (but see Q 9:33). The remedies may include setting up a for-profit subsidiary.[4] This option is not available to private foundations, however, because of the excess business holdings rules.

The statement that there is no mechanical formula for measuring what is *primary* was a generalization; it was not precisely accurate. In the case of tax-exempt title-holding companies, the maximum amount of unrelated business income that they can have in a year without endangering tax exemption is 10 percent.[5] This rule does not apply, however, with respect to any other type of tax-exempt organization. For most exempt organizations, 10 percent is too narrow a limitation on permissible unrelated business activity.

CAUTION: As far as private foundations are concerned, however, the limitation on unrelated business activity is zero (Q 9:28).

Q 9:3   How does an exempt organization know whether an activity is a related one or an unrelated one?

This is both one of the easiest and hardest questions in the law of tax-exempt organizations.

The easy answer is that an unrelated activity is one that does not substantially advance the exempt purposes of the organization. That is, it is an activity that the organization engages in principally for the purpose of earning money, rather than furthering one or more programs. The fact that the money earned is used for exempt purposes does not alone make the activity itself related (but see Q 9:33). The more complex answer is that the activity must be evaluated against as many as five levels of analysis. These are:

1. Is the activity a *trade or business* (Q 9:6)?
2. Is it *regularly* carried on (Q 9:13)?
3. Is the conduct of the activity *substantially related* to the conduct of exempt functions (Q 9:18)?
4. Is the activity exempted from taxation by one or more statutory exceptions (Q 9:22)?
5. Is the income from the activity exempted from taxation by one or more statutory exceptions (Q 9:23)?

Q 9:4   What is the rationale underlying the unrelated income rules?

The basic structure of these rules was enacted in 1950. The essence of this body of law is the separation of the income of a tax-exempt organization into two categories: income from related business and income from unrelated business. The income from unrelated business generally is taxed as if it was earned by a for-profit, taxable company.

The primary objective of these rules is to eliminate a source of *unfair competition* with the for-profit sector by placing the unrelated business activities of exempt organizations on the same tax basis as those conducted by nonexempt organizations, where the two are in competition.[6] Some courts place considerable emphasis on the factor of competition when assessing whether an undertaking is an unrelated business (Q 9:10). The existence or nonexistence of competition, however, is not a statutory requirement for the presence of unrelated business.

It is ironic that, in actuality, the enactment of these rules has not quelled the cries of "unfair competition" from the business sector, particularly small business owners. Over five decades later, the issue is not so much that unrelated business by nonprofits is competitive; rather, the competition is often derived from *related* businesses. In part, this is the result of shifts in the definition of related and unrelated activities, and of the entry of for-profit organizations into fields of endeavor previously confined to nonprofit entities. Some small business advocates want competitive practices prohibited, as a way of "leveling the playing field." These individuals are of the view that unrelated income taxation is not enough; they fret about the fact that some consumers are attracted to, and thus bring their business to, nonprofit entities just because they are nonprofit—a situation informally known as the *halo effect.*

Thus, the purpose of the unrelated income tax itself is to equalize the economics of a transaction, irrespective of whether the vendor of a good or service is tax-exempt or taxable. If an organization can sell a product and not pay income tax on the sales proceeds, that organization can charge a lower price for that product and have more "profit" remaining than an organization selling the same product and have to pay taxes as a cost of doing business. This ability, and occasional practices of price undercutting, is the basis for the claim of "unfair competition."

Q 9:5   Are these claims of unfair competition leading to anything, such as law changes?

It doesn't look like it, at least not in the immediate future. A few years ago, when the small business lobbying on this subject was at its peak, some thought that Congress would toughen the unrelated business rules. There was a series of hearings before the Subcommittee on Oversight, of the House Committee on Ways and Means, in 1986–1987. The chairman of the subcommittee pushed hard for legislation but could not build a consensus for the proposals. The nonprofit community lobbied effectively against the various proposed law changes, the small business lobby did a poor job of sustaining its efforts, and the movement for revising these laws atrophied.

The individual who was then the subcommittee chairman is no longer in Congress, and there seems to be little interest, in either the House of Representatives or the Senate, in law change in this area. Still, efforts to make it more difficult for nonprofits to compete are unfolding in several states.

Q 9:6   What is the trade or business requirement?

A statutory definition of *trade or business* is specifically applicable in the unrelated business setting. The phrase means any activity that is carried on for the production of income from the sale of goods or the performance of services.[7] That definition is, of course, quite broad and encompasses nearly everything that a tax-exempt organization does.

In fact, the law regards a tax-exempt organization as a bundle of activities. They may be related or unrelated, but they are still *businesses.*

Q 9:7   Does this mean that the law considers the programs of exempt organizations as businesses?

Yes. Each of the programs of a tax-exempt organization is considered a separate business. In fact, what an organization regards as a single program may embody several businesses. For example, the bookstore operated by a college is a combination of businesses. These include sales of books, cosmetics, computers, appliances, and clothing. The same is true with respect to hospital and museum gift shops, and associations' sales of items to their members. In the case of charitable organizations, many of their fund-raising activities are businesses.

It is difficult to convince the IRS that a particular activity is not a business. The most likely instances where an exempt organization can prevail on this point are with respect to its investment activities and infrequent sales of assets. Occasionally, a court will be more lenient, as illustrated by an opinion finding that an association's monitoring activities with respect to insurance programs for its membership, where the insurance and claims processing functions were elsewhere, did not rise to the level of a trade or business.[8]

Moreover, an activity does not lose its identity as a trade or business just because it is carried on within a larger aggregate of similar activities or within a larger complex of other endeavors that may or may not be related to the exempt purposes of the organization.[9] This means that an activity cannot be hidden from scrutiny, as to whether it is a business, by tucking it in with other activities. The IRS has the authority to review each business of an exempt organization in isolation, in search of unrelated activity. That is, it can—figuratively speaking—fragment an organization into as many businesses as it can define. In the jargon of the field, this is known as the *fragmentation rule.*

Q 9:8   When the federal tax law regards an exempt organization as a composite of businesses, isn't that different from how nonprofit organizations see themselves?

There is no question about that. Unfortunately, the matter gets murkier. Actually, the statutory definition of *business* states that the term *trade* or *business* "includes" that definition of it. That word has opened the door for the courts and the IRS to add requirements and possibilities that may cause an activity to be a business. Some courts use additional criteria, such as competitive activity or commerciality, and then jump all the way to the conclusion that the activity is an unrelated business.

For example, in a completely different area of the tax law, concerning whether a gambler gambling only for personal ends is engaged in a business for expense deduction purposes, the Supreme Court held that, for an activity to be considered a trade or business, it must be carried on with a profit motive.[10] The Court specifically wrote that this definition of trade or business was not to be used in other tax settings. But, the lower courts promptly ignored that admonition and engrafted that rule onto the definition of exempt organizations' unrelated income purposes.[11]

Q 9:9   Why would a tax-exempt organization object to that additional element of the definition, concerning a profit motive? Wouldn't that rule always favor exempt organizations, causing some activities to not be businesses in the first instance?

Actually, it doesn't always work that way. In some instances, a tax-exempt organization *wants* an activity to be considered an unrelated business. This is because income from unrelated activity and losses from other unrelated activity can be aggregated to produce a single, bottom-line item of net income or net loss.

For example, suppose an exempt organization has two unrelated activities. One produces $100,000 of net income, the other generates $70,000 of net losses. On the unrelated business income tax return, the income and losses from the two businesses are blended, and the organization pays the unrelated income tax on only $30,000. This works, however, only when both activities are in fact *businesses.*

Suppose the second of these activities consistently, year in and year out, yields losses. The IRS will usually take the position that, because the activity always results in an annual loss, it is not being conducted with the requisite profit motive. If that position is sustained, the activity is not considered a *business,* in which case the $70,000 of loss could not be offset against the $100,000 of gain. Then the organization would have to pay the unrelated income tax on the full $100,000.

All of this is happening even though the tax regulations state that the fact that a trade or business does not produce a net profit is not sufficient to exclude it from the definition of a trade or business.[12]

Q 9:10   What are some of the other elements being engrafted onto this definition?

Sometimes, a business is found when a tax-exempt organization is in competition with for-profit enterprises.[13] The existence of profits may lead a court to the conclusion that an undertaking is a business (usually an unrelated business).[14] The IRS may assert the presence of unrelated business just because a fee is charged for the product or service.[15] Moreover—and this is becoming a growing practice—courts will jump to the conclusion that an unrelated business exists where the activity is undertaken in a *commercial* manner.

Q 9:11   What is a *commercial activity*?

The commerciality doctrine has been conceived by the courts, although it is not fully articulated. There is, with one relatively minor exception, no mention of *commerciality* in the Internal Revenue Code (Q 9:12). The same is the case with respect to the tax regulations.

The doctrine essentially means that a tax-exempt organization is engaged in a nonexempt activity when that activity is conducted in a manner that is considered *commercial*. An activity is a commercial one if it is undertaken in the same manner as it would be if it were being conducted by a for-profit (commercial) business. The most contemporary explication of the commerciality doctrine sets forth these criteria:

- The tax-exempt organization sells goods or services to the public.
- The exempt organization is in direct competition with one or more for-profit businesses.
- The prices set by the organization are based on pricing formulas common in the comparable commercial business setting.
- The organization utilizes advertising and other promotional materials and techniques to enhance sales.
- The organization's hours of operation are basically the same as those of for-profit enterprises.
- The management of the organization is trained in business operations.
- The organization uses employees rather than volunteers.
- There is an absence of charitable giving to the organization.[16]

Q 9:12   What are the statutory and regulatory references to the commerciality doctrine?

In 1986, Congress added to the federal tax law a rule stating that an organization cannot qualify as a tax-exempt charitable entity or a social welfare entity if a substantial part of its activities consists of the provision of commercial-type insurance.[17] While that term is not defined by statute, it generally means any insurance of a type provided by commercial insurance companies. The reach of this aspect of commerciality has been accorded broad interpretation in the courts.[18]

As far as the regulations are concerned, there is a brief mention of commerciality in the rules pertaining to whether an activity is regularly carried on (Q 9:13).[19] There it is stated that business activities of an exempt organization ordinarily will be deemed to be regularly carried on "if they manifest a frequency and continuity, and are pursued in a manner, generally similar to comparable commercial activities of nonexempt organizations."[20]

Q 9:13   What are the rules as to whether a business activity is *regularly carried on*?

An activity cannot give rise to unrelated business taxable income—even if it is a business (Q 9:6)—unless and until it is *regularly carried on*. This test is a derivation of the rationale for the unrelated business rules (Q 9:4): An activity cannot be competitive with for-profit business if it is not regularly carried on.

Thus, income from an unrelated business cannot be taxed where that business is merely sporadically or infrequently conducted. The frequency and continuity of the activity, the manner in which the activity is pursued, and the continuing purpose of deriving income from the activity largely determine whether the activity is regularly carried on.[21]

Q 9:14   How is regularity measured?

There is no precise means of measurement in determining whether a business is regularly carried on. An activity that consists of a single, one-time-only transaction or event is certainly irregular. For this reason, a sole sale of an item of property often is not taxable. Most fund-raising events, like annual dances, theater outings, sports tournaments, and auctions, usually are not taxed because of this rule.

Beyond that, it is a judgment call. A business occupying only a few days in a year is not regularly carried on. For example, the tax regulations offer a quaint example of the operation of a sandwich stand by a hospital auxiliary for two weeks at a state fair. That business, according to the regulations, is not regularly carried on. But it cannot be said with any certainty when too many days of activity cause the line to be crossed. The regulations add that the operation of a commercial parking lot for one day in each week of a year is a regularly carried on business.[22] Operation on 52 days out of 365, or operation on one day each week, obviously reflects an operation that is regularly carried on.

Q 9:15   Are there any other aspects of this level of analysis?

Yes, there are three other aspects of regularity in the unrelated business context.

One is that, where a business activity is, in the commercial sector, carried on only during a particular season, the duration of this season, rather than a full year, is the measuring period for an exempt organization.[23] For example, an organization selling Christmas trees or Christmas cards would measure regularity in relation to the length of the Christmas season. Likewise, an operation of a horse racing track would be measured in relation to the horse racing season.

Q 9:16   What are the other two aspects of regularity?

One is that the IRS has come to the view that there is more to the measurement of regularity than just the time expended in connection with the event itself. The IRS takes into consideration the amount of time the tax-exempt organization spends in preparing for the event—*preparatory time*—and the time expended afterward in connection with the event—*winding-down time.*[24] If an exempt organization were to sell a product commercially for a few days each year, in assessing regularity it is—according to the IRS view— supposed to include the preparatory time of lining up the product, creating advertising, soliciting purchasers, and the like as well as the winding-down time spent assessing the operation and arranging for the return of unsold items. The same is true, the IRS says, in connection with sale of a service.

Q 9:17   Do some operations get converted into regular ones by using that approach?

That can be the case. But there's more. The law in general recognizes the concept of a *principal* and an *agent.* A principal is a person who hires another person to act in his, her, or its stead, for the principal's benefit; the second person is an agent. Generally, the law considers the acts of an agent to be those of the principal. This means that the acts of an agent are attributed to the principal.

In the unrelated business setting, it is common for a tax-exempt organization to contract with a company to perform a service. If the company is considered an agent of the organization and the company's function is in connection with an unrelated business, the IRS will likely take the position that the time spent by the company is attributable to the exempt organization in determining whether the unrelated activity was regularly carried on.[25]

For example, in one case, a university contracted with a publisher to produce programs for its home football games. The contract reserved advertising space in the programs for the university, income generated by sales of that space was reserved for the university, and the university retained an advertising agency to sell its space. The IRS determined that the revenues from the sale of the advertisements constituted unrelated business income to the university because, by reason of a clause in the contract, the advertising agency was an agent of the university. By reason of the agency relationship, the agency's activities were attributable to the university for purposes of determining whether the university regularly carried on the business of selling program advertising. A court, however, has rejected this approach to the determination of regularity.[26] Nonetheless, the IRS has openly disagreed with this holding and is adhering to its position in issuing rulings.[27]

Q 9:18   What about the third level of analysis, concerning the substantially related requirement?

This is where the issue usually is: whether the business that is regularly carried on is *related* or *unrelated.*[28] The general rule is that the income from a regularly conducted trade or business is subject to tax unless the income-producing activity is substantially related to the accomplishment of the organization's tax-exempt purpose.

In determining whether an activity is related, an examination is made of the relationship between the business activity and the accomplishment of the organization's exempt purpose. The fact that the income from the business is used for exempt programs does not make the activity a related one. (But see Q 9:33.)

A trade or business is *related* to tax-exempt purposes only where the conduct of the business has what the tax law terms a *causal relationship* to the achievement of an exempt purpose. The business is *substantially* related only if the causal relationship is recognizably large or material.[29] Thus, for the conduct of a trade or business from which a particular amount of gross

income is derived to be substantially related to an exempt purpose, the production or distribution of the goods or the performance of the services from
which the gross income is derived must contribute importantly to the accomplishment of these purposes. Where the production or distribution of goods
or the performance of services does not contribute importantly to the accomplishment of the organization's exempt purposes, the income from the sale
of the goods or services does not derive from the conduct of a related business.

Q 9:19   How is relatedness determined?

There is no formula in this setting. Judgments as to whether there is a causal
relationship and whether there is substantiality are made in the context of the
facts and circumstances involved. Unfortunately, however, there is not much
"straightforwardness." This aspect of the tax law is very complex and murky.

Q 9:20   What are some examples of these judgments?

There are dozens of IRS rulings and court opinions in this area. Let's take a
look at the field of associations, for example.

In one instance, a local bar association sold standard legal forms to its
member lawyers for their use in the practice of law. These forms were purchased from a state bar association. The IRS ruled that the sale of the forms
was an unrelated business because it did not contribute importantly to the
accomplishment of the association's exempt functions.[30] There is, however,
a court opinion to the contrary.[31] Another court held that the sale of preprinted
lease forms and landlords' manuals by an exempt association of apartment
owners and managers was a related business.[32]

This IRS ruling illustrates that, just because an association's membership
uses a product in their own businesses, the sale of the product does not
become a related business for the association. When an association of credit
unions published and sold a consumer-oriented magazine to its members, the
IRS held that to be an unrelated business because the magazine was distributed to the depositors of the members as a promotional device.[33]

Other instances of unrelated businesses of associations include the sale
of equipment to members,[34] the operation of an employment service,[35] the
conduct of other registry programs,[36] the selling of endorsements (including
the right to use the association's name and logo),[37] and the charging of dues
to certain categories of purported associate members.[38]

Over the years, one of the issues that has generated considerable attention for associations is whether the provision of insurance for members is an
unrelated business. From the outset of the controversy, the IRS was of the
position that it was. Associations prevailed at the beginning,[39] but the tide
shifted. Now the courts uniformly uphold the IRS on this subject: Compensation to associations for assistance in making insurance available to their
members is almost always taxable.[40]

In one instance, the IRS examined seven activities of an exempt association and found each of them to be an unrelated business. These activities

were the sale of vehicle signs to members, the sale to members of embossed tags for inventory control purposes, the sale to members of supplies and forms, the sale to members of kits to enable them to retain sales tax information, the sale of price guides, the administration of a group insurance program, and the sale of commercial advertising in the association's publications.[41]

The outcome isn't always that the business is unrelated. In one case, the IRS concluded that the sale of television time to governments and nonprofit organizations at a discount by an exempt association of television stations was a related business.[42]

Q 9:21   Are there any other aspects of the substantially related test?

There are four other aspects of this test. One of them is the *size and extent test.*

In determining whether an activity contributes importantly to the accomplishment of an exempt purpose, the size and extent of the activity must be considered in relation to the size and extent of the exempt function it purports to serve.[43] Thus, where income is realized by a tax-exempt organization from an activity that is in part related to the performance of its exempt functions, but that is conducted on a scale larger than is reasonably necessary for performance of the functions, the gross income attributable to that portion of the activities in excess of the needs of exempt functions constitutes gross income from the conduct of an unrelated business.

An example of this test involved an exempt association that had a membership of businesses in a particular state. One of its income-producing activities was the supplying of member and nonmember businesses with job injury histories on prospective employees. Rejecting the association's contention that this service contributed to accomplishment of exempt purposes, the IRS ruled that the activity was an unrelated business, in that the services went "well beyond" any mere development and promotion of efficient business practices.[44]

As an illustration of the application of this test where the IRS concluded that the business was entirely related, the IRS considered a tax-exempt organization that provided a therapeutic program for emotionally disturbed adolescents. It operated a retail grocery store that was almost completely staffed by adolescents to help secure their emotional rehabilitation. The IRS ruled that the store operation was not an unrelated business because it was operated on a scale no larger than reasonably necessary for its training and rehabilitation program.[45]

Another of these aspects is the *same state test.* As a general rule, the sale of a product that results from the performance of tax-exempt functions does not constitute an unrelated business where the product is sold in substantially the same state it is in upon completion of the exempt functions.[46] This rule is significant for organizations that sell articles made by disabled individuals as part of their rehabilitation training. By contrast, where a product resulting from an exempt function is exploited in business endeavors beyond what is reasonably appropriate or necessary for disposition in the state it is in upon completion of tax-exempt functions, the activity becomes transformed into an unrelated business.[47] For example, an exempt organization maintaining a dairy herd for scientific purposes may sell milk and cream produced in the ordinary course of operation of the project—the cows must be milked—without unrelated income taxation. If the organization, however, were to utilize the milk and cream in the further manufacture of food items, such as ice cream or pastries, the sale of these products would likely be the conduct of an unrelated business.[48]

NOTE: Another illustration of this rule appeared in an IRS ruling concerning a tax-exempt salmon research facility. The facility would, from time to time, have excess salmon and would sell the fish to wholesalers. The IRS ruled that the sales were not taxable, because the organization was selling the salmon in the same state they were in when obtained by the facility (i.e., caught in the ocean). Someone, however, obviously spending far too much time in fast food restaurants, came up with the idea of *salmon nuggets*. The salmon meat was rolled into clumps, which were then breaded and fried. The IRS ruled that the sale of these nuggets was an unrelated business, inasmuch as the salmon being sold in this fashion were no longer in the same state they were in when they were acquired as part of the facility's exempt functions.[49]

Another of these subtests of substantiality is the *dual use test*.[50] This concerns an asset or facility that is necessary to the conduct of exempt functions but is also employed in an unrelated endeavor. Each source of the income must be tested to see whether the activities contribute importantly to the accomplishment of exempt purposes. For example, a museum may have a theater auditorium for the purpose of showing educational films in connection with its program of public education in the arts and sciences; use of that theater for public entertainment in the evenings would be an unrelated business. Likewise, a school may have a ski facility that is used in its physical education program; operation of the facility for general public would be an unrelated business.

The fourth of these subtests is the *exploitation test*.[51] In certain instances, activities carried on by an exempt organization in the performance of exempt functions generate goodwill or other intangibles that are capable of being exploited in unrelated endeavors. When this is done, the mere fact that the income depended in part on an exempt function of the organization does not make it income from a related business. This type of income will be taxed as unrelated business income, unless the underlying activities themselves contribute importantly to the accomplishment of an exempt purpose. For example, income from advertising in a publication with exempt function content generally is taxable income resulting from an exploitation of an exempt resource.

Q 9:22 What types of activities are exempt from unrelated income taxation?

An interesting feature of the federal tax laws pertinent to tax-exempt organizations is the series of *modifications* that are available in calculating taxable unrelated business income.[52] Although these modifications largely exclude certain types of income from taxation (Q 9:23), they also exclude three types of research activities from the tax. This set of exclusions is somewhat of an oddity, in that research activities generally are exempt functions.

One exclusion is for research for the federal government, or any of its agencies or instrumentalities, or any state or political subdivision of a state. Another exclusion is for research performed for any person; however, the research institution must be a college, university, or hospital. The third exclusion is as broad as the second: The organization must be operated primarily for the purpose of carrying on fundamental research, and the results of the research must be freely available to the general public.[53]

The law also excludes from taxation revenue derived from the lending of securities by exempt organizations to brokers.[54]

Eleven other statutory exceptions shelter types of activities from unrelated income taxation. One is for a business in which substantially all of the work in carrying on the business is performed for the tax-exempt organization without compensation.[55] Any unrelated business can be protected from taxation by this exception, including the business of advertising. This exception can be useful in shielding fund-raising functions (special events) from taxation.

TIP: The concept of *compensation* is broadly applied. In one instance, the revenue from gambling events was held taxable because the workers, all of whom were volunteers, were frequently tipped by the patrons.[56]

Another exception is for a business that is conducted by a tax-exempt charitable organization, or a state college or university, primarily for the convenience of its members, students, patients, officers, or employees.[57] This broad exception—known as the *convenience doctrine*—is relied on heavily by colleges, universities, and hospitals. Much of the income from sales of items in college and university bookstores and hospital gift shops is rendered nontaxable because of this rule.

Another exception is for a business that sells merchandise, substantially all of which was contributed to the exempt organization.[58] This exception is generally utilized by thrift shops that sell donated clothing, books, and the like to the general public.[59]

Still other exceptions are for certain businesses of associations of employees conducted for the convenience of their members,[60] the conduct of entertainment at fairs and expositions by a wide range of exempt organizations,[61] the conduct of trade shows by most exempt organizations,[62] the performance by hospitals of certain services for smaller hospitals,[63] the conduct of certain bingo games by most tax-exempt organizations,[64] qualified pole rentals by exempt mutual or cooperative telephone or electric companies,[65] the distribution of low-cost articles incidental to the solicitation of charitable contributions,[66] and the exchanging or renting of membership or donor mailing lists between tax-exempt charitable organizations.[67]

Q 9:23 What types of income are exempt from unrelated income taxation?

The *modifications* (Q 9:22) shield a wide variety of forms of income from unrelated income taxation. This protected income generally encompasses annuities, capital gains, dividends, interest, rents, and royalties.[68] For the most part, there is little controversy in this area as to the definition of these income items, inasmuch as the terms are amply defined elsewhere in the federal tax law.

There has been, nonetheless, an underlying festering controversy. For years it has been the view of the IRS that the exclusion is available only where the income is investment income or is otherwise passively received. This approach to these modifications rests on the rationale for the unrelated income rules, which is to bring parity to the economics of competitive activities involving nonprofit and for-profit organizations (Q 9:10).[69] Passive income, by definition, is not derived from competitive activity and thus should not be taxed. But the IRS wishes to tax net income from the active conduct of commercial business activities.

This dichotomy presents itself in connection with the exclusion for rental income. Where a tax-exempt organization carries on rental activities in the nature of a commercial landlord, the exclusion is not available.[70] The exclusion, however, is not normally voided, simply because the exempt organization provides normal maintenance services. In practice, this opportunity for taxation is obviated by the use of an independent building management and leasing company.

There can be disputes as to whether an income flow is truly rent or is a share of the profits from a joint venture; revenue in the latter form is generally taxable. A contemporary illustration of this distinction is the litigation surrounding crop-share leasing. The IRS has lost all of the cases to date; the courts have held that the funds received by the exempt organization were in the form of excludable rent and not from a partnership or joint venture.[71]

The contemporary battles in this context are being waged over the scope of the exclusion for royalties. In part, this is because exempt organizations have more latitude than with any other type of income in structuring transactions to shape the resulting income. In this instance, the objective is to make the income fit the form of a royalty or at least dress it up to look like a royalty. For the most part, the dilemma is presented because the statute does not define the term *royalty*.

The IRS, until recently, persisted with its position that a royalty, to be excludable, must be passively received by the exempt organization. This issue, however, has been reviewed by the courts on several occasions; the exempt organizations involved have prevailed each time. The courts are ruling that a royalty is a payment for the use of valuable intangible property rights and are tolerating an insubstantial amount of promotional and administrative activity by the exempt organization receiving the royalty; they are rejecting the passive-active dichotomy, at least in the realm of the royalty exclusion.[72]

One set of these cases that was instrumental in developing the law in this area involved use of the royalty exclusion to shield from taxation funds derived from the use of mailing lists, where the special exception is unavailable.[73] Another significant set of cases concerned use of the royalty exclusion to protect income generated from an affinity card program.[74] The government's losses continued in the aftermath of these decisions.[75]

Finally, the IRS realized that this series of defeats was insurmountable—that the courts were not going to accept its interpretation of the scope of the tax-excludable royalty. The IRS National Office, late in 1999, communicated with its exempt organizations specialists in the field, essentially capitulating on the point. A memorandum distributed to them stated bluntly that "[c]ases should be resolved in a manner consistent with the existing court cases."[76] This memorandum added that "it is now clear that courts will continue to find the income [generated by activities such as mailing list rentals and affinity card programs] to be excluded royalty income unless the factual record clearly reflects more than unsubstantial services being provided." Two factors were highlighted by the IRS as establishing nontaxable royalty income: where the involvement of the exempt organization is "relatively minimal" and where the exempt organization "hired outside contractors to perform most services associated with the exploitation of the use of intangible property."

TIP: An issue under consideration at the IRS is whether there should be an allocation, of a single payment, between compensation for the use of intangible property (royalty income) and compensation for more than insubstantial services (presumably taxable).

One approach to follow while this aspect of the law is being sorted out is to bifurcate the arrangement: execute two contracts, one reflecting passive income/royalty payments and the other as payments for services rendered.[77] The income paid pursuant to the second contract would presumably be taxable. The organization would endeavor to allocate to the royalty contract as much of the income as reasonably possible. The difficulty with this approach is the form-over-substance rule: Two contracts of this nature are easily collapsed and treated as one for tax purposes.

Q 9:24   Are there any exceptions to the rules stating these exemptions?

Yes, for tax-exempt organizations in general, there are two exceptions. One pertains to the payment of otherwise excludable income from a controlled organization. The general rule is that payments of annuities, interest, rent, and/or royalties by a controlled corporation to a tax-exempt controlling organization are taxable as unrelated income, when these items are deductible by the payor corporation.[78] This is the case even though these forms of income are otherwise passive in nature. For this purpose, an organization controls another where the parent entity owns more than 50 percent of the ownership interest in the subsidiary.[79] This control element can be manifested by stock or by an interlocking of directors, trustees, or other representatives of the two organizations.[80]

The other exception is found in the rules concerning unrelated debt-financed property (Q 9:30).[81] Where income is debt-financed income, the various exclusions referred to above (Q 9:23) are unavailable.[82]

Q 9:25   Are there any exceptions to these exceptions?

Yes, there is one. The rule concerning the taxation of income from a controlled subsidiary (Q 9:24) does not apply where the funds are dividends, because dividends are not deductible by the payor corporation.[83] Thus, where other types of income are deductible by the controlled entity that provides the income, the exempt organization that receives the income must regard it as unrelated business income.

Q 9:26   Are private foundations allowed to engage in any business activity?

Well, they are certainly allowed to engage in *related* business activities. This includes, of course, grant-making for charitable purposes. These activities also encompass charitable activities and funding by means of functionally related businesses (Q 5:3) and program-related investments (Q 5:4).

A private foundation, however, is not permitted to actively engage in unrelated business activity. This is the case no matter how small the undertaking might be. The reason for this is that the unrelated activity is considered a business form known as the *sole proprietorship*. By definition, the foundation would "own" 100 percent of that business. This would be a violation of the excess business holdings rules (Chapter 5).[84]

A private foundation may own an interest in a business enterprise (Q 9:27), such as shares of stock in a commercial enterprise. These interests, however, may not exceed the levels prescribed pursuant to the excess business holdings rules.

Q 9:27   What is a *business enterprise*?

In general, the term *business enterprise* includes the active conduct of an unrelated trade or business, including any activity that is regularly carried on for the production of income from the sale of goods or the performance of services (Q 5:1, Q 9:6).[85] Where an activity carried on for profit constitutes an unrelated business, no part of the business may be excluded from the classi-fication of a business enterprise merely because it does not result in a profit.[86]

Q 9:28 If private foundations are not permitted to engage in business activity, what is the relevance of the unrelated business income rules to them?

There are ways in which a private foundation can, without adverse tax con-sequences, engage in a business (or businesslike) activity. These ways are based on the concept that the activity does not constitute a *business enter-prise* (Q 5:1, Q 9:27).

The principal way for a private foundation to engage in allowable and nontaxable business activity is to participate in a business activity in which at least 95 percent of the gross income of the business is derived from *passive sources*.[87] Gross income from passive sources includes the items excluded from taxation under the modification rules for dividends, interest, payments with respect to securities loans, amounts received as considera-tion for entering into agreements to make loans, annuities, royalties, rents, capital gains, and gains from the lapse or termination of options to buy or sell securities.[88]

There are two refinements to these rules:

1. A bond or other evidence of indebtedness does not constitute a holding in a business enterprise, unless the bond or other evidence of indebtedness is otherwise determined to be an equitable interest in the enterprise.[89]
2. A leasehold interest in real property does not constitute an interest in a business enterprise, even though rent payable under the lease is dependent, in whole or in part, on the income or profits derived by another person from the property, unless the leasehold interest con-stitutes an interest in the income or profits of an unrelated business.[90]

Thus, as long as the income is generated as one or more forms of these or other types of passive income, the income will not—as a general rule—be taxed as unrelated business income. This exception, then, usually shields most forms of investment income received by private foundations from unre-lated income taxation.

Consequently, as a general proposition, a private foundation may freely invest in (or receive as a contribution and retain) securities without becoming subject to the unrelated business income rules. The same is generally true with respect to rental property, although the income may be taxed if the rental property is used in an active business operation, if the rent is based on the lessee's net income or profits, or if the property is indebted (Q 9:30). As to royalties, as long as the income is passive in nature, it is not taxable; other-wise, a full understanding of the scope of this exclusion must await the next IRS pronouncement, made in the aftermath of considerable litigation.

Gross income from passive sources also includes income from the sale of goods (including charges or costs passed on at cost to purchasers of the goods or income received in settlement of a dispute concerning or in lieu of the exercise of the right to sell the goods) if the seller does not manufacture, produce, physically receive or deliver, negotiate sales of, or maintain inventories in the goods. For example, where a corporation purchases a product under a contract with the manufacturer, resells it under contract at a uniform markup in price, and does not physically handle the product, the income derived from that markup meets the definition of passive income. By contrast, income from individually negotiated sales, such as those made by a broker, would not meet the definition, even if the broker did not physically handle the goods.[91]

If, in a year, less than 95 percent of the income of a trade or business is from passive sources, a private foundation may, in applying this 95 percent test, substitute for the passive source gross income in the year the average gross income from passive sources for the 10 years immediately preceding the year in question. Thus, stock in a passive holding company is not considered a holding in a business enterprise even if the company is controlled by the foundation; instead, the foundation is treated as owning its proportionate share of any interests in a business enterprise held by the company.[92]

Q 9:29 Can a private foundation own a for-profit subsidiary for the purpose of conducting unrelated business?

Generally, no. A private foundation normally cannot own a subsidiary because of the prohibition on excess business holdings (Chapter 5). A private foundation may, however, be able to own a controlled organization that generates passive income.

This possibility may be obviated where a private foundation incurred debt to acquire or improve a property (Q 9:30). That is, the resulting income may be taxed, in whole or in part, as unrelated business income, notwithstanding the fact that it is passive income. (This type of income, however, nonetheless retains its character as passive income for purposes of the excess business holdings rules.[93])

Q 9:30 Do the unrelated debt-financed income rules apply with respect to private foundations?

Absolutely. The modifications exempting passive investment income from the unrelated business income tax (Q 9:23) do not apply to the extent that the investment is made with borrowed funds or the purchase is what is termed *debt-financed.* This rule is applicable to private foundations. A classic example of a permitted foundation investment impacted by this rule is a rental building financed by a mortgage.

The term *debt-financed property* means—with certain exceptions— property that is held to produce income (usually dividends, interest, or rent) and with respect to which there is an *acquisition indebtedness* at any time during the tax year (or during the preceding 12 months if the property was disposed of during the year).[94] Acquisition indebtedness, with respect to debt-financed property, means the unpaid amount of the indebtedness incurred:

- By the foundation in acquiring or improving the property,
- Before any acquisition or improvement of the property if the indebtedness would not have been incurred but for the acquisition or improvement of the property, and
- After the acquisition or improvement of the property, if the indebtedness would not have been incurred but for the acquisition or improvement, and the incurrence of the indebtedness was reasonably foreseeable at the time of the acquisition or improvement.[95]

If property is acquired by a private foundation subject to a mortgage or other similar lien, the indebtedness thereby secured is considered an acquisition indebtedness incurred by the organization when the property is acquired, even though the organization did not assume or agree to pay the indebtedness.[96] In the case of mortgaged property acquired as a result of a bequest or devise, however, the indebtedness secured by this type of mortgage is not treated as an acquisition indebtedness during the 10-year period following the date of acquisition.[97]

A like rule applies with respect to mortgaged property received by gift, where the mortgage was placed on the property more than five years before the gift and the property was held by the donor more than five years before the gift.[98] Indebted property that is not producing any recurrent annual income but is being held to produce appreciation in underlying value is subject to this rule—meaning that the capital gains are taxable.[99]

Acquisition indebtedness does not include indebtedness the incurrence of which is inherent in the performance or exercise of the purpose or function constituting the basis of the organization's tax-exempt status.[100] Acquisition indebtedness also does not include an obligation to pay a qualified charitable gift annuity.[101]

Further exempted from treatment as debt-financed property are the following types of properties:

- Property where substantially all (i.e., at least 85 percent) of its use is related to the exercise or performance by the organization of its tax-exempt purpose or, if less than substantially all of its use is related, to the extent that its use is related to exempt purposes.[102]
- Property to the extent that the income is derived from research activities and therefore is excluded from taxation (Q 9:22).[103]
- Property to the extent that its use is in a business exempted from tax because substantially all of the work is performed without compensation.[104]

- Property to the extent that its use is in a business carried on primarily for the convenience of the organization's members, students, patients, officers, or employees.[105]
- Property to the extent that its use is in a business that is the selling of merchandise, substantially all of which was donated to the organization.[106]
- Property to the extent that its income is already subject to tax as income from the conduct of an unrelated trade or business.[107]

NOTE: A federal court of appeals held that securities purchased on margin by a supporting organization (Q 12:15) constitute debt-financed property, which generates unrelated business income.[108] One of the arguments offered by the organization was that the investment income is not taxable because the securities it purchased on margin are substantially related to its exempt purpose (an exception to the definition of debt-financed property) and its purchase of securities on margin is inherent to its exempt purpose (the exception to the definition of acquisition indebtedness). The court agreed that investment of the assets of the organization is inherent in its tax-exempt purpose of benefiting the supported organization. The court, however, did not accept the view that margin-financing of the acquisition of securities was a related activity.

In computing unrelated business taxable income of a private foundation (or, for that matter, any type of tax-exempt organization), there must be included with respect to each debt-financed property that is unrelated to the organization's exempt function—as an item of gross income derived from a trade or business—an amount of income from the property, subject to tax in the proportion in which the property is financed by the debt. Basically, deductions are allowed with respect to each debt-financed property in the same proportion.[109]

Q 9:31   How is the unrelated business income tax calculated?

In general, the unrelated business income tax is determined in the same manner as with for-profit entities. The unrelated income tax rates payable by most tax-exempt organizations are the corporate rates.[110] Some organizations, such as trusts, are subject to the individual income tax rates.[111] There is a specific deduction of $1,000.[112]

This tax[113] falls on *net* unrelated business income.[114] An exempt organization is allowed to subtract its business expenses from gross unrelated income in arriving at taxable net unrelated income. The law generally states that a deductible expense must be *directly connected* with the carrying on of the business; an item of deduction must have a proximate and primary relationship to the carrying on of the business.[115] This standard is more rigorous than the one applied to for-profit and individual taxpayers, where the law allows the deductibility of expenses that are reasonably connected with the taxable endeavor. In practice, however, exempt organizations often follow the standard of reasonableness, particularly when allocating expenses. Because of the looseness of the tax regulations, this approach has been upheld in the courts.[116]

There is one exception to the directly connected test. This exception is for the charitable contribution deduction allowed in computing taxable unrelated income. In general, this deduction cannot exceed 10 percent of the unrelated business taxable income otherwise computed.[117]

These taxes are paid by means of an unrelated business income tax return (Q 9:32). Tax-exempt organizations must make quarterly estimated payments of this tax.[118]

Q 9:32   How is the unrelated business Income tax reported?

The return filed by nearly all tax-exempt organizations with the IRS on an annual basis is an *information* return. For private foundations, this form is Form 990-PF (Chapter 10). This type of return is not used to report taxable income. For that purpose, a *tax* return is required. The IRS has devised a tax return for reporting unrelated business taxable income. This form is Form 990-T. It must be filed in addition to the annual information return.

Q 9:33   Can the receipt of unrelated business income cause a private foundation to lose its tax-exempt status?

A concise answer to this question is yes. In fact, this is true with respect to any type of tax-exempt organization. In the case of a private foundation, however, the tax on excess business holdings is likely to be applied before a consideration of the unrelated business income tax.

At the same time, consideration should be given to what is arguably the most extraordinary IRS private letter ruling issued in 2000.[119] In this ruling, the IRS held that the operations of a gift shop and tea room by a organization operating to assist needy women are unrelated businesses, rejecting arguments that they are related businesses because of the enhancements they bring to the operation of the organization's consignment shop. Nonetheless, these enterprises were found to be in furtherance of charitable purposes, enabling the organization to remain tax exempt.

The purpose of the organization is to "establish and maintain . . . a place for the reception, exhibition and sale of articles, [which are] the product and manufacture of industrious and meritorious women." Another of its purposes is to "assist needy and deserving women in their efforts to earn an honest livelihood by their own industry."

This organization has three activities, all approximately the same size. One is a consignment shop, operated by volunteers and paid employees, where goods made by needy women are displayed and sold. Another is a gift shop, operated by volunteers and employees, which purchases decorative items from for-profit vendors for resale to the public. The third function is a tea room, operated by volunteers and employees, which is a luncheon facility (dining room and kitchen) selling to the general public.

The IRS reviewed these facts from the standpoint of the organization's purpose: the charitable objective of enabling needy women to support themselves. The consignment shop was held to be a related business, in that it provides necessary services to members of a charitable class.

The gift shop is a regularly carried on business. As to relatedness, the organization asserted that the items in the shop enhance the consignment items, attract customers, and provide funds to support the consignment activity. The items in the gift shop are sophisticated, tasteful, and fashionable; the thought was that, by being in the same showroom with the consignment items, they attract "quality clientele" who would not otherwise visit the consignment shop, which has the aura of a "craft fair." The IRS did not accept these arguments, finding no substantial causal relationship to exempt purposes. Thus, the gift shop was held to be an unrelated business.

The tea room also is a regularly carried on business. Relatedness was asserted in that it attracts the type of persons to the facility who will be willing to buy the consignment items. This argument failed as well. The IRS turned to the *commerciality doctrine* (Q 9:11) for guidance to the conclusion that the eating facility is "presumptively commercial." The factors considered were that the enterprise competes directly with other restaurants, uses profit-making pricing formulas, engages in advertising, has hours of operation competitive with commercial establishments, and there are no plans to solicit contributions. Thus, the tea room was held to be an unrelated business.

NOTE: These three businesses were said to be of approximately equal size. For example, the revenue from each one was about the same for the year under examination; as for percentages, the tea room accounted for 34 percent of the revenue, the consignment shop generated 33 percent, and the gift shop yielded 28 percent. (The rest came from gifts and dues.) Thus, 62 percent of the organization's revenue was derived from unrelated business. Yet, in the exemption setting, the IRS agreed that the purposes of the gift shop and tea room help further the organization's charitable function. That is, they raise funds for the organization's charitable program and attract purchasers for the products produced through that program.

Thus, even though the fact that income from an activity is used for exempt purposes does not alone make the activity a related one, it appears that that argument can be used to preserve an organization's tax-exempt status. In this ruling, even though about two-thirds of an organization's activities were unrelated, the IRS permitted the organization to remain tax-exempt.

CHAPTER 10

Annual Information Return

The universal form used by the IRS, by states, and by many others to scrutinize the activities of private foundations is Form 990-PF. Beginning in 2000, the form entered the electronic age and is available for all to see, and if they wish download and print, on the Internet at *Guidestar.org*. Form 990-PF's 12 pages and the 27 pages of IRS instructions exemplify the complexity of reporting and compliance requirements for a private foundation. This form reminds private foundations that they are taxpayers and subject to a broad set of special rules. Suggestions for its accurate and clear preparation are presented in this chapter.

Here are the questions that are most frequently asked (or that should be asked) about the private foundation annual information return—and the answers to them.

Q 10:1   Do private foundations have to file an annual return with the IRS?

Each private foundation, including a charitable trust, is required by law to file Form 990-PF annually regardless of gross revenues received during the year. Even a foundation with a non–interest-bearing checking account is required to file. The basic financial information—the revenues, disbursements, assets, and liabilities—are classified into meaningful categories to allow the IRS, funders, states, and persons who ask to inspect the returns to statistically evaluate the scope and type of a foundation's activity. Second, a myriad of questions fish for failures to comply with the payout, self-dealing, taxable expenditure, excess business holdings, jeopardizing investment, and other special rules (Chapters 3–7). The various parts of the form are inactive and do not follow in logical order.

NOTE: Form 990-T is also filed by a foundation receiving more than $1,000 of unrelated business income (Chapter 9).

Q 10:2   When and where is Form 990-PF due to be filed?

The due date for filing this annual IRS report gives tax practitioners and foundations a reprieve. Form 990-PF is due to be filed within 4½ months after the end of the foundation's fiscal year, rather than the 2½ months allowed for Form 1120 (for-profit corporations) and the 3½ months for Form 1041 (trusts). An extension of time can be requested if the organization has not completed its year-end accounting soon enough to file by the initial deadline. For both Forms 990-PF and 990-T, however, the filing of an extension does *not* extend the time to pay the tax. All information returns for tax-exempt organizations, including foundations, are filed in the following central center: Internal Revenue Service Center, Ogden, UT 84201-0027.

CAUTION: Late filing can be costly. A penalty of $20 a day (up from $10) is due if the return is filed late by organizations with gross receipts under $1 million a year, not to exceed the greater of $10,000 or 5 percent of the annual gross receipts for the year of late filing.[1] The penalty also can be imposed if the form is filed incompletely. The penalty for a large organization (more than $1 million of annual gross receipts) is $100 a day up to a maximum penalty of $50,000.

Q 10:3   What are the most important issues raised by information submitted with the return?

The return is designed to allow the IRS to scrutinize a foundation's compliance with a variety of special rules. It begins with an income statement and a balance sheet accompanied with detailed descriptions of many of the categories. Beginning with a list of contributors by name and type of property given, the return contains the name, proceeds, and cost of each asset sold during the year, descriptions of the nature of payments to directors and trustees, lawyers, accountants, and other professionals, a detailed list of grant recipients, and a myriad of other information. Two pages of questions fish for failures to comply with the tax rules. The type of issues the form seeks to address include the following and many more presented in the questions of this chapter:

- Does the amount of salaries paid to directors, trustees, and other disqualified persons indicate self-dealing may have occurred?
- Is the level of expenses attributable to investment income high?
- Has the foundation made payments for charitable programs of a sufficient amount to satisfy its minimum distribution requirements?
- Does the difference between the book and market value of the assets or reported losses on sales of assets reflect jeopardizing investments?

- Is a private operating foundation meeting both the income and the asset tests?
- Does the grant listing indicate that the foundation should have exercised expenditure responsibility?
- Does the foundation receive a significant amount of unrelated business income, evidencing its lack of charitable purpose?
- Has the foundation lent money to its insiders?

Q 10:4   Other than the IRS, who scrutinizes Form 990-PF?

Everyone who cares to can ask to see a foundation's Form 990-PF. The scanned forms are also viewable and printable on the Internet at *Guidestar.org* for any and all to scrutinize. Accurate and complete preparation of this annual tax form should be given top priority because a foundation's public reporting responsibilities have entered another dimension and deserve careful attention. In March 1997, the IRS contracted with the Urban Institute of Washington, D.C., to receive and place on CD-ROM Forms 990 for the years 1996 through 2001. In a coordinated effort, Philanthropic Resources, Inc., began in 1998 to digitize the information so that it could be sorted and searched. The IRS is also studying an electronic filing system for 990s so as to eliminate the paperwork and allow it to more effectively monitor exempt organizations in a statistical and focused fashion.

Since March 13, 1999, private foundations are subject to the same return disclosure rules as public charities (Q 11-22–11:28). A foundation must permit anyone that knocks on its door to see the latest three years of 990-PFs and its Form 1023. A copy of the returns must be provided if the requester is willing to pay a modest fee. Written requests also must be honored for copy of them. This new public disclosure regime has replaced the former 180-day availability period that had to be announced in a newspaper.

State attorneys general have the opportunity to scrutinize the return that is required by federal tax law to be provided to them each year. Although in many states the returns are not examined, information gleaned from the returns has inspired investigations into foundation affairs. A private foundation must file Form 990-PF with each state with which it is registered to conduct business, the state in which the foundation's principal office is located, and the state in which the foundation was incorporated or created.

Last, Part XV of Form 990-PF is scrutinized by a wide variety of grant seekers to ascertain the type of organizations the foundation supports. In this part, the foundation lists all of the grants it has paid out during the year and those it has approved for future payment. Widely disseminated databases are created by sorting and summarizing the information submitted in Part XV. To aid fund-raising efforts, the Foundation Center publishes a national directory of the facts and figures gleaned from Part XV. Foundation directories published on a statewide and area basis also report the information. Public libraries in many cities have a Philanthropic Research Center with Form 990-PF and other fund-raising books and grant-seeking aids.

SUGGESTION: Part XV of Form 990-PF should be prepared by the foundation's program officers or whoever is responsible for choosing grant recipients, not by the accountants who prepare the rest of the return. It is imperative that the information reflect the foundation's mission and intentions. If the foundation has formal grant guidelines, they are described and possibly attached. The display of grants paid out during the year in Part XV (3) should be presented according to type of programs supported, such as healthcare, churches, child abuse, medical research, battered women, the poor, and the like. The objective is to clearly describe the type of organizations the foundation wants to support to reduce the number of unnecessary applications for funding it receives.

Q 10:5   What types of information are reported on Form 990-PF?

A wide range of information is reported. A brief synopsis of the purpose of the various parts follows:

- The foundation's income and expenses for the year and the resulting balance sheet are shown in Parts I, II, and III, as explained in depth later.
- Beginning with Part IV, the form accommodates the special calculations, requirements, and rules placed on private foundations. Part IV calculates the foundation's gain or loss on sales of assets using its tax rather than its financial basis. Because the foundation must use the donor's basis for contributed property, the net gains are often higher than book gains as discussed in the next question.
- Part V calculates the foundation's qualification for a reduced tax rate of 1 percent based on an increase in current year charitable distributions in excess of its historic payouts (Q 8:18).
- Part VI calculates the foundation's excise tax on investment income. It reflects the fact that the foundation with tax of more than $500 must pay the tax in advance following the estimated tax system used by normal taxpayers.
- Part VII-A and B contain a host of questions to determine the foundation's ongoing qualification for tax-exempt status by asking whether it has violated any of the special private foundation rules and if it has changed its organizational documents, its purposes, or its status as a private charity.
- Part VIII reports finite details of compensation paid to persons that serve the foundation. It should be carefully prepared (Q 10:11).
- Part IX-A and B describe the foundation's direct charitable activities and program-related investments. For a private and exempt operating foundation, this information justifies its classification. The return asks that relevant statistical information, such as the number of organizations

and other beneficiaries served, conference convened, research papers produced, and so on, be submitted. Words should not be spared in painting a picture of the foundation's exempt purposes when it spends money on its own programs.

- Parts X, XI, XII, XIII, and XIV determine the foundation's satisfaction of the annual payout requirements.
- Part XV can be the most significant part for many foundations. As described (Q 10:4), this part lists the grants paid out by the foundation and paints a picture of the type of programs the foundation supports. It is significant because the information is widely used by fund seekers.
- Part XVI-A and B identify the character of the foundation's income as passive and related investment income, program service revenue, or unrelated business income (Q 10:16). If more than $1,000 of revenue is reported in column (b), the IRS will expect the foundation to file a Form 990-T.
- Part XVII is almost always inapplicable to a private foundation. This part asks the foundation to indicate its relationship to business leagues, civic associations, or other types of noncharitable, tax-exempt organizations and political organizations.

Q 10:6 What are the special characteristics of Part I of Form 990-PF?

Each of the columns in Part I serves a different purpose in the IRS regulatory scheme for private foundations. Deciding what goes where and why is not a logical process. Different accounting methods are used for reporting information in different columns, and some items are included in more than one column, while others are not. All foundations complete columns (a) and (d).

Column (a), Revenue and Expenses "Per Books"

This column agrees with financial reports prepared for the board or for public dissemination by the organization. The cash or accrual method of accounting is permitted, in keeping with the system regularly used to prepare financial statements for other purposes. In-kind contributions of services or use of property, even though properly booked for financial statement purposes, are excluded. Capital gains are calculated using "book basis" rather than "tax basis," which is reported in column (b), line 7 or 8 (Q 8:12).

Column (b), Net Investment Income

Column (b) reports the income and allocable expenses used to calculate the foundation's investment excise tax and associated deductions (Q 8:13). Exempt operating foundations do not complete column (b) because they do not pay the investment excise tax (Q 14:10). Only four types of revenues— interest, dividends, rents, and royalties—and capital gains from the properties producing such income are subject to the tax (Q 8:3–8:10).

The most common difference between columns (a) and (b) regards capital gains. Column (a) reports gains calculated using the foundation's book basis, often the value of donated property on the date it was received as a gift. Tax basis for donated property, however, is equal to the donor's basis, customarily a much lower number (Q 8:12). Column (b) does not include:

- Unrelated business income separately reported on Form 990-T
- Program service revenue
- Gain from sale of exempt function assets, or
- Profits from fund-raising events

Column (c), Adjusted Net Income

This column became obsolete for most private foundations in 1976. It is still important for two types of private foundations:

1. Private and exempt operating foundations (Q 14:2, Q 14:10) calculate their *adjusted net income* used in the tests shown in Part XIV for comparison to active program expenditures (Q 14:3). They must spend 85 percent of their adjusted net income on charitable projects. This column includes net investment income, plus short-term capital gains and unrelated business income, less long-term capital gains and the investment income tax.
2. Foundations receiving program service income also use this column to isolate the income and associated expenses. To the extent that the foundation's programs generate revenues, only expenses in excess of such revenues are reportable in column (d). This column must end in zero.

Column (d), Disbursements for Charitable Purposes

Amounts reported in this column are significant because the total is carried to Part XII to tally up the foundation's qualifying distributions (Chapter 4). As the title says, this column contains the foundation's expenditures for charitable purposes—grants it pays out and spending for administrative and direct program costs. Expenses allocable to investment and program services revenues reported in columns (b) and (c) are not also reported. The cash method must be used for this column.

Q 10:7   Do any special rules apply to reporting of expenses by a private foundation?

Proper allocation of expenses between investment and charitable program costs is a significant aspect of completing Form 990-PF. A foundation basically has only two types of expenses—amounts spent to enable it to produce investment income and disbursements for charitable purposes, also called *exempt function expenses.* Many foundation expenses, such as directors' and trustees' fees, personnel, accounting and legal fees, office rental, and other costs, are allocable both to its investments and its charitable programs. Good records (Q 10:7) can be used to allocate these expenses. The characteristics of the two types of foundation expenses follow:

1. The ordinary and necessary expenses of producing investment income are reported in column (b) to offset revenues in calculating the foundation's excise tax on investment income. Investment-related expenses thereby reduce the foundation's tax burden. The rules for identifying such expenses are those applicable to deductible expenses for individual and business income tax returns (Q 8:14).[2]
2. Expenses for charitable purposes include grants paid to other charitable organizations, scholarship and fellowship payments, costs of conducting active charitable programs, and an allocable part of the foundation's administrative expenses.

NOTE: Between 1985 and 1990, Congress placed a limit on a foundation's administrative expenses. When a the general and administrative expenses exceeded a limit equal to .65 percent of its assets, they could not be counted. They were disallowed as a reduction of investment income and also could not count toward the distribution requirements. The IRS soon found the limits ineffective. They had been designed to curb abusive situations often found in larger organizations, such as excessive compensation, but the formula missed that mark. It was the smaller foundations that had high costs but had correspondingly high qualifying distributions. Finally, the IRS admitted that the calculations were complicated and burdensome to foundations and did not recommend their continuance.

Q 10:8   Is there any special order in which the parts of Form 990-PF should be prepared?

Form 990-PF has evolved over 30 years as the rules governing private foundations have developed, retaining original concepts and adding new ones. Certain interdependent calculations do not follow in logical order. The most efficient order in which to prepare the return is the following:

1. Parts I, II, III, and IV
2. Skip to Parts VII, VIII, IX-A and B, XV, XVI-A and B, XVII, and XVIII
3. Part X
4. Part XII
5. Part V
6. Part VI
7. Part XI
8. Part XIII or XIV

Q 10:9   Are there any steps a foundation can take to ease this reporting burden?

Preparation of the return is much easier for a foundation that has documentation and cost accounting records to capture revenues and costs in categories and to distinguish between the investment and program functions. Techniques to provide verifiable bases to identify the character of expenses are useful. Additionally, a basis for allocating those many expenses that are attributable both to managing the foundation's assets and to conducting its charitable programs is necessary (Q 8:14). At a minimum, a foundation might find it useful to maintain the following:

- A staff salary allocation system to record the time employees spend on tasks each day. The possibilities are endless. Computer programs for recording time are readily available. Although some persons are reluctant to keep such records, the reports should be completed often enough to ensure accuracy, preferably weekly. In situations where personnel perform repetitive tasks, preparing one week's report for each month or one month each year might be sufficient. The desired result is the percentage of time spent on various foundation functions—investments, programs, and administration.
- Office/program space utilization charts to assign occupancy costs can be prepared. All physical building space rented or owned can be allocated according to its usage. Floor plans can be tabulated to arrive at square footage of the space allocable to each activity center or department. In some cases, the allocation is based on staff/time ratios. For dual-use space, records must reflect the number of hours or days space is used for each purpose.
- Direct program or activity costs should be captured whenever possible. The advantages include reduction of investment and unrelated business income tax and proof of qualifying distributions. A minimal amount of additional time should be required by administrative staff to accumulate costs by programs. A departmental accounting system is imperative. A system for recording telephone calls, print shop usage, travel and meeting expenses, and the like should quantify such charges by activity. As another example, separate accounts can be established with vendors for each department.
- Joint project allocations must be made on a reasonable and fair basis, recognizing the cause-and-effect relationship between the cost incurred and where it is allocated. Four possible methods of allocating include:

  1. Activity-based allocations (identifying departmental costs);
  2. Equal sharing of costs (e.g., if three projects, divide by three);
  3. Cost allocated relative to stand-alone cost (e.g., what it would cost if that department had to hire and buy independently); and
  4. Cost allocated in proportion to cost savings.

- Supporting, administrative, or other management costs should be allocated to departments to which the work is directly related. The private foundation's size and the scope of administrative staff involvement in actual programs determine the feasibility of such cost attributions. Staff salaries are most often allocable. Say, for example, the executive director is also the editor of the foundation's journal. If a record of time spent is maintained, his or her salary and associated costs could be attributed partly to the publication.
- A computer-based fund accounting system is preferable, in which department codes are automatically recorded as monies are expended. The cost of the software is easily recouped in staff time saved, improved planning, and possibly tax savings due to a reduction in income and excise taxes.

Q 10:10 What tax accounting method must a foundation use in preparing Form 990 PF?

The instructions for Form 990-PF direct a foundation to use the same accounting method on the return to figure revenue and expenses as it regularly uses to keep its books and records.[3] The method must, however, clearly reflect income. Once a foundation adopts either the cash or accrual method for 990-PF reporting to calculate its investment excise tax, it must file Form 3115 to change the method. A foundation that changes its method of reporting contributions and grants to comply with the Financial Accounting Standards Board (FASB) standards, however, is not required to file Form 3115.[4] The prior year effect of such a change is reported on Part III of Form 990-PF, rather than on the beginning balance sheet.

The cash method of accounting must be used by a private foundation to tally its minimum distribution requirements (Q 4:10). Thus, the information submitted in column (d) of the front page of Form 990-PF may be different from that in column (a). A foundation that follows the accrual method of accounting will report a grant in column (a) when the obligation to make a grant is approved and pledged to a grantee. The grant is included in column (d) for purposes of calculating satisfaction of the payout requirement, however, only when the grant is actually paid out in cash. Most foundations use the cash method to avoid this problem.

Q 10:11 What parts of Form 990-PF reveal when a self-dealing transaction has occurred?

Self-dealing (Chapter 3) can occur when a financial transaction takes place between the private foundation as those that fund and control it, its disqualified persons (Chapter 2). The most common lines on which such payments are reported are lines 13–16 of Part I—compensation for personal services rendered on behalf of the foundation. The amounts must be reasonable, and comparable to what other foundations of the same size and type pay, for the services rendered. National surveys that provide the average paid for work performed by size, type, and locale of foundations are used to measure the prospects of excessive amounts.

The foundation's balance sheet presented in Part II might reflect a loan to or from a disqualified person. The form asks that attributes of such loans be reported in detail—principal amount, interest rate, repayment terms, collateral, and most important the purpose of the loan. The only type of loan permitted is an interest-free loan from a disqualified person to the foundation for its use in conducting charitable activities (Q 3:7).

Most important, Part VIII reports the names of officers, directors, key employees, independent contractors, and essentially anyone paid personal service compensation in excess of $50,000 is listed. Their names, position, time spent working on the job, basic compensation, benefits, and expense allowances are individually reported. Careful reporting of these details is important to avoid the suggestion of self-dealing.

Last, in Part VII-B, the foundation must overly say whether it had any financial transactions with insiders and, if so, why.

Q 10:12 What part of Form 990-PF indicates whether the foundation meets its payout requirements?

Part XIII, called Undistributed Income, compares the minimum distribution requirement (Chapter 4) calculated in Part XI to the qualifying distributions reported in Part XII. It is desirable that amounts only be reported in columns (a), (c), and (d) of this part because column (b) represents deficiencies in prior-year payments. The form reflects the fact that a foundation seldom meets its distribution requirement to the penny, but instead usually has some amount of excess distributions. In fact, some foundations have a carryover of multiple years' worth of excess distributions because they choose to pay out more to charity than is required. Such excesses can be carried over for five years, as shown in Part XIII.

Q 10:13 Does Form 990-PF identify excess business holdings?

No, not specifically. Excess business holdings (Chapter 5) occur when a foundation's ownership, combined with those of its insiders, exceed certain percentage limitations. A detailed description, such as 100 shares of XYZ common shares, is submitted for those foundation assets reflected on the balance sheet in Part II. The percentage those 100 shares represent, however, is not reported on the asset listings. The only way excess holdings are evidenced is if the foundation voluntarily, in Part VII, answers the question positively that yes, indeed, it does have excess business holdings.

Q 10:14 Are jeopardizing investments identified on Form 990-PF?

There are several ways a bad investment, or one jeopardizing a foundation's charitable assets (Chapter 6), can be spotted on the form. Although the rules say jeopardy is determined at the time the investment is made, it is the ultimate results that often raise the question.

- The first signal of a jeopardy investment is a loss on lines 6–8 of the income statement in Part I.
- Another clue is a comparison of the beginning asset balances in column (a) of the balance sheet in Part II with the column (b) ending balances and the fair market value listed in column (c). Certainly if the ending fair market value is much less than the cost, one would ask why. It is important to note that this tool cannot be used for a foundation that uses the accrual basis of accounting for reporting its financial condition (box checked in item J at the top of the first page). In such cases, the assets are written up or down to market value so that jeopardy would be suggested by changes on lines 3 and 5 of Part III.
- The foundation Is required to attach a detailed listing of its assets to Part II. Each stock, bond, building, collectible, and the like is described. Jeopardy can exist if the foundation fails to diversify its investments, meaning it holds several different stocks, bonds, and the like. If the form reports the foundation invests all of its assets in one stock or only holds only real estate, one might find jeopardy.
- Last, the foundation is asked in Part VII-B, Question 4, whether it has jeopardizing investments.

Q 10:15 How can Form 990-PF reveal that a foundation has made a taxable expenditure?

Many parts of the form ask questions and request explanations of activities that might indicate that a taxable expenditure—basically, one that does not serve a charitable purpose (Chapter 7)—has occurred.

- Parts I and II of the form report expenses by generic category—salaries, travel, printing, grants paid, and the like. So a taxable expenditure would not necessarily be identified in these parts. A violation might be spotted in the parts where the foundation describes the purpose of its expenditures.
- Part VII-A specifically asks whether the foundation attempted to influence any national, state, or local legislation. A yes answer indicates a taxable expenditure.
- Part VII-A also asks whether the foundation has spent more than $100 for political purposes—again, an impermissible act.
- Part VII-B asks whether any one of the five specific types of taxable expenditures occurred.
- Parts IX-A and IX-B ask the foundation to describe its direct charitable activities and its program-related investments. Saying the foundation buys food to feed a particular family (not a charitable class) would indicate impermissible expenditures. Investment in the venture capital firm of the foundation might be difficult to describe as charitable.

- Last, but certainly a troublesome type of expenditure, is a grant to an organization that doesn't qualify for some reason. Part XV (3) and (4) list grant recipients. The form asks whether an individual grant recipient has any relationship to the foundation's insiders (Q 9:11). The foundation status of a recipient—either private or public—is reported. If a grant to a private charity is listed and an expenditure responsibility agreement is not included in the return, a taxable expenditure occurs (Q 9:23).

Q 10:16 Where does Form 990-PF signal the IRS that the private foundation may have unrelated income?

On Part XVI-A and B, entitled *Analysis of Income-Producing Activities and Relation of Activities to the Accomplishment of Exempt Purposes,* a foundation characterizes its income according to its relatedness to its exempt purposes. The IRS added this part in 1989 to allow it to find unrelated business income (Chapter 9) that is not identified in Part I. The excess business rules prohibit a foundation holding an investment in a business that operates as a proprietorship. A foundation, however, might earn income treated as a permissible unrelated business from indebted rental property or shares of Subchapter S corporation stock. This unrelated income is reported in columns (a) and (b). If the total amount in column (b) exceeds $1,000, Form 990-T must be filed to report the income and pay normal tax on any net profits.

NOTE: The typical foundation only submits information in column (d) of Part XVI, where interest, dividends, rents, and capital gains on investments are reported. A foundation that receives program service revenues, such as admission to visit a historic site or sale of educational materials, would report that income in column (e) and explain how the activity furthers its exempt purposes.

Q 10:17 How does a foundation report changes in its organizational documents or its mission?

When the foundation changes its charter, bylaws, or its trust instrument, Part VII-A, question 3, asks it to say so and to attach the changes. Similarly, but less commonly, a foundation might change its mission and begin to conduct activities it has "not previously reported to the IRS" and must answer "yes" to question 2 of Part VII-A. This question is sometimes hard to answer when the foundation's activity has evolved or expanded but has not necessarily changed in its focus or overall purpose. When there is any doubt, it is prudent to answer "yes" and attach an explanation.

The issue raised by these questions is whether the foundation wants written IRS approval for its evolving or new activity or document changes. Simply answering this question "yes" and attaching a detailed description of a change does not result in an IRS response, in most cases. The exempt organization must decide whether to instead report its changes to the Ohio Service Center with a request for determination of its impact on exempt status. Two examples of situations in which it is customary to seek overt approval from Cincinnati, and two that do not, follow:

- A private operating foundation (Chapter 14) converts itself into a standard private foundation or vice versa.
- A foundation plans to give away all, or a substantial part of, its assets and cease to exist (Chapter 13).
- A grant-making foundation that decides to add colleges to its list of educational institutions it funds may or may not be considered a new activity.
- A change in the bylaws to add name outside directors in addition to the family members is not a change the impacts tax-exempt status.

Q 10:18 When would a private foundation file an amended return?

A foundation that finds it has incorrectly reported its income and expenses subject to the investment income tax and/or its expenditures reported as qualifying charitable payments might choose to file an amended return to reflect the accurate amounts. The choice depends on the materiality, or the magnitude, of the mistake. If the foundation has underpaid its tax, interest would be due on the unpaid balance for the period between the normal and the delayed payment date. Say a foundation finds it failed to report $5,000 of bond interest (or overstated an expense) so that an additional tax on the underreported amount of $100 is due. Simply adding the underreported amount to the succeeding year in which the mistake is discovered and paying the tax might be acceptable. If, instead, the understatement of tax was more a much greater amount, the foundation might amend its return. The decision has to be made based on the facts of each situation in view of the potential interest due on the amount.

A mistake in reporting charitable disbursements or in valuing charitable assets impacts the foundation's satisfaction of the mandatory payout rules. Again the correction method depends on the magnitude of the mistake. The law forgives any penalties for under distribution due to the asset valuation or other unintentional mistakes. It is almost impossible for a foundation to precisely meet its distribution amount each year, so usually there is some excess carried over each year (Q 4:19–4:21). It is, therefore, acceptable to report a correction as an adjustment to the excess distribution carryover if the amount is relatively insignificant and did not cause a failure to meet the payout requirement. If the mistake did cause a failure, the foundation is expected to file Form 4720 to report the error (Q 10:19).

Q 10:19 How does a private foundation report a violation of the rules?

Very importantly, a foundation that discovers it has violated one of these rules should voluntarily report the facts and circumstances involved to the IRS.

The foundation each year must answer a pageful of questions in Part VII-B to say if it has committed any sins. The law provides abatement provisions that allow forgiveness by the IRS of all of the penalties except for those pertaining to self-dealing. A foundation that inadvertently commits an impermissible act can escape penalties, if it corrects the problem itself. If any of the answers to the questions in Part VII-B reveal a violation, the foundation is directed to file Form 4720 to report the problem. The nature of the problem and the reasons the foundation should not be penalized (assuming they can be mustered) are reported on Form 4720.

CHAPTER 11

Disclosure and Substantiation Rules

Private foundations—like most charitable and other tax-exempt organizations—are subject to a host of rules by which they must disclose information about their governance and program operations. Charitable giving to them also can trigger disclosure requirements.

Some of these rules infrequently apply in the private foundation context. These are rules that are implicated when fund-raising ensues—and private foundations do not normally engage in fund-raising. Still, even the infrequent gift requires disclosure. Other rules, pertaining to disclosure of important tax documents, apply extensively. This latter body of law includes rules that are quite new, having taken effect in early 2000.

Here are the questions that are often asked (or that should be asked) about the disclosure and substantiation rules as they apply with respect to private foundations—and the answers to them.

Q 11:1 Are there any fund-raising disclosure rules for private foundations?

There are no rules applicable to private foundations requiring disclosure of fund-raising activities as such. Private foundations, of course, rarely engage in fund-raising in any event. A foundation that undertook substantial and ongoing fund-raising probably would no longer be a private foundation but would evolve into a donative-type publicly supported charity (Q 12:4).

There are fund-raising disclosure rules for many types of tax-exempt organizations.[1] These rules are not applicable to charitable organizations, however, and thus are not applicable to private foundations.

Also, there are fund-raising disclosure rules for charitable organizations, in the form of the substantiation and quid pro quo contribution rules (Q 11:5, 11:14). Further, there are rules pertaining to the offering of certain information or services (Q 11:2).

Q 11:2   What are the rules regarding the offering of information or services?

A tax-exempt organization must, under certain circumstances, disclose that information or services that it is offering is available without charge from the federal government.[2] While this rule is technically applicable to private foundations, it is rare that a foundation offers this type of information or services of this nature to the general public.

This rule requires a tax-exempt organization to, when it offers to sell (or solicits money for) specific information or a routine service for any individual that could be readily obtained by the individual without charge (or for a nominal charge) from an agency of the federal government, make an express statement, in a conspicuous and easily recognizable format, that the information can be so obtained.

This requirement is applicable only if the information to be provided involves the specific individual solicited. Thus, for example, the law applies with respect to obtaining the Social Security earnings record or the Social Security identification number of an individual solicited. The requirement is inapplicable with respect to the furnishing of copies of newsletters issued by federal agencies or providing copies of or descriptive material on pending legislation.

Also, this requirement is inapplicable to the provision of professional services, such as tax return preparation, grant application preparation, or medical services, as opposed to routine information retrieval services, to an individual even if they may be available from the federal government without charge or at a nominal charge.[3]

Q 11:3   What are the penalties for violation of these rules?

There is a monetary penalty, which is applicable for each day on which the failure occurred. The penalty is the greater of $1,000 or 50 percent of the offers and solicitations that occurred on any day on which the failure occurred and with respect to which there was this type of failure.[4]

Q 11:4   What does it mean to *substantiate* a charitable contribution?

The essence of the substantiation requirements—which are a matter of federal tax law—is that there is no federal income tax charitable contribution deduction for any charitable gift of $250 or more, unless the donor has a contemporaneous written acknowledgment—*substantiation*—of the contribution from the donee charitable organization.[5] These rules were written as a principal means of preventing individuals from claiming tax deductions in situations where gifts were not in fact made—either because there was not a transaction at all (cheating) or because the payment was not a gift (perhaps a misunderstanding of the law). Thus, the focus here is on gifts to public charities. Nonetheless, gifts to private foundations are not accorded any preference and thus are subject to this substantiation requirement.

Q 11:5   What are the federal income tax charitable gift substantiation rules?

An *acknowledgment* of this type must include the following information:

- The amount of money (if any) contributed.
- A description (but not the value) of any property, other than money, contributed.

> **NOTE:**   Thus, the donee charitable organization is not required to value the property for the donor—and should not do so. Valuation of the donated property is the responsibility of the donor. The donee organization, however, has to place a value on the contributed property for purposes of its financial records.

- Whether the charity provided any goods or services to the donor in exchange, in whole or in part, for the contribution.
- A description and good-faith estimate of the value of any goods or services provided in exchange for the gift.

> **NOTE:**   It is unlikely, in the private foundation setting, that a foundation would provide a good or a service to a donor. Moreover, if the donor is a disqualified person (Chapter 2), the provision of a good or service may constitute an act of self-dealing (Chapter 3).

> **CAUTION:**   If goods or services are not provided, the substantiation document must state that fact.

- If the goods or services consist solely of intangible religious benefits, a statement to that effect.[6]

> **NOTE:**   The term *intangible religious benefit* means any intangible religious benefit that is provided by an organization organized exclusively for religious purposes and that generally is not sold in a commercial transaction outside the donative context.[7]

A charitable organization that knowingly provides false written substantiation to a donor may be subject to the penalties for aiding and abetting an understatement of tax liability.[8]

It is obvious, then, that this substantiation requirement is applicable with respect to just about every gift—most likely, *every* gift—received by a private foundation.

Q 11:6   What is a *separate contribution*?

Separate gifts to a charitable organization are regarded as independent contributions and are not aggregated for purposes of measuring the $250 threshold. Donations made through payroll deductions are considered separate payments from each paycheck.[9]

The IRS is authorized to establish antiabuse rules to prevent avoidance of the substantiation requirements—for example, by writing separate small checks to the same charitable organization on the same date. The IRS has not, however, promulgated rules of this nature.

Q 11:7   Must the written acknowledgment be in a particular form?

No, the law does not mandate any particular form for the written acknowledgment. Most charitable organizations want to tastefully thank their donors in any event and thus incorporate the substantiation elements into a thank-you letter. Any other form of a writing will serve, however, such as a card or computerized printout.

Q 11:8   What does the word *contemporaneous* mean?

For the substantiation to be *contemporaneous,* it must be obtained no later than the date the donor files a tax return for the year in which the contribution was made. If the return is filed after the due date or on an extended due date, the substantiation must have been obtained by the due date or extended due date.[10]

Q 11:9   What does the phrase *goods or services* mean?

The phrase *goods or services,* at least in this context, means money, property, services, benefits, and/or privileges.[11]

Q 11:10   What does the phrase *in consideration for* mean?

The concept of *consideration* is taken from the law of contracts. A contract, to be valid (i.e., enforceable), must provide consideration to the parties to the agreement. *Consideration* is what each party receives as a consequence of participating in the agreement; the various forms of consideration provided have to be of approximate equal value for the requisite bargain to be present.

If a person makes a payment of money or a transfer of property to a charitable organization and receives goods or services in exchange, that payment or transfer is not a gift.[12] It is a payment made pursuant to a contractual relationship. Examples would be payment of tuition to a school or for healthcare services to a hospital. The substantiation rules are designed in part to ferret out transactions of this nature, to preclude persons from claiming charitable deductions for transfers to charity that are not gifts.

NOTE: If the goods or services provided have a value that is less than that of the money or property transferred, the difference can be regarded as a charitable gift (Q 11:14).

The substantiation rules thus apply to payments made in consideration for some benefit provided by the charitable organization involved. They are applicable where a good or service is provided *in consideration for* (i.e., in exchange for) a payment or transfer to a charity. The principle is that the "donor" expects the good or service to be provided at the time the payment or transfer is made.

This leads to a difficult point, concerning benefits provided to donors after the gifts were made, where there was no prior notification of the benefit, such as a recognition dinner. This type of an after-the-fact benefit generally does not need to be taken into account in determining the amount (if any) of the charitable deduction.

CAUTION: Some reality may have to be injected here. If the charitable organization always provides a recognition dinner for certain donors, at some point, an "expectation" can be presumed, even when there is no express promise of it at the time of the gift. Lines of demarcation in this area will be drawn on the basis of facts and circumstances.

Q 11:11   What is a *good-faith estimate*?

The statute embodying the substantiation rules does not define the phrase *good-faith estimate*. The accompanying regulations are not of much help on the point. There the phrase is said to mean the charitable organization's "estimate of the fair market value of any goods or services, without regard to the manner in which the organization in fact made that estimate."[13]

NOTE: This definition does not contain the requirement that the estimate be made in good faith.

Whatever the phrase means, it is something less than a formal appraisal of the value of the property.

Q 11:12 How do these rules apply to planned gifts?

The substantiation rules do not apply to gifts to charity made by means of charitable remainder trusts (Q 17:28) and charitable lead trusts (Q 17:32).[14] This is because donors to these trusts are not required to designate a specific charitable organization as the beneficiary at the time money or property is transferred to the trust. Thus, there may not be a charitable organization available to provide the requisite written acknowledgment. Also, even where a specific charitable beneficiary is designated, the designation often is revocable. By contrast, the law requires that one or more charitable organizations must maintain a pooled income fund (Q 17:31), so contributions made by means of these vehicles must be substantiated.

Q 11:13 What is the sanction for noncompliance with the substantiation rules?

If the substantiation rules are not timely complied with (Q 11:8), the sanction is that the donor is not entitled to the federal income tax charitable contribution deduction that would otherwise be available.[15]

COMMENT: At a hearing in 1995, the House Ways and Means Committee considered a proposal to repeal these gift substantiation rules. The Department of the Treasury expressed its opposition to the proposal on two grounds: The rules are intended to "stop known abuse" of the charitable deduction by those who seek to deduct payments to charity that are actually not contributions and (2) the requirements provide the IRS with an "effective mechanism" for verifying that a payment to a charitable organization "genuinely" represents a charitable contribution. The Ways and Means Committee promptly abandoned any serious idea of repealing these rules.

NOTE: A marvelous illustration as to how these rules can work was provided in the case of an individual who, when audited by the IRS, was able to produce canceled checks showing that he had indeed made payments of $500 to $1,000 weekly to his church—just as he had claimed on his tax returns. That might have been sufficient for this "donor" to prevail. But the agent decided to check with the minister to verify that the money actually had been transferred to the church. In fact, it had—but the minister added a critical item of information: The "donor" was a "coin collector who bought the change that worshippers dropped in the collection plate each week."[16]

Q 11:14 What is a *quid pro quo contribution*?

A *quid pro quo contribution* is a payment made partly as a contribution to a charitable organization and partly for goods or services (Q 11:9) provided to the donor by the charitable organization.[17]

Q 11:15 What is the consequence of a quid pro quo contribution?

If the quid pro quo contribution is in excess of $75, the charitable organization involved must provide a written disclosure statement to the donor. This statement must inform the donor that the amount of the contribution that is deductible for federal income tax purposes is limited to the excess of any money, or the excess of the value of any property, the donor transferred to the charity over the value of the goods or services provided by the charity.[18] The disclosure must provide the donor with a good-faith estimate (Q 11:16) of the value of the goods or services the donor received.

The charitable organization must furnish the statement in connection with either the solicitation or the receipt of the quid pro quo contribution. The disclosure must, as noted, be in writing and presented in a manner that is reasonably likely to come to the attention of the donor. A disclosure in small print within a larger document may not satisfy this requirement.

Q 11:16 What is a *good-faith estimate*?

Again (Q 11:11), the statute does not define the phrase *good-faith estimate* in this context. The tax regulations state that a good-faith estimate of the value of goods or services (Q 11:9) provided by a charitable organization is an estimate of the fair market value of the goods or services. These regulations add that an organization can use a reasonable methodology in making a good-faith estimate—as long as it applies the methodology in good faith.[19]

Q 11:17 Are there any exceptions to these rules?

Yes. There are seven exceptions. The first three apply where the only goods or services provided to a donor are those having an incidental value. The exceptions are:

1. Where the fair market value of all the benefits received is not more than 2 percent of the contributions or $50, whichever is less.[20]

   NOTE: This $50 threshold is indexed for inflation. For 2001, the amount is $76.
   ---

2. Where the contribution is $25 or more and the only benefits received by the donor in return during the calendar year have a cost, in the

aggregate, of no more than that of a low-cost article.[21] A *low-cost article* is one that does not cost more than $5 to the organization that distributes it or on whose behalf it is distributed.[22]

NOTE: The $25 contribution threshold, indexed for inflation, is $38 for 2001. The cost of a low-cost article, also adjusted for inflation, is $7.60 for 2001.

---

3. Where, in connection with a request for a charitable contribution, the charity mails, or otherwise distributes free, unordered items to patrons, and the cost of the items (in the aggregate) distributed to any single patron in a calendar year is not more than a low-cost article.
4. Where no donative element is involved in the transaction with the charitable organization. Illustrations of this are payments of tuition to a school, payments for healthcare services to a hospital, and the purchase of an item from a museum gift shop.
5. Where an *intangible religious benefit* is involved (Q 11:5).[23] For this exception to be available, the benefit must be provided by an organization exclusively for religious purposes and must be of a type that generally is not sold in a commercial transaction outside the donative context. An example of a religious benefit is admission to a religious ceremony. This exception also generally applies to *de minimis* tangible benefits, such as wine provided in connection with a religious ceremony. This intangible religious benefit exception does not apply to items such as payments for tuition for education leading to a recognized degree, travel services, or consumer goods.
6. Annual membership benefits offered for no more than $75 per year that consist of rights or privileges that the individual can exercise frequently during the membership period.[24] These benefits include free admission to the organization's events, free parking, and discounts on the purchase of goods.
7. Annual membership benefits offered for no more than $75 per year that consist of admission to events during the membership period that are open only to members of the charitable organization and for which the organization reasonably projects that the cost per person (excluding any overhead) for each event is within the limits established for low-cost articles.[25]

Q 11:18 How does a charitable organization value the participation of a celebrity for purposes of the quid pro quo contribution rules?

If the celebrity performs at the event, employing the talent for which he or she is celebrated (e.g., singing or stand-up comedy), the fair market value of the performance should be determined in calculating any benefit and thus any charitable deduction. If the celebrity does nothing or something else (for which he or she is not celebrated), his or her presence can be disregarded.

For example, in the case of a tour of a museum guided by an artist whose paintings are featured there, the value of the tour can be ignored, inasmuch as the artist's fame derives from being a painter, not a tour guide.[26]

Q 11:19 What is the sanction for violation of these rules?

A penalty can be imposed on a charitable organization that does not meet these disclosure requirements.[27] For failure to make the required disclosure in connection with a quid pro quo contribution of more than $75, there is a penalty of $10 per contribution, not to exceed $5,000 per fund-raising event or mailing. A organization may be able to avoid this penalty if it can show that the failure to comply was due to reasonable cause.

Q 11:20 It was mentioned earlier that the annual information returns are public documents. What does that mean?

For years, private foundations have been under a disclosure regime that was different from that applicable to all other types of tax-exempt organizations. Essentially, this entailed publication of a notice in a newspaper of general circulation that its most recent annual information return was available for public inspection for a 180-day period.[28]

As of March 13, 2000, however, that disclosure requirement was radically revised. As of that date, the disclosure rules for private foundations were basically made the same as is the case with respect to other tax-exempt organizations.

Q 11:21 How did this law change come about?

For years, tax-exempt organizations, other than private foundations, have been required to make their annual information returns and applications for recognition of tax exemption available for public inspection. As to annual information returns, a tax-exempt organization is required to make a copy of each return available for inspection during regular business hours by any individual at its principal office for three years. Similar rules apply with respect to public inspection of copies of applications for recognition of exemption, along with supporting documents and IRS communications.[29]

Congress decided to augment this disclosure regime significantly. Thus, the Taxpayer Bill of Rights 2, which was signed into law on July 30, 1996, brought a document dissemination requirement.[30] Essentially, this requirement obligates an organization to, upon request of an individual in person or in writing, provide copies of the most recent three annual information returns and the application for recognition of exemption. The effective date of this body of law was, however, postponed until 60 days after the accompanying regulations were issued in final form. The regulations were issued in proposed form on September 25, 1997,[31] and were issued in final form on April 9, 1999,[32] with an effective date of June 8, 1999.

Congress surprised the private foundation community by, as part of legislation enacted in 1998, extending to private foundations the same rules regarding public dissemination of documents that apply to other tax-exempt organizations. The accompanying tax regulations were issued in proposed form on August 10, 1999,[33] and were issued in final form on January 12, 2000,[34] with an effective date of March 13, 2000.

Q 11:22 What are the document dissemination rules?

The general rules, coupled with the rules described above, are that a private foundation, like nearly every other tax-exempt organization, must, as of the effective date of the law (Q 11:21), do the following:

- Make its application for recognition of tax exemption available for public inspection without charge at its principal, regional, and district offices during regular business hours (Q 11:21).
- Make its annual information returns available for public inspection without charge in the same offices during regular business hours. Each return must be made available for a period of three years, beginning on the date the return is required to be filed or is actually filed, whichever is later.
- Provide a copy without charge, other than a reasonable fee for reproduction and actual postage costs, of all or any part of any application or return required to be made available for public inspection to any individual who makes a request for the copy in person or in writing.

An *application for recognition of exemption* includes Form 1023 (Chapter 16) and supporting documents. The term does not include an application filed before July 15, 1987, unless the organization that filed it had a copy of it on that date. The *annual information return* includes Form 990-PF.[35]

COMMENT: The regulations employ the term *application for exemption.* The correct term is *application for recognition of exemption.* There is considerable significance to the distinction between the two terms.

This is a slight aspect of these regulations that one in a peevish mood might find annoying. This is based on the not unreasonable expectation that a government agency will make accurate reference, in its regulations, to a form over which it has administrative responsibility.

Despite the reference in these regulations, the term is not *application for tax exemption.*[36]

If one's peevish mood persisted, one could get worked up to the point of believing that this is a deliberate attempt on the part of the IRS to perpetuate the myth that it has the power to grant tax-exempt status, when it fact its authority is confined to granting *recognition of* tax-exempt status.

Generally, a private foundation must provide copies of the documents, in response to an in-person request, at its principal, regional, and district offices during regular business hours. Also generally, the foundation must provide the copies to a requestor on the day the request is made.

In the case of an in-person request, where unusual circumstances exist so that fulfillment of the request on the same business day places an unreasonable burden on the exempt organization, the copies must be provided on the next business day following the day on which the unusual circumstances cease to exist or the fifth business day after the date of the request, whichever occurs first. *Unusual circumstances* include receipt of a volume of requests that exceeds the foundation's daily capacity to make copies, requests received shortly before the end of regular business hours that require an extensive amount of copying, and requests received on a day when the foundation's managerial staff capable of fulfilling the request is conducting special duties. *Special duties* are activities such as student registration or attendance at an off-site meeting or convention, rather than regular administrative duties.

If a request for a document is made in writing, the private foundation must honor it if the request

- Is addressed to, and delivered by mail, electronic mail, facsimile, or a private delivery service to a principal, regional, or district office of the foundation, and
- Sets forth the address to which the copy of the document should be sent.

A private foundation receiving a written request for a copy must mail it within 30 days from the date it receives the request. If, however, a foundation requires payment in advance, it is only required to provide the copy within 30 days from the date it receives payment. A foundation must fulfill a request for a copy of the organization's entire application or annual information return or any specific part or schedule of its application or return.

Q 11:23 Is a private foundation required to disclose the names and addresses of its donors?

Yes. A list of the names and addresses of those who make contributions to a private foundation must be attached to the annual information return for the year of the gifts (Q 10:3). This list must be among the material that is to be disseminated upon request.[37]

NOTE: All other charitable organizations are not required to disclose the names and addresses of their donors to the public.

Q 11:24 May a private foundation charge a fee for providing copies of these documents?

A private foundation may charge a reasonable fee for providing copies of these documents. A fee is *reasonable* if it is no more than the per-page copying fee charged by the IRS for providing copies. It also can include actual postage costs. The requestor may be required to pay the fee in advance.[38]

Q 11:25 What happens if a private foundation fails to comply with these rules?

If a private foundation denies an individual's request for inspection or a copy of an application or return, and the individual wishes to complain about that to the IRS, he or she may send a statement to the appropriate IRS district office, describing the reason why the individual believes the denial was in violation of these requirements.[39]

NOTE: The term *complain* is not in the regulations. There, reference is made to an individual who wants to "alert" the IRS "to the possible need for enforcement action."

The penalties for failure to comply with these rules equal $20–$100 each day up to a maximum of $10,000–$50,000.[40]

Q 11:26 Are there exceptions to this dissemination requirement?

Yes. A private foundation is not required to comply with requests for copies of its application for recognition of tax exemption or an annual information return if the organization has made the document widely available.[41]

NOTE: The rules as to public inspection of the documents (Q 11:22) nonetheless continue to apply.

Q 11:27 What does the term *widely available* mean?

A private foundation can make its application for recognition of tax exemption or an annual information return *widely available* by posting the document on a World Wide Web page that the foundation establishes and maintains. It also can satisfy the exception if the document is posted as part of a database of similar documents of other exempt organizations on a World Wide Web page established and maintained by another entity.

The document is considered widely available only if

- The World Wide Web page through which it is available clearly informs readers that the document is available and provides instructions for downloading it,
- The document is posted in a format that, when accessed, downloaded, viewed, and printed in hard copy, exactly reproduces the image of the application or return as it was originally filed with the IRS, except for any information permitted by statute, and
- Any individual with access to the Internet can access, download, view, and print the document without special computer hardware or software required for that format, and can do so without payment of a fee to the foundation or to another entity maintaining the World Wide Web page.[42]

The organization maintaining the World Wide Web page must have procedures for ensuring the reliability and accuracy of the document that it posts on the page. It must take reasonable precautions to prevent alteration, destruction, or accidental loss of the document when printed on its page. In the event a posted document is altered, destroyed, or lost, the organization must correct or replace the document.

Q 11:28 What does the term *harassment campaign* mean?

If the IRS determines that a private foundation (or other tax-exempt organization) is the subject of a harassment campaign and compliance with the requests that are part of the campaign would not be in the public interest, the organization is not required to fulfill a request for a copy that it reasonably believes is part of the campaign.[43]

A group of requests for an organization's application or returns is indicative of a *harassment campaign* if the requests are part of a single coordinated effort to disrupt the operations of the organization rather than to collect information about the organization. This is a facts-and-circumstances test; factors include:

- A sudden increase in the number of requests
- An extraordinary number of requests made by means of form letters or similarly worded correspondence
- Evidence of a purpose to deter significantly the organization's employees or volunteers from pursuing the organization's exempt purpose
- Requests that contain language hostile to the organization
- Direct evidence of bad faith by organizers of the purported harassment campaign
- Evidence that the organization has already provided the requested documents to a member of the purported harassment group

- Demonstration by the private foundation that it routinely provides copies of its documents upon request.[44]

A private foundation may disregard any request for copies of all or part of any document beyond the first two received within any 30-day period or the first four received within any one-year period from the same individual or the same address, irrespective of whether the IRS has determined that the organization is subject to a harassment campaign.[45]

The regulations stipulate the procedure to follow for applying to the IRS for a determination that the organization is the subject of a harassment campaign.[46] (There is no form.)

NOTE: This is a matter of compliance between the private foundation and the IRS. That is, an individual requestor lacks the requisite authority to sue a private foundation that refuses to provide the requested documents.[47]

The organization may suspend compliance with respect to the request, as long as the application is filed within 30 days after harassment is suspected, until the organization receives a response from the IRS.[48]

CHAPTER 12

Public Charities

The federal tax law places charitable organizations into one of two categories: public and private. The latter are termed *private foundations* (Q 1:1). Although the law presumes that all charitable organizations are private foundations,[1] nearly all charities are public charities. The law provides for three basic classifications of public charities; there are, however, many types within each classification. Because the body of federal tax law concerning private foundations is so onerous, it is important for a charitable organization to achieve public charity status if it can.

Here are the questions that are most frequently asked (or that should be asked) about the difference between public charities and private foundations, how to acquire and maintain public charity status, and the oft-maligned supporting organization—and the answers to them.

Q 12:1   What are the categories of public charities?

Basically, there are three categories of public charities (Q 1:2): institutions (Q 12:2), publicly supported organizations (Q 12:3), and supporting organizations (Q 12:15).

Q 12:2   What is an *institution*?

Institutions are charitable organizations that are clearly not private foundations, simply by virtue of their programs and structure.[2] These entities are churches, associations and conventions of churches, integrated auxiliaries of churches, colleges, universities, schools, hospitals, certain other healthcare providers, medical research organizations, certain supporting foundations for governmental colleges and universities, and a variety of governmental units.

Q 12:3   What is a *publicly supported organization*?

Basically, a publicly supported organization is a charitable entity that receives, on a continuous basis, a broad base of financial support (often contributions and grants) from the general public. Because of the nature of their funding, publicly supported charities generally are the antithesis of private foundations (Q 1:1).

Fundamentally, there are two types of publicly supported charities. One is the donative publicly supported charitable organization (Q 12:4). The other is the service provider publicly supported charitable organization (Q 12:5).

Q 12:4   What is a *donative publicly supported charitable organization*?

A *donative publicly supported charitable organization* is an organization that receives a substantial amount of its support in the form of direct or indirect gifts and grants from the general public or from the U.S. government, a state, or a political subdivision.[3] In this setting, *substantial* generally means at least one-third.[4] The denominator of this support ratio includes investment income; fee-for-service revenue (Q 12:5) is not included in either the numerator or denominator. These calculations are made on the basis of a four-year moving average. (Generally, the source(s) of the balance of the financial support received by this type of organization is irrelevant to the concept of public support.)

NOTE: The tax regulations state that types of organizations that generally qualify for this classification of publicly supported charities are (not "include") "publicly or governmentally supported museums of history, art, or science, libraries, community centers to promote the arts, organizations providing facilities for the support of an opera, symphony orchestra, ballet, or repertory drama, or for some other direct service to the general public, and organizations such as the American Red Cross or the United Givers Fund."[5] In fact, however, the types of entities that qualify as donative publicly supported charities is much broader.

Support (Q 12:6) from any one source is public support to the extent that the amount does not exceed an amount equal to 2 percent of the support fraction denominator. For example, if an organization received $400,000 over its most recent four years, its public support would be the contributed or granted amounts that did not exceed $8,000 per source (.02 × $400,000). If the organization is able to show that at least $133,334 of the $400,000 came from public support, it can be considered a donative publicly supported organization

---

CAUTION: If an organization receives a substantial part of its support in the form of fee-for-service revenue, however, it cannot qualify as a donative publicly supported organization, even if it meets the support test for the small amount of contributions it receives.[6]

---

for the two years immediately succeeding the four measuring years.[7] Unusual grants (Q 12:7) are excluded from the computation.

Some additional rules apply to the computation of support for donative publicly supported organizations:

- Grants from other donative publicly supported organizations and from governmental units constitute public support in full (i.e., they are not limited by the 2 percent rule).[8]
- Gifts and grants that exceed the 2 percent limitation constitute public support to the extent of the 2 percent limitation amount.[9]
- There are attribution rules in determining sources of support (e.g., gifts from a husband and wife are considered as derived from one source).[10]

To illustrate the second of these rules, if the organization in the above example received a $10,000 contribution from one source, $8,000 of it would be public support. The full $10,000 would be part of the denominator of the support fraction denominator.

Two other categories of donative publicly supported organizations are recognized in the law: those that are public charities by virtue of the *facts and circumstances test* (Q 12:5) and community foundations.[11] A community foundation is a charitable organization that receives funding from and makes grants within a discrete community.

Q 12:5   What is the *facts and circumstances test*?

A charitable organization, to satisfy the facts and circumstances test, must have at least 10 percent of public support and have characteristics that demonstrate public interaction with the organization.[12] Factors that are taken into account in this regard include the following:

- The organization is attracting new and additional public support on a continuous basis.
- The extent to which the public support ratio is greater than the 10 percent threshold.
- The extent of public support.
- Whether the organization provides facilities or services for the benefit of the general public on a continuing basis.
- Public involvement in the programs.
- A board of directors reflective of the community.

NOTE: The facts and circumstances test is an underutilized aspect of the law of tax-exempt organizations. Many practitioners seem unaware of its existence. Thus, the test is often overlooked as a basis for public charity status. To its credit, the IRS has been fair and generous in recognizing the ability of organizations to qualify under this test. An organization can either seek a ruling on the point or attach a statement, claiming this status, on its annual information return.

Q 12:6   What types of financial support qualifies as *support*?

As noted (Q 12:4), fee-for-service revenue (Q 12:8) does not constitute public support in this context.[13] Thus, public support for a donative publicly supported charitable organization generally is in the form of gifts and grants.

There can be controversy in this setting. For example, *support* for these purposes includes funding from a governmental unit. In fact, however, not all support from a governmental unit is public support in this context. To so qualify, the amount must be in the nature of a *grant*. This means that the purpose of the payment is primarily to enable the organization to provide a service to or maintain a facility for the direct benefit of the public. If the payment is made to serve the direct and immediate needs of the payor, it is not a grant; the funds involved are fee-for-service revenue.[14]

NOTE: Confusion can abound here. Often the distinction is said to be between a *grant* and a *contract*. It is true that an amount paid pursuant to a contract is more likely to be considered fee-for-service revenue. At the same time, however, the name placed by the parties on the document is not determinative of the nature of the underlying funding for this purpose. A payment can still be a grant, even though the document involved is termed a contract (as can happen, e.g., with a government research grant).

Another example of this dichotomy is the matter of *membership fees*. Generally, membership fees are dues, that is, funds paid to purchase services or admission to facilities. Dues of this nature are fee-for-service revenue (or exempt function revenue) and thus not public support. If, however, the payments are basically for the general support of the organization, they are forms of public support for donative publicly supported organizations.[15]

Q 12:7   What is an *unusual grant*?

The answer does not lie in the nomenclature: These payments should be termed *unexpected grants*. For that matter, the payments are not always grants—they can be gifts. An unusual grant essentially is a grant (or gift) that has these characteristics:

- The amount involved, such as a contribution or bequest, is substantial.
- The payment came from a disinterested party.
- The amount was attracted by reason of the publicly supported nature of the organization.
- The grant, gift, or the like was "unusual or unexpected" with respect to the amount involved.
- The amount would, by reason of its size, adversely affect the status of the organization as being publicly supported.[16]

CAUTION: An item of gross investment income cannot be excluded from the public support ratio as an unusual grant.

A number of facts and circumstances are taken into account in determining whether a contribution or grant is an *unusual grant*. These include:

- Whether the contribution was made by any person who created the organization, previously contributed a substantial amount, or stood in a position of authority with respect to the organization. A contribution by someone else is given more favorable consideration.
- Whether the contribution was a bequest or inter vivos transfer. Bequests are given more favorable consideration.
- Whether the contribution was in the form of cash, readily marketable securities, or exempt function assets.
- Whether the organization has exempt function programs and a public solicitation effort, and has been able to attract a significant amount of public support.
- Whether the organization may reasonably be expected to attract a significant amount of public support after the particular contribution. Ongoing reliance on unusual grants is not favored.
- Whether, before the contribution was received, the organization met the general one-third public support test (Q 12:4).
- Whether the contributor or a person related to the contributor continues, directly or indirectly, to exercise control over the organization.
- Whether the organization has a representative governing body.
- Whether any material restrictions or conditions (Q 15:18) have been imposed by the transferor in connection with the transfer.[17]

NOTE: No single factor is necessarily determinative as to whether a payment is an unusual grant.

Q 12:8   What is a *service provider publicly supported charitable organization*?

A *service provider publicly supported organization* is the other basic type of publicly supported charity.[18] This type of organization normally receives at least one-third of its support in the form of gifts, grants, and exempt function revenue from the general public. The ratio calculation is made on the basis of a four-year moving average. The denominator of the ratio consists of the various forms of public support, plus net unrelated business income, investment income, tax revenues levied for the benefit of the organization, and the value of certain services or facilities furnished by a governmental unit.[19] Gift and grant support from any one source is public support to the extent that the amount derived did not come from a *disqualified person* (Chapter 2). Unusual grants (Q 12:7) are excluded from the computation.[20]

The term *disqualified person* includes an organization's directors, trustees, officers, key employees having responsibilities similar to those of officers, substantial contributors, family members of these individuals, and certain entities related to or affiliated with these persons (Q 2:1). A *substantial contributor* is a person who contributed or granted more than $5,000 to the charitable organization, where that amount was more than 2 percent of the gifts and grants to the organization during the period of its existence (Q 2:2). In almost all cases, once a person is classified as a substantial contributor, that classification remains irrespective of the growth of the charity (Q 2:3).

Public support can include *exempt function revenue* (or fee-for-service revenue).[21] This is revenue in the form of gross receipts from admissions, sales of merchandise, performance of services, or furnishing of facilities, in an activity that is not an unrelated business. Revenue of this nature, however, is not public support to the extent that the receipts from any person or from any bureau or similar agency of a governmental unit in any tax year exceed the greater of $5,000 or 1 percent of the organization's support in that year.[22] Also, this type of support from disqualified persons is not public support.[23]

Using the figures of the above example (Q 12:4), an organization attempting to qualify as a service provider publicly supported charity also would have to receive at least $133,334 in public support during the four-year measuring period. This support could be in the form of gifts, grants, and/or exempt function revenue. None of this support, however, could be from substantial contributors, board members, or other disqualified persons.

A service provider publicly supported organization cannot normally receive more than one-third of its support from gross investment income.[24]

CAUTION: A service provider publicly supported organization that utilizes a supporting organization (Q 12:15) must be cautious: Funds transferred from the supporting organization may, in whole or in part, retain their character as investment income for this purpose.[25]

Q 12:9   What is an *advance ruling*?

An *advance ruling* is a ruling issued by the IRS to a new charitable organization that is expecting to qualify as a publicly supported organization (in either category, donative (Q 12:4) or service provider (Q 12:8)). This ruling is part of the basic ruling recognizing tax-exempt status and charitable donee status (Q 16:4). Being new, the organization does not, of course, have a financial history on which to base a determination as to whether it is publicly supported. Consequently, the IRS makes this initial determination of the organization's publicly supported charity status on the basis of a budget provided by the organization; where that information appears credible, the IRS will rule that the organization is reasonably expected to constitute a publicly supported organization. The term *advance* is used because the ruling is issued before actual development of the necessary financial data that will indicate whether the organization is in fact publicly supported. In this sense, the ruling is a probationary or tentative ruling as to publicly supported charity status.

NOTE 1:   The IRS does not look behind the financial information provided in the context of a request for an advance ruling. The budget figures are (in the authors' experience) always accepted. What would happen, however, if the numbers submitted turned out to be willfully false? Charges of perjury and fraud, presumably.

NOTE 2:   The concept of an advance ruling does not apply with respect to recognition of tax exemption or charitable donee status. Advance rulings are issued to both putative donative publicly supported organizations and service provider publicly supported organizations.

If a new charitable organization wishes to be regarded by the IRS as a publicly supported charity, it must receive an advance ruling, where it is in existence for only one year. (That *year* must be less than eight months.[26]) Where the organization has a financial history that is longer, it is entitled to, but need not pursue, a definitive ruling (Q 12:11).

TIP: This area of the law can be confusing, because of its source. The IRS does not follow the existing regulations on the subject. Instead, it uses different rules that can be found only in the instructions accompanying the application for recognition of tax exemption.

The period of time the advance ruling is in effect is the *advance ruling period*—the organization's first five years.

NOTE: This use of the term *year* can be tricky. For purposes of being able to gain a definitive ruling with only one year of existence, the *year* must, as noted, be a period of at least eight months. When *measuring* an entity's advance ruling period, however, as noted, the first year can be a period of any length—months, weeks, or some number of days. This may mitigate against forming, late in a year, a charitable entity that is intended to be publicly supported.

Once the advance ruling period has expired (at the close of the appropriate year) and if the organization has satisfied one of the public support tests, the advance ruling will ripen into a definitive ruling. The organization is expected to apply for a definitive ruling within 90 days after the close of the advance ruling period. The requisite financial information should be provided on IRS Form 8734.

NOTE: This form has deficiencies. One or more separate schedules may have to be attached, to reflect computations such as the reporting of funding that is not, in the case of donative publicly supported organizations, limited by the 2 percent threshold (Q 12:4) and exempt function revenue that is, in the case of service provider publicly supported organizations, limited by the 1 percent threshold (Q 12:8). Worse, the form makes no provision for the reporting of the public support ratio. Thus, this should be done in a letter of transmittal.

Q 12:10 At the end of the advance ruling period, will the IRS automatically request information regarding the organization's public support, or does the organization need to initiate contact with the IRS?

The responsibility to apply to the IRS for a definitive ruling within 90 days following the close of the advance ruling period (Q 12:9) lies with the organization. The IRS will not initiate contact with the charitable organization on this point at this time, beyond sometimes sending a copy of the requisite form. Although it is not specifically required, the IRS prefers that the necessary information be tendered on that form.

Once the information is submitted, it is rare for the IRS to request additional information. That is, the IRS will normally accept the public support information on its face. If the information reflects sufficient public support, the IRS will issue a definitive ruling (Q 12:11). If the information shows that the organization did not receive adequate public support during the advance ruling period, the IRS—without inquiry—will (or, at any rate, should) classify the organization as a private foundation. This is because the organization has failed to rebut the presumption that it is a private foundation.[27]

As noted (Q 12:9), it is important for an organization in this position to accompany the form with a cover letter explaining why the organization meets the public support test (assuming it does) and to include the precise public support ratio. On occasion, if an organization has not met a public support test during the advance ruling period but seems clearly on the way to doing so in the succeeding year, the IRS will issue a favorable definitive ruling.

Q 12:11 What is a *definitive ruling*?

A *definitive ruling* is a ruling issued by the IRS to a charitable organization that qualifies as a publicly supported organization. This ruling is part of the basic declaration that recognizes tax-exempt status and charitable donee status. Definitive rulings are issued to both donative publicly supported organizations (Q 12:4) and service provider publicly supported organizations (Q 12:8).

An eligible charitable organization is entitled to a definitive ruling if it has completed at least one tax year (consisting of at least eight months) and meets the requirements for one of the categories of publicly supported organization. A charitable organization, however, that has been in existence for a period of that duration and has not yet achieved the necessary level of public support to qualify as a publicly supported organization, yet expects to qualify as a publicly supported organization, can obtain an advance ruling that it is reasonably expected to be a publicly supported organization.[28]

Q 12:12 Does it matter which category of publicly supported charity an organization uses?

Once a charitable organization meets the criteria of either type of publicly supported organization (donative or service provider), the IRS generally does not care which category the organization is in at any point in time. For example, an organization may receive an advance ruling that it is a donative publicly supported organization and subsequently be able to qualify only as a service provider publicly supported organization. Or, once a definitive ruling as to one of the classifications is received, the organization may annually shift from one category of publicly supported charity to the other.

In general, it is preferable, if possible, for a charitable organization to be classified as a donative publicly supported organization (Q 12:4). Policymakers and regulators tend to look more favorably on charitable organizations that are supported primarily by gifts and grants.

NOTE: As an example, an organization was denied a state's property tax exemption solely for the reason that it received only a nominal amount of financial support in the form of contributions. The organization clearly was a charitable entity: It provides free mental health services to indigents. (An entity cannot get more charitable than that.) Tax-exempt status for this organization was restored, however, following litigation.[29]

Charitable organizations that receive significant amounts of fee-for-service revenue are far more susceptible to allegations that they are operating in a commercial manner (Q 9:11).

Whatever its actual category, a charitable organization may prefer to be regarded as a donative publicly supported organization rather than a service provider publicly supported organization. (Generally, there is no advantage to classification as a service provider publicly supported organization instead of a donative publicly supported organization.) There is one caution here: Only a donative publicly supported organization is eligible to maintain a pooled income fund (Q 17:31). This eligibility extends, however, to organizations *described in* the rules pertaining to donative publicly supported organizations.[30] If a charitable organization has received a definitive ruling that it is a service provider publicly supported organization, but it meets the support requirements for a donative publicly supported organization, it may maintain a pooled income fund.

TIP: The IRS prefers to classify publicly supported organizations as donative ones. On occasion, an organization that has applied for service provider status will find that the IRS wants to accord it donative status instead. Unless it is clear that the organization will not meet the service provider entity rules or there is a specific reason for wanting the service provider category, it is best to go along with the IRS on this point.

Q 12:13 What happens when an organization ceases to be a publicly supported charity?

If a charitable organization ceases to qualify as a publicly supported entity, the technical rule is that it automatically becomes a private foundation.[31] This can happen in one of two ways:

1. The organization may reach the end of its advance ruling period (Q 12:9) and lack the requisite public support.
2. The organization may have a definitive ruling that it has publicly supported charity status (Q 12:4, Q 12:8) but, at a point in time, fail to continue to qualify under either category of publicly supported charity.

In either circumstance, the organization will become a private foundation unless some other category of public charity status is available. One possibility is that the organization can (temporarily or otherwise) qualify as a donative publicly supported organization by reason of the facts and circumstances test (Q 12:5). Another is that the organization can find a mate and become structured as a supporting organization (Q 12:15). Still another—the least likely—is that the organization can become one of the institutions (i.e., an educational organization structured as a school) (Q 12:2).

If a charitable organization in this circumstance cannot avoid private foundation status, it is hardly the "end of the world" for the entity. It may be possible for the organization to become a hybrid entity (a blend of public charity and private foundation), usually a private operating foundation (Q 14:2) or an exempt operating foundation (Q 14:10). A charitable organization that becomes classified as a private foundation can at any time demonstrate compliance with one of the bases for public charity status, terminate its private foundation status, and proceed on a definitive ruling or advance ruling basis.

NOTE: This is a most peculiar aspect of the law and IRS enforcement of it. Untold numbers of charitable organizations routinely lose their publicly supported charity status and never report this fact to the IRS. (This puts the organization in the position of filing the wrong

---

annual information return (Chapter 10) (Form 990 instead of 990-PF) and not paying the private foundation tax on net investment income (Chapter 8).) This may entail the violation of other private foundation rules, such as failure to make the requisite payout (Chapter 4). The IRS is rather nonchalant about all this. In one instance, an organization started filing the private foundation annual return and paid the investment income tax; the IRS did not know what to do with the check because its records showed the organization to be a public charity. In another case, when an organization failed public support tests and sought another advance ruling (Q 12:9), the IRS "senior agent" did not know what to do and admitted it, writing the organization's lawyer to report that the matter "was a unique situation in that most organizations do not notify the Service when they may be considered a private foundation."

Q 12:14 What should an organization do when it realizes, during the course of its advance ruling period, that it will not qualify as a publicly supported organization as of the close of that period?

There is no law on this point. In practice, a charitable organization that has an advance ruling, and realizes along the course of its advance ruling period that it cannot qualify as a publicly supported organization, can try to utilize the facts and circumstances test (Q 12:5), convert to a supporting organization (Q 12:15), or, as a less likely choice, become an institution, such as a school (Q 12:2). If the organization qualifies for the alternative status, the IRS will issue a ruling to that effect and will not attempt to assess tax on the organization's investment income (Chapter 8) for the early years. The fact that the organization did not meet a public support test during the initial months of the advance ruling period will be ignored.

One aspect of this matter is clear: The organization should not simply allow the advance ruling period to expire in these circumstances without taking action. Occasionally, where the organization meets a public support test by taking into account the year following the advance ruling period but has not timely filed the support information (Q 12:9), the IRS will still issue a definitive ruling. But this action is wholly within the discretion of the IRS personnel, and that outcome should not be assumed.

CAUTION: A charitable organization that expects to meet a public support test as of the close of its advance ruling period, but then does not, is likely to not have the requisite private foundation provisions in its articles of organization (Q 16:19). Unless this matter is remedied by state law, the organization will lose its tax-exempt status.[32] It is thus imperative to place the private foundation provisions in the governing instrument as a "fall-back" position where the state does not impose the rules as a matter of law.

Q 12:15 What is a *supporting organization*?

A *supporting organization* generally is a charitable organization that would be a private foundation but for its structural or operational relationship with one or more charitable organizations that are either public institutions (Q 12:2) or publicly supported organizations (Q 12:4, Q 12:8).[33]

NOTE: As will be discussed, however, certain noncharitable tax-exempt organizations can be supported entities (Q 12:23).

This type of organization must be organized, and at all times thereafter operated, exclusively for the benefit of, to perform the functions of, or to carry out the purposes of at least one of these public charities, which are *supported organizations*. Also, it must be operated, supervised, or controlled by or in connection with one or more supported organizations. A supporting organization may not be controlled directly or indirectly by one or more disqualified persons (Chapter 2) other than foundation managers (Q 2:6) and one or more supported organizations.

The supporting organization must meet an *organizational test,* which basically requires that its articles of organization limit its purposes to those of a supporting entity and not empower the organization to support or benefit any other organizations.[34] The supported organization(s) must be specified in the articles, although the manner of the specification depends on the nature of the relationship with the supported organization(s) (Q 12:16). Also, the supporting organization must adhere to an *operational test:* It must engage solely in activities that support or benefit one or more supported organizations (Q 12:17).[35]

Q 12:16 What are the requisite relationships between a supporting organization and a supported organization?

There are three of these relationships, defined as

1. Operated, supervised, or controlled by
2. Supervised or controlled in connection with
3. Operated in connection with

Irrespective of the relationship, the supporting organization always must be responsive to the needs or demands of one or more supported organizations and constitute an integral part of or maintain a significant involvement in the operations of one or more supported organizations.[36]

The relationship encompassed by the phrase *operated, supervised, or controlled by* contemplates the presence of a substantial degree of direction by one or more supported organizations over the policies, programs, and activities of the supporting organization.[37] This relationship—which is basically that of parent and subsidiary—is normally established by causing at least a majority of the directors or officers of the supporting organization to be composed of representatives of the supported organization or to be appointed or elected by the governing body, officers, or membership of the supported organization.

TIP: This is the most common relationship of the three. It is the easiest and most direct control relationship to construct, and it assures the supported organization that the benefits it expects from the supporting entity will be received. It also happens to be the relationship preferred by the IRS.

The relationship manifested by the phrase *supervised or controlled in connection with* contemplates the presence of common supervision or control by persons supervising or controlling both entities, to ensure that the supporting organization will be responsive to the needs and requirements of the supported organization(s).[38] This relationship—one of "brother and sister" entities—requires that the control or management of the supporting organization be vested in the same persons who control or manage the supported organization(s).

The relationship envisioned by the phrase *operated in connection with* contemplates that the supporting organization is responsive to and significantly involved in the operations of the supported organization(s).[39] Generally, the supporting organization must meet both a *responsiveness test* and an *integral part test.*

The responsiveness test is satisfied where the supporting organization is responsive to the needs or demands of one or more supported organizations.[40] The test can be satisfied where the supporting organization and the supported organization(s) are in close operational conjunction. There are several ways to show this. They include (1) having one or more of the officers or directors of the supporting organization elected or appointed by the officers or directors of the supported organization(s) or (2) demonstrating that the officers or directors of the supporting organization maintain a close and continuous working relationship with the officers and directors of the supported organization(s). The officers and directors of the supported organization(s) must have a significant voice in the investment policies of the supporting organization; the timing of and manner of making grants, and the selection of grant recipients by the supporting organization; and the direction of the use of the income or assets of the supporting organization.

The responsiveness test also may be met where (1) the supporting organization is a charitable trust under state law, (2) each specified supported organization is a named beneficiary under the trust's governing instrument, and (3) each supported organization has the power, under state law, to enforce the trust and compel an accounting.

A supporting organization satisfies the integral part test where it maintains a significant involvement in the operations of one or more supported organizations and the beneficiary organization(s) are dependent on the supporting organization for the type of support it provides.[41] This test is met where the activities engaged in by the supporting organization for or on behalf of the supported organization(s) are activities to perform the functions of, or to carry out the purposes of, the supported organization(s) and, but for the involvement of the supporting organization, would normally be engaged in by the supported organization(s).

There is a second way to meet the integral part test.

TIP: Although these requirements are considerably complex, these rules represent the furthest reaches under which a charitable organization can avoid private foundation status. This is an area where abuse can occur (particularly, disqualified person control over the supporting organization, which is prohibited (Q 12:24)). Thus, the IRS does not like these arrangements, having gone so far as to, in its exempt organizations continuing professional education text for fiscal year 2001, designate these entities "razor edge" supporting organizations.

Under this approach, the supporting organization makes payments of substantially all of its income to or for the use of one or more supported organizations, and the amount of support received by one or more of the supported organizations is sufficient to ensure the attentiveness of the organization(s) to the operations of the supporting organization. The phrase *substantially all* means at least 85 percent.[42] A substantial amount of the total support from the supporting organization must go to those supported organizations that meet an attentiveness requirement with respect to the supporting organization.

In general, the amount of support received by a supported organization must represent a sufficient part of its total support so as to ensure the requisite attentiveness. If the supporting organization makes payments to or for the use of a department or school of a university, hospital, or church, the total support of the department or school is the measuring base, rather than the total support of the beneficiary institution.

Even where the amount of support received by a supported organization does not represent a sufficient part of its total support, the amount of support from a supporting organization may be sufficient to meet the requirements of the integral part test if it can be demonstrated that, in order to avoid the interruption of the conduct of a particular function or activity, the beneficiary organization will be sufficiently attentive to the operations of the supporting organization. This may be the case where either the supporting organization or the beneficiary organization earmarks the support received from the supporting organization for a particular program or activity, even if the program or activity is not the beneficiary organization's primary program or activity, so long as the program or activity is a substantial one.

All pertinent factors—including the number of the supporting organizations, the length and nature of the relationship between the beneficiary organization and the supporting organization, and the purpose to which the funds are put—are considered in determining whether the amount of support received by a beneficiary organization is sufficient to ensure its attentiveness to the operations of the supporting organization. Inasmuch as, in the view of the IRS, the attentiveness of a supported organization is motivated by reason of the amount of funds received from the supporting organization, the more substantial the amount involved (in terms of a percentage of the total support of the supported organization), the greater the likelihood that the required degree of attentiveness will be present. Other evidence of actual attentiveness by the supported organization is, however, of almost equal importance. The mere making of reports to each of the supported organizations does not alone satisfy the attentiveness requirement of the integral part test.

Where none of the supported organizations is dependent on the supporting organization for a sufficient amount of the beneficiary organization's support, the integral part test cannot be satisfied, even though the supported organizations have enforceable rights against the supporting organization under state law.

Q 12:1/ What are the functions of a supporting organization?

With the emphasis on *support,* the most common function of a supporting organization is as a funding mechanism for the supported organization(s).[43] In some instances, the supporting organization is the endowment fund for one or more beneficiary organizations. Endowments can be established by a public charity's transfer of some or all of its investment assets to a newly created supporting entity.

NOTE: There seems to be a persistent belief that a public charity cannot spawn a supporting organization. This is not the case. For example, in the endowment fund setting, there may be considerable merit in having the fund in a separate entity, such as for liability purposes and/or to place the assets in the hands of trustees who are more concerned with long-term operations than immediate budgetary pressures.[44] Healthcare providers and other public charities use the supporting organization vehicle to establish "holding companies" for more effective management.[45]

The law in this area speaks also of providing a *benefit* to a supported organization (Q 12:15). Aside from providing the supported organization with money, an organization can support or benefit another organization by carrying on its own programs or activities to support or benefit a supported organization. For example, a supporting organization supported a medical school at a university by operating teaching, research, and services programs as a faculty practice plan.[46] As another illustration, as part of its relationship with a public charity that provided residential placement services for mentally and physically handicapped adults, a supporting organization established and operated an employment facility for the handicapped and an information center about various handicapping conditions.[47] In another instance, a hospital caused a supporting organization to purchase a motel and convert it into a facility where patients, and their family and friends, can reside during the period leading up to an operation.[48]

A supporting organization may engage in fund-raising activities, such as charitable gift solicitations, special events (e.g., dinners and theater outings), and unrelated business activities, and grant the funds for the supported organization(s) or to other permissible beneficiaries.[49]

NOTE: Presumably the same rules as to the unrelated business law apply here (Chapter 9). That is, there are limitations on the amount of unrelated business activity in which a supporting organization can engage. This rule does not confer on supporting organizations the ability to engage in unlimited amounts of unrelated business activity.

Q 12:18 Does the supported organization have to be identified in the organizational document of the supporting organization?

Usually, but not always. Generally, it is expected that the articles of organization of the supporting organization will designate the (or each of the) supported organization(s) by name. The manner of the specification depends on the nature of the relationship between the supported and supporting organizations (Q 12:16).[50]

If the relationship is one of *operated, supervised, or controlled by* or *supervised or controlled in connection with,* designation of a supported organization by name is not required as long as two rules are followed:

1. The articles of organization of the supporting organization require that it be operated to support or benefit one or more supported organizations that are designated by class or purpose.
2. The class or purpose includes one or more supported organizations to which one of the two relationships pertains, or organizations that are closely related in purpose or function to the supported organizations to which one of the relationships pertains.

If the relationship is one of *operated in connection with,* generally the supporting organization's articles must designate the specified supported organization by name.

TIP: Irrespective of the relationship, it is usually preferable—from the standpoint of all organizations involved—for the supported organization(s) to be designated by name in the supporting organization's articles.

Where the relationship between the organizations is other than op*erated in connection with,* the articles of organization of a supporting organization may (1) permit the substitution of an eligible organization within a class for another organization either in the same class or in a different class designated in the articles, (2) permit the supporting organization to operate for the benefit of new or additional organizations in the same class or in a different class designated in the articles, or (3) permit the supporting organization to vary the amount of its support among different eligible organizations within the class or classes of organizations designated by the articles.

An organization that is *operated in connection with* one or more supported organizations can satisfy this specification requirement even if its articles permit an organization that is designated by class or purpose to be substituted for an organization designated in its articles, but only where the substitution is "conditioned upon the occurrence of an event which is beyond the control of the supporting organization." This type of an event would be loss of tax exemption, substantial failure or abandonment of operations, or dissolution of the supported organization(s) designated in the articles. In one instance, a charitable entity failed to qualify as a supporting organization because its articles permitted substitution too freely: Whenever, in the discretion of its trustee, the charitable undertakings of the supported organizations become "unnecessary, undesirable, impracticable, impossible or no longer adapted to the needs of the public," substitution was permitted.[51]

Q 12:19 How many supported organizations can a supporting organization support?

There is no specific limitation on the number of supported organizations that can be served by a supporting organization. Whatever the number, there must be a requisite relationship between the supporting organization and each of the supported organizations (Q 12:16). As a practical matter, this relationship requirement serves as somewhat of a limitation on the number of supported organizations that can be clustered around a supporting organization. Yet there is a supporting organization that serves over 300 public charitable entities.

Q 12:20 Can a supporting organization support or benefit a charitable organization or other person, in addition to one or more specified supported organizations?

Yes, although the opportunities for doing this are limited. The constraint comes from the fact that the law requires that a supporting organization be operated *exclusively* to support or benefit one or more qualified public entities (Q 12:15). The limitation also stems from the requirement of the requisite relationship and the specification rules (Q 12:16, Q 12:18). In general, a supporting organization must engage *solely* in activities that support or benefit one or more supported organizations.

A supporting organization may make payments to or for the use of, or provide services or facilities for, individual members of the charitable class that is benefited by a specified supported organization. Also, a supporting organization may make a payment through another, unrelated organization to a member of a charitable class benefited by a specified supported organization, but only where the payment constitutes a grant to an individual rather than a grant to an organization. At the same time, a supporting organization can support or benefit a charitable organization (other than a private foundation) if it is operated, supervised, or controlled directly by or in connection with a supported organization.[52] A supporting organization will, however, lose its status as such if it pursues a purpose other than supporting or benefiting one or more supported organizations.

A supporting organization can carry on an independent activity as part of its support function (Q 12:17). This type of support must be limited to permissible beneficiaries, as described above.

In practice, however, it is quite common for supporting organizations to make payments to noncharitable entities as part of their support activities. For example, a supporting organization can procure and pay for services that are rendered to or for the benefit of a supported organization. The supporting organization also can engage in fund-raising activities, such as special events, for the benefit of a supported organization. In that capacity, the supporting organization can contract with and pay for services such as advertising, catering, decorating, and entertainment.

Q 12:21 Can a supporting organization support another supporting organization?

Although the law is not crystal clear on the point, the answer probably is no. The law requires that a supporting organization operate for the benefit of, to perform the functions of, or to carry out the purposes of one or more public institutions (Q 12:2) or publicly supported organizations (Q 12:4, Q 12:8).[53] A literal reading of this law could lead one to the conclusion that a supporting organization may not be supported in this manner because it is not a public institution or publicly supported, or other qualified, organization.

It is quite possible, however, that, by supporting a supporting organization, a supporting organization could simultaneously benefit or carry out the purposes of a public institution or publicly supported organization. In fact, the regulations state that any charitable organization (other than a private foundation) can be a beneficiary of a supporting organization where the recipient organization is operated or controlled by a qualified supported organization.[54] The IRS is of the view, however, that this regulation was not intended to allow one supporting organization to support another—under any circumstances. Thus, it would not be advisable to structure this type of an arrangement without first obtaining a ruling from the IRS.

Q 12:22 Can a supporting organization support a private foundation?

Here the answer is a flat no. The supported organization(s) must be an institution (Q 12:2), a publicly supported organization (Q 12:4, Q 12:8), perhaps (in rare instances) another supporting organization (Q 12:15), or another qualified supported organization (Q 12:23).

Q 12:23 Can a charitable organization be a supporting organization with respect to a tax-exempt organization that is not a charitable one?

Yes. A charitable organization can support or benefit an exempt organization other than a charitable entity where the supported organization is a tax-exempt social welfare organization,[55] a tax-exempt labor organization,[56] or a tax-exempt association that is a business league.[57] For this arrangement to be successful, however, the supported organization must meet the public support test applied to service provider publicly supported charitable organizations (Q 12:8).[58] This rule is largely designed to establish non-private foundation status for "foundations" and other funds that are affiliated with and operated for the benefit of these eligible noncharitable exempt organizations.

COMMENT: This type of supporting organization highlights a significant fact: A supporting organization is a tax-exempt charitable entity. This means it must engage in activities that qualify it for tax-exempt status (e.g., educational or scientific functions), *and* it must engage in activities that provide the requisite support and benefit. This usually is not a problem where the supporting and supported entities are both tax-exempt charitable organizations. The situation can be more problematic, however, where the supported organization is not charitable; the supporting organization must be careful that it doesn't overdo the support function, to the point that it is engaging substantially in non-exempt activities or furthering nonexempt purposes.

Q 12:24 Are any limitations placed on the composition of the board of directors of a supporting organization?

Yes. The general concept is that a supporting organization will be controlled, through a structural or programmatic relationship, by one or more eligible organizations. Thus, a supporting organization may not be controlled, directly or indirectly, by one or more disqualified persons (Chapter 2)—other than, of course, foundation managers and one or more supported organizations.[59] A supporting organization is controlled by one or more disqualified persons if, by aggregating their votes or positions of authority, they may require the organization to perform any act that significantly affects its operations or may prevent the supporting organization from performing the act. Generally, a supporting organization is considered to be controlled in this manner if the voting power of disqualified persons is 50 percent or more of the total voting power of the organization's governing board or if one or more disqualified persons have the right to exercise veto power over the actions of the organization. All pertinent facts and circumstances are taken into consideration in determining whether a disqualified person indirectly controls an organization.

An individual who is a disqualified person with respect to a supporting organization (such as being a substantial contributor (Q 2:2)) does not lose that status because a supported organization appointed or otherwise designated him or her a foundation manager of the supporting organization as the representative of the supported organization.

Q 12:25 Provide some examples of how disqualified persons are considered to control supporting organizations.

There are many ways disqualified persons can control a supporting organization; these range from the obvious to the devious. The clearest way to do this, of course, is to have a majority of the board of directors consist of disqualified persons. That certainly is impermissible. Here are some other structures.

In one instance, the IRS concluded that the board of directors of a supporting organization was indirectly controlled by a disqualified person. The organization's board of directors was composed of a substantial contributor to it, two employees of a business corporation of which more than 35 percent of the voting power was owned by the substantial contributor (making the corporation itself a disqualified person (Q 2:16)), and one individual selected by the supported organization. None of the directors had any veto power over the organization's actions. While conceding that the supporting organization was not directly controlled by the disqualified person, the IRS said that "one circumstance to be considered is whether a disqualified person is in a position to influence the decisions of members of the organization's governing body who are not themselves disqualified persons." The IRS concluded that the two individuals who were employees of the disqualified person corporation should be considered disqualified persons for purposes of applying the 50 percent control rule. This led to a ruling that the organization was indirectly controlled by disqualified persons and therefore could not qualify as a supporting organization.[60]

This control element can be the difference between the qualification of an organization as a supporting organization or as a common fund private foundation. The right of the donors to designate the recipients of the organization's grants can constitute control of the organization by them; supporting organization classification is precluded where this control element rests with substantial contributors.[61]

CAUTION: This matter of indirect control by disqualified persons is very much a facts-and-circumstances test. The IRS is particularly sensitive to the possibility that creative structuring is being used to mask control of a supporting organization by one or more disqualified persons. As the discussion that follows indicates, the IRS tends to be rather strict on this point.

In the IRS's exempt organizations continuing professional education text for fiscal year 2001, this element of control is discussed. Two fact patterns are under scrutiny by the IRS:

1. Complex trustee structures
2. Asset control

Complex Trustee Structures

The IRS is on the lookout for what it terms "complex trustee structures." This includes situations where (1) disqualified persons select the nondisqualified persons, "independents," or "community members" for the board of the supporting organization; (2) committees controlled by disqualified persons nominate board members; or (3) a bylaws provision stating that disqualified person board members cannot be removed, even for cause.

The IRS focused on the following fact situation. An organization, intending to qualify as a supporting organization (the *operated in connection with* type), provides support to specified supported organizations in its board's discretion. Grants over $100,000 to single recipients within a 12-month period, however, must be approved by (1) the vote of at least two-thirds of the organization's board of trustees or (2) two majority votes of the board, one preceding and one following the annual reconstitution of the board. This board consists of two Class A trustees, consisting of the founder of the organization and either one of his or her family members or an employee of an entity that the founder owns. There are also three Class B trustees, none of whom can be disqualified persons.

This board of trustees will be reconstituted annually. The Class A trustees select the successor Class A trustees. Class B trustees are selected by majority action of the "trustee electors" from among nominations approved by the Class B nominating committee. The trustee electors, who elect their successors, will be officers or directors of a supported organization, but cannot include disqualified persons. The organization's nominating committee consists of two individuals selected by the Class A trustees and one selected by the trustee electors, and may include trustees. A majority of the nominating committee approves the slate of candidates, which includes at least two candidates for each position to be filled. The trustee electors then vote on the slate. If the trustee electors do not elect a Class B trustee position, then the nominating committee proposes a different slate of candidates for each unfilled position. If the trustee electors do not fill the Class B trustee position after two slates, the Class A trustees elect the Class B trustee to fill the unfilled position. Trustees of either class may be removed but only for cause and only by the affirmative vote of two-thirds of the trustee electors. A trustee may delegate in writing his or her rights to any other trustee.

The organization's founder's approval is required, as long as he or she is legally competent, to amend the organization's governing instrument. If the founder is incompetent or dead, the organization's board can amend the instrument with an 80 percent vote. Given this individual's power over the trustee selection process, he or she can effectively prohibit grants exceeding $100,000 to a single recipient within a 12-month period. Moreover, a trustee may delegate his or her voting rights on substantive matters to the founder in making distributions upon dissolution. The governing instrument provides that the founder's charitable preferences will be used as a guide to the organization's grant-making.

In this situation, the IRS holds that the organization cannot qualify as a supporting organization, since it fails the control test in that it is indirectly controlled by a disqualified person. The founder directly controls his or her own position on the board and indirectly controls the other Class A trustee position through a family or employment relationship. Also, the founder exercises indirect control over the three Class B trustee positions through his or her control over the slate of nominees for those positions. Although the founder cannot ensure that a particular individual will be on the organization's board (because two candidates must be offered for each open position), he or she can ensure that particular individuals will not be on the board.

The founder is said by the IRS to, in effect, have veto power over the return of any or all of the incumbent Class B trustees to the board, such as trustees who may not agree with his or her ideas on the direction of the organization. Inasmuch as the board is reelected every year, the founder can, wrote the IRS, depend on a board that will endorse his or her views and proposals. By controlling the nomination process, the founder also, said the IRS, maintains the ability to steer grants to the charities of his or her choice. Finally, the founder's control was seen as manifested by the instrument's expressed intent that the organization not survive the founder's death or incompetence for very long and that the board use his or her charitable preferences as a guide in making distributions upon dissolution.

Asset Control

Control by a disqualified person can be over the assets of a supporting organization. The length of time particular securities or other assets are retained by a supporting organization, and the manner of exercising voting rights with respect to stocks in which members of its governing body also have some interest, are factors bearing on the control issue.[62]

The IRS offered this example. The owner of a business loans money to his wholly owned corporation in exchange for a promissory note issued by the corporation. The note is secured by real estate owned by the corporation and used in its business. The corporation has purchased key man insurance to pay off the debt in the case of the owner's death. The owner transfers the note to a supporting organization (the operated in connection with type). The owner and his wife serve as two of the five directors of the supporting organization; one director is appointed by the supported organization. The owner, of course, is a disqualified person with respect to the supporting organization, as a substantial contributor and a foundation manager.

The IRS concluded that, because the owner controls the business, he controls the note. If he wished, he could consume all of the business's income and liquid assets through salary and dividends, leaving nothing to be paid on the note. The owner also could operate the business in an imprudent manner, such as an untimely expansion of the business's product or service without adequate capital support, which could work to the detriment of the supporting organization.

The supporting organization asserts that it holds the note, secured by the real estate and the life insurance policy. The IRS observed, however, that the insurance can be canceled or cashed in by the business and that the owner's control of the business allows him control over the real estate. Thus, any number of actions taken by the owner could impair the security. For example, the owner, in operating the business, could incur debt (or have incurred debt) secured by the real estate with a priority equal to or higher than the priority of the security held by the supporting organization. Further, the owner could impair the going concern value of the business in a manner that impairs the market value of the business's real estate.

The IRS stated that, in this example, the nature of the note held by the supporting organization and the donor's connection to the note are facts that are relevant in determining whether there is indirect control of this supporting organization by the disqualified person. Inasmuch as the owner exercises, in large part, control over the supporting organization's asset, the IRS expressed its view that "it would be difficult not to conclude" that the owner is exercising indirect control over this supporting organization.

Q 12:26 Should a supporting organization be separately incorporated?

The law does not require that a supporting organization be incorporated. In most instances, however, supporting organizations are incorporated, for the same reasons most nonprofit corporations use the corporate form—avoidance of personal liability for directors and officers.[63] One context in which the trust form may be advisable is where it may be needed as a way to satisfy the responsiveness test (Q 12:16).

NOTE: If a bank is involved, either as a trustee and certainly if it is the sole trustee, the trust form will likely be advocated by those with the bank. Banks and like financial institutions prefer the trust form, because of ease of administration and investing.

Q 12:27 Should a supporting organization have bylaws?

This answer depends on the type of organization that the supporting organization is. If it is a corporation or an unincorporated association, it should have bylaws. Charitable trusts do not usually have bylaws, although when the trust form is used for a supporting organization, a set of bylaws or a document akin to bylaws is advisable.

NOTE: There is a specific organizational test in this setting (Q 12:15). The language required by this test, however, must be contained in the articles of organization; inclusion only in the bylaws is insufficient.

Q 12:28 Who elects or appoints the directors of a supporting organization?

Selection of directors (or trustees) depends on the type of supporting organization, that is, on the nature of the relationship between the supporting entity and the supported organization(s) (Q 12:16). If the relationship is that of *operated, supervised, or controlled by,* at least a majority of the board of the supporting organization would be elected or appointed by the supported organization. The entirety of the supporting organization's board can be selected in this manner, or the minority members can be selected by the majority members.

If the relationship is that of *supervised or controlled in connection with,* the boards of directors of the two organizations will be the same. Thus, the organizational documents of the supporting organization would state that its governing board is the same group that comprises the board of the supported entity.

Where the relationship is embraced by the phrase *operated in connection with,* the board of directors of the supporting organization can possibly be wholly independent of the supported organization from the standpoint of its governance. Thus, the board can be structured in any way that is deemed appropriate by the parties involved.

REMINDER: The board of directors of a supporting organization cannot be controlled by disqualified persons with respect to it (Q 12:24).

It may be necessary to have one or more of the directors of the supporting organization elected or appointed by the directors of the supported organization, to facilitate compliance with the responsiveness test (Q 12:16).

Q 12:29 Can a supporting organization maintain its own financial affairs (such as by means of a separate bank account and separate investments)?

The supporting organization not only can maintain its own financial affairs but it should. This type of entity is a separate organization, and its legal status (including tax exemption) is predicated on that fact. Thus, separate financial resources are (or should be) always the case. This is particularly true with respect to supporting organizations that support or benefit noncharitable entities (Q 12:23). Separate annual information returns are also required.

NOTE: Under the rules followed by certified public accountants, a supporting organization almost always is a *related party* with respect to its supported organization. Thus, even though there will be separate annual information returns, any financial statements generally will be consolidated.

One of the overarching requirements often is that the supported organization have a significant involvement in the operations of the supporting organization (Q 12:16). This is likely to mean that the board of the supported organization has direction over the investment policies of the supporting organization. For example, for purposes of meeting the responsiveness test, the officers and directors of the supported organization(s) may have to have a significant voice in the investment policies of the supporting organization, the timing of grants, the manner of making them, and the selection of recipients by the supporting organization, and in otherwise directing the use of the income or assets of the supporting organization (*id.*).

Q 12:30 What financial reports and disclosure should a supporting organization make to the supported organization?

The law on this point is next to nonexistent. For the most part, this is a management matter rather than a legal one. State law may apply, particularly if the supporting entity is a charitable trust.

To the extent the federal rules address the point, it is a function of the relationship between the supported organization and the supporting organization. In general, the supporting organization must be responsive to the demands of the supported organization (Q 12:16). Thus, the law generally requires that the supporting organization provide whatever financial information about itself that the board of the supported organization "demands." Where the relationship is one of *operated, supervised, or controlled by* or *supervised or controlled in connection with,* the board of the supported organization is in the position of receiving any information about the supporting organization—financial or otherwise—that it wants.

Financial disclosure to the supported organization becomes most problematic when the relationship is evidenced by the phrase *operated in connection with.* In this situation, the board composition of the supporting organization may be such that financial information is not readily available to the board of the supported organization. A problem may arise in the context of meeting the attentiveness requirement of the integral part test. The mere making of reports to a supported organization, however, does not alone enable the supporting organization to meet this requirement (*id.*). Thus, where the *operated in connection with* relationship is involved, the sharing of financial information may be largely political, that is, whatever the parties can work out.

Q 12:31 What oversight should the supported organization perform?

No oversight requirement is imposed by law on the supported organization (other than the supervision that may flow out of fiduciary responsibility duties). The relationship responsibilities all fall on the supporting organization, as part of the justification for its nonprivate foundation status. The supporting organization always must be responsive to the needs or demands of one or more supported organizations and must constitute an integral part of or maintain a significant involvement in the operations of one or more supported organizations (Q 12:16).

Good management practice dictates that the supported organization be concerned with, and do what it can to conserve, the state and nature of the resources held by the supporting organization. Where the relationship is one of *operated, supervised, or controlled by or supervised or controlled in connection with,* any management oversight duties that the supported organization may wish to undertake are readily available.

Q 12:32 How does an organization acquire public charity status?

Most commonly, an organization acquires public charity status at the same time it acquires recognition of tax-exempt status as a charitable organization (Chapter 16). As part of the organization's filing of an application for recognition of exemption, it selects the category of public charity that it wants. If the IRS agrees that the organization qualifies as a type of public charity, it includes that classification on the determination letter or ruling that it issues. (This is the process by which a charitable organization rebuts the presumption that it is a private foundation (Q 12:1).) Depending on the category of public charity, the organization will receive either an advance ruling (Q 12:9) or a definitive ruling (Q 12:11).

Q 12:33 How does an organization maintain its public charity status?

The manner in which an organization maintains its public charity status depends in large part on the type of public charity that it is. If it is an institution (Q 12:2) or a supporting organization (Q 12:15), it remains a public charity as long as it continues to satisfy the programmatic or structural criteria that originally gave rise to the classification. If it is a publicly supported organization (Q 12:4, Q 12:8), it must provide its public support information to the IRS each year. This is done as part of the annual information return; there is a schedule by which both donative publicly supported charitable organizations and service provider publicly supported organizations display support information for a four-year measuring period. An organization must only demonstrate that it qualifies under one of the categories each year, irrespective of the category that is reflected on its ruling.

Q 12:34 Why is it so important to be classified as a public charity and avoid private foundation status?

There are *no disadvantages* to public charity status; all of the disadvantages in the law lie in classification as a private foundation. The disadvantages vary according to the nature of the organization; for some organizations, all of the disadvantages are important.

One of the principal disadvantages to private foundation status is the fact that, as a practical matter, private foundations will not make grants to other private foundations. A private foundation grantor must exercise *expenditure responsibility* as part of this type of grant (Q 7:24), and most private foundations do not have the resources to undertake, and do not want the risk of, expenditure responsibility grants. Also, in some instances, this type of grant will not qualify under the mandatory payout requirements (Chapter 4). Any charitable organization that is structured as a private foundation has basically denied itself access to funding by private foundation grants.

Another disadvantage to private foundation status is that contributions to private foundations may be less deductible than those to public charities (Chapter 17). For example, in a single tax year, an individual may make deductible gifts of money to public charities in amounts up to 50 percent of his or her adjusted gross income, whereas gifts of money to private foundations are subject to a 30 percent limitation. Similarly, gifts of appreciated property to public charities are deductible up to a 30 percent limitation, but the limitation generally is 20 percent in the case of private foundations (Q 17:6, Q 17:7).

Other disadvantages to private foundation status include

- Compliance with the massive federal tax rules regulating the operations of private foundations (Chapters 3–7)
- Payment of a 2 percent tax on net investment income, including capital gain (Chapter 8)
- The requirement of filing a more complex annual information return (Chapter 10)

On occasion, a charitable organization—not understanding the rules in this area—indicates on the application for recognition of exemption (Chapter 16) that it is a private foundation, when in fact it will clearly be qualifying as a publicly supported charity. The IRS can be unnecessarily harsh on the point, rarely permitting the organization to amend the application and instead forcing it to formally terminate its private foundation status, including "starting over" with an advance ruling (Q 12:9). This can cause enormous funding problems in the early years when reliance is placed on private foundation grants (Q 7:18). Thus, a charitable organization should be certain, when selecting foundation status, that that is the correct classification.

CHAPTER 13

Termination of a Private Foundation

A foundation might terminate its status as a private charity for a number of reasons and in several different ways. Some foundations have charter provisions that require termination after a designated number of years. Second-generation trustees may choose to divide up a private foundation's assets into several foundations. A foundation's mission may be accomplished by spending its assets to buy a historic building and donating the site to a preservation society. In a rare circumstance, there could be some action impermissible if the organization remains a private foundation. The IRS also can cause the involuntarily termination of a foundation for reasons of repeated violations of the private foundation sanctions. In any case, the private foundation must carefully follow the rules for terminating its existence, as missteps can be costly. The termination rules are complex and are evolving.

Here are the questions that are most frequently asked (or that should be asked) about the private foundation termination rules—and the answers to them.

Q 13:1 Are there any special rules governing the termination of private foundation status?

When the directors or trustees decide, for whatever reason, that they cannot continue to operate a private foundation, the foundation may go out of existence in several different ways. All of the foundation's assets can be given away to a public charity, to a municipality, or to another private foundation. A foundation might spend up its assets for charitable purposes, such as buying food to feed the hungry. It also might turn itself into a public charity by reforming its governing documents to qualify as a supporting organization or by seeking public funding that will equal at least one-third of its annual revenues. Although unusual, a foundation can convert itself into a public charity by beginning to operate a church, school, or hospital. A foundation can be split into two or more different parts to allow its differing board members to each have their own foundation. Unless the termination is involuntarily caused by the IRS (Q 13:7), the IRS provides only a few rules governing such life changes for a foundation. The most important criteria follow.

DEDICATION TO CHARITABLE PURPOSES: The assets that are distributed by a terminating foundation must continue to be used exclusively in a manner that accomplishes a charitable purpose, just as they are required to be used while they are held during the foundation's lifetime.

NO CONTROL: The terminating foundation must in fact go out of existence. Its directors or trustees cannot retain control over the use of the assets by the recipient charity (Q 13:4).

Q 13:2   Must a foundation seek advance IRS approval for changes in its status?

For most types of foundation transformations, IRS approval is not technically required, although many advisors recommend advance notification and request approval. The reason for this caution is the onerous language of the tax code entitled "Termination of Private Foundation Status."[1] The code says the "status of any organization as a private foundation shall be terminated only if (1) such organization notifies the Secretary [IRS] . . . of its intent to accomplish such termination, or (2) (A) with respect to such organization, there have been either willful repeated acts (or failure to act), giving rise to liability for tax under chapter 42, and (B) the Secretary notifies such organization that" it is subject to a termination tax. The termination tax is equal to all of the aggregate tax benefits gained by the foundation's substantial contributors for their donations to the foundation. The foundation and its contributors certainly want to avoid the costly and undesirable tax that can be imposed on the second type of change, called an *involuntary termination.* Simplified procedures are promised to be issued by the IRS.

Prior IRS notification is required by the tax code for a foundation that wants to make a voluntary termination of its private foundation status by conversion of itself into a public charity in what is called a *60-month termination.* Essentially, the foundation does not cease to exist, it simply changes its tax classification from private to public. The information listed below (Q 13:5) is submitted with a request that the IRS issue an advance ruling approving the change.

Q 13:3   How does a foundation inform the IRS of a change in its status?

The procedure for informing the IRS of changes that occur throughout the life of a tax-exempt organization is to submit data with the annual information return. Form 990-PF each year asks whether a "liquidation, termination, dissolution, or substantial contraction occurred during the year." If so, the foundation is instructed to attach a detailed explanation and the legal documents evidencing the actions taken and any other facts pertinent to the changes that occurred. Thus, a foundation that gives away all of its assets for charitable purposes is expected to simply inform the IRS of its actions.

When the foundation distributes all of its assets to another charitable organization, the payments are treated as charitable grants and reported alongside the foundation's normal grant and program disbursements made during the year. The total value of the distributed assets is treated as a qualifying amount for purposes of satisfying the 5 percent payout calculation. Sufficient information to evidence that the foundation has not retained impermissible control over the distributed assets as described in the next question may be attached.

NOTE: It is not customary for the IRS to acknowledge notice of this type of termination furnished in the Form 990-PF filed in Ogden, Utah. A foundation that desires an overt approval for the transfer also can send the information to the Cincinnati, Ohio, office with a request for approval. The request can simply ask the IRS to update its database to reflect the fact that the foundation has voluntarily terminated its existence.

Q 13:4 What rules apply when a foundation transfers its assets to a public charity?

A foundation that wishes to cease to exist can transfer or donate all of its assets to one or more public charities. The tax code says the foundation can accomplish a voluntary termination by transferring its assets to a type of charity— one classified as a donative publicly supported charity (Q 12:4) that has been in existence for at least 60 continuous months. This category of public charity includes churches, schools, hospitals, municipalities, state college support organizations, and donative charities. Public charities so classified because they are supported by admission charges from activities they conduct, such as symphony societies, theaters, healthcare providers other than hospitals, research organizations, and many others, are not mentioned as a qualifying recipient for a terminating distribution. The code is also silent regarding supporting organizations. Nonetheless, as noted at the end of this question, they do qualify to receive a gift of all of the assets of a foundation wishing to cease to exist.

Advance notice seeking IRS approval prior to terminating a foundation with a distribution of assets to a public charity (Q 12:1) is not necessary. The one requirement is that the gift be complete. A detailed description indicating the six factors listed below are present should be included in Form 990-PF for the year in which the assets are transferred. The tax regulations say "All right, title, and interest in and to all of the net assets" must be transferred. No material restrictions or conditions can be imposed preventing free and effective use of the assets by the public charity. The following questions are used to find restrictions:

1. Is the public charity owner, in fee, of the assets it receives from the foundation?
2. Are the assets held and administered by the public charity for its exempt purposes?
3. Are the assets free of any liabilities, leases, or other obligations limiting their usefulness to the recipient organization?
4. Does the public charity's governing body have ultimate authority and control over the assets and the income derived therefrom for its tax-exempt purposes?
5. Is the governing body of the public charity organized and operated separately and independently of the private foundation?
6. Are members of the public charity board chosen by the public charity?[2]

Restrictions that do not hamper the recipient charity's control and dedication of the assets to exempt purposes can be imposed in connection with a terminating gift, including:

- The foundation can require the public charity create a segregated and identifiable fund to hold the assets so long as the controls listed above are not present.
- The foundation can stipulate that the fund be named after the terminating foundation, its founders, or any other person or business. A name is considered an intangible, not capable of value, asset.
- The charitable purpose for which the transferred funds are to be used can be designated—a restriction can be placed on the assets that devotes their use to saving the environment, to educating immigrants, to housing the poor, or to one or more other specific charitable purposes.
- The transferor foundation also can require that the property be retained and not sold when it is important to the charitable purpose, such as a nature preserve, art collection, or historic property.

NOTE: Although the tax code only contains rules for making a terminating distribution to certain public charities (Q 12:2, Q 12:4), a terminating distribution also can be made to other categories of public charities (Q 12:8, Q 12:15). The terms of the transfer should contain similar conditions as those described above. Essentially, the foundation must make a complete gift retaining no future control over the assets. Proof of public status should be maintained in the files of the terminating private foundation.

Q 13:5   Can a private foundation turn itself into a public charity?

A private foundation can change its method of operation or sources of support and become a public charity.[3] Basically, the foundation adopts plans to qualify itself as a public organization and submits an application for approval to the key district office. A detailed list of information describing all aspects of the transformation is submitted to the IRS for approval.

CAUTION: Timing here is very important—the termination notice must be filed in advance of the year in which it is effective.

A conversion of this type is called a *60-month termination* because the requirements are to be met throughout and by the end of the continuous period of 60 months. The foundation need not necessarily qualify as a public charity at the beginning of the termination period, but it must have a good plan to do so. The terminating foundation agrees to extend the statute of limitations during the 60 months and pay excise taxes for any year in which its reformation plans fail to qualify it as publicly supported. Actually, a converted private foundation (as for all public charities) can lose public status in any future year in which it fails to meet the test, whether it's the sixth, sixteenth, or whatever year beyond 60 months.

A variety of circumstances could arise to make conversion to a public charity desirable. For example, a delay in the start-up of operations and attendant fund-raising programs might cause an organization classified as public during its advance ruling period to fail to receive over one-third of its support from the general public. The current-year support levels might qualify it as public, but the cumulative totals for the first five years do not. In such a situation, it becomes classified as a private foundation during its advance ruling period. If notice is given in a timely fashion, the organization should be able to continue its public status by starting anew with a 60-month termination.

Another example would be a privately endowed operating foundation, say a museum that plans to undertake a major public campaign to expand its operations. It is privately funded in the early years, but converts to public charity status as soon as its public funding is adequate. A private foundation also can begin to conduct activities that enable it to change its status to a public charity, such as operation of a hospital or school.

Q 13:6   Can one foundation transfer its assets to another foundation?

A private foundation desiring to cease to exist, to enable its trustees to pursue their divergent charitable interests, or to otherwise transform itself can transfer all of its assets to one or more existing or newly created private foundations.[4] The rules make this type of transfer simple because the old foundation is deemed not to terminate. Assets transferred to the recipient foundation carry transferee liability and retain characteristics possessed by the transferring foundation. Any previously undistributed income, for example, must be distributed by the recipient foundation; likewise, prior excess distributions can be carried over to reduce distribution requirement of the recipient foundation. Most significantly, the recipient bears any burden for a termination tax in the unlikely event that one is assessed.[5]

Countless private letter rulings[6] make it clear that the division of all assets of one private foundation to two other private foundations, to enable the trustees to pursue their divergent charitable interests, does not terminate the transferor's private foundation status or result in a termination tax. This conclusion applies when two facts exist: (1) The transferor has not given notice of intent to terminate and (2) there is no evidence that the original private foundation has violated any of the private foundation sanctions so as to cause the IRS to terminate it involuntarily.

Neither the old nor the newly created organization is treated as newly created (a seemingly impossible situation) in a private foundation split-up. The attributes of the old organization are attributed proportionately to each of the "new-old" private foundations.[7] The tax attributes that carry over to a successor private foundation include excess qualifying distributions. The amount of the carryover attributable to one of several distributees is calculated in proportion to the value of assets each receives from the terminating foundation.[8] The following sample of the private letter rulings issued by the IRS in 1991 offer examples of split-ups that have been blessed by the IRS:

- A merger of two private operating foundations to manage a recreational complex[9]
- Three new organizations—one public organization to receive half of the assets and two private foundations each to receive one-fourth of the assets—formed from one private foundation[10]
- A private foundation's legal structure converted to a nonprofit corporation from its original form as a charitable trust[11]
- One private foundation split into three private foundations[12]
- A combination of three commonly controlled foundations into one,[13] or two into one[14]

A private foundation is not required to give the IRS notice of its intention to terminate, but if it makes no notice, it continues to be treated as a private foundation for all purposes.[15] However, as pointed out in the regulations, if the foundation has given away all of its assets, the tax will be zero because the foundation will have no assets.[16]

Tax attributes, some positive and some negative, that the receiving foundation inherits are listed below. Some of the rules apply to the same extent and in the same manner that they would have applied to the transferor foundation had the transfer not been made. If there is more than one transferee organization, the attributes may be allocated according to the value of the assets received by each foundation.

- Transferor's excess qualifying distributions carryover can be used to offset the transferee's payout requirements and any deficiencies must be made up.[17] The transfer itself counts as a qualifying distribution in the year of transfer if the assets go to an uncontrolled private foundation.

- Tax basis of assets carried over and not stepped up to market value.[18]
- The time period allowed for disposition of excess business holdings carries over.[19]
- Expenditure responsibility reporting requirements cease once a foundation disposes of its assets except when its assets are transferred to a foundation controlled by the same parties.[20]

A transferee effectively controlled by the same person or persons who control the transferor is treated as the same foundation and has, in addition to those listed above, the following privileges and burdens:

- Special rules and privileges or savings provisions with respect to the private foundation rules, such as using the historic grant payout rate to reduce the excise tax rate, can be taken advantage of by a commonly controlled transferee.[21]
- Expenditure responsibility reporting requirements do carryover to a transferee foundation that is effectively controlled by the same person or persons as the transferor.[22]

Q 13:7   Can the IRS involuntarily terminate a private foundation?

The tax code allows the IRS to involuntarily terminate a foundation for reasons of repeated violations of the private foundation sanctions. The ultimate penalty for failure to play by the excise tax rules Congress designed to curtail private foundation activities is an involuntary termination and imposition of a so-called *third-tier tax*. When a private foundation has willfully repeated flagrant act(s) or failure(s) to act giving rise to the imposition of the first- and second-tier sanctions in the private foundation rules (Q 1:4), the IRS can notify the private foundation that it is liable for a termination tax.[23] The termination tax equals the lower of the aggregate tax benefit received by all of the foundation's donors and the foundation itself resulting from charitable status, or the foundation's net assets, whichever is less. The IRS can abate this tax if the private foundation transfers all of its assets to a public organization in a termination described in Q 13:4. The tax also can be abated if corrective action under state law occurs to ensure that the assets will be used for tax-exempt purposes.[24] The IRS is required to notify state officials of its intention to impose the termination tax[25] and essentially give the state an opportunity to intervene and preserve the assets for charitable purposes.

For this severe penalty to apply, there must have been at least two acts or failures to act, which are voluntary, conscious, and intentional.[26] The offense must appear to a reasonable person to be a gross violation of the sanctions, and the managers must have been aware that they were violating the rules.

Q 13:8   Is it conceivable that a private foundation can turn itself into a taxable entity?

Listed first in the statute, but the least likely choice for termination, is a voluntary termination by conversion to a taxable entity. A foundation can notify the IRS of its intent to terminate and request abatement or pay tax, which, of course, it probably will have to pay. In most cases, the assets remain dedicated to charitable purposes under charter provisions or a trust instrument and, thereby, under state law. Once notice is given, the foundation is treated as a newly created organization. If, for some unlikely reason, it wanted to resecure tax-exempt status, it would have to file another application for recognition of tax exemption to be recognized as exempt.[27]

CHAPTER 14

Types of Foundations

All types of private foundations are first and foremost charitable organizations qualified for tax exemption. Charities are further classified as being private foundations or public institutions under rather complicated rules (Chapter 12). In this chapter, the different types of private foundations are defined.

Here are the questions that are most frequently asked (or that should be asked) about the various types of private foundations—and the answers to them.

Q 14:1   What is a *standard* private foundation?

A private foundation is defined by what it is not. The definition negatively says a private foundation is a charity that cannot qualify as one of three different categories of public charities. The detailed requirements for qualification as a public charity have been discussed (Chapter 12). Briefly, Type 1 public charities are called inherently public because they include churches, schools, hospitals, and governmental entities that are treated as public entities without regard to the sources of their financial support or who controls them. Type 2 public charities are those that receive financial support from a many sources, and Type 3 public charities are those that exist to provide financial support and (generally) are controlled by one or more specified public charities.

The standard private foundation, instead, receives its financial support from investment income and donations from a limited number of persons and does not conduct activities that qualify it as a public charity. A distinctive characteristic in comparison to a public charity is also the fact that it is controlled by its disqualified persons—those that create, fund, and manage it; most public charities are controlled by a board made up of unrelated persons.

Q 14:2   What is a *private operating* foundation?

A private operating foundation is essentially a cross between a private foundation and a public organization. A private operating foundation is a charity that "does its own thing," or, in the language of the statute, "actively conducts activities constituting the purpose or function for which it is organized and operated."

In other words, a private operating foundation makes qualifying distributions by sponsoring and managing its own charitable projects rather than making grants to other organizations to conduct the programs. It might operate a museum, historic restoration project, library, research institute, provide disaster relief, and a myriad of other charitable programs. Many private operating foundations are privately funded entities started by a person of means who has strong ideas about charitable objectives he or she wants to accomplish through self-initiated projects. Their expenditures may be financed by annual gifts from its creators, investment income on its accumulated funds, or a combination of both.

NOTE: If a privately funded organization operates a church, school, or hospital, it likely can qualify as a public charity.

The most significant attribute of a private operating foundation is sometimes the most difficult quality to possess. To qualify as a private operating foundation, the foundation must focus—it must be *significantly involved* in its own projects in a continuing and sustainable fashion. To be involved might mean the foundation purchases property, goods, and services to conduct its own programs. It might hire a staff of researchers, teachers, curators, or other program specialists. Incidentally, its staff can be partly or wholly made up of volunteers and can include its funders or trustees, if their work involvement is genuine.

The typical operating foundation acquires and maintains program assets used in its programs—buildings, artworks, research facilities, and the like. A private operating foundation might, for example, buy, restore, and rent historic houses to preserve them. To conduct the restoration project it engages realtors, architects, and contractors and other specialists needed to acquire and fix up the property. It pays utility, maintenance, and insurance costs, engages property managers, and pays administrative expenses necessary to operate the properties. Optimally, a private operating foundation is identified in the public eye with and by its projects.

A private operating foundation must meet two annual distribution requirements—one based on its income levels and another on either its assets or sources of its revenues. Most importantly for its funders, donations to a private operating foundation are afforded the higher deductibility limits allowed for gifts to public charities (Q 14:7).

Q 14:3 What special distribution tests apply to a private operating foundation?

A private operating foundation must make expenditures for its active programs under an income test and also meet one of three different asset tests. The income test requires a private operating foundation spend at least 85 percent of its annual *adjusted net income* or two-thirds of the standard private foundation distribution requirement (essentially 3⅓ percent of its investment assets)(Q 4:1) on its self-initiated charitable programs. *Adjusted gross income* is calculated using the following formula:

$$A - B - C - D = \text{Adjusted net income}$$

- A = Gross income of all types for the year (not limited to income subject to the investment income tax).
- B = Long-term capital gains.
- C = Contributions received.
- D = Ordinary and necessary expenses paid or incurred for the production or collection of gross income or for the management, conservation, or maintenance of property held for the production of such income.

In addition to the income test, a private operating foundation must meet an asset test, an endowment test, or a support test. The *asset test* measures the portion of the foundation's assets devoted to the active conduct of its charitable activities. To meet this test, at least 65 percent of the fair market value of the operating foundation's assets must be program-related—an art collection, buildings, or stock of a controlled corporation substantially all of the assets of which are directly used in conducting the charitable programs. The concepts of exempt function and dual-use assets used in calculating the minimum distribution requirement for a standard private foundation are followed to identify assets qualifying for this test (Q 4:5). Assets that are not capable of being valued, such as a botanical garden, can be included at the historical cost for the facility.[1]

The *endowment test* essentially measures whether the operating foundation spends a sufficient portion of its annual income on its active projects. Under this test, the private operating foundation's annual distributions must equal at least two-thirds of its minimum investment return (3⅓ percent of investment assets versus 5 percent for a standard private foundation). The endowment test is designed to prevent a standard private foundation from seeking private operating foundation status to take advantage of a lower income test. Assuming a private foundation holds marketable securities that pay no dividends, the income test, taken alone, would require no current charitable spending. A private operating foundation with a portfolio of low current yield securities would have to distribute part of its principal or contributions received to meet this test, just like a standard private foundation, only at a lower level.

Under the *support test,* the private operating foundation's revenues must come from donations from the general public and from five or more non-controlled charitable organizations, with none giving more than 25 percent of the private operating foundation's support. An organization wishing to meet this test must carefully study the regulations.

The income and asset tests are applied each year for a four-year period that includes the current and past three years. The private operating foundation has a choice of methods to calculate its compliance with the tests, but it must use the same method for both tests:

- All four years can be aggregated so that the distributions for four years are added together. The private operating foundation must use only one of the asset, endowment, or support tests for all four years.
- For three of the four years, the private operating foundation meets the income test and any one of the asset, endowment, or support tests.

Q 14:4   What happens if a private operating foundation fails these tests?

If the private operating foundation fails to qualify for a particular year, it is treated as an ordinary private foundation for that year. It can return to private operating foundation classification as soon as it again qualifies under both the income test and the assets, endowment, or support test. There is no requirement that a private operating foundation applying method 2 make up the deficient year.[2] New organizations generally must meet the test in their first year. If application for recognition of exemption is made prior to the completion of the proposed private operating foundation's first fiscal year, the IRS will accept the organization's assertion, based on a good-faith determination, that it plans to qualify. The application and its instructions contain a workpaper for submitting the appropriate information. Failure in the first year can be remedied, if the private operating foundation does in fact qualify in its second, third, and fourth years.

Q 14:5   Can a private operating foundation make grants to a standard private foundation?

A grant to a standard private foundation is presumed to be indirect conduct of exempt activity, even if the activity of the grantee foundation helps the private operating foundation accomplish its goals. While one or more other foundations may be involved in some manner, an operating foundation must expend a prescribed amount of its funds directly. The regulations provide that: "Qualifying distributions are not made by a foundation directly for the active conduct unless such distributions are used by the foundation itself, rather than by or through one or more grantee organizations."[3]

It is important to note that a private operating foundation is not prohibited from making grants to other organizations; such grants simply do not count toward satisfying the private operating foundation's distribution requirements. So long as the private operating foundation distributes the requisite annual amount for its active programs, it may, in addition, make grants to other organizations. A special limitation applies if the operating foundation's minimum investment return is less than its adjusted net income. If its active project distributions are less than adjusted gross income, more than 85 percent of the total qualifying distributions must be active.[4] The point is that as long as the private operating foundation meets the income and asset tests, it may spend additional amounts on any form of charitable activity it chooses.

Q 14:6   Can a private operating foundation make grants to individuals?

Payments to individuals under a scholarship program, a student loan fund, a minority business enterprise capital support project, or similar charitable effort can qualify as active program for a private operating foundation.[5] The facts and circumstances surrounding the project must indicate that the private operating foundation is *significantly involved.* Merely selecting, screening, and investigating applicants for grant or scholarships is insufficient. When the recipients perform their work or studies alone, such as in pursuit of a doctoral degree, or exclusively under the direction of their college or some other organization, the individual grants are not considered to be direct qualifying payments.

Significant involvement of the private operating foundation and its staff exists when the individual grants are a part of a comprehensive program. The test is qualitative rather than quantitative. A qualifying private operating foundation might, for example, have as its mission the relief of poverty and human distress. It designs activities to ameliorate conditions among the poor, particularly during national disasters. It provides food and clothing to indigents without the assistance of an intervening organization or agency, under the direction of its salaried and volunteer staff of administrators, researchers, or other personnel who supervise and direct the activity. Such an active program would qualify the foundation as an operating one.

Another example is a foundation formed to train teachers for institutions of higher education. Fellowships are awarded to students for graduate study leading toward advanced degrees in college teaching. Pamphlets encouraging prospective college teachers and describing the private operating foundation's activity are widely circulated. Seminars, attended by fellowship recipients, private operating foundation staff and consultants, and other interested parties, are held each summer, and papers from the conference are published. Despite the fact that a majority of the organization's money is spent for fellowship payments, the program is comprehensive and suitable to qualify as an active project.[6]

Q 14:7   What are the advantages of classification as a private operating foundation?

Private operating foundations have a number of special advantages:

Contribution deduction limits are preferential. The charitable deduction rules provide the same deduction for money and property donated to a private operating foundation as are allowed for public charity. A philanthropist can shelter up to 50 percent of his or her income with gifts of cash to a private operating foundation as compared to 30 percent for a standard private foundation. The full fair market value of real estate, artworks, and other appreciated property is deductible for a gift to a private operating foundation. Except for readily marketable securities, the deduction for gifts of noncash property to a standard private foundation is limited to the donor's basis.[7]

Distributable amount may be lower. The minimum distribution requirement for a private operating foundation may be lower than for normal private foundations. In some cases, given a sufficient return on investment, a private operating foundation can better build an endowment over the years. It must distribute only 85 percent of its actual net income when it is lower than minimum distribution requirement and need only to pay out two-thirds of its minimum distribution requirement.

Grants from standard private foundation can be retained. Last, grants to an operating foundation from a standard private foundation can be retained and need not be redistributed to enable the grant to count toward satisfying the granting foundation's payout requirement.

Q 14:8   What are the disadvantages of classification as a private operating foundation?

The primary *disadvantage* is the requirement that the private operating foundation must meet both the income test and the asset, endowment, or support test each year before the last day of the year. A standard private foundation need not pay out its minimum distributable amount until the end of the next succeeding year. Some relief for this disadvantage is afforded by an alternative test that allows a private operating foundation to meet the distribution requirement on a three-out-of-four-year basis (Q 14:3).

A disadvantage for some foundation managers is the need to sustain self-initiated programs by maintaining a staff and managing programs. The requirement to be actively, rather than passively, involved is a commitment some find hard to sustain.

Q 14:9   Can a standard private foundation convert itself into an operating foundation?

A standard private foundation can convert itself into an operating foundation by ceasing to support other organizations and developing its own active programs. An IRS advance ruling is not required to approve such a conversion. The foundation is technically qualified by definition if it meets the tests by changing its method of operation or mix of assets. Such a conversion, however, can take four years and careful planning.[8] Most important, the charitable distributions have to be accelerated due to the loss of the one-year time lag allowed for standard private foundations not available to private operating foundations. For a converting standard private foundation, mandatory distributions also may be accelerated with the payment of both the prior year distributable amount and active program distributions before year end.

Q 14:10 What is an *exempt operating* foundation?

An exempt operating foundation is one that currently possesses the attributes of a private operating foundation (conducts active programs) and has three distinguishing characteristics.

1. It has been publicly supported for at least 10 years in the past.
2. It is governed by a board of independent trustees or directors that broadly represent the general public, at least 75 percent of whom are not disqualified persons.
3. None of its officers is a disqualified person.[9]

Q 14:11 Why was the exempt operating foundation category created?

By virtue of the structure of the federal tax law, private foundations are encouraged to make grants to public charities that qualify as one of the *institutions* (Q 12:2). This means that grant-making to other types of public charities—principally publicly supported charities—is less stimulated.

This system favors institutions such as churches, colleges, universities, and hospitals. Other traditional public charity/institutions are not so favored. These include museums, libraries, and opera societies. (Organizations of this nature usually are publicly supported charities.) Congress has never seriously considered writing definitions of these terms yet was somewhat sympathetic to the plight of these "quasi" institutions. Thus, it instead created the category of exempt operating foundation to provide a generic definition of these entities, so as to encourage grant-making to them.

Also, to make these organizations feel more like public charities, they were exempted from the tax on investment income (Chapter 8), should it be applicable.

Q 14:12 What are the advantages of being classified as an exempt operating foundation?

The most significant monetary advantage of an exempt operating foundation is the fact that it is excused from paying excise tax on its investment income. Secondarily, but important to an exempt operating foundation that seeks funding, is the fact that a standard private foundation need not exercise expenditure responsibility for grants made to an exempt operating foundation.

Q 14:13 What are the disadvantages of being classified as an exempt operating foundation?

The primary disadvantage of classification as an exempt operating foundation is the fact that disqualified persons cannot control it.

Q 14:14 What is a *pass-through* foundation?

A grant from one standard private foundation to another is not counted as a qualifying distribution by the granting foundation if the recipient standard foundation keeps the funds. For the foundation that makes the grant to report the distribution as counting toward its 5 percent payout test, the amount of the grant must be redistributed, or "passed through," to enable the donor foundation to count it as a qualifying distribution (Q 4:12). This pass-through foundation serves somewhat the same function as the conduit foundation that redistributes a gift from a for-profit donor to enable the donor to receive a charitable deduction.

Q 14:15 What is a *conduit* foundation?

A standard private foundation becomes a conduit foundation for any year in which it receives a donation of property and essentially does not keep the property—it serves simply as a conduit to allow its donor to receive a full charitable donation deduction. To understand this type of foundation, it helps to remember a fact: The charitable deduction for appreciated property, other than readily marketable securities, to a standard private foundation is limited to the donor's basis. This limit is lifted and the full market value of the property is deductible if the foundation redistributes or gives away the full value of the gift or the property itself to another charity (either private or public) by the fifteenth day of the third month after the end of the year in which it receives the donation. It cannot count the redistribution in satisfying its normal 5 percent payout requirement.[10] A conduit foundation attaches a statement to Form 990-PF for the year in which it treats distributions as being made out of corpus for purposes of permitting a donor to claim a full fair market deduction.

If the conduct foundation redistributes the property itself, the appreciation over the donor's basis is not subject to the investment income tax (Q 8:10). If the foundation sells the property and redistributes the proceeds of sale, the donor's gain is taxed because the foundation must use the donors basis to calculate its gain. Excess distribution carryovers (Q 4:19–4:21) also can be counted as a qualifying distribution by a conduit foundation.[11] The regulations specifically allow a foundation to elect to treat as a current distribution out of corpus any amount distributed within one of the five prior taxable years that was treated as a distribution out of corpus and not availed of for any other purpose.

CHAPTER 15

Alternatives to Private Foundations

Private foundations are marvelous charitable entities, enabling individuals and corporations to support philanthropic ends while retaining the ability to control the flow of charitable funds and target the desired charitable causes. They are unique; at the same time, they are critical to the functioning of the nation's nonprofit sector. In the appropriate set of circumstances, the private foundation clearly is the charitable vehicle of choice.

Yet, as in all things, perfection is difficult to achieve: although splendid, there are some disadvantages to structuring a charitable entity as a private foundation. There are some alternative vehicles that, again in the appropriate circumstances, are or may be preferable to the private foundation. Principally, they are the *supporting organization* and the *donor-advised fund.* The latter may be some form of *charitable gift fund.*

An individual contemplating establishment of a private foundation should, before doing so, be advised of the various alternatives. To a lesser degree, this is also the case with respect to corporations. (Although public charities often form *foundations,* these are not private foundations and this range of alternatives normally is not suitable in that context.) Even individuals with private foundations should be aware of these choices; one or more may be suitable in addition to the foundation. Occasionally, a private foundation is converted to one of these other types of entity (most often a supporting organization).

Here are the questions that are often asked (or that should be asked) about entities that are alternatives to private foundations.

Q 15:1 Why would one consider an alternative to a private foundation?

Before specifically answering that question, it is helpful to review the elements to generally consider when contemplating the establishment of a charitable organization. They are:

- The location of the organization. Every entity has to be organized some-where; the focus here is on the state in which the entity is to be formed. Usually that is the state in which the organization is to be operated. An organization may have a presence in more than one state. As to the state in which it is formed, it is a *domestic* organization. As to all other states in which it may have activities (often termed *doing business*), the organization is a *foreign* organization.
- The form of the organization. Basically, a charitable organization must, to be tax-exempt under federal law, be a nonprofit corporation, a trust, or an unincorporated association. Private foundations are almost always either corporations or trusts.
- The function of the organization. This element essentially concerns the program activities of the charitable organization. It may, however, entail other undertakings, such as fund-raising. As to private founda-tions, for example, the general dichotomy is between those entities that engage solely in grant-making and those that operate their own programs (Q 14:2).
- The board of directors or trustees of the organization. This factor includes the origin and number of board members, how the board is structured, who elects the members of the board, and the length of their term(s) of office.
- The tax-exempt status of the organization. Presumably, tax exemption under the federal tax law is desired and will be applied for (Chapter 16).[1] Tax exemption also should be pursued under state law. At the state level, tax exemptions may be available for income, sales, use, tangible personal property, intangible personal property, real property, and other items.
- The organization will certainly want to be qualified under the federal tax law as an organization to which deductible contributions may be made. As a practical matter, this status is achieved when the organi-zation acquires recognition of tax-exempt status (see the previous factor). Technically, however, this is a separate qualification.[2] Chari-table donee status under state law should also be sought; most states follow the federal law criteria.
- The public charity status of the organization. Is the entity to be a private foundation, or is it to be one of the forms of public charity (Chapter 12)? This element should be considered at the time of formation of the organization; it also is a subject to be considered throughout the orga-nization's existence, such as the maintenance of publicly supported charity status.
- The organization is probably going to have an obligation to file, pur-suant to federal tax law, an annual information return (Chapter 10). This type of organization also is required to make these documents accessible to the public (Chapter 11).
- The organization is likely to have annual reporting obligations under state law.

- If the organization is going to engage in fund-raising, it will have a considerable amount of federal law to contend with (Chapter 11), as well as one or more state charitable solicitation acts.[3]
- The factor of board member liability. If there is to be a board of directors or trustees, the extent of their personal liability for serving on the board should be understood. This liability can be eliminated or at least narrowed by incorporation of the entity or by means of insurance and/or indemnification. The law in some states offers complete or limited immunity for volunteer board members.[4]
- If the organization has employees, there are a variety of responsibilities imposed upon it by the tax and labor laws, such as withholding, reporting, overtime compensation, vacation and sick time, health and retirement benefits, and suitable working conditions.
- There is always the potential of application of other laws, such as the postal, antitrust, and securities laws [5]

With these general elements in mind, the question can be considered: Why would someone consider an alternative to a private foundation? As noted, the fundamental generic alternative to a private foundation is a public charity.

Thus, it is appropriate to next review the advantages of public charity status rather than private foundation status. They are:

- Public charities can avoid the private foundation rules. Private foundations are subject to a battery of rules as to their program activities, investments, and other operations (Chapters 3–8). These rules are complex and can be onerous; a misstep can lead to substantial taxation. As a general rule, however, these rules are not applicable to public charities.

NOTE: One of these sets of rules applicable only to private foundations is those concerning self-dealing (Chapter 3). The excess benefit transactions rules, however, are much like the self-dealing rules; the excess benefit transactions rules, enforced by the intermediate sanctions penalties, are applicable with respect to public charities.[6]

- Public charities have greater flexibility as to administration of their program activities. There is almost no law on this point (other than that the activities stay within the ambit of what is considered by the law to be charitable, educational, religious, scientific, and the like). By contrast, private foundations must expend at least a base percentage of their income for charitable purposes (Chapter 4) and must be concerned that the expenditures are for appropriate ends (Chapter 7). As an illustration, a private foundation making grants to individuals is expected to be in compliance with a much more intricate body of law on the point than is the case with public charities (Q 7:10–7:17).

- Often contributions to public charities are more deductible in a given year than to private foundations. This can be the outcome because of the percentage limitations placed on the annual deductibility of charitable gifts by individuals (Q 17:4–17:7).
- The enhanced deductibility of charitable gifts made to public charities also can occur as the result of certain rules making gifts of property to private foundations far less deductible than if the property was contributed to a public charity (Q 17:3).
- The annual information return filed by public charities (usually Form 990) is generally simpler to prepare than the annual information return filed by private foundations (Form 990-PF) (Chapter 10).
- Public charities are not subject to a general tax on their investment income.[7] Private foundations, by contrast, are subject to a tax on their net investment income (Chapter 8).

There are, of course, advantages as to qualification as a private foundation. They are:

- A greater acceptance of the idea that the donor to the charity (individual, family, or corporation) maintains control of the charity. Thus, for example, all of the trustees of the foundation can be family members of the donor or members of the board of directors of a for-profit corporation owned by the donor.
- The donor basically retains control of the use of the private foundation's income and assets. This does not mean that the donor(s) can use this income or assets for private ends. Donors in this situation can and do, nonetheless, have much more direct involvement in the selection of charitable activities and the funding of them than is the case with involvement in the functions of public charities.
- The employees of a private foundation can be members of the donor's family. This affords an individual the opportunity to provide his or her sons and/or daughters with gainful employment. These individuals are disqualified persons with respect to the private foundation (Chapter 2) and thus subject to the self-dealing rules (Chapter 3). Nonetheless, if the services are necessary to achievement of the exempt purposes of the foundation and the compensation is reasonable, the employment of these individuals should not result in self-dealing.
- A private foundation can facilitate an individual's status in the community (or perhaps nationally) as a philanthropist, far more so than can a public charity. The foundation usually bears the donor's name (or the name of the donor's family or business). Individuals and organizations approach these donors, seeking assistance from the private foundation. They are more likely to be invited to social and sporting events, and otherwise integrated into the community as an important element of it. They could achieve this end by making gifts personally to the

various charities, but the existence of the private foundation as a dis-crete entity can provide the donor and his or her family members a special aura.

To look at all this from a different perspective, the principal disadvan-tages to private foundation status are that the charitable organization is subject to the private foundation rules, there are greater limitations as to deductibility of gifts, there is a tax on the private foundation's net investment income, and the information return to be filed with the IRS is more complex.

Q 15:2   Can a supporting organization be an alternative to a private foundation?

Absolutely. In fact, overall, the supporting organization (Q 12:15) reigns today as the premier preferable vehicle as an alternative to a private foundation. In general, the utility of a supporting organization in this setting is that, while it can look and function much as a private foundation, it is a public charity.

Q 15:3   What are the other alternatives to a private foundation?

If a charitable organization is to be an entity other than a private foundation and other than a supporting organization, it could be another type of public charity. The realistic choices here include qualification as a school or as a form of publicly supported charity. Other options of this nature include a uni-versity, college, hospital, medical research organization, or church, but these alternatives require the meeting of special and unique rules, and thus are not often authentic alternatives. (In general, see Chapter 12.)

Another alternative to the private foundation is the donor-advised fund (Q 15:9). Technically, these funds are subaccounts within a larger entity. This larger entity may be a community foundation, a charitable gift fund (Q 15:11), or some other organization maintaining donor-advised funds as the entirety or some of its activities.

Still another of these alternatives is the charitable remainder trust (Q 17:28). Because of the nature of this entity, however, it is the least feasible of the alternatives to private foundations.

Q 15:4   What are the advantages of supporting organization classifica-tion rather than private foundation classification?

The essential defining feature of a supporting organization in relation to a private foundation is that the former is a *public charity* (Q 12:15). It is thus tax-exempt as a charitable entity and contributions to it are deductible under the federal tax law to the fullest allowable extent (Q 17:5, Q 17:7). Of major impor-tance is the fact that the supporting organization is not subject to the private foundation rules, even though it usually functions in many ways much the same as a private foundation (grant-making).

Thus, generally, there is no payout obligation imposed on a supporting organization, as is the case for private foundations (Chapter 4). There is no tax on investment income (Chapter 8), and the supporting organization has greater flexibility as to the administration of its charitable programs (Chapter 7). The annual information return filed by supporting organizations is generally easier to prepare than the one filed by private foundations (Chapter 10).

Q 15:5 What are the disadvantages of supporting organization classification rather than private foundation classification?

From the standpoint of comparison to a private foundation, the chief disadvantage is that the entity cannot be controlled by disqualified persons (Q 12:24). (For the most part, the supporting organization must be under the control of the organization or organizations it supports.) When an individual, or group of individuals, is contemplating the establishment of a private foundation, and the alternative of the supporting organization is introduced, the principal reason that the supporting organization approach is rejected is this factor. As noted (Q 15:1), one of the principal advantages of the private foundation is the ability of its funders, and family members, to maintain control over the charitable organizations and the use of its income and assets. For donors of significant amounts of money or property, this often is a pivotal factor influencing the choice—tilting the selection in favor of the private foundation.

Otherwise, the similarity between the two categories is considerable. For example, the supporting organization can have the name of an individual, family, or corporation. It can be an employer of the donor's children (as long as the control rule is not violated). And, as discussed next, both types of entities are or can be grant-makers.

A supporting organization, by definition, functions to support one or more entities (Q 12:17). Usually, these entities are specified in the governing instruments of the supporting organization (Q 12:18). With limited exceptions (Q 12:20), therefore, the grant-making by the supporting organization is confined to these identified supported organizations. The supporting organization thus lacks flexibility as to selection of its grantees. The typical private foundation, by contrast, is free to support whatever charity or charities it wishes to support at any point in time.

There is another disadvantage to qualification as a supporting organization at this time. There have been some abuses of the supporting organization (Q 12:25). This is leading to scrutiny of them by members of Congress, the IRS, the Treasury Department, and the media. At this time, it is difficult to predict

---

COMMENT: The principal issue—the one as to control by disqualified persons—is clear under present statutory law and thus not likely to be addressed by Congress. Rather, the law may be revised so that some of the private foundation rules are made applicable to donor-advised funds (Q 15:21).

---

what, if any, changes may be made to the supporting organization requirements, but it may be assumed that any change would reduce the utility of the supporting organization.

The scrutiny being given to supporting organizations, while intense and portentous, should not, however, by itself, be used as a reason for not establishing a supporting organization under the appropriate (and lawful) circumstances.

Q 15:6   Can a charitable remainder trust be an alternative to a private foundation?

Yes, but only in a sense. First, a little background. A charitable remainder trust (Q 17:28) is a *split-interest trust* that has been established to create a remainder interest in property, with that interest in the gift property designated for one or more charitable organizations. The donor(s) receive a charitable contribution deduction for the transfer of the remainder interest.

A qualified charitable remainder trust must provide for a specified distribution of income, at least annually, to one or more beneficiaries, at least one of which is not a charitable organization. The flow of income must be for a life or lives, or for a term not to exceed 20 years. An irrevocable remainder interest must be held for the benefit of the charity or paid over to it. The noncharitable beneficiaries are the holders of the income interests, and the charitable organization has the remainder interest.

Conventionally, once the income interest or interests expire, the assets in a charitable remainder trust are distributed to, or for the use of, the charitable organization that is the remainder interest beneficiary. It does not happen very often, but the property in the trust may, instead of being distributed to the charity, be retained in the trust for application for charitable purposes.

NOTE: If the second option is selected, the trust will have to be qualified for tax-exempt status as a charitable entity. It is almost certain to constitute a private foundation in that form.

Q 15:7   What are the advantages of classification as a charitable remainder trust rather than a private foundation?

There aren't many. As noted (Q 15:6), the charitable remainder trust is a planned giving vehicle that is designed to be a passive split-interest trust, holding property and making distributions to the income beneficiaries until the time comes to transfer the assets in the trust to the charity that is the remainder beneficiary. About the only advantage is that, if the remainder beneficiary is a public charity, the extent of deductibility of the transfer is based on the more favorable rules pertaining to contributions to public charities rather than the rules as to gifts to private foundations (Q 17:5, Q 17:7).

Q 15:8   What are the disadvantages of classification as a charitable remainder trust rather than a private foundation?

The disadvantages of classification as a charitable remainder trust rather than a private foundation clearly outweigh whatever advantage there may be (Q 15:7). Basically, they are two different types of entities. The use of a charitable remainder trust in this context is unlikely if only because it is quite difficult, if not impossible, to operate charitable program activities out of this type of trust.

A transfer of money or property to a private foundation gives rise to a charitable deduction—whatever it may be—for the entire amount transferred to the charity. In the case of the contribution by means of a charitable remainder trust, the charitable deduction for it is limited to the value of the remainder interest to be transferred to the charitable beneficiary at the close of the income payment period. This is known as a *partial interest gift* (Q 17:27).

In any event, many of the private foundation rules (Q 1:4) are applicable to charitable remainder trusts.[8] This is because Congress was fearful that sophisticated tax planners would use charitable remainder trusts as a means to sidestep the private foundation restrictions. In practice, this rarely happens: The charitable remainder trust simply is not a viable alternative to the conventional private foundation.

Q 15:9   What is a *donor-advised fund*?

A *donor-advised fund* is a fund (not a separate entity) that is inside a charitable organization. These funds are created and maintained within public charities, such as community foundations, colleges and universities, churches, and charitable gift funds. Indeed, these funds were initiated by community foundations, which have existed since the early 1900s, beginning with The Cleveland (Ohio) Foundation, which was formed in 1914. Today there are about 400 community foundations and a growing number of charitable gift funds (Q 15:11), accounting for billions of dollars in assets and income.

Thus, this vehicle has been part of the federal tax law of charity for nearly a century, yet only recently has it become the subject of considerable scrutiny and criticism. Indeed, there are three federal tax issues involved (Q 15:16, Q 15:17, Q 15:19), all based on the fundamental fact that the donor-advised fund is a popular alternative to a private foundation. Some choose to state the matter somewhat differently, regarding donor-advised funds as a means of sidestepping or avoiding the private foundation rules.

A donor-advised fund is not a separate legal entity. Rather, as noted, it is a fund within an organization, which is a public charity. This type of fund is often referred to as an *account* or sometimes as a *subaccount* of the host organization. A contribution to a donor-advised fund is, under present law (Q 15:17), treated as made to a public charity.

These accounts can be in the name of an individual, family, corporation, or cause, or used facilitate anonymous gifts. They often bear the name of the contributor or the contributor's family or business. Because of its name, a donor-advised fund can appear to be a separate legal entity—seemingly a charitable organization with many of the attributes of a private foundation.

The donor-advised fund is to be contrasted with the *donor-directed fund*. In the case of a donor-directed fund, the donor or a designee of the donor retains the right to direct the investment of the fund's assets and/or to direct grants from the fund for charitable purposes. By contrast, with the donor-advised fund, the donor has the ability (but not a legal right) to make recommendations (proffer advice) as to investment policy and/or the making of grants.

The donor-advised fund has, as noted, long been a staple of community foundations. In recent years, other types of charitable organizations and commercial investment companies have created donor-advised funds, recognized as public charities by the IRS. As long as the use of these funds was confined to community foundations, there was no controversy; the attention accorded these funds, including criticism, started when their use was extended to other public charities.

These funds can be viable alternatives to the formation of private foundations. The individual or individuals involved may wish to avoid the administrative responsibilities (including the annual reporting and other regulatory requirements) of operating a private foundation. Another factor may be that the amount of money or property involved is too small to warrant the establishment of a private foundation.

Q 15:10 Can a donor-advised fund be an alternative to a private foundation?

Yes. A donor-advised fund, in the correct set of circumstances, can be an alternative to a private foundation. The greater likelihood, however, is that the preferential alternative is the supporting organization (Q 15:2).

Q 15:11 What is a *charitable gift fund*?

The term *charitable gift fund* is not a legal term. A charitable gift fund is another name for a donor-advised fund. Sometimes the term is used to describe a donor-advised fund that has an operational affiliation with an investment company. One of the most successful of the donor-advised funds is the one established by Fidelity Investments: the Fidelity Investments Charitable Gift Fund. The term *charitable gift fund* has evolved in the aftermath of the development of that fund.

Q 15:12 Is the concept of the donor-advised fund defined in the law?

Basically, no. The Internal Revenue Code and the income tax regulations offer only two significant methods for donors to charitable organizations to exercise any posttransfer control or direction over the use of money or property irrevocably transferred to charity for which the donor is entitled to a charitable deduction in the year of the transfer. One method is use of a special type of private foundation that is, in essence, a donor-directed fund (see below). This entity is referred to as the *common fund foundation.*

The other method is utilization of the community foundation or community trust.[9] The community foundation regulations and another regulation (see below) only allow donor designation at the time of the gift and donor advice (not donor direction) after the date of the gift.

Relevant to the concept of a charitable gift and the matter of reciprocal benefits to donors is the fact that the federal law, as noted, distinguishes between donor-advised funds and donor-directed funds. To reiterate, the latter type of fund involves an arrangement between a charitable organization and a donor where the donor retains one or more rights as to the subsequent investment and/or disposition of the subject of the gift. By contrast, a donor-advised fund does not have the feature of donor-direction but allows the donor to tender advice as to subsequent investment and/or disposition of the subject of the gift.

There is little specific law on donor-advised funds and donor-directed funds, however. The closest reference in the Internal Revenue Code to the concept is the provision authorizing the common fund foundation; deductible charitable contributions are allowed in these circumstances.[10] This is the case even though the donor and his or her spouse can annually designate public charities to which the foundation must grant the income and principal of the original contribution. Thus, the common fund foundation is a type of private foundation that is closely comparable to a donor-directed fund. (There is nothing in the Internal Revenue Code that defines an entity comparable to a donor-advised fund.)

In the case of community foundations, which hold themselves out as a bundle of donor-advised funds, a donor at the time of the gift (i.e., at the time of creation of the component fund) is permitted to designate the charitable purpose of the gift or the specific charity that will receive the income or principal, consistent with the community foundation's exempt purposes.[11] These regulations do not permit the donor to direct, aside from the original designation, which charity may receive distributions or the timing of the distributions to the charitable recipient.[12] The donor may also offer nonbinding advice to the community fund manager regarding payouts from the component fund. (When a donor offers advice of this nature, the IRS is likely to carefully examine the facts involved to determine whether the giving of the "advice" by the donor is in actuality an indirect reservation of a right to direct the distributions (Q 15:15).)

There is, nonetheless, a determination from the IRS that is somewhat pertinent to this analysis.[13] This private letter ruling involved a private foundation, the trustees of which determined to transfer all of its assets to a community foundation, which in turn would place the assets in a donor-advised fund. (The private letter ruling does not define this term.) The private foundation would remain in existence for the sole purpose of advising the community foundation on the use of the fund for charitable purposes. The IRS ruled that the retention of this ability to make this type of recommendation would not constitute a prohibited material restriction as that term is used for purposes of the private foundation termination tax (Chapter 8).

A private foundation can make a grant (qualifying distribution) to a donor-advised fund in satisfaction of the foundation's mandatory payout requirements (Chapter 5). These distribution requirements can be satisfied even though the private foundation's governing board retains the ability to make recommendations as to the subsequent granting of the money.[14]

The law concerning *prohibited material restrictions* (Q 15:18) is very similar to the concepts distinguishing donor-directed funds and donor-advised funds. This body of law is in the federal income tax regulations.[15] The test under these restrictions is whether the transferee of assets is prevented from freely and effectively employing the transferred assets or the income from them for charitable purposes. For example, if the transferor reserved the right to direct one or more public charities to which the transferee must distribute the transferred assets and/or income, that would constitute a prohibited material restriction. The same is true with respect to restrictions on the ability of the transferee to maintain or manage the assets or to any other condition that is imposed on the transferee that prevents it from exercising ultimate control over the assets received by the transferor.

The above-referenced IRS determination[16] holds that the ability to make the recommendation expressed by the trustees of the private foundation does not constitute a prohibited material restriction.[17]

Q 15:13 What are the advantages of classification as a donor-advised fund rather than a private foundation?

There are several advantages to use of a donor-advised fund rather than a private foundation. They are:

- The organization housing the funds is a public charity. Therefore, the tax deduction for charitable giving to the donor-advised fund is governed by the more generous percentage limitations (Q 17:5, Q 17:7). Likewise, property may be contributed to the subaccount, with the charitable deduction generally based on the fair market value of the property (Q 17:7). In general, then, each subaccount constituting a donor-advised fund is treated, for charitable giving purposes, as a public charity.
- There is no need to establish and maintain an organization. This fact eliminates the expenses of establishing an entity, such as incorporation, legal, and accounting fees.

NOTE: The host public charity will charge a small annual maintenance fee for each subaccount and perhaps a start-up fee.

- There is no requirement for filing an application for recognition of tax-exempt status (Chapter 16). The subaccount takes on the tax-exempt status (and the public charity status) of the host public charity.
- There is no requirement for filing an annual information return (Chapter 10). The program and economic activity of the subaccount is reflected in the annual information return filed by the host public charity.
- Most, if not all, other administrative responsibilities associated with operating a separate legal entity are eliminated.
- The program activity in the donor-advised fund is grant-making. Thus, the fund can function in many ways like a private foundation, yet it is not subject to the private foundation rules (Q 1:4).

CAUTION: This statement is made in reflection of existing statutory law. As discussed (Q 15:20), however, the IRS is administratively attempting to impose some of the private foundation rules on host public charities and their donor-advised funds.

- Since there is no separate legal organization, there is no board of directors or trustees for the donor-advised fund. Thus, there are no worries about board liability.
- The donor-advised fund can have the name of the donor, donor's family, donor's business, or the like, making it appear to the outside world as a private foundation.
- The amount of money and/or property involved in establishing the fund may be too small to warrant starting a private foundation, yet the donor-advised fund facilitates the use of a philanthropic vehicle anyway.

Q 15:14 What are the disadvantages of classification as a donor-advised fund rather than a private foundation?

There are some disadvantages to use of a donor-advised fund. Some of them are the reverse of the advantages (Q 15:13). These disadvantages are:

- The donor-advised fund usually cannot be used for program activities other than grant-making. Thus, for example, one of these subaccounts is not a suitable alternative for a private operating foundation (Q 14:2).
- The donor-advised fund will not have employees. It is, therefore, of little utility in providing employment for family members.
- The donor-advised funds are under the control and direction of the board of directors or trustees of the host public charity. Thus, the donor cannot select the board (or perhaps not be on the board), as is the case with a private foundation.
- The donor, having made the gift, has no subsequent control over the contributed funds and/or property.

- The IRS frowns on grants from donor-advised funds to private foundations or to foreign charities.
- Donor-advised funds are raising a number of legal issues (Q 15:15). They are currently under scrutiny by members of Congress, congressional committee staff, the Treasury Department, the IRS, and the media. It is not clear what, if any, legislative changes may emerge from this analysis.

Q 15:15 What are the legal issues being raised by donor-advised funds?

The legal issues being raised by donor-advised funds are the following:

- Are the organizations that host them really charitable entities, or are they another form of (nonexempt) commercial financial institution (Q 15:16)? This issue has raised primarily by the stand-alone entity that has the creation and maintenance of donor-advised funds as its primary or sole function.

> **NOTE:** Some who disparage these types of collectives of funds term them *accommodation charities.*

- Are transfers of money and/or property to donor-advised funds actually *gifts,* or do the transferors retain sufficient control over the subsequent use of the money or property so that there has not been the requisite parting of right, title, and interest in the money or property? (Q 15:17)
- Do the organizations that host donor-advised funds, assuming they are charitable entities (Q 15:16), qualify as publicly supported charities, or should the funding be considered support only for the "ultimate" charitable recipient? (Q 15:19)

> **NOTE:** If the latter, the charitable organization would be considered a mere conduit and a private foundation (unless it was organized and operated as a supporting organization.

Q 15:16 What are the details of the issue as to the charitable status of organizations with donor-advised funds?

This issue concerns organizations that have as their primary or sole function the origination and maintenance of donor-advised funds. These are the stand-alone collectives of donor-advised funds, including charitable gift funds (Q 15:11).

> **NOTE:** Technically, this issue could extend to the tax-exempt status of community foundations, but there have not been any challenges by the IRS of this nature to date.

The view of the IRS is that an organization that is a collective of donor-advised funds is an association of transferors for which financial services are commercially performed for fees. This perspective holds that there is little or no charitable activity being undertaken. The distribution of funds from the subaccounts is not really seen as grant-making. The extent of "control" (Q 15:18) by "donors" (Q 15:17) is perceived as violative of the doctrine of private benefit or even private inurement.

The IRS has not had much success with this argument in the courts. In fact, the first case on the issue led to a monumental loss. The IRS challenged the donor-advised fund technique in court, attempting to deny tax-exempt status to a public charity maintaining donor-advised funds, contending that the entity was merely an association of donors for which commercial services were being performed for fees and that it was violating the prohibitions on private inurement and private benefit.[18] The IRS asserted that the organization's "activities are all originated, funded, and controlled by small related groups, by single individuals, or by families" and that "these individual donors retain full control of the funds."

The court, however, found that donors to the organization "relinquish all ownership and custody of the donated funds or property" and that the organization is "free to accept or reject any suggestion or request made by a donor." Indeed, the court enthused that the "goal" of the organization "is to create an effective national network to respond to many worthy charitable needs at the local level which in many cases might go unmet" and that its activities "promote public policy and represent the very essence of charitable benevolence as envisioned by Congress in enacting" tax-exempt status for charitable organizations.

Ten years later, the IRS prevailed on the point.[19] The entity involved was structured much the same as the collective of donor-advised funds in the previous case. The trustee of the fund was bound by the donor's enforceable conditions as to disposition of its funds to ultimate charities. The fund was ruled to not be tax-exempt as a charitable organization. The court wrote: "The manner in which the [f]und's investment activity would be conducted makes clear that one of the purposes of the [f]und is to allow persons to take a charitable deduction for a donation to the [f]und while retaining investment control over the donation." This opinion did not differentiate between material and other restrictions (Q 15:18).

Yet the IRS's victory in this case was short-lived. This decision was appealed, which led to settlement negotiations. The trustee of the fund agreed, as requested by the IRS, to eliminate the language in the fund's document that gave donors the control that was found by the lower court to be unwarranted private benefit. Nonetheless, for over one year, the IRS refused to grant the fund recognition of tax-exempt status, eventually causing the court of appeals, in frustration, to vacate the district court's decision and to direct that court to issue an order that the fund is an exempt charitable entity.[20]

The government was of the view that this amendment did not "sufficiently address the inadequacies" of the fund's operations. It was contended that the administrative record showed that the fund would not "take complete control over the contributions." Rather, the government asserted that the fund will "adhere to the directions of its donors regarding the investment and the ultimate distribution of the contributed funds." This amendment does not, the government asserts, prevent the fund from "providing investment services and acting as an administrative conduit for its donors' funds."[21]

It may be that this issue as to tax exemption of donor-advised funds will be the subject of, and will be shaped by, further litigation.[22]

Q 15:17 What are the details of the issue as to the tax law status of transfers to organizations with donor-advised funds?

One of the legal issues raised by donor-advised funds is whether the transfer to the fund constitutes a gift. That is, the question arises as to whether the transfer to the fund is incomplete, in that the donor, by reserving an ability to advise, has retained some form of "right" that precludes the transfer from being a completed gift.

There must be a *gift* before there can be a *charitable gift.* Integral to the concept of the charitable contribution deduction is the fundamental requirement that the payment of money or property to a charitable organization be transferred pursuant to a transaction that constitutes a gift. While the Internal Revenue Code does not define the word *gift,* the federal income tax regulations contain this definition: A *contribution* is a "voluntary transfer of money or property that is made with no expectation of procuring financial benefit commensurate with the amount of the transfer."[23]

This definition is reflective of the observation of the U.S. Supreme Court years ago that a gift is a transfer motivated by "detached or disinterested generosity."[24] Any condition (see below) by which the donor retains complete dominion and control over the transferred property makes the gift incomplete.[25] An incomplete gift cannot give rise to a deductible contribution.

The Supreme Court also ruled, in the context of determining the concept of a *charitable gift,* that a "payment of money [or a transfer of property] generally cannot constitute a charitable contribution if the contributor expects a substantial benefit in return."[26] Subsequently, the Supreme Court wrote that an exchange having an "inherently reciprocal nature" is not a gift and thus cannot be a charitable gift where the recipient is a charity.[27] At the same time, where a benefit to a donor arising out of a transfer to a charitable organization is *incidental,* the benefit will not defeat the charitable deduction.[28]

Thus, a *charitable gift* can be defined as a voluntary transfer of money or property to a charitable organization without actual or anticipated receipt by the donor of more than incidental economic considerations or benefits in return. The value inherent in any economic consideration or benefit received in return, other than an incidental one, must be subtracted from the value of the total gift to determine the value of the actual gift (the deductible portion).

In most situations, once a donor has made a gift to a charity, the gift becomes the property of the charitable organization and the donor retains none or perhaps a little authority over the use (including investment) or expenditure of the funds. The issue in this context is the extent of any donor control that may arise when a gift is made to a donor-advised fund, that is, is made but the donor or a designee retains the ability to make recommendations as to subsequent transfers of the fund's income.

This issue is receiving intense scrutiny by Congress, the Department of the Treasury, and the IRS at this time. The principal reason for this development is the advent of the *charitable gift fund* (Q 15:11).

The traditional type of donor-advised funds are those that, as noted, are component entities of community foundations. A monumental rivalry for millions of dollars in charitable gifts is under way between community foundations and charitable gift funds, and this activity is helping to stimulate and maintain the government's scrutiny in this area. This focus has brought intense scrutiny of donor-advised funds.

This use of charitable gift funds involves the law concerning conditional gifts. A *conditional gift* is one that is made subject to the occurrence of an event, either before (*condition precedent*) or after (*condition subsequent*). This matter concerns conditions subsequent, namely, gifts made to a charitable organization containing binding covenants on the charitable donee.

Usually, with respect to the tax consequences of conditional gifts, the only party that may be subject to any risk is the donor who is taking a full charitable deduction yet may not lawfully be allowed to do so. The tax-exempt status of the charitable donee may, however, be implicated (Q 15:16).

Conditions subsequent that are not negligible can defeat the income tax charitable deduction. In one case, donors gifted real property to a charitable trust but retained control over its future occupancy and sale; the entire federal income tax charitable contribution deduction was disallowed because of these retained rights (although they were incapable of valuation).[29] The charitable deduction for a gift of a rare book collection to a charity was disallowed because the donor retained an unlimited right of access to the collection and the right to deny access to it to others.[30] An illustration of a negligible or incidental condition subsequent was a gift of theatrical materials to a public library, where the materials could not be copied or removed from the library without the donor's permission.[31]

This body of law, as to whether a completed gift has been made, is reflected in the private foundation termination rules. In those rules is embedded the doctrine of the *prohibited material restriction*.

Q 15:18 What are the *prohibited material restrictions* rules?

One of the reasons for focus on these types of donor funds is the need for a judgment as to whether a transaction that is otherwise a charitable gift is not, in law, a completed gift at all because the donor retains too much control over the subsequent use and disposition of the gift money or property. At least in the context of donor-advised gift funds (and thus presumably in most other donor fund contexts, including donor-directed funds), the IRS uses the criteria provided in the private foundation termination rules to determine whether a completed gift has been made or not.

A charitable organization can terminate its private foundation status by transferring all of its income and assets to one or more public charities (Chapter 12). An issue that can arise is whether the "transfer" is in fact a completed one. The income tax regulations provide criteria for making this determination.

The regulations concerning termination of private foundation status focus on whether a grantor private foundation has transferred "all of its right, title, and interest in and to" the funds (including any property) granted.[32] In order to effectuate such a transfer, a grantor private foundation "may not impose any material restriction or condition" that prevents the grantee from "freely and effectively employing the transferred assets, or the income derived therefrom, in furtherance of its exempt purposes."[33] Whether a particular condition or restriction imposed upon a transfer of assets is *material* or not must be determined from all of the facts and circumstances of the transfer.[34]

The presence of some or all of the following *nonadverse factors* (or positive characteristics) are not considered as preventing the grantee from "freely and effectively employing the transferred assets, or the income derived therefrom, in furtherance of its exempt purposes":

- *Name.* The transfer is to a fund that is given a name or other designation which is the same as or similar to that of the grantor private foundation or otherwise memorializes the creator of the foundation or his or her family.
- *Purpose.* The income and assets of the fund are to be used for a designated purpose or for one or more particular public charities, and that use is consistent with the public charity's charitable purpose.
- *Administration.* The transferred money or property is administered in an identifiable or separate fund, some or all of the principal of which is not to be distributed for a specified period, if the grantee public charity is the legal and equitable owner of the fund and the governing body of the public charity exercises ultimate and direct authority and control over the fund.[35]
- *Retention Requirement.* The grantor private foundation transfers property the continued retention of which by the grantee is required by the transferor if the retention is important to the achievement of charitable purposes.[36]

The presence of any of seven factors—the *adverse factors*—is considered as preventing the grantee from "freely and effectively employing the transferred assets, or the income derived therefrom, in furtherance of its exempt purposes." Only two of the factors are pertinent to this analysis.[37]

The first of these adverse factors concerns control over distributions. The issue is whether the transferor private foundation, a disqualified person with respect to it (i.e., a board member, officer, or substantial contributor), or any person or committee designated by, or pursuant to the terms of an agreement with, such a person (collectively, the *grantor*) reserved the right, directly or indirectly, to name the persons to which the transferee public charity must distribute or to direct the timing of the distributions.[38]

With respect to this factor, the IRS is to carefully examine whether the seeking of advice by the transferee from, or the giving of advice by, any grantor after the assets have been transferred to the transferee constitutes an indirect reservation of a right to direct the distributions. In this case, the reservation of this type of a right will be considered to exist where the only criterion considered by the public charity in making a distribution of income or principal from a grantor's fund is advice offered by the grantor. Whether there is a reservation of this type of right is to be determined on the basis of all of the facts and circumstances. In making this determination, the elements contained in the six factors, in addition to the five factors (both of which are discussed next), are to be taken into consideration.[39]

The presence of some or all of the following factors—the *six factors*—indicates that the reservation of this type of right does not exist:

1. There has been an independent investigation by the staff of the public charity evaluating whether the grantor's advice is consistent with specific charitable needs most deserving of support by the recipient charity (as determined by it).
2. The public charity has promulgated guidelines enumerating specific charitable needs consistent with the charitable purposes of the public charity.
3. The grantor's advice is consistent with these guidelines.
4. The public charity has instituted an educational program publicizing these guidelines to donors and other persons.
5. The public charity distributes funds in excess of amounts distributed from the grantor's fund to the same or similar types of organizations or charitable needs as those recommended by the grantor.
6. The solicitations for funds of the public charity specifically state that the public entity will not be bound by advice offered by the grantor.[40]

The presence of some or all of the following factors—the *five factors*—indicates that the reservation of a right exists:

1. The solicitation of funds by the public charity states or implies that the grantor's advice will be followed.
2. A pattern of conduct on the part of that charity creates an expectation that the grantor's advice will be followed.
3. The advice of a grantor (whether restricted to a distribution of income or principal from the grantor's trust or fund or not) is limited to distributions of amounts from the grantor's fund (and certain factors are not present—namely, the first two of the six factors).
4. Only the advice of the grantor as to distributions from the grantor's fund is solicited by the public charity, and no procedure is provided for considering advice from persons other than the grantor with respect to the fund.

5. For the year involved and all prior years, the public charity follows the advice of all grantors with respect to their funds substantially all of the time.[41]

The other factor of the adverse factors that may be relevant pertains to any agreement that is entered into between the transferor private foundation and the transferee public charity "which establishes irrevocable relationships with respect to the maintenance or management of assets transferred to the public charity . . . "[42] This factor is additionally described by a reference to relationships "such as continuing relationships with banks, brokerage firms, investment counselors, or other advisors with regard to the investments or other property transferred to the public charity."[43]

(Of the seven factors, the remaining five are irrelevant to this matter. They are those pertaining to certain mandatory actions or withholding of actions, assumptions of leases, retentions of investment assets, rights of first refusal, and any other condition that prevents the transferee public charity "from exercising ultimate control over the assets received from the transferor private foundation for purposes consistent with its exempt purposes."[44])

The presence of any of the seven factors is, as noted, considered as preventing the transferee from "freely and effectively" utilizing the transferred assets or income from them in furtherance of charitable purposes. To have application of these rules be deemed to cause something less than a full transfer for purposes of termination of private foundation status and thus for purposes of determining whether a transfer is a qualifying distribution (Chapter 4), however, a restriction, right, or condition also must be material.[45]

Whether a particular condition or restriction imposed on a transfer of assets is *material* or not must be determined from all of the facts and circumstances of the transfer.[46] The tax regulations state that some of the "more significant" facts and circumstances to be considered in making this determination—the *materiality factors*—are whether:

- The public charity is the owner in fee of the assets it received from the private foundation.
- The assets are to be held and administered by the public charity in a manner consistent with one or more of its exempt purposes.
- The governing body of the public charity has the ultimate authority and control over the assets and the income derived from them.
- The governing body of the public charity is organized and operated so as to be independent from the transferor.[47]

As to the fourth of these factors, it also must be determined from all of the facts and circumstances.[48] Some of the "more significant" of these facts and circumstances to be considered—the *independence factors*—are:

- Whether, and to what extent, members of the governing body are comprised of individuals selected by the transferor private foundation or its

disqualified persons, or are themselves disqualified persons with respect to the foundation.
- Whether, and to what extent, members of the governing body are selected by public officials acting in their capacities as such.
- How long a period of time each member of the governing body may serve in that capacity.[49]

In one instance, a private foundation proposed to provide an endowment to fund the operating expenses of a public charity, including those for construction of a facility. The funds were to be paid to an escrow agent, who would hold the funds until certain conditions were satisfied. The purpose for establishment of the endowment, before construction took place, was to assure bondholders and contributors that funds would be available to support the entity. In finding the restrictions to not be "material," the IRS observed that the private foundation had given up any right to control use of the funds in the grantee's possession, other than through the restrictions set forth in the escrow agreement; the private foundation retained no right of reversion or other interest in the transferred assets; ultimate distribution of the funds would occur within a reasonable period of time; and the ultimate grantee was a public charity.[50]

Q 15:19   What are the details of the issue as to the public charity status of organizations with donor-advised funds?

Another issue being raised by the functions of charitable organizations that maintain donor-advised funds—particularly those that maintain these funds as their sole function—is whether these entities qualify as publicly supported charities.

Community foundations, charitable gift funds, and other entities maintaining donor-advised funds to a significant extent are classified as donative-type publicly supported charities (Q 12:4). This is because the contributions to these organizations, albeit earmarked for donor-advised funds, are treated, in whole or in part, as public support for the charity. The IRS, however, has been fretting over the propriety of treating donor-advised funds as publicly supported charities on the theory that these charities may not be *supported* in a technical, legal sense.

When a grant is made from a donor-advised fund to a charity—which may be termed the *ultimate beneficiary*—the grant amount can be regarded (in whole or in part) as public support for the ultimate beneficiary. For some time, it was the view of the IRS that these gifts to charities maintaining donor-advised funds amounted to public support for both the "intermediate" and "ultimate" beneficiary charities.[51] As the controversy widened, however, the IRS withdrew its views on the subject.[52]

This issue has been festering. This fact is reflected in an IRS publication issued in 1995.[53] The IRS is not troubled by the concept that "earmarked" gifts are forms of public support for the "ultimate" charitable recipient. It is the treatment of these gifts as public support for the "intermediate" entity—the collective of donor-advised funds—that gives the IRS pause.

The IRS's publication feigns objectivity in places, then loses even that in others. Thus, it was written: "There is no authority in the regulations or elsewhere that the earmarked funds are treated as support for the intermediary organizations as well as the ultimate recipient." It is true that the law is silent on the point, but that does not necessarily mean that this dual characterization of the funds for tax purposes is inappropriate. This is particularly the case with donor-advised funds, where the gifts are not really "earmarked." The statement is thus loaded, rendered predisposed to the conclusion.

This analysis posited a second approach, in that it applied the distinction between contributions *to* a charitable organization and those *for the use of* a charitable organization. The idea is that only contributions to a charitable organization can be treated as public support, since the charity is free to use the gifts in its charitable program. The IRS essay asserts that an "earmarked" gift and a gift "for the use of" a charity are similar in that "both have qualities of property held in trust." That is, this view asserts that the "intermediary" entity is the functional equivalent of a trustee for the "ultimate" charity, so that these "earmarked" contributions ought not to be regarded as public support for the intermediate entity—the organization housing charitable gift funds.

There are fundamental problems with this approach. This analysis often fails to differentiate between donor-advised funds and donor-directed funds. Given the limited recommendatory authority associated with the former, it is not credible to assert that the arrangement involves a trust relationship. Also, it is common for donors to make restricted gifts, where the restriction is a programmatic one (e.g., for research or scholarships); there is no authority for a proposition that these restrictions give rise to a trust. Moreover, the statutory definition of *support*[54] does not embody this dubious dichotomy in this context between gifts to and for the use of charity.

COMMENT: Notwithstanding all of this concern, when the time came for the IRS to rule on the issue, it ruled in favor of the charitable organization. That is, the agency held that contributions to the organization, destined for its donor-advised fund, qualified as support from the general public.[55]

Q 15:20 What private foundation rules is the IRS trying to impose on public charities that maintain donor-advised funds?

The following representations are being required by the IRS, at least in certain instances:

- The organization will see to it that its grants for each year will equal or exceed 5 percent of its average net assets on a fiscal-year rolling basis. This, of course, is adherence to the private foundation payout requirement (Chapter 4). If this level of grant activity is not attained, the organization will identify the named accounts (donor-advised funds) from which grants over the period totaled less than 5 percent of each account's average assets. The organization will contact the donor advisors of these accounts to request that they recommend grants of at least this amount. If a donor advisor does not provide the qualified grant recommendations, the organization is authorized to transfer an amount up to 5 percent of assets from the named account to one or more charities selected by the organization.

- The organization will include language in its promotional materials stating that it will investigate allegations of improper use of grant funds for the private benefit of donor advisors.
- The organization will include language in its letters to grantees to the effect that grants are to be used by grantees exclusively in furtherance of charitable purposes and cannot be used for the private benefit of donor advisors. This is intended to parallel the prohibitions on private foundations as to the making of taxable expenditures (Chapter 7).

Q 15:21 Are these issues as to donor-advised funds likely to be resolved by legislation?

It could happen. A proposal being bandied about would permit a charitable organization that has as its primary activity the operation of these funds to qualify as a public charity, but only where three requirements are met. (Neither this proposal nor any other has been formally introduced in Congress.)

1. There could not be any material restriction that prevents the organization from freely and effectively employing the assets in its donor-advised funds, or the income therefrom, in furtherance of its exempt purposes. The definition of *material restriction* generally would be based on that used in the tax regulations pertaining to the private foundation termination rules (Q 15:18). Nonetheless, the existence of a material restriction would not be presumed from the fact that a charity regularly follows a donor's advice.

2. Distributions from donor-advised funds could be made only to public charities, private operating foundations, and governmental entities.

3. Annual distributions from donor-advised funds would have to equal at least 5 percent of the net fair market value of the organization's aggregate assets held in these funds. There would be a carryforward of excess distributions for up to 5 years.

A similar rule would apply to organizations that maintain donor-advised funds, but not as a primary activity. In this situation, however, if these requirements are not satisfied with respect to the donor-advised funds, the organization's public charity status would not be affected, but the assets maintained by the organization in the funds would be subject to the private foundation rules, including taxes.

The term *donor-advised fund* would be defined as any segregated fund or account maintained by a charity for contributions received from a particular donor (or donors) as to which there is an understanding that the donor or donor's designee may advise the charity regarding the distribution of any amounts held in the fund. This term would not, however, include any fund or account as to which the advice is limited to the use to be made by the charity for its own operations of amounts held in the fund.

This proposal also would amend the definition of disqualified person under the intermediate sanctions rules to clarify that a person who is a donor or a designated advisor to a particular donor-advised fund maintained by a public charity (and that individual's family members and controlled entities) will be treated as having substantial influence with respect to any transactions involving that fund (and thus be deemed a disqualified person for that reason). There would be a similar revision of the law in connection with the definition of disqualified persons in the private foundation law context.

There would not be any inference as to the tax law treatment of transfers to donor-advised funds or the application of current law rules to transactions involving donor-advised funds for the period prior to the effective date of the proposal as enacted.

CHAPTER 16

Tax Exemption Recognition Process

Under the federal income tax system, every element of gross income received by a person—whether a corporate entity or a human being—is subject to taxation, unless there is an express statutory provision that exempts from tax either that form of income or that type of person.

Many types of nonprofit organizations are eligible for exemption from the federal income tax. But the exemption is not forthcoming merely because an organization is not organized and operated for profit. Organizations are tax-exempt where they meet the requirements of the particular statutory provision that authorizes the tax-exempt status. Organizations that are *charitable* in nature are eligible to be recognized as tax-exempt organizations. This includes private foundations.

A great myth is that the IRS grants tax-exempt status. This is not the case—and the correct concept, concerning recognition of exempt status, is frequently puzzling. The government's forms in this setting can appear daunting. Various and additional rules for charitable organizations can add to the perplexity.

Here are the questions that are most frequently asked (or that should be asked) about the exemption application recognition process—and the answers to them.

Q 16:1 A private foundation is, of course, a nonprofit organization. Are all nonprofit organizations tax-exempt organizations?

No. A nonprofit organization basically is a creature of state law (e.g., a nonprofit corporation or charitable trust) and is an entity that may not engage in forms of private inurement (Q 1:39). While nearly every tax-exempt organization is a nonprofit entity, it is not enough to achieve tax-exempt status to simply be a nonprofit organization.

Q 16:2   How does a *nonprofit organization* become a *tax-exempt organization*?

To qualify for tax-exempt status under the federal tax law, a nonprofit organization must meet the criteria of at least one provision of the Internal Revenue Code describing tax-exempt organizations. That is, in general, an organization that meets the appropriate statutory criteria qualifies—for that reason alone—as a tax-exempt organization.

Most tax-exempt organizations under the federal tax law are those that are described in section 501(c)(1)-(27) of the Internal Revenue Code. Other Code provisions that provide for income tax exemption are sections 521 and 526-529. Depending on how these provisions are parsed and the breadth of the term *tax-exempt organization* used, at least 63 categories of tax-exempt organizations are provided for in the federal income tax law.[1] Private foundations are organizations referenced in Code section 501(c)(3).

Q 16:3   Concerning tax exemption, what taxes are involved?

For the most part, a reference to a tax-exempt organization is to an entity that is exempt from the federal income tax. There are other federal taxes from which nonprofit organizations are exempt, but the federal income tax exemption is certainly the principal one. There are state tax exemptions as well, including state income tax exemptions.

State law, moreover, provides exemptions from sales, use, tangible personal property, intangible personal property, real property, and other taxes.

Frequently, the law providing exemption for nonprofit organizations from state income tax tracks the rules for exemption from federal income tax. (The criteria for exemption tend to become more rigorous when a property tax exemption is involved, particularly the real property tax exemption.) Therefore, the federal rules usually are the place to start.

Private foundations are always exempt from state income tax. Whether they are exempt from any other state taxes is dependent on the nature of the law in the particular state.

Q 16:4   Is a nonprofit organization required to apply to the IRS for tax-exempt status?

A very literal answer to this question is no. Despite what is often thought, the IRS does not grant tax-exempt status. Tax exemption is a feature of an organization that is available to it by operation of law.

What the IRS does is grant recognition of tax-exempt status. This role of the IRS in recognizing the exempt status of organizations is part of its overall responsibility for evaluating the tax status of organizations.

Q 16:5   What does *recognition* of tax exemption mean?

Whether a nonprofit organization is entitled to tax exemption, on an initial or continuing basis, is a matter of law. The U.S. Congress—not the IRS—defines the categories of organizations that are eligible for tax exemption, and it is up to Congress to determine whether a category of exemption from tax should be continued, in whole or in part. Except for state and local governmental entities, there is no constitutional right to a tax exemption.

As noted (Q 16:4), the IRS does not grant tax-exempt status. Congress, by means of sections of the Internal Revenue Code that it has enacted, performs that role. Rather, the function of the IRS in this regard is to recognize tax exemptions that Congress has created.

Consequently, when an organization makes application to the IRS for a ruling or determination as to tax-exempt status, it is requesting the IRS to recognize a tax exemption that already exists (assuming the organization qualifies). Similarly, the IRS may determine that an organization is no longer entitled to tax-exempt status and act to revoke its prior recognition of exempt status.

For many nonprofit organizations that are eligible for a tax exemption, it is not required that the exemption be recognized by the IRS. Whether a nonprofit organization seeks an IRS determination on the point is a management decision, which usually takes into account the degree of confidence the individuals involved have in the eligibility for the exemption and the costs associated with the application process. Most organizations in this position elect to pursue recognition of tax-exempt status.

Q 16:6   Must an organization, desiring to be a charitable one, seek recognition of tax-exempt status?

With few exceptions, such as for churches and small organizations, charitable organizations must, to be tax-exempt and to be charitable donees, seek (successfully) recognition of the exemption from the IRS.[2] Thus, by contrast, entities such as social welfare organizations,[3] labor organizations,[4] trade and professional associations,[5] social clubs,[6] and veterans' organizations[7] need not (but may) pursue recognition of tax-exempt status.

Q 16:7   Must a private foundation acquire recognition of tax-exempt status?

Yes. A private foundation, being a charitable entity, must—to be tax-exempt—seek recognition of exempt status from the IRS and be successful in doing so. None of the various exceptions that is available in this context is applicable to private foundations.

NOTE: The exception for small organizations (Q 16:6) is not available for private foundations.[8]

Q 16:8   How is this recognition of tax exemption initiated?

Unlike most requests for a ruling from the IRS (which are commenced by a letter to the agency), a request for recognition of tax exemption is initiated by filing a form, entitled "Application for Recognition of Exemption." Charitable organizations, including private foundations, file Form 1023. Most other organizations file Form 1024.

Q 16:9   What are the *organizational tests*?

Every charitable organization[9] must satisfy a basic *organizational test.* This test has three elements: (1) the purposes of the organization as stated in its organizing document (termed *articles of organization*) must be exempt ones, (2) the organization must not be empowered to engage in nonexempt activities (other than insubstantially), and (3) the organization's articles of organization must contain a clause directing the distribution of its assets in the event of dissolution.[10]

There is, in addition, a separate organizational test for private foundations. Essentially, this test requires that the dictates of the private foundation rules (Q 1:4) be embodied in each foundation's articles of organization.[11] Many states have laws, however, that impose these rules on private foundations; in those situations, the foundations are deemed to be in compliance with this organizational test.[12]

TIP: Even if one of these statutes is in force with respect to a private foundation, it is a recommended practice that the elements of this test be reflected in its articles of organization.

A organization that is a supporting organization (Q 12:15) must adhere to the requirements of an organizational test for these entities.[13]

Q 16:10   What is the *operational test*?

In addition to the organizational test (Q 16:9), a charitable organization must satisfy an *operational test.* This test mandates actual operation by the organization in ways that ensures it is being operated primarily in exempt functions.[14] For private foundations, the private foundation rules (Q 1:4) serve as a second operational test. Supporting organizations also must adhere to a separate operational test.[15]

Q 16:11   What is the *recognition application procedure*?

The IRS has promulgated specific rules by which a ruling or determination letter may be issued to an organization in response to the filing of an application for recognition of its tax-exempt status.

A recognition of exemption by the IRS from an office outside Washington, D.C., is termed a determination letter.[16] This type of recognition from the IRS's National Office in Washington, D.C., is termed a ruling.[17] In practice, both of these types of determinations are often generically referred to as rulings.

A ruling or determination will be issued to an organization as long as the application and supporting documents establish that it meets the particular statutory requirements. The application must include a statement describing the organization's purposes, copies of its governing instruments (e.g., in the case of a corporation, its articles of incorporation and bylaws), and either a financial statement or a proposed multiyear budget.

The application filed by a private foundation and other organizations also must include a summary of the sources of its financial support, its fund-raising program (usually not something a private foundation has), the composition of its governing body (usually board of trustees or directors), its relationship with other organizations (if any), the nature of its services or products and the basis for any charges for them, and its membership (if any). A private foundation is unlikely to have members, however.

An application for recognition of exemption should be regarded as an important legal document and prepared accordingly. Throughout an organization's existence, it will likely be called on to provide its application for recognition of exemption to others for review. Indeed, a nonprofit organization is required by federal law to provide a copy of this application to anyone who requests it (Q 11:22).

Q 16:12 What information must be provided by means of the application for recognition of tax exemption?

The application for recognition of tax exemption filed by charitable organizations (Form 1023) comes in a packet.

NOTE: This analysis of the application for recognition of tax exemption is based on Form 1023 dated September 1998. The reader may wish to obtain a copy of this form and have it available for purposes of this discussion.

This packet includes instructions for preparation of the form and the form itself (in duplicate). Only one copy of Form 1023 need be filed with the IRS; the other copy may be used in drafting the application.

Part I

Part I of Form 1023 requests certain basic information about the applicant organization, such as its name, address, and date of formation. Every tax-exempt organization, including a private foundation, must have an employer identification number (even if there are no employees); this is obtained by filing Form SS-4. Form SS-4 may be filed as soon as the organization is formed and organized, or it may be filed with Form 1023.

The contact person (question 3) may be either someone directly involved with the organization, such as an officer or director, or an independent representative of the organization, such as a lawyer or accountant. If this type of a representative is being used, he or she must be granted a power of attorney, which is filed with the application, on Form 2848.

The organization must state the month in which its annual accounting period ends (question 4). The determination of a fiscal year should be given some thought; most organizations use the calendar year (in which case the answer is "December"). Whatever period is selected, the organization should be certain that the same period is stated on Form SS-4 and used when compiling its multiyear budget. (See below.)

The date of formation is to be provided (question 5). If incorporated, for example, this date will be the date the state agency received the private foundation's articles of incorporation. This date can be significant for public charities in relation to the 15-month rule. (See below.)

Question 10 of Form 1023 requires an applicant organization to identify its *type*. Generally, the organization must be one of three types: nonprofit corporation, trust, or unincorporated association. A private foundation will be a corporation or a trust.

If the private foundation maintains a Web site, that address must be provided in the answer to question 1e.

If a corporation, the attachments will be the articles of incorporation and bylaws, any amendments to these documents, and the certificates of incorporation and amendment (if any) issued by the state. If a trust, the attachments will be the trust document(s).

Part II

The organization must provide a narrative of its activities (question 1). Usually, this is an essay that is descriptive of the organization's programs and should be carefully written. Good practice is to open with a description of the organization's purposes, followed by one or more paragraphs summarizing its program activities. This response should be as full as is reasonable and may well occupy more space than is provided, in which case the response can be in the form of a separate exhibit. A private foundation describes the scope (if any) of its grant-making program and the types of anticipated grant recipients.

The applicant charitable organization must identify, in order of size, its sources of financial support (question 2). The answers are, for charities generally, contributions from the general public, other contributions, grants, dues, other exempt function (fee-for-service) revenue, and/or investment income. For a private foundation, however, this matter is simpler, in that the choices are fewer. Most private foundations are initially funded with one gift; thereafter, ongoing income is in the form of investment income. A private foundation is unlikely to receive exempt function revenue and certainly would not receive dues.

The organization is requested to describe its actual and planned fund-raising program (question 3). A public charity would be likely to summarize its use of, or plans to use, undertakings and assistance such as selective mailings, fund-raising committees, volunteers, and professional fund-raisers. This type of organization can describe a very detailed fund-raising program, or it can state that is has yet to develop a semblance of a fund-raising program. For a private foundation, by contrast, there almost always is no fund-raising program, and thus this question is to be answered accordingly.

The names and addresses of the organization's officers and directors (perhaps, in the case of a private foundation, termed trustees) must be provided, along with the amount (if any) of their annual compensation (question 4). As to compensation, this includes all compensation, not just that for serving as an officer or director (or trustee). This, of course, can be a sensitive topic, particularly with respect to the self-dealing rules (Chapter 3).

Question 5, concerning relationships with other organizations, can be very important for some organizations. As a general rule, it does not matter whether the charitable organization has a special relationship with, or is controlled by, another organization. For example, some charitable organizations are controlled by other types of tax-exempt organizations, such as social welfare organizations or trade associations, or are controlled by for-profit corporations, such as corporation-related foundations. This is not likely, however, to be relevant for private foundations.

Question 8 inquires as to the organization's assets used in the performance of its exempt functions. Since these assets do not include property producing investment income, the answer for a private foundation is likely to be "None." If the foundation is a private operating foundation (Q 14:2), however, the answer is likely to be quite different.

Question 11, concerning membership groups, is basically self-explanatory. It relates to organizations that have a true membership, however, not merely arrangements where the concept of a "membership" is used as a fund-raising technique. This, too, is almost certain to be irrelevant for a private foundation.

Part III

Question 5 of Part I, concerning the date of formation of an organization, can be of no particular importance or it can be of extreme importance, depending on the circumstances. The basic rule, reflected in question 1, is that the recognition of exemption will be retroactive to the date of formation of the charitable organization where the application if filed with the IRS within 15 months from the end of the month in which the organization was established.[18] For example, if the organization is created on January 15, 2002, and the application for recognition of exemption is filed on or before April 30, 2003, the recognition of exemption (if granted) will be retroactive to January 15, 2002, irrespective of when the determination is made by the IRS. To continue with this example, however, if the application is filed on or after May 1, 2003, the recognition of exemption generally would, under the 15-month rule, be effective only as of the date the application was received by the IRS. (Nonetheless, as discussed below, the emergence of a 27-month rule has somewhat alleviated the time pressures in this context.)

As to the matter of tax-exempt status, the 15-month rule may not be of any particular importance, in that the charitable organization can qualify as a tax-exempt social welfare organization[19] (which does not require recognition of tax-exempt status) until the date of its classification as a charitable organization. This alleviation of the tax-exemption problem, however, as reflected in question 7, is of no assistance with respect to the posture of the organization as a charitable donee or as a nonprivate foundation (if the latter is applicable). Donors making gifts during the interim period will, upon audit, find their charitable deductions disallowed. Private foundations, by contrast, cannot utilize this approach. Although their tax exemption could be preserved in this fashion, there would not be a charitable deduction for the initial funding of it, which would be unacceptable.

There is another dimension to this topic. A private foundation making grants to charitable organizations during this interim period may be subject to taxation for failure to exercise expenditure responsibility (Q 7:19)—if the funding went to an organization that failed to adhere to the 15/27-month rule. Thus, it is imperative that an organization desiring to be recognized as a charitable organization from its date of formation either file a completed application for recognition of tax exemption prior to the expiration of the 15-month period or utilize an exception to this rule (discussed next).

There are, nonetheless, some exceptions to the 15-month rule. The most fundamental one is an automatic 12-month extension of time within which to file the application (question 3)[20]; this has essentially converted the standard to a 27-month rule. In some instances, the IRS can accord relief in this area (question 5). Certain small organizations, churches, conventions or associations of churches, integrated auxiliaries of churches, and other organizations are exempted from this application requirement (question 2). As noted, however (Q 16:7), none of these exceptions is available for private foundations.

Questions 7 through 9 can be of very large consequence. This is where the public charity/private foundation rules come into play (Chapter 3). Where the applicant charitable organization is a private foundation, the answer to question 7 is yes. If the organization is seeking classification as a private operating foundation, it should so indicate in response to question 8 and complete Schedule E.

If the organization, however, believes it can avoid private foundation status by reason of being one of the entities listed in question 9, it must select either a definitive ruling (Q 12:11) or an advance ruling (Q 12:9). Private foundations always skip the advance ruling requirement and obtain a definitive ruling. New charitable organizations (i.e., those with a tax year of less than eight months) that are seeking to be classified as publicly supported entities, an advance ruling (selected by responding to question 10) is the correct choice. This is because they lack the financial history to demonstrate actual public support, which is required before a publicly supported organization can receive a definitive ruling. If the applicant believes it will be supported principally by gifts and grants (Q 12:4), it should check the box correlating with question 9(h). The box of question 9(i) is for organizations that are expecting support in the form of a blend of gifts, grants, and exempt function income (Q 12:8).

Either type of putative publicly supported organization must demonstrate its initial qualification for nonprivate foundation status by convincing the IRS that it will receive the requisite extent of public support. This is done by submitting a proposed budget. This budget summarizes contemplated types of revenue (e.g., gifts, grants, exempt function revenue, and investment income) and types of expenses (e.g., expenditures for program, compensation, occupancy, telephone, travel, postage, and fund-raising) for each of five years. For this purpose, a year is a period consisting of at least eight months. (For new organizations, this budget is submitted in lieu of the financial statements reflected in Part IV of Form 1023.) The five-year period is the advance ruling period. Thus, as question 10 reflects, an organization with a tax year of at least eight months, but which has a period of existence of less than five years, can obtain either an advance or definitive ruling.

In designing the budget, the five years involved are the fiscal years of the organization. The applicant organization should be certain that the fiscal year used to develop the budget is the same period referenced in the response to question 4 of Part I. Also in this process, the organization should be certain that the types of revenue stated in the budget correspond to the types of revenue summarized in the response to question 2 of Part III.

The advance ruling pertains only to the applicant organization's status as a publicly supported entity. That is, it is not an advance ruling as to tax-exempt status or charitable donee status. Thus, the advance ruling period is a probationary or conditional ruling, as to "public" status. Once the advance ruling period expires and the organization has in fact received adequate public support during the five-year period, that fact will be reported to the IRS, which will in turn issue a definitive ruling that it is a publicly supported charity. Just as the advance ruling is conditional, the definitive ruling is permanent (unless upset by a subsequent loss of qualification or change in the law). Again, all of this is inapplicable to the applicant private foundation; nonetheless, these rules should be understood by the foundation executive because they are applicable to the foundation's grantees.

The publicly supported charitable organization must, during and after the expiration of the advance ruling period, continue on an ongoing basis to show that it qualifies as a publicly supported charity, assuming it wants to retain that status. This is done by reporting the financial support information that has been being reported on the annual information return (Chapter 10).

It does not matter which type of publicly supported organization the charitable entity is at any point in its existence; the principal objective is to qualify, at any one time, under one category or another. Thus, an organization can shift from one classification of publicly supported organization to another throughout its duration. Likewise, a charitable organization can, without concern, select one category of publicly supported organization when it completes Part III and satisfy the requirements of the other category only as of the close of the advance ruling period.

If an organization selects a category of publicly supported charitable organization when it prepares Part III and finds at the close of the advance ruling period that it did not meet either set of requirements for publicly supported status, it will be categorized as a private foundation, unless it can demonstrate eligibility for otherwise avoiding private foundation status. This can be done if the organization qualifies as an entity such as a church, school, hospital, or supporting organization (see below).

If the organization files as a type of public charity but fails to garner the requisite public support during the advance ruling period and thus becomes classified as a private foundation following the close of its advance ruling period, it will have to pay the excise tax on its net investment income (Chapter 8) for each of the years in the advance ruling period (and thereafter). For the IRS to be able to assess the tax retroactively, the taxpayer must agree to waive the running of the statute of limitations, which otherwise would preclude the IRS from reaching that far back. The waiver is granted by the execution of Form 872-C (in duplicate), which is part of the Form 1023 package.

An applicant organization that qualifies as a church, school, hospital, supporting organization, or the like is eligible to receive a definitive ruling at the outset. This is because its financial support is not the factor used in classifying it as a public entity. Instead, its public status derives from what it does programmatically.

An organization can receive a definitive ruling that it is publicly supported if it has been in existence for, as noted, a tax year of at least eight months and received the requisite public support during that period. The organization in this situation would submit a completed Part IV for each of these years.

Every organization that is requesting a definitive ruling must evidence its selection of nonprivate foundation status by answering questions 11 through 14 of Part III. Question 10 is to be answered by organizations seeking an advance ruling. Certain organizations are required to submit a schedule (question 14); these organizations include churches (Schedule A), schools (Schedule B), supporting organizations (Schedule D), private operating foundations (Schedule E), scholarship-granting organizations (Schedule H), and successors to for-profit entities (Schedule I).

Summary

This application for recognition of tax exemption as a charitable organization, if properly completed, amounts to a rather complete portrait of the programs, fund-raising plans, and other aspects of the applicant organization. That is why it is important to devote some time and thinking to the preparation of the form. It is, as noted (Chapter 11), a public document, and, during the course of the organization's existence, the organization may well be called on to supply a copy of the application. Since those who request the document are likely to be prospective donors or grantors, or representatives of the media, it is particularly important that it be properly prepared.

Q 16:13 Are any aspects of this application unique to private foundations?

For the most part, no. Certainly, the main body of the application has nothing that is exceptional with respect to private foundations. Indeed, the document is clearly focused, in its design, on public charities (Q 1:2), with its questions about undertakings such as fund-raising, dues solicitations, payments for services or benefits provided, influencing legislation, and political campaign activities.

The only aspects of the application that are unique—in any sense—to private foundations are found in the schedules. There, as noted, schedules must be filed by private operating foundations (Schedule E) and entities that provide scholarship benefits and the like (Schedule H).

Q 16:14 Where are these applications filed?

Applications for recognition of exemption are filed with the IRS Service Center in Cincinnati, Ohio. Infrequently, there will be occasion to file the application with the National Office of the IRS.

Q 16:15 How long does it take the IRS to process an exemption application?

It is difficult to generalize as to the length of time required by the IRS to process an application for recognition of tax exemption. Three of the critical factors generally are the complexity and/or sensitivity of the case, the completeness of the application (and related documents) (Q 16:21), and the workload of the IRS representative who will be reviewing the file and preparing the ruling. Normally, a private foundation's application for recognition of tax exemption does not involve the factor of complexity, so a foundation's application is likely to be processed more quickly than an application filed by a public charity.

For rather straightforward filings, like that of a standard private foundation, the organization should plan on an IRS processing period of about three months. The IRS may have questions, and this can lengthen the period. Once in a while, a case is referred to the IRS's National Office, and that development can have a bearing on the overall time period.

Having said all this, it is in reality difficult to predict in any particular filing how long it will take for a ruling (a favorable one) to be issued. An application virtually brimming with hearty exempt organization issues can sail through the process, without any IRS inquiries, and result in a ruling in a few weeks. Yet a simple case, one lacking in any issues of substance, can be worried over by an IRS exempt organizations specialist for an agonizingly long period of time.

There is a process by which an applicant organization can request the IRS to expedite the processing of the application. For this to work, the organization must convince the IRS that there is a substantive reason as to why its application should be considered out of order (e.g., a large gift or grant that will be lost if recognition is not quickly extended). About the only time this process can work in the case of a private foundation is where the foundation is being created toward the end of a year and the contributor(s) want the charitable contribution deduction for that year.

Understandably, out of overall fairness, the IRS is reluctant to grant expedited consideration of these applications, so the case for a quick processing must be a persuasive one. The IRS has been known, however, to formally decline to expedite consideration of an exemption application—and then process it speedily anyway.

Q 16:16 How long does an exemption ruling remain in effect?

These rulings are not accompanied by an expiration date. Generally, an organization whose tax-exempt status has been recognized by the IRS can rely on that determination as long as there are no substantial changes in its character, purposes, or methods of operation. Of course, a change in the law can void a ruling or cause a reevaluation of it.

Determining whether one of these changes is *substantial* is not always easy and can be a matter of considerable judgment. An applicant organization should endeavor to disclose as much information as is reasonably possible, to preclude a later contention that some material fact was omitted. Once the ruling is obtained, it is a recommended practice to periodically review the application, to see whether it reflects current programs and other practices. A ruling from the IRS is only as valid as the facts on which it is based—and a substantial change in purposes and the like could void or at least threaten the validity of the ruling.

Q 16:17 What happens if there is a substantial change in an organization's character, purposes, or methods of operation?

If there is a substantial change in an organization's character, purposes, or methods of operation, the rule of law is that the IRS is to be notified of the change or changes—obviously so that the IRS can reevaluate the organization's exempt status. This notification is required to take place in proximity to the change.

In practice, however, this rule is rarely followed. As the years go by, organizations can evolve into and out of varying programs and purposes, and/or change management and methods of operation, and never give a thought to what was said in the exemption application (or, for that matter, in the articles of organization or bylaws). This is not a good practice; a periodic review in this regard is recommended. There are organizations in operation today that have strayed so far from their original purposes and operations, and into nonexempt activities, that they would have their exempt status revoked were the IRS to learn the facts. Even if these changes are not substantial, they are to be reported to the IRS as part of the filing of the annual information return (Chapter 10).

Q 16:18 Will the IRS issue a ruling to an organization in advance of its operations?

In general, yes. The basic rule is this: A determination letter or ruling (Q 16:11) will be issued by the IRS to an organization where its application for recognition of exemption and supporting documents establish that it meets the requirements of the category of exemption that it claimed. Tax-exempt status for an organization will be recognized by the IRS in advance of operations where the entity's proposed activities are described in sufficient detail to permit a conclusion that the organization will clearly meet the pertinent statutory requirements.

The organization should not merely restate its purposes or state only that its proposed activities will be in furtherance of the organization's purposes. This approach does not satisfy the requirements and serves only to put the IRS on notice that the application has been prepared by those who lack experience with the rules.

The applicant organization is expected to fully describe the activities in which it expects to engage, including the standards, criteria, procedures, or other means adopted or planned for carrying out the activities, the anticipated sources of receipts, and the nature of contemplated expenditures. As noted (Q 16:12), for a private foundation, this normally is a rather straightforward process.

Where, however, an organization cannot demonstrate, to the satisfaction of the IRS, that its proposed activities will qualify it for recognition of exemption, a record of actual operations may be required before a ruling is issued.

Q 16:19 How much information must be provided to the IRS?

There is no precise standard in this regard. The IRS expects a "detailed narrative description of all the activities of the organization—past, present, and planned."[21] Thus, an organization that took this issue to court lost in its bid to acquire recognition of exemption because it "failed to supply such information as would enable a conclusion that when operational, if ever . . . [the organization] will conduct all of its activities in a manner which will accomplish its exempt purposes."[22] The entity was chided by the court for offering only "vague generalizations" about its ostensibly planned activities.[23]

Likewise, this court concluded that an organization could not be exempt because it did not provide a "meaningful explanation" of its activities to the IRS.[24] In another instance, a court found that an organization's failure to respond "completely or candidly" to many of the inquiries of the IRS precluded it from receiving a determination as to its tax-exempt status.[25]

NOTE: This court subsequently observed that, in order to obtain recognition of tax exemption as a charitable organization, the entity must "openly and candidly disclose all facts bearing upon the organization, its operations, and its finances so that the Court may be assured that it is not sanctioning an abuse of the revenue laws by granting a claimed exemption."[26]

An organization, however, is considered to have made the required "threshold showing" where it describes its activities in "sufficient detail" to permit a conclusion that the entity will meet the pertinent requirements, particularly where it answered all of the questions propounded by the IRS.[27]

This aspect of the process essentially comes down to this: The law "requires that the organization establish measurable standards and criteria for its operation as an exempt organization"; this standard does not necessitate "some sort of metaphysical proof of future events."[28]

In any event, this is not the time to hold back information; it is foolish for an organization—private foundation or other entity—to fail to be recognized as an exempt organization on the ground that it refused to submit suitable information. The organization should be willing to tell its story fully, treating the application as a business plan (Q 16:22). This document is, after all, a public one (Q 11:22), and its proper preparation should be regarded as a first step in presenting the organization's justification for existence and tax-exempt status.

This is, in essence, a burden-of-proof issue—with the burden on the would-be exempt organization. Moreover, there is a negative presumption: When the representatives of an organization fail to submit the appropriate factual information to the IRS, an inference arises that the facts involved would denigrate the organization's cause.

Q 16:20 What happens if the IRS decides the application is incomplete?

If an application for recognition of tax exemption does not contain the requisite information, the IRS's procedures authorize it to return the application to the applicant organization without being considered on its merits.

NOTE: The application will be returned to the organization—not to anyone on a power of attorney (e.g., a lawyer or accountant), with obvious implications. A competent representative of a nonprofit organization in this regard should have no experience with this rule.

The application for recognition of tax exemption as submitted by a would-be exempt organization will not be processed by the IRS until the application is at least *substantially completed* (Q 16:21).

Q 16:21 What is a *substantially completed* application?

An application for recognition of exemption is a substantially completed one when it:

- Is signed by an authorized individual.
- Includes an employer identification number or a completed application for the number (Form SS-4).
- Includes information regarding any previously filed federal income tax and/or exempt organization information returns.
- Includes a statement of receipts and expenditures and a balance sheet for the current year and the three preceding years (or the years the organization has been in existence, if less than four years), although if the organization has not yet commenced operations, or has not completed one full accounting period, a proposed budget for two full accounting periods, and a current statement of assets and liabilities is acceptable.
- Includes a narrative statement of proposed activities and a narrative description of anticipated receipts and contemplated expenditures.

- Includes a copy of the document by which the organization was established, signed by a principal officer or is accompanied by a written declaration signed by an authorized individual certifying that the document is a complete and accurate copy of the original or otherwise meets the requirement that it be a conformed copy.
- If the organizing document is a set of articles of incorporation, includes evidence that it was filed with and approved by an appropriate state official (e.g., a copy of the certificate of incorporation) or includes a copy of the articles of incorporation accompanied by a written declaration signed by an authorized individual that the copy is a complete and accurate copy of the original document that was filed with and approved by the state, and stating the date of filing with the state.
- If the organization has adopted bylaws, includes a current copy of that document, certified as being current by an authorized individual.
- Is accompanied by the correct user fee (Q 16:24).[29]

The application for recognition of exemption submitted by charitable organizations requests information concerning the composition of the entity's governing body, any relationship with other organizations, the nature of its fund-raising program, and a variety of other matters.

Q 16:22 Is the application for recognition of exemption an important document for a private foundation?

Yes, this application is a significant legal document for a private foundation (or, for that matter, for any tax-exempt organization), and it should be prepared and retained accordingly.

OBSERVATION: An unduly high proportion of private foundations and other tax-exempt organizations cannot locate a copy of their application for recognition of tax exemption. Something about this document seems to subject it to an exceedingly high likelihood of being lost soon. Copies should be on hand, as the law requires the public disclosure of them (Q 11:22).

The proper preparation of an application for recognition of tax exemption involves far more than merely responding to the questions on a government form. It is a process not unlike the preparation of a prospectus for a business in conformity with the securities law requirements. Every statement made in the application should be carefully considered. Some of the questions may force the applicant organization to focus on matters that solid management practices should cause it to consider, even in the absence of the application requirements. The application is a nicely constructed and factually sweeping document, and it should be approached and prepared with care and respect.

The prime objectives in this regard must be accuracy and completeness; it is essential that all material facts be correctly and fully stated (Q 16:21). Of course, the determination as to which facts are material and the marshaling of these facts requires judgment. Moreover, the manner in which the answers are phrased can be extremely significant; this exercise can be more one of art than of science.

The preparer or reviewer of the application should be able to anticipate the concerns the contents of the application may cause the IRS and to see that the application is properly prepared, while simultaneously minimizing the likelihood of conflict with the IRS. Organizations that are entitled to tax-exempt status have been denied recognition of exemption by the IRS, or have caused the process of gaining recognition to be more protracted, because of inartful phraseologies in the application that motivated the IRS to muster a case that the organization does not qualify for exemption.

Therefore, the application for recognition of tax exemption should be regarded as an important legal document and prepared accordingly. The fact that, as observed, the application is available for public inspection only underscores the need for thoughtful preparation.

Q 16:23 How long does it take to prepare an application for recognition of tax exemption?

It is impossible to generalize on this point. The pertinent factors include the complexity of the organization, the extent to which the factual information and supporting documents are readily available, and the skill and expertise of those who prepare and review the document. As has been referenced previously (Q 16:13), normally the application for recognition of exemption filed by a private foundation is not as complex as one filed by a public charity.

Nonetheless, apparently there is a way to produce some averages of time expenditures in this regard. The Form 1023 instructions reveal that it is the view of the IRS that the estimated average time required to keep records so as to be able to prepare the application (not including any schedules) is 44 hours and 14 minutes; to learn about the law in this regard or the form is 1 hour and 44 minutes; and to prepare the application and send it to the IRS is 4 hours and 23 minutes.

NOTE: Perhaps this *Answer Book* can shorten one or more of these time estimates somewhat. The second of these estimates is the most challenging. It will take a quick learner, indeed, to master the underlying law of private foundations and public charities in under two hours.

Q 16:24 Is there a charge for the processing of an application for recognition of exemption?

Yes, the IRS levies a user fee for processing an organization's application for recognition of exemption. This fee must be paid at the time of the filing of the application and must be accompanied by a completed user fee form (Form 8718).

The fee for the processing of one of these applications is $500, where the applicant has gross receipts that annually exceed $10,000. For smaller organizations, the fee is $150. Obviously, in the case of a private foundation, the fee will be the larger one.

Q 16:25 Can an application for recognition of exemption be referred to the IRS's National Office?

Yes. The IRS representative considering the application must refer to the National Office of the IRS an application for recognition of tax exemption that (1) presents questions the answers to that are not specifically covered by the Internal Revenue Code, Department of Treasury regulations, an IRS revenue ruling, or court decision published in the IRS's *Internal Revenue Bulletin,* or (2) has been specifically reserved by an IRS revenue procedure and/or *Internal Revenue Manual* instructions for handling by the National Office for purposes of establishing uniformity or centralized control of designated categories of cases. In these instances, the National Office is to consider the application, issue a ruling directly to the organization, and send a copy of the ruling to the appropriate IRS office.[30]

NOTE: One of the purposes of the recent centralization efforts by the IRS in this context is to centralize the processing of exemption applications so as to consolidate expertise and increase the efficiency of the process.

Q 16:26 Can the applicant organization seek the assistance of the National Office?

Yes. If, during the course of consideration of an application for recognition of tax exemption, an applicant organization believes that its case involves an issue as to which there is no published precedent, the organization may ask the IRS to request *technical advice* from the IRS's National Office.[31]

Q 16:27 Can an application for recognition of exemption be withdrawn?

Yes. An application for recognition of tax exemption filed with the IRS may be withdrawn, upon the written request of an authorized representative of the organization, at any time prior to the issuance of an initial adverse ruling.

CAUTION: Where an application is withdrawn, it and all supporting documents are retained by the IRS.[32]

Q 16:28 If an organization is denied recognition of exemption, may it later reapply?

Absolutely—the key is correction of the problem or problems that caused the denial in the first instance.

An organization may reapply for recognition of tax exemption if it was previously denied recognition, where the facts involved are materially changed so that the organization has come into compliance with the applicable requirements. The revised application must include information demonstrating that the organization is now in compliance with the law and that the organization will not knowingly operate in a manner that would disqualify it from exemption.

Q 16:29 What is the effective date of these rulings?

A determination letter or ruling recognizing tax exemption (Q 16:11) usually is effective as of the date of formation of the organization, where its purposes and activities during the period prior to the date of the determination letter or ruling were consistent with the requirements for tax exemption.

NOTE: Remember, there are special rules in this regard for charitable organizations, including private foundations (Q 16:12).

If the organization is required to alter its activities or to make substantive amendments to its enabling instrument, the determination letter or ruling recognizing its tax-exempt status is effective as of the date specified in the determination letter or ruling. If a nonsubstantive amendment is made, tax exemption ordinarily is recognized as of the date the entity was formed.

Q 16:30 To what extent can an organization rely on its ruling?

In general, an organization can rely on a determination letter or ruling from the IRS recognizing its tax exemption. Reliance is not available, however, if there is a material change, inconsistent with tax exemption, in the character, purpose, or method of operation of the organization.

Q 16:31 How does a private foundation remain tax exempt?

Subject only to the authority of the IRS to revoke recognition of exemption for good cause (e.g., a change in the law), a private foundation that has been recognized by the IRS as being tax-exempt can rely on the determination as long as there are no substantial changes in its character, purposes, or methods of operation. Should material changes occur, the foundation should notify the IRS and may have to obtain a reevaluation of its exempt status.

CHAPTER 17

Charitable Contribution Deductions

Private foundations and the charitable contribution deduction rules have a tenuous existence. Many private foundations do not care about them, in that the only charitable gift they received was the one initially funding them—and that occurred years ago. Other private foundations receive gifts from time to time. Some are the potential recipient of planned gifts, such as distributions from charitable remainder trusts and charitable lead trusts.

Private foundations may be interested in the charitable contribution deduction rules if only because of their applicability to the public charities they fund. This interest is based at least in part on the recognition that the charitable deduction often shapes the form and timing of gifts and enables donors to give more generously than would otherwise be the case.

Thus, the private foundation executive should have at least a grasp of the basics of this body of law. This area of the law, being fluid, is constantly undergoing change, and the executive should check with legal counsel from time to time when making decisions, or when prospective donors are making decisions, based on what is thought to be the state of the law. Nonetheless, the executive should have a basic grounding in the tax law surrounding the charitable deduction—and the purpose of this chapter is to provide that framework.

Here are the questions that are most frequently asked (or that should be asked) about the charitable contribution deduction rules—and the answers to them.

Q 17:1   What are the charitable contribution deductions?

The federal tax law provides three sets of charitable contribution deductions. Most state laws make available one or more of these deductions as well.

The federal charitable contribution deduction that attracts the most attention is the income tax charitable deduction.[1] There are, however, two other charitable contribution deductions: one that is part of the federal gift tax law[2] and one that is part of the federal estate tax law.[3]

Q 17:2   Are all tax-exempt organizations eligible to receive tax-deductible contributions?

No. The categories of organizations that are eligible for *exemption* from the federal income tax is considerably more extensive than the categories of organizations that are eligible to receive contributions that are *deductible* under the federal tax law.

For example, for federal *income* tax purposes, there are only five categories of entities that are charitable donees for this purpose:

1. Charitable organizations that are such for tax exemption purposes, including educational, religious, and scientific entities.[4]

NOTE: The range of charitable organizations for deductible charitable giving purposes is almost the same as that for income tax exemption purposes. There is one minor exception: Organizations that *test for public safety* are charitable, but only for exemption purposes.[5] Contributions to them are not tax deductible gifts.

---

2. Governments, namely, a state, a possession of the federal government, a political subdivision of either, the federal government itself, and the District of Columbia, as long as the gift is made for a public purpose.
3. An organization of war veterans and an auxiliary unit of or foundation for a veterans' organization.
4. Many fraternal societies that operate under the lodge system, as long as the gift is to be used for charitable purposes.
5. Membership cemetery companies and corporations chartered for burial purposes as cemetery corporations.[6]

Generally, contributions to other types of tax-exempt organizations are not deductible.

TIP: Although contributions to exempt organizations other than those in these five categories generally are not deductible, this limitation is rather easily sidestepped by the creation of a related charitable entity, often loosely termed a *foundation.* Tax-exempt organizations that effectively use related foundations for purposes of attracting deductible charitable gifts include trade, business, and professional associations,[7] and social welfare organizations.[8] In some instances, an otherwise nonqualifying organization is allowed to receive a contribution that is deductible where the gift money or property is devoted to charitable purposes.

NOTE: The "foundations" referred to above are not private founda-tions. They are public charities (Q 12:1). Some are publicly supported organizations (Q 12:3). Often, however, they are supporting organiza-tions (Q 12:15).

COMMENT: It is common for a charitable organization—one that itself is eligible to receive deductible gifts—to utilize a related founda-tion. This is done for management and fund-raising, not tax, purposes. Organizations that follow this approach include hospitals and other healthcare providers, colleges, universities, schools, and various reli-gious organizations. Again, however, these entities are not private foundations.

Q 17:3   Are contributions to private foundations deductible?

Generally, yes. A private foundation is a *charitable* organization (Q 1:1). It is thus an organization in the first of the five categories referenced earlier (Q 17:2). There are, however, a myriad of special rules governing the deduct-ibility of charitable contributions to private foundations.

Q 17:4   What are the federal income tax rules for deductibility of a con-tribution of money to a private foundation by an individual?

A charitable contribution is, of course, often made with money. Some prefer the word *cash.* (Some don't care about the terminology as long as they obtain the currency.) While this type of gift is usually deductible, there are limitations on the extent of deductibility in any one tax year.

REMINDER: For a charitable contribution of money to be deductible by an individual under the federal income tax law, he or she must itemize deductions.

The limitations in this area are based in part on the concept of the *con-tribution base.* An individual's contribution base essentially is the same as the amount of his or her *adjusted gross income.*[9] Technically, an individual's *con-tribution base* is his or her adjusted gross income, computed without regard to any net operating loss carryback to the taxable year.[10]

NOTE: Throughout, reference will be made to *adjusted gross income* rather than the more technical term *contribution base.*

The charitable contribution deduction for individuals is subject to the 3 percent limitation on overall itemized deductions.[11] A gift of money may have to be *substantiated* (Q 11:5) and/or may be a *quid pro quo contribution* (Q 11:14). A planned gift can be made in whole or in part with money (Q 17:27).

In the case of an individual, where a charitable gift is made with money and the charitable donee is a charitable organization that is a private foundation, the extent of the charitable contribution deduction under the federal income tax law, for the year of the gift, cannot exceed 30 percent of the donor's adjusted gross income.[12] Any excess portion can be carried forward and deducted over a period of up to 5 subsequent years.[13]

Thus, for example, if an individual had adjusted gross income in the amount of $100,000 for 2002 and made a gift of money to a private foundation in that year in the amount of $20,000, the gift would be fully deductible (assuming no other gifts and no application of any other limitations) for 2002. If this gift was instead $40,000 in 2002, the charitable deduction for 2002 would generally be $30,000 (30 percent of $100,000) and the excess amount of $10,000 would be carried forward, to be potentially deductible for 2003.

Q 17:5   What are the federal income tax rules for deductibility of a contribution of money to a public charity by an individual?

In the case of an individual, where a charitable gift is made with money and the charitable donee is a public charity, the extent of the charitable contribution deduction under the federal income tax law, for the year of the gift, cannot exceed 50 percent of the donor's adjusted gross income.[14] Any excess portion can be carried forward and deducted over a period of up to five subsequent years.[15]

NOTE: The foregoing rule also is applicable with respect to certain types of private foundations, usually private operating foundations (Q 14:2).

Thus, for example, if an individual had adjusted gross income in the amount of $100,000 for 2002 and made gifts of money to one or more public charities in that year totaling $40,000, the gifts would be fully deductible (assuming no other gifts and no application of any other limitations) for 2002. If this donor were more generous and contributed $60,000 during 2002, the charitable deduction for 2002 would generally be $50,000 (50 percent of $100,000) and the excess amount of $10,000 would be carried forward, to be potentially deductible for 2003.

COMMENT: An individual may, in any one year, make charitable gifts to a number of charitable organizations, some public and some not. Each gift deduction must be separately calculated using the

---

appropriate limitation. No matter the combination, the total amount of deductible giving in a year cannot exceed the 50 percent maximum.[16]

NOTE: If a husband and wife file a joint return, the deduction for charitable contributions is the aggregate of the contributions made by the spouses, and the percentage limitations are based on the aggregate contribution of the spouses.[17]

Q 17:6   What are the federal income tax rules for deductibility of a contribution of property to a private foundation by an individual?

The rules pertaining to charitable contributions by individuals of property are more complex than those involving gifts of money (Q 17:4, Q 17:5). This type of gift is usually deductible, but there are several limitations on the extent of deductibility in any tax year.

In the case of an individual, where a charitable gift is made with property and the charitable donee is a charitable organization that is a private foundation, the extent of the charitable contribution deduction under the federal income tax law, for the year of the gift, generally cannot exceed 20 percent of the donor's adjusted gross income.[18] Any excess portion can be carried forward and deducted over a period of up to five subsequent years.[19]

Thus, for example, if an individual had adjusted gross income in the amount of $100,000 for 2002 and made a gift of property to a private foundation in that year in the amount of $15,000, the gift would be fully deductible (assuming no other gifts and no application of any other limitations) for 2002. If this gift was instead $30,000 in 2002, the charitable deduction for 2002 would generally be $20,000 (20 percent of $100,000) and the excess amount of $10,000 would be carried forward, to be potentially deductible for 2003 (still subject to the 20 percent limitation).

Moreover, there is a *deduction reduction rule* that generally applies in this context. That rule is this: Where property is contributed to or for the use of a private foundation, the amount of the contribution deduction must be reduced by the amount of the long-term capital gain inherent in the property.[20]

There is, however, a significant exception to that rule. It concerns *qualified appreciated stock,* which essentially means publicly traded securities.[21] This type of stock can be contributed to a private foundation with the charitable deduction based on the full fair market value of the stock (as long as all of the inherent gain is long-term capital gain).[22]

NOTE: This special rule has a fitful history. Initially, Congress would extend it for a period of time. It would expire, leaving prospective donors to wonder (fret as to) whether it would be resuscitated. Then Congress would resurrect it, only to have it once again expire. Mercifully, in 1998, Congress made the rule permanent.

Q 17:7   What are the federal income tax rules for deductibility of a contribution of property to a public charity by an individual?

The primary set of these limitations imposes percentage maximums, applied in the same fashion as is the case with respect to gifts of money (Q 17:5). Thus, for individuals, where a charitable gift consists of property and the charitable donee is a public charity, the extent of the charitable deduction under the federal income tax law generally cannot exceed 30 percent of the donor's adjusted gross income.[23] Any excess portion can be carried forward and deducted over a period of up to five subsequent years.[24]

NOTE: Again, the foregoing rule also is applicable with respect to certain types of private foundations, usually private operating foundations (Q 14:2).

Thus, for example, if an individual had adjusted gross income in the amount of $100,000 for 2002 and made gifts of property to one or more public charities in that year totaling $20,000, the gifts would be fully deductible (assuming no other gifts and no application of any other limitations) for 2000. If this donor instead made gifts of this nature in the amount of $40,000 in 2002, the charitable deduction for 2002 would generally be $30,000 (30 percent of $100,000) and the excess amount of $10,000 would be carried forward, to be potentially deductible for 2003.

One of the most appealing features of the federal income tax law in this context is that a charitable contribution of property that has appreciated in value often is deductible based on the full fair market value of the property. The capital gain inherent in the appreciated property, which would be taxable had the property instead been sold or otherwise disposed of, goes untaxed.[25]

NOTE: For this benefit to be available, the property must be *capital gain property* rather than *ordinary income property.*[26] As a generalization, this distinction is based on the tax treatment of the revenue that would result if the property was sold. That is, the revenue would either be *long-term capital gain,* or *ordinary income* or *short-term capital gain.* (Generally, long-term capital gain property is a capital asset held for more than 12 months.[27]) Where the property is ordinary income property, the charitable contribution deduction must be reduced by the amount of gain that would either be ordinary income or short-term capital gain; in other words, the deduction is confined to the donor's basis in the property.[28]

As an illustration, an individual purchased an item of (capital gain) property in 2000 for $20,000 and, as of January 1, 2002, it is worth $40,000. He or she contributes this property to a public charity in 2002 and receives a potential charitable contribution deduction of $40,000. The capital gain of $20,000 that would have been triggered had the property been sold escapes taxation.

The charitable deduction is a *potential* one because the actual deduction is determined by applicable of the percentage limitation. If this donor's adjusted gross income for 2002 was $100,000, the charitable deduction would be $30,000 and the excess of $10,000 would be carried forward to 2003 (still subject to the 30 percent limitation).

TIP: This rule pertaining to the favorable tax treatment for gifts of appreciated property is equally applicable in the planned giving setting (Q 17:27). In many situations (but not all), the deductible remainder interest is based on the full fair market value of the contributed property, and the appreciation element (gain) is not taxed.

Again, a gift of property may have to be *substantiated* (Q 11:4) or be a *quid pro quo contribution* (Q 11:14), and/or there may have to be an appraisal of the value of the property. A planned gift is often made, in whole or in part, with (appreciated) property.

Q 17:8   Are there any exceptions to this rule?

There is one exception. The law provides an opportunity for an individual donor to elect application of the 50 percent limitation (Q 17:5) where the 30 percent limitation (Q 17:7) would otherwise apply. That is, a donor who is an individual may elect for a tax year to reduce his or her potential federal income tax charitable contribution deduction, occasioned by the gift or gifts of capital gain property to charity made during the year, by the amount of what would have been long-term capital gain had the property been sold, in exchange for use of the 50 percent limitation.[29]

This election may be made with respect to contributions of capital gain property carried over to the tax year involved even though the donor has not made any contributions of capital gain property in the year. If this election is made, the 30 percent limitation and the carryover rules with respect to it are inapplicable to the contributions made during the year.[30] This means that the 50 percent limitation applies.

COMMENT: Of course, in deciding whether to make this election, the individual must determine whether the 50 percent limitation or the 30 percent limitation is most suitable for him or her (or perhaps both) under the circumstances. Usually, the principal factor is the extent to which the property has appreciated in value; this election can be preferable where the property has not appreciated much in value. Another factor is whether the donor is seeking the maximum charitable contribution deduction for a contribution year. Since capital gain property generally is deductible using the fair market value of the property

---

(Q 17:7), the 30 percent limitation can operate to reduce what would otherwise be a larger charitable contribution deduction if the 50 percent limitation applied. This election enables a donor to calculate the deduction by using the fair market value of the property rather than merely the basis in the property.

CAUTION: Once this election is made, it cannot be revoked. In one instance, donors calculated their charitable deduction for a significant gift of property, which was highly appreciated in value by making this election. This decision resulted in a charitable deduction for the year of the gift and for two subsequent years. Two years later, they recalculated their charitable deduction stemming from the gift by using the 30 percent limitation and filed amended tax returns, This approach gave them a smaller charitable deduction for the year of the gift and the following two years, but it also produced a charitable contribution deduction for each of the next three tax years. The IRS, upheld in the courts, was of the view that donors are bound by this election; thus, the election, found improvident in hindsight, cannot be undone.[31]

Q 17:9   What are the federal income tax rules as to timing of the deductibility of a charitable contribution by an individual?

A federal income tax charitable contribution deduction for a gift made by an individual arises at the time of, and for the year in which, the making of the contribution. Usually the gift is made (completed) when the subject of the gift (e.g., money or a check) is transferred or delivered to the donee.[32] When a gift is made using a credit card, the contribution becomes deductible for the year in which the donor charged the gift on the account (rather than the year when the account including the charged amount is paid).[33]

The rules can be more complicated when the gift is of some other form of property. This is particularly the case where there is a formal system for the transfer of title. For example, an individual may make a contribution of a security (an item of intangible personal property) to a charitable organization—and create a federal income tax charitable contribution deduction—where the properly endorsed certificate evidencing the security is delivered to the charitable organization. Delivery also can be accomplished by a transfer of a security to an agent of the charitable donee.

CAUTION: When a gift is of stock, timing can have several consequences. It can determine who is the proper recipient of the dividends (taxable income to the donor). Timing also can affect taxation of any capital gain associated with the stock; if the donor is deemed to have control of the stock when it was sold, the capital gain will be attributed to (read: taxed to) the donor.[34]

Similarly, there is, of course, a formal legal system for the recording and transfer of title to parcels of real estate; transfers of real property are generally effected by means of deeds. As to the timing of the charitable deduction, the contribution for a gift of real property generally comes into being on the date the donor delivers a deed to the property to the charitable donee.[35]

Q 17:10 What are the federal income tax rules for deductibility of a charitable contribution by a for-profit corporation?

The answer to this question depends on the type of for-profit corporation that is the donor. There are essentially two types of these corporations. The larger corporations are sometimes referred to as *regular* corporations. Because these entities are the subject of Subtitle A, Chapter 1, Subchapter C of the Internal Revenue Code, they are often denominated *C corporations*.[36]

The other type of corporation is the *small business* corporation. These entities are the subject of Subtitle A, Chapter 1, Subchapter S of the Code and thus are often termed *S corporations*.[37] A major distinction between these two categories of corporations is that the S corporation is not a taxable entity; it is a *flow-through* type of organization and thus is treated as a partnership for tax purposes.[38]

The first answer (Q 17:11) assumes the donor is a C corporation. The rules as to a gift by an S corporation are summarized elsewhere (Q 17:13).

Q 17:11 What are the federal income tax rules for deductibility of a charitable contribution by a C corporation?

A C corporation may make a charitable gift of money. That contribution may not exceed, in any tax year, 10 percent of the corporation's pretax net income.[39] Carryover rules are available.[40] Generally, these rules also apply in instances of charitable gifts of other property.

There are, however, special rules limiting the deductibility of corporate gifts. In optimal circumstances, the allowable charitable contribution deduction is an amount equal to as much as twice the corporation's basis in the property. These special rule—providing what is termed an *augmented deduction*—pertain to gifts of the following types of property:

- Inventory, with the deduction enhanced when the property is to be used for the care of the ill, the needy, or infants[41]
- Tangible personal property to be used for scientific research (a *qualified research contribution*)[42]
- Computer technology and equipment for elementary or secondary school purposes[43]

NOTE: The third of these rules is inapplicable to a contribution made during a tax year beginning after December 31, 2000.[44]

Q 17:12 What are the federal income tax rules for deductibility of a charitable contribution by a partnership?

The taxable income of a partnership generally is computed in the same manner as is the case with individuals. The charitable contribution deduction, however, is not allowed to partnerships.[45] Rather, each partner takes into account separately the partner's distributive share of the partnership's charitable contributions.[46]

A partner's distributive share of charitable contributions made by a partnership during a tax year of the partnership is allowed as a charitable deduction on the partner's tax return for the partner's tax year with or within which the tax year of the partnership ends.[47] The aggregate of the partner's share of partnership contributions and the partner's own (directly made) contributions are subject to the various percentage limitations on annual deductibility (Q 17:4–17:7).

Moreover, another aspect of the tax law becomes invoked when a charitable gift is made out of a partnership: adjustment of the partner's basis in his or her (or its) interest in the partnership. This requires, by way of explanation, some background on this subject.

When a partnership makes a charitable contribution of property, the basis of each partner's interest in the partnership is decreased (but not below zero) by the amount of the partner's share of the partnership's basis in the property contributed.[48]

The adjusted basis of a partner's interest in a partnership must be increased by the sum of the partner's distributive share for the tax year and prior tax years of the taxable income of the partnership, the income of the partnership that is exempt from tax, and the excess of the deductions for depletion over the basis of the property subject to depletion.[49] The adjusted basis of a partner's interest in a partnership must be decreased (but not below zero) by distributions by the partnership as well as by the sum of the partner's distributive share for the tax year and prior tax years of the losses of the partnership and expenditures of the partnership that are not deductible in computing taxable income and not properly chargeable to capital account.[50]

These adjustments to the basis of a partner's interest in a partnership are necessary to prevent inappropriate or unintended benefits or detriments to the partners. Generally, the basis of a partner's interest in a partnership is adjusted to reflect the tax allocations of the partnership to that partner. This adjustment ensures that the income and loss of the partnership are taken into account by its partners only once. Also, adjustments must be made to reflect certain nontaxable events in the partnership.[51] For example, a partner's share of nontaxable income (e.g., exempt income) is added to the basis of the partner's interest because, absent a basis adjustment, the partner could recognize gain with respect to the tax-exempt income (e.g., on a sale or redemption of the partner's interest) and the benefit of the tax-exempt income would be lost to the partner. Likewise, a partner's share of nondeductible expenditures must be deducted from the partner's basis in order to prevent that amount from giving rise to a loss to the partner on a sale or redemption of the partner's interest in the partnership.

In determining whether a transaction results in exempt income[52] or a nondeductible noncapital expenditure,[53] the inquiry must be whether the transaction has a permanent effect on the partnership's basis in its assets, without a corresponding current or future effect on its taxable income.

With this as background, perhaps an example will elucidate these points. A and B each contribute an equal amount of money to form a general partnership. Under the partnership agreement, each item of income, gain, loss, and deduction of the partnership is allocated 50 percent to A and 50 percent to B. This partnership has unencumbered property, having a basis of $60,000 and a fair market value of $100,000. The partnership contributes the property to a charitable organization.

NOTE: This property is not of the type that requires reduction of the charitable deduction by elements of ordinary income or capital gain (Q 17:6).

As discussed, the contribution of this property by this partnership is not taken into account in computing the partnership's taxable income. Consequently, the contribution results in a permanent decrease in the aggregate basis of the assets of the partnership that is not taken into account by the partnership in determining its taxable income and is not taken into account for federal income tax purposes in any other manner. Therefore, the contribution of the property, and the resulting permanent decrease in partnership basis, is an expenditure of the partnership that is not deductible in computing its taxable income and not properly chargeable to capital account.

Reducing the partners' bases in their partnership interests by their respective shares of the permanent decrease in the partnership's basis in its assets preserves the intended benefit of providing a deduction for the fair market value of appreciated property without recognition of the appreciation. By contrast, reducing the partners' bases in their partnership interests by the fair market value of the contributed property would subsequently cause the partners to recognize gain (or a reduced loss), such as on a disposition of their partnership interests, attributable to the unrecognized appreciation in this contributed property at the time of the contribution.

In the example, under the partnership agreement, partnership items are allocated equally between A and B. Accordingly, the basis of A's and B's interests in the partnership is each reduced by $30,000 (50 percent of $60,000).

Q 17:13 What are the federal income tax rules for deductibility of a charitable contribution by an S corporation?

S corporations (Q 17:10) are treated, for federal tax purposes, essentially the same as partnerships (Q 17:12). Thus, the charitable contribution deduction is not allowed to the S corporation but is taken by each shareholder on an allocable basis.

Q 17:14 What are the federal income tax rules for deductibility of a charitable contribution by a limited liability company?

Limited liability companies are treated, for tax purposes, essentially the same as partnerships (Q 17:12).[54] Thus, the charitable contribution deduction is not allowed to the limited liability company but is taken by each member on an allocable basis.

Q 17:15 What are the federal income tax rules as to timing of the deductibility of a contribution by a corporation?

Presumably, this question pertains to a charitable contribution made by a *regular* corporation (Q 17:10).

Generally, a federal income tax charitable contribution deduction for a gift made by a corporation arises at the time of, and for the year in which, the deduction is made. A corporation that reports its taxable income using the accrual method of accounting may, however, at its election, deduct charitable contributions paid within 2½ months after the close of its tax year, as long as

- The board of directors of the corporation authorized the making of the charitable contribution during the tax year, and
- The charitable contribution is made after the close of the tax year of the corporation and within the 2½-month period.[55]

This election must be made at the time the tax return for the tax year is filed. This is done by reporting the contribution on the return. A written declaration must be attached to the return stating that the resolution authorizing the contribution was adopted by the board of directors during the tax year involved. This declaration must be verified by a statement signed by an officer authorized to sign the return that it is made under penalties of perjury. There also must be attached to the return when filed a copy of the resolution of the board of directors authorizing the contribution.[56]

To satisfy this rule, contributions of property need not be segregated by year. Also, there is no requirement that the donees be identified at the time the resolution is adopted.[57]

Q 17:16 Is the use of the gift property relevant in determining the amount of the charitable contribution deduction?

In some circumstances, the actual use of the property can be a factor in determining the amount of the charitable contribution deduction. The rule is that where the property contributed is tangible personal property and where the charitable donee uses the property for a noncharitable purpose, the contribution deduction must be reduced by the amount of the long-term capital gain inherent in the property.[58]

CAUTION: This rule can be problematic in the private foundation context. It is likely that greater troubles will ensue if a private foundation engages in noncharitable activities. The difficulties here are far more likely in the public charity setting. An example is the charitable auction. It is common for someone to make a gift of an item to be auctioned by the charity. The property that is the subject of the gift is often a painting, some other work of art, an item of furniture, and the like — things that are tangible personal property. Sale soon after donation is an unrelated use. Thus, the charitable deduction for gifts of this nature is usually confined to the donor's basis in the property (Q 17:17).

Q 17:17 Is there anything unique about gifts of works of art to charitable organizations?

Certainly there usually is a federal income tax contribution deduction for a gift of a work of art to a charitable organization. In general, this deduction is an amount equal to the fair market value of the property (Q 17:7).

There are, however, two exceptions that are particularly applicable in this context:

1. The work of art that is contributed may be the creation of the donor, in which case the deduction is confined to the donor's basis in the property (Q 17:20).
2. The work of art may be put to an unrelated use by the charitable recipient, in which case the deduction is confined to the donor's basis in the property.

Of these two exceptions, the second is most likely to occur. A work of art is an item of *tangible personal property*. There is a special rule as to gifts of this nature, which may be reiterated in this context. The rule is this: Where a gift of tangible personal property is made to a charity, the amount of the charitable deduction that would otherwise be determined must be reduced by the amount of gain that would have been long-term capital gain if the property contributed had been sold by the donor at its fair market value, determined at the time of the contribution, where the use by the donee is unrelated to its tax-exempt purposes.

The greatest controversy surrounding the charitable deduction of a work of art is likely to be the value of the item. Not infrequently, there is a dispute between the IRS and a donor as to the fair market value of a work of art. Usually, these disputes are settled; sometimes they are resolved by a court — most frequently the U.S. Tax Court.

COMMENT 1:   The appropriate value of an item of property is a question of fact, not law. Judges are not trained as appraisers; therefore, this field is rife with the use of expert witnesses. Not infrequently, the value of property in these circumstances is arrived at with the court splitting the difference between the value advanced by the donor's expert and that asserted by the government's expert.[59]

COMMENT 2:   This is a field where donors can get rather creative and promoters of various art-based tax shelters proliferate. In turn, judges can become frustrated, cynical, or wry. Here is an example of the latter: "This was an interesting tax-saving arrangement devised as an art transaction, but the art will have to be treasured for art's sake and not as a tax deduction."[60]

Q 17:18 What is the tax law consequence of a loan of a work of art to a charitable organization?

As the question indicates, rather than *contribute* a work of art to a charitable organization, a person may decide to *loan* the artwork to a charity. This type of transfer does not give rise to a federal *income* tax charitable contribution deduction. The transaction is, nonetheless, a gift.

The transaction is disregarded as a transfer for *gift* tax purposes, however, where

- The recipient organization is a charitable entity.
- The use of the artwork by the charitable donee is related to the purpose or function constituting the basis for its tax exemption.
- The artwork involved is an archeological, historic, or creative item of tangible personal property.[61]

Q 17:19 Is there a federal income tax deduction for a gift of real property for conservation purposes?

Yes. A relevant problem, however, is that private foundations cannot be the direct recipients of these gifts. These rules may be pertinent, however, to a private foundation's grantee, and thus they are briefly summarized.

Special federal tax rules pertain to contributions to charity of real property for conservation purposes. These rules are an exception to the general

---

NOTE: The rules about to be discussed are in the context of the *income tax* charitable contribution deduction for qualified conservation contributions. There are, however, somewhat comparable rules in the *estate tax* and *gift tax* charitable deduction settings.

---

rule that there is no charitable contribution for contributions of *partial interests* in property (Q 17:27). This exception involves the *qualified conservation contribution.*[62]

A qualified conservation contribution has three fundamental characteristics: It is a contribution

1. Of a *qualified real property interest.*
2. To a *qualified organization.*
3. Exclusively for *conservation purposes.*

A qualified real property interest is one of the following interests in real property:

• The entire interest of the donor in the property (other than a qualified mineral interest)

> **NOTE:** A *qualified mineral interest* is the donor's interest in subsurface oil, gas, or other minerals, and the right to access to these minerals.

> **CAUTION:** A real property interest is not treated as an entire interest in the property (other than a qualified mineral interest) if the property in which the donor's interest exists was divided prior to the contribution in order to enable the donor to retain control of more than a qualified mineral interest or to reduce the real property interest contributed (with an exception for certain minor interests).

• A remainder interest (Q 17:28)
• A restriction (granted in perpetuity) on the use which may be made of the real property

> **NOTE:** A form of qualified real property interest is the *perpetual conservation restriction.* This is a restriction granted in perpetuity on the use which may be made of real property, including an easement or other interest in real property that under state law has attributes similar to an easement (e.g., a restrictive covenant).

A qualified organization is an entity that is one of the following:

• A unit of government
• A publicly supported charitable organization that is the *donative* type (Q 12:4)

- A publicly supported charitable organization that is the *service provider* type (Q 12:8)
- A *supporting organization* (Q 12:15) that is controlled by one or more of the foregoing three types of organizations

In addition, to be a qualified donee, an organization must have a commitment to protect the conservation purposes of the donation and have the resources to enforce the restrictions. A qualified organization is not required to set aside funds to enforce the restrictions that are the subject of the contribution. In the instrument of conveyance, the donor must prohibit the donee from subsequently transferring the interest unless it requires, as a condition of the subsequent transfer, that the conservation purposes which the contribution was originally intended to advance be carried out.

The term *conservation purpose* means one of the following:

1. Preservation of land areas for outdoor recreation by, or for the education of, the general public

   ---
   NOTE: This purpose includes the preservation of a water area for the use of the public for boating or fishing, or a nature or hiking trail for the use of the public.
   ---

2. Protection of a relatively natural habitat of fish, wildlife, or plants, or similar ecosystem

   ---
   NOTE: This standard allows for alteration of the habitat or environment to some extent by human activity. For example, the preservation of a lake formed by a man-made dam qualifies if the lake is a natural feeding area for a wildlife community that includes rare, endangered, or threatened native species.
   ---

3. Preservation of open space (including farmland and forest land) where the preservation
   - Is for the scenic enjoyment of the general public, or
   - Is pursuant to a clearly delineated federal, state, or local governmental conservation policy, and
   - (As to either category) will yield a significant public benefit

   ---
   NOTE 1 A governmental policy in this regard must be more than a general declaration of conservation goals by a single official or legislative body. The requirement is met by contributions that further a specified, identified conservation project; that preserve a wild or scenic river; or that protect the scenic, ecological, or historic character of land that is
   ---

contiguous to or an integral part of the surroundings of existing recreation or conservation sites.

NOTE 2:   The tax regulations contain criteria for evaluating and applying phrases such as *scenic enjoyment* and *significant public benefit.*

4. Preservation of a historically important land area or a certified historic structure

NOTE 1:   A *historically important land area* includes:
- An independently significant land area, including any related historic structures that meet the National Register Criteria for Evaluation.
- Any land area within a registered historic district, including any buildings on the land area that can reasonably be considered as contributing to the significance of the district.
- Any land area adjacent to a property listed individually in the National Register of Historic Places, in a case where the physical or environmental features of the land area contribute to the historic or cultural integrity of the property.

NOTE 2:   A *certified historic structure* is a building, structure, or land area that is listed in the National Register, located in a registered historic district, and certified by the Secretary of the Interior or the Secretary of the Treasury as being of historic significance to the district.

To satisfy these rules, a contribution must be *exclusively* for conservation purposes. A conservation deduction will not be denied, however, where an incidental benefit inures to the donor merely as a result of conservation restrictions limiting the uses to which the donor's property may be put. One of the requirements in this regard is that the conservation purpose must be protected in perpetuity.

COMMENT: As an example of this last requirement, a court held that a grant of an easement over the facades of the donors' interests in a condominium apartment building was not a qualified conservation contribution because it was not contributed exclusively for conservation purposes, in that the easement was not protected in perpetuity because a security interest in the building had priority over the easement.[63]

This type of gift raises (once again) the matter of valuation (Q 17:17). The amount of the charitable contribution deduction, in the case of a contribution of a donor's entire interest in conservation property (other than a qualified mineral interest), is the fair market value of the surface rights in the property contributed.

Two subrules:

1. In the case of a contribution of a remainder interest in real property, depreciation and depletion of the property must be taken into account in determining the value of the interest.
2. The value of a charitable contribution of a perpetual conservation restriction is the fair market value of the restriction at the time of the contribution.

If a donor makes a qualified conservation contribution and claims a charitable contribution deduction for it, the donor must maintain written records of

- The fair market value of the underlying property before and after the contribution.
- The conservation purpose furthered by the contribution.

NOTE: This is a *substantiation* requirement. This requirement is in addition to the general charitable contribution substantiation requirements (Q 11:4–11:5).

Q 17:20 Is there a federal income tax charitable contribution deduction for a gift of property created by the donor?

Yes, but. An individual may make a contribution to a charitable organization of an item of property that was created by the donor, such as a painting or a manuscript. The charitable deduction for this type of gift is not based on the fair market value of the property (Q 17:7). Instead, it is confined to the donor's cost basis in the property.

This result is occasioned by the rule that requires a reduction in the charitable contribution deduction, created by a gift of property, by an amount equal to the amount of gain that would not have been long-term capital gain had the property been sold by the donor at its fair market value at the time of the contribution. The federal tax law excludes from the definition of the term *capital asset* a copyright, a literary, musical, or artistic composition, a letter or memorandum, or similar property, held by

- An individual whose personal efforts created the property.
- In the case of a letter, memorandum, or similar property, a person for whom material of this nature was prepared or produced, or

- A person in whose hands the basis of the property of this nature is determined, for purposes of determining gain from a sale or exchange, in whole or in part by reference to the basis of the property in the hands of a person described in either of the foregoing two categories.[64]

Thus, as noted, this charitable contribution deduction is confined to the amount equal to the cost to the donor of the creation of the item of property.

Q 17:21 What about gifts to private foundations from retirement plans?

The transfer of retirement plan assets to private foundations and other charitable organizations (and to charitable remainder trusts (Q 17:28)) is a subject of some complexity—and the law in this field may be dramatically changing. The subject entails not only income tax issues but also retirement plan law (chiefly, the Employee Retirement Income and Security Act), estate taxation, and the law of tax exempt organizations.

As a general rule, the income and/or assets in a retirement plan must be distributed to the beneficiary beginning at age 70½.[65] There is a penalty for untimely or inappropriate payments.[66] Thus, when a transfer of funds is made from a retirement vehicle to a charitable organization, the penalty is triggered. Also, there is no federal income tax charitable contribution deduction for the payment.

NOTE: At the behest of the Bush Administration, the 107th Congress (2001–2002) will be considering legislation to revise the law in this area, to make charitable transfers from retirement plans more attractive from a tax perspective.

Q 17:22 Is there a federal income tax charitable contribution deduction for a gift of services?

No. The federal tax law does not allow a charitable contribution deduction for the value of services provided to a charitable organization as a gift.[67] For example, a lawyer may contribute to a charitable organization, as an item to be bid on at the charity's fund-raising auction, his or her services in the writing of a will. There is no charitable contribution deduction for the value (based on the lawyer's hourly rate) of this type of gift.[68]

NOTE 1:   There is another reason why a gift of services is not deductible: There is no charitable deduction for gifts of *property* created by the donor (Q 17:20).[69]

NOTE 2:   If the organization was a publicly supported charity, it could not take the value into account in calculating public support.

NOTE 3:   By contrast, in some instances, the out-of-pocket expenses incurred by volunteers may be deductible as charitable contributions. This can occur where the expenses are necessary to the accomplishment of the organization's charitable purposes.[70] Nonetheless, there is no charitable contribution deduction for traveling expenses (including amounts expended for meals and lodging) while away from home, whether paid directly or by reimbursement, "unless there is no significant element of personal pleasure, recreation, or vacation in such travel."[71]

Q 17:23 Is there a charitable contribution deduction for a gift of the right to use materials, equipment, or facilities?

No. The federal tax law does not allow a charitable contribution deduction for the value of materials, equipment, or facilities provided to a charitable organization as a gift.[72] For example, the owner of an office building may contribute office space in the building to a charity. There is no charitable contribution deduction for this type of gift. Likewise, the owner of a beach house may contribute to a charity, as an item to be bid on at a fund-raising auction, a two-week stay at the house. No contribution deduction is available for this type of gift.

NOTE 1:   In one case, an individual claimed a charitable contribution deduction for the fair rental value of a portion of a garage used to house a fire engine owned by a county. The deduction was denied.[73]

NOTE 2:   In another instance, a charitable organization sponsored an auction as a fund-raising event. One of the items contributed to the charity was the right to use a vacation home for one week, with the donor of the home being its owner. The IRS ruled that the value of the fair rental amount forgone by the property owner could not be the basis for a federal income tax charitable contribution deduction.[74] (Making matters worse, the IRS also ruled that use of the property by the successful bidder at the auction is considered "personal use" by the owner, for purposes of determining any business expense deduction allowable with respect to the property.[75])

NOTE 3:   If the organization is a publicly supported charity, it could not take the value into account in calculating public support.

Q 17:24 What is a *restricted* gift?

A *restricted* gift is a contribution to a charitable organization where one or more restrictions (limitations, conditions) are imposed on the use or application of the gift. In a broad sense, there are two types of restricted gifts. One category of restricted gift is where the restriction is imposed on the gift by the donor. The other category is where the restriction on the gift was imposed by the board of trustees or directors of the recipient charitable organization. Usually, the term *restricted* gift is employed only to describe the first type of restricted gift.

Where the restriction was imposed by the donor, it becomes the obligation of the charitable organization—once it has accepted the encumbered gift—to use the restricted money or property in a manner that conforms to the restriction. This is because the gift restriction is considered to be imposed by contract.

COMMENT: If, of course, the restriction is imposed by the charity's governing board, the board (or a subsequent one) can remove the restriction—as long as in doing so the body does not violate the established legal rights of others.

Typical restrictions of this nature include the mandate that the gift or its proceeds be used for scholarships, a chair at a university, an award program, the construction and/or maintenance of a building, or an endowment fund (Q 17:25).

Aside from the terms of the restriction, there is an overarching need to be certain that the gift property is used for charitable ends (unless it is investment property). Difficulties in this area can be reduced to the extent the restriction is general. If even a funded program is discontinued, there may be other uses of the property that are within the range of the restriction.

NOTE: This may require some creative reading of the restriction. Again, the ease of compliance with the language of the restriction is in direct correlation with the breadth of the restriction.

If there is no one living to challenge an actual or alleged deviation from the restriction, the organization should consider use of the restricted property in a manner as close to the bounds of the restriction (but presumably not in literal compliance) as possible. This is a "judgment call," based on the facts and circumstances at the time. Above all, the organization should be prudent and act in good faith when making this type of management decision.

If there is no reasonable way to conform with the restriction, the organization has these options:

- If the donor is still alive, obtain a written waiver of the restriction, perhaps replacing it with a restriction that the organization can currently satisfy.
- Make a grant of the funds and/or property to another organization that can satisfy the restriction.
- Take the matter into court in a effort to have the restriction revised or eliminated.

There are other tax issues to contend with. Generally, restrictions of the type referenced above will not jeopardize, in whole or in part, the donor's charitable contribution deduction. If the restriction would cause the charity to do something illegal or contrary to public policy, the restriction may not be enforceable. Or, to the other extreme, compliance with the restriction may endanger the charity's tax-exempt status and/or transgress one or more of the private foundation rules (Q 1:4). (A question may arise, however, as to why the organization accepted the gift.)

A restriction accompanying a gift may raise a question as to whether, in fact, the transaction amounts to a completed gift. At stake here is the donor's charitable deduction, inasmuch as there must be a true gift before there can be a charitable contribution deduction. This can be a particular problem where the donor has an ongoing involvement in the expenditure and/or investment of the gift funds or property. There can be an argument that the restriction prevents the transaction from being a completed gift—that is, a transfer by which the transferor parts with all of his or her right, title, and interest in the property—so that there is no gift and thus no charitable contribution deduction. Other areas of the law where questions of this nature are being raised concern supporting organizations (Q 12:15) and donor-advised funds (Q 15:9).

Q 17:25 What is an *endowment* gift?

An *endowment* gift is a form of restricted gift (Q 17:24). It is a gift that is restricted for placement in one or more endowment funds of the recipient charitable organization. Again, this type of restriction can be imposed on the gift by the donor or by the governing board of the charitable organization. Also, again, usually the term *endowment* gift is used only to describe the first type of restricted gift.

An endowment gift is a contribution where the charity is obligated to place the gift into one or more funds. Usually the principal of the gift (the money and/or property transferred) must be retained in the fund and invested. That is, the gift item is not to be spent for program purposes. The income from the principal, however, is usually available for program purposes.

The endowment fund need not be a separate legal entity. It is a component of the charitable organization, best evidenced by a board resolution. Its tax-exempt status is that of the organization itself. It is often desirable to have a separate bank and/or investment account for the endowment fund. Some organizations choose nonetheless to cause the endowment fund to be in a separate entity, which itself is a charitable organization. Often, this separate entity is a supporting organization (Q 12:15).

The endowment fund can be supportive of the charitable organization's entire range of programs. It also can be supportive of just one aspect of the organization, such as maintenance of a building, funding of a scholarship program, or funding of a research effort. A charitable organization can have several endowment funds.

CAUTION: A trap lurks in this blend of the concept of an endowment fund and the use of a supporting organization. As is discussed elsewhere, certain tax-exempt organizations that are not charitable ones can have a supporting organization (Q 12:23). A common model is a membership association that is tax-exempt as a business league[76] with a supporting organization. Is this instance, the supporting organization cannot be an or maintain an endowment fund that is generally supportive of the association—because that would be a substantial noncharitable purpose (even though it would be a form of support or benefit). Nonetheless, the supporting organization could maintain an endowment fund to be supportive of only the charitable and educational programs of the association. With that approach, the supporting organization could make restricted grants to the association.

Q 17:26 What is a *bargain sale*?

A *bargain sale* is a transfer of property to a charitable organization, with the transaction in part a sale or exchange of the property and in part a charitable contribution of the property.[77] Basically, a bargain sale is a sale of an item of property to a charitable organization at a price that is an amount that is less than the fair market value of the property, with the amount equal to the fair market value of the property less the amount that is the sales price regarded as a contribution to the charitable organization.[78]

CAUTION: The deduction reduction rule (Q 17:7) can apply in the bargain sale setting.

There must be allocated to the contribution portion of the property that element of the adjusted basis of the entire property that bears the same ratio to the total adjusted basis as the fair market value of the contributed portion of the property bears to the fair market value of the entire property. Further, for these purposes, there must be allocated to the contributed portion of the property the amount of gain that is not recognized on the bargain sale, but that would have been recognized if the contributed portion of the property had been sold by the donor at its fair market value at the time of its contribution to the charitable organization.[79]

Q 17:27 Is a donor, to receive a charitable contribution deduction for a gift, required to give the entirety of the donor's interest in the property?

No. In certain circumstances, a donor may make a gift to a charitable organization of only a portion of the donor's interest in the property. There can be a charitable contribution deduction arising as a result of the gift, for the portion of the gift destined for charity.

This type of a gift is known as a *partial interest* gift. This means, of course, that the donor is contributing only a portion of the interest in the property to charity. For a charitable deduction to be available, however, some very technical rules must be complied with.

Generally, there is no charitable deduction for a partial interest gift.[80] Here, though, is a situation where the exception to the rule is larger than the application of the general rule. The prevailing way to make a partial interest gift is to so by means of a *split-interest trust.* This is the vehicle commonly used to conceptually divide the property into the two component interests: income interest and remainder interest.

Usually, a qualified split-interest trust is required if a charitable contribution deduction is to be available.[81] Split-interest trusts are charitable remainder trusts (Q 17:28), pooled income funds (Q 17:31), and charitable lead trusts (Q 17:32).

There are some exceptions to these general requirements of a split-interest trust in this type of giving. The principal exception is the charitable gift annuity, which utilizes a contract rather than a trust (Q 17:33). Other approaches also can generate a charitable contribution deduction (Q 17:34).

Thus, in this setting, it is not enough to create a remainder interest for a charity. It is critical to create a remainder interest, the gift of which yields a charitable contribution deduction. There are only a few ways in which a remainder interest can be the subject of a charitable contribution deduction. Absent qualification of an eligible partial interest (almost always a qualifying remainder interest), there is no charitable contribution deduction for the gift.

17:28   What is a *charitable remainder trust*?

A *charitable remainder trust* is one of the types of split-interest trusts (Q 17:27).[82] As the name indicates, it is a trust that has been used to create a remainder interest (*id.*), with that interest in the gift property designated for one or more charitable organizations. Each charitable remainder trust is designed and written specifically for the particular circumstances of the donor(s). The donor(s) receives a charitable contribution deduction for the transfer of the remainder interest.

A qualified charitable remainder trust must provide for a specified distribution of income, at least annually, to one or more beneficiaries, at least one of which is *not* a charity. The flow of income must be for a life or lives, or for a term not to exceed 20 years. An irrevocable remainder interest must be held for the benefit of the charity or paid over to it. The noncharitable beneficiaries are the holders of the income interests, and the charitable organization has the remainder interest. Most types of property can be contributed to a charitable remainder trust.

Conventionally, once the income interests expire, the assets in a charitable remainder trust are distributed to, or for the use of, the charitable organization that is the remainder interest beneficiary. It does not happen very often, but the property in the trust may, instead of being distributed to the charity, be retained in the trust for use for charitable purposes.

CAUTION: If the second option is selected, the trust will have to be qualified for tax-exempt status as a charity. It is almost certain to constitute a private foundation (Q 1.1).

Usually, a bank or similar financial institution serves as the trustee of a charitable remainder trust. This institution should have the capacity to administer the trust, make appropriate investments, and timely adhere to all income and gain distributions and reporting requirements. In some instances, the charitable organization that is the remainder interest beneficiary acts as the trustee.

CAUTION: This is a subject of state law. In some states, a charitable organization cannot serve as a trustee. State law, then, obviously must be looked into before a trust arrangement is finalized.

A donor or related party may be the trustee of a charitable remainder trust. Caution must be exercised here, however, to avoid triggering the *grantor trust* rules, which, among other outcomes, cause the gain from the sale of appreciated property by the trust to be taxed to the grantor/donor.[83]

Generally, a charitable remainder trust is a tax-exempt organization.[84]

Q 17:29 Are there different types of charitable remainder trusts?

Yes. At the present time, there are five types of charitable remainder trusts. One of these is the *charitable remainder annuity trust* (CRAT) and the other four are variations of the *charitable remainder unitrust* (CRUT). The prime distinction among these trusts is the manner in which the income to be paid from the trust to those holding income interests is determined.

NOTE: Another important distinction between a CRAT and a CRUT is that additional contributions can be made to a CRUT but not to a CRAT.

A qualified CRAT must have the following features:

- The income payments from the trust are in the form of a fixed amount—an annuity—or what the law terms a *sum certain.*
- This sum certain must be at least 5 percent of the initial net fair market value of all property placed in the trust and may not exceed 50 percent of that value.
- This sum certain (or *annuity amount*) must be paid, at least annually, to one or more persons (at least one of which is not a charity).
- If the annuity amount beneficiary is an individual, that person must be living at the time of creation of the trust.
- The annuity amount payment period may be for a term of years, not in excess of 20, or for the life or lives of the annuity amount beneficiary or beneficiaries.
- No amounts, other than the annuity amounts, may be paid to or for the use of any person other than a charitable organization.
- Following the close of the annuity payment period, the remainder interest in the trust must be transferred to, or for the use of, a charitable organization or retained by the trust for a charitable use.
- The value of the remainder interest (Q 17:27) must be at least 10 percent of the initial net fair market value of all property placed in the trust.[85]

As an example of the annuity amount, a CRAT is funded with $100,000 worth of property; the income payout amount is set at $5,000. Thus, $5,000 must be paid annually to one or more income interest beneficiaries.

NOTE 1:   It is said throughout that the income interest amounts must be paid *annually.* This refers to the total amount of income that is required to be paid out each year. The actual payout may be more frequent, such as semiannually or quarterly.

NOTE 2:   In addition to the above rules concerning qualified CRATs, to the extent the remainder interest is in *qualified employer securities,*[86] the securities may be transferred to an employee stock ownership plan[87] as long as the transfer constitutes a *qualified gratuitous transfer.*[88]

One of the CRUTs is the standard CRUT, or SCRUT. A qualified SCRUT must have the following features:

- The income payments from the trust are an amount equal to a fixed percentage of the net fair market value of its assets, valued annually.

- This fixed percentage must be at least 5 percent of the net fair market value of the assets, valued annually, and may not exceed 50 percent of that value.
- This income amount (or unitrust *amount*) must be paid, at least annually, to one or more persons (at least one of which is not a charity).
- If the unitrust amount beneficiary is an individual, that person must be living at the time of creation of the trust.
- The unitrust amount payment period may be for a term of years, not in excess of 20, or for the life or lives of the unitrust amount beneficiary or beneficiaries.
- No amounts, other than the unitrust amounts, may be paid to or for the use of any person other than a charitable organization.
- Following the close of the unitrust payment period, the remainder interest in the trust must be transferred to, or for the use of, a charitable organization or retained by the trust for a charitable use.
- With respect to each contribution of property to the trust, the value of the remainder interest (Q 17:27) in the property must be at least 10 percent of the net fair market value of the property as of the date the property is contributed to the trust.[89]

The SCRUT is also thus known as the *fixed percentage CRUT.*[90] Thus, the amount paid out each year to the income interest beneficiaries can fluctuate from year to year. As an example of a standard unitrust amount, a SCRUT is funded with $100,000 worth of property; the percentage selected is 5 percent. In year 1, the income payout amount is $5,000. Thus, $5,000 must be paid that year to one or more income interest beneficiaries. The value of the trust's assets for year 2 is $105,000; the payout amount is $5,250. The value of the trust's assets for year 3 is $110,000; the payout amount is $5,500. The value of the trust's assets for year 4 is $95,000; the payout amount is $4,750.

There are two types of CRUTs that are known as *income exception* CRUTs. This means that the payout rules for SCRUTs need not be followed. This approach is usually used where the contributed property does not generate enough income (perhaps none) to enable the trust to comport with the 5 percent rule.

One of these types of CRUTs enables the income to flow to the income interest beneficiary or beneficiaries once there is any income generated in the trust.[91] This amount may be less than the 5 percent amount. Here, the unitrust amount is the lesser of the fixed percentage amount or the trust's annual net income. The income payments begin once a suitable amount of income begins to flow into the trust. That is, the income payments may begin at a future point in time and are only prospective. This form of CRUT is the net income CRUT—or NICRUT.[92]

For example, the property transferred to a NICRUT has a fair market value of $100,000, but it is non–income-producing (e.g., it is unimproved real estate). Two years elapse before the property can be sold. The property is sold early into year 3 and the proceeds invested; the investment return for that year is 3 percent. This NICRUT would make no distributions in years 1 and 2, and distribute the 3 percent amount in year 3.

The other of these types of CRUTs is similar to the NICRUT but the trust instrument provides that, for the years in which there was no or an insufficient distribution, the trust can, once the investment policy generates adequate income, not only begin to pay the income interest beneficiaries the full amount of the determined unitrust payments but also make payments that make up for the distribution deficiencies in prior years.[93] This type of trust can thus make catch-up—or make-up—payments once the non–income-producing asset is sold. Thus, in this case, the unitrust amount is determined under the net income method, with that amount also including any amount of income that exceeds the current year's fixed percentage amount to make up for any shortfall in payments from prior years when the trust's income was less than the fixed percentage amount. This net income make-up CRUT is the NIMCRUT.[94]

For example, the property transferred to a NIMCRUT has a fair market value of $100,000, but it is non–income producing (e.g., it is unimproved real estate). The fixed percentage is 5 percent. Two years elapse before the property can be sold. The property is sold early into year 3 and the proceeds invested; the investment return for that year is 3 percent. In years 4 and 5, the return is 5 percent. In years 6 and 7, the return is 8 percent. This NIMCRUT would make no distributions in years 1 and 2, distribute the 3 percent amount in year 3, distribute the 5 percent amount in years 4 to 7, and start using the excess (over 5 percent) income amounts received in years 6 and 7 to make up for the deficiencies in payouts in years 1 to 3.

NOTE: Again, these trusts do not normally pay income taxes (Q 17:28). Thus, if the non–income-producing property was highly appreciated in value, the sales proceeds are not reduced by capital gains taxes, which means that the full amount of the sales proceeds can be invested in income-producing property. This produces the maximum asset base to generate income in furtherance of the NIMCRUT approach.

TIP: The makeup feature selected will have an impact on the charitable deduction for the gift of the remainder interest. Because the makeup feature that allows for retroactive payments can provide more income to the income beneficiary (or beneficiaries) than the prospective makeup feature, the income interest is likely to be greater and, correspondingly, the remainder interest is that much less. The result: a smaller charitable deduction when the retroactive income makeup provision is used.

The fourth type of CRUT is the flip unitrust—the FLIPCRUT. In the case of a FLIPCRUT, its governing instrument provides that the CRUT will convert (flip) once from one of the income exception methods—the NICRUT or NIMCRUT—to the fixed percentage method—the SCRUT—for purposes of calculating the unitrust amount.[95] The conversion is allowed, however, only if the specific date or single event triggering the flip (*triggering event*) is outside the control of, or not discretionary with, the trustee or any other person or persons.[96]

Permissible triggering events with respect to an individual include marriage, divorce, death, or birth.[97] The sale of an unmarketable asset, such as real estate, is a permissible triggering event. Examples of impermissible triggering events include the sale of marketable assets and a request from the unitrust amount beneficiary or that recipient's financial advisor that the CRUT's payout mechanism be converted to the fixed percentage method.

The conversion to the fixed percentage method must occur at the beginning of the tax year that immediately follows the tax year in which the triggering date or event occurs.[98] Any make-up amount is forfeited when the trust converts to the fixed percentage method.

The term *unmarketable assets* means assets other than cash, cash equivalents, or assets that can be readily sold or exchanged for cash or cash equivalents. Unmarketable assets include real property, closely held stock, and unregistered securities for which there is no available exemption under the securities laws permitting public sale.[99]

Thus, where these rules are satisfied, a donor can fund a CRUT with unmarketable assets that produce little or no income. The donor likely wants the income beneficiary or beneficiaries of the CRUT to receive a steady stream of payments based on the total return available from the value of the assets. Of course, these payments cannot be made until the unmarketable assets can be converted into liquid (marketable) assets that can be used to generate income to pay the fixed percentage amount.

Using these FLIPCRUT rules, a donor can establish a CRUT that uses one of the two income exception methods in calculating the unitrust amount until the unmarketable assets are sold. Following the sale, the CRUT's payout method would be altered so that the fixed percentage method is used to calculate the unitrust amount. Thus, the permissible FLIPCRUT patterns are a NICRUT flipped to a SCRUT or a NIMCRUT flipped to a SCRUT.

NOTE 1:   The conversion permitted by this law is the only allowable type of CRUT flip. (Any other type of conversion will cause the trust to fail to constitute a charitable remainder trust.) Thus, for example, a SCRUT cannot convert to a NICRUT or a NIMCRUT. For that matter, a CRAT cannot convert to a CRUT, nor can a CRUT convert to a CRAT.

NOTE 2:   The rules as to qualified gratuitous transfers of qualified employer securities also apply in the case of CRUTs.

Q 17:30 What types of charitable organizations can be remainder interest beneficiaries of charitable remainder trusts?

There are no limitations on the types of charitable organizations that can be beneficiaries of charitable remainder trusts. That is, these organizations can be either public charities (Q 1:2) or private foundations (Q 1:1).

TIP: The percentage limitations on deductible charitable giving (Q 17:4–17:7) need to be taken into account. For example, a contribution of appreciated property to a public charity is subject to the 30 percent limitation, while the same gift made to a private foundation is subject to a 20 percent limitation. These percentages do not apply just when a gift is made outright; they apply when the gift is made by means of a charitable remainder trust. Here can be a problem: If the trust instrument does not expressly confine the charitable beneficiary or beneficiaries to a public charity or public charities, the 20 percent limitation will be imposed on the deduction, because of the possibility that the property will be transferred to a private foundation (Q 17:6). (Also, the gift deduction may be confined to the donor's basis in the property [Q 17:7].)

Q 17:31 What is a *pooled income fund*?

A *pooled income fund* is a type of split-interest trust (Q 17:27). It is a trust (fund) that is used to create remainder interests destined for charity.[100] Contributions to pooled income funds are generally confined to cash and readily marketable securities.

A donor to a qualified pooled income fund receives a charitable contribution deduction for contributing the remainder interest in the donated property to charity. This use of the fund creates income interests in noncharitable beneficiaries. The remainder interests in the gift properties are destined for the charitable organization that maintains the fund.

Private foundations, however, are not permitted to maintain pooled income funds. Only certain types of public charities are allowed to do so.[101]

Q 17:32 What is a *charitable lead trust*?

In essence, a *charitable lead trust* is the reverse of a charitable remainder trust (Q 17:28): With the lead trust, the income interest is contributed to charity and the remainder interest is destined for noncharitable beneficiaries.[102] Thus, the charitable lead trust is a form of split-interest trust (Q 17:27).

Under these arrangements, an income interest in property is contributed to a charitable organization for a term of years or for the life of one or more individuals. These individuals must be the donor, the donor's spouse, or one who, with respect to all noncharitable remainder interest beneficiaries, is either a lineal ancestor or the spouse of a lineal ancestor of these beneficiaries.[103] The remainder interest in the property is reserved to return, at the expiration of the income interests (the *lead period*), to the donor or to be transferred to one or more other remainder interest beneficiary or beneficiaries.

The charitable lead trust can be used to accelerate into one year a series of charitable contributions that would otherwise be made annually. In some circumstances, a charitable deduction is available for the transfer of an income interest in property to a charitable organization by means of a charitable lead trust. There are stringent limitations, however, on the deductible amount of charitable contributions of these income interests. Frequently, there is no charitable contribution deduction; the donor's motive for establishing the trust is estate planning.

Q 17:33 What is a charitable gift annuity?

Unlike most other forms of planned giving—which are based on a type of split-interest trust (Q 17:28, Q 17:31, Q 17:32)—the *charitable gift annuity* is arranged in an agreement between the donor and the charitable donee. The donor agrees to make a payment and the donee agrees, in return, to provide the donor (and/or someone else) with an annuity. (Again, an *annuity* is a payment of a fixed amount, usually annually (Q 17:29).)

With one payment, the donor is actually engaging in two transactions: the *purchase* of an annuity and the making of a charitable *gift*. The gift component gives rise to the charitable contribution deduction. One sum (which may include one or more items of property) is transferred; the amount in excess of the portion necessary to purchase the annuity is the charitable gift portion. Because of the dual nature of the transaction, the charitable gift annuity transfer constitutes a *bargain sale* (Q 17:26).

The annuity resulting from the creation of a charitable gift annuity arrangement is a fixed amount paid at regular intervals (as noted, at least once annually). The exact amount is calculated to reflect the age of the beneficiary, which is determined at the time the calculation is made, and the annuity rate selected.

NOTE: As a matter of law, a charitable organization is free to offer whatever rate of return it wishes (staying within the ambit of reasonableness). Most charities utilize the rates periodically set by the American Council on Gift Annuities. These voluntary rates are in place to avoid unseemly "price wars" among charities pursuing these gifts. The establishment and "enforcement" of these uniform rates triggered litigation in which the Council was charged with antitrust and securities law violations. In an effort to eliminate the bases for these types of lawsuits, Congress responded in 1995 with the Philanthropy Protection Act (amending the securities laws) and the Charitable Gift Annuity Antitrust Relief Act (amending the antitrust laws), the latter augmented by the Charitable Donation Antitrust Immunity Act of 1997.[104]

A portion of the annuity paid is tax-free because it is a return of capital. Where appreciated property is contributed, there will be recognition of capital gain reflecting the appreciation that is attributable to the value of the annuity. If the donor is the annuitant, the capital gain can be reported ratably over the donor's life expectancy. The tax savings occasioned by the charitable contribution deduction may, however, shelter any capital gain (resulting from creation of the annuity) from taxation.

Because the arrangement is by contract between the donor and donee, all of the assets of the charitable organization are subject to liability for the ongoing payment of the annuities.

NOTE: This is an important distinction between charitable gift annuities and other giving approaches. With most planned giving techniques, the resources for payment of income are confined to those in a split-interest trust. Here the resources of the charity are on the line for the annuities.

For this reason, some states impose a requirement that charitable organizations establish a reserve for the payment of gift annuities. This is one reason many charitable organizations are reluctant to embark on a gift annuity program. Organizations can, however, eliminate much of the risk surrounding ongoing payment of annuities by reinsuring them.

NOTE: In general, an obligation to pay an annuity is a debt. Thus, the charitable organization involved would have acquisition indebtedness for purposes of the unrelated debt-financed income rules, were it not for a special rule.[105] To come within this rule (which gift annuity programs should and usually do), the value of the annuity must be less than 90 percent of the value of the property in the transaction, there can be no more than two income beneficiaries, there can be no guarantee as to a minimum amount of payments and no specification of a maximum amount of payments, and the annuity contract cannot provide for an adjustment of the amount of the annuity payments by reference to the income received from the transferred property or any other property.

TIP: A charitable organization that provides commercial-type insurance as a substantial part of its activities cannot be tax-exempt; this activity, even when of a lesser magnitude, is an unrelated business. Arguably, a charitable gift annuity is not a form of commercial-type insurance. To eliminate uncertainty on the point, however, there is an exception from these rules for these annuities.[106] To be eligible for this exception, a charitable deduction must be involved and the above exception from the unrelated debt-financed income rules must be available.

Q 17:34 Are there other ways to make deductible gifts of remainder interests?

Yes; there are three of them:

1. An individual may give a remainder interest in his or her personal residence or farm to charity. The individual receives a charitable deduction for this gift without using a trust. (Indeed, a trust cannot be used in this context.)[107]
2. A trust is not required for a deductible gift of a remainder interest in real property when the gift is made in the form of a *qualified conservation contribution*.[108]
3. A contribution of an undivided portion of one's entire interest in property is not regarded as a contribution of a partial interest in property.[109]

Q 17:35 What is the estate tax charitable contribution deduction?

A charitable deduction is allowed an estate[110] for the value of all estate transfers of the decedent to or for the use of the following entities:

- Organizations organized and operated exclusively for religious, charitable, scientific, literary, or educational purposes; to foster amateur sports competition (but not athletic facilities or equipment); and to encourage art and the prevention of cruelty to children or animals, where there is no inurement of net earnings to persons in their private capacity, no substantial amount of lobbying activity, and no participation in political campaigns[111]
- The United States, any state (including the District of Columbia), and political subdivisions of these governments, where the funds are used exclusively for public purposes
- Fraternal societies for use exclusively for religious, charitable, scientific, literary, or educational purposes, including encouragement of art and the prevention of cruelty to children or animals, and not a disqualified organization because of substantial lobbying or political campaign activities
- Veterans' organizations organized by an act of Congress, or their departments, local chapters, or posts, where there is no private inurement.[112]

A private foundation qualifies under the first of these categories.

NOTE: Unlike the federal income tax charitable deduction, where there is a limit on the amount that may be deducted each year (Q 17:4–17:7), there is no limit imposed on the federal estate tax charitable deduction.

A charitable deduction is allowed for a transfer of a split interest in property (Q 17:27) to a charitable organization where the remainder interest transferred is in the form of a charitable remainder annuity trust or charitable remainder unitrust (Q 17:28), a pooled income fund (Q 17:31), a guaranteed annuity, or an annual fixed percentage distribution of the fair market value of property (Q 17:29).

Contributions of split interests in copyrighted tangible works of art are not denied a charitable contribution deduction where the artwork is conveyed separately from the copyright in the work.[113] The split interest of the artwork and its copyright are treated as separate properties. The contribution must be made to a qualified charitable organization where the use of the property is related to the organization's function. Here a *qualified* organization is a charitable entity other than a private foundation.

Q 17:36 Is there a gift tax charitable deduction?

Yes. Just as there is a federal estate tax charitable deduction (Q 17:35), there is a federal gift tax charitable deduction.[114]

There is a deduction from the gift tax for gifts to or for the use of:

- Organizations organized and operated exclusively for religious, charitable, scientific, literary, or educational purposes; to foster amateur sports competition (but not athletic facilities or equipment); and to encourage art and the prevention of cruelty to children or animals, where there is no inurement of net earnings to persons in their private capacity, no substantial amount of lobbying activity, and no participation in political campaigns[115]
- The United States, any state (including the District of Columbia), and political subdivisions of these governments, where the funds are used exclusively for public purposes
- Fraternal societies for use exclusively for religious, charitable, scientific, literary, or educational purposes, including encouragement of art and the prevention of cruelty to children or animals, and not a disqualified organization because of substantial lobbying or political campaign activities
- Veterans' organizations organized by an act of Congress, or their departments, local chapters, or posts, where there is no private inurement

A private foundation qualifies under the first of these categories.

A charitable deduction is allowed for a transfer of a split interest in property (Q 17:27) to a charitable organization where the remainder interest transferred is in the form of a charitable remainder annuity trust or charitable remainder unitrust (Q 17:29), a pooled income fund (Q 17:31), a guaranteed annuity, or an annual fixed percentage distribution of the fair market value of property (Q 17:29).

If, as of the date of a gift, however, a transfer for charitable purposes is dependent on the performance of some act or the happening of a precedent event in order that it might become effective, a gift tax charitable deduction is not allowable unless the possibility that the charitable transfer will not become so effective is so remote as to be negligible.[116] Further, if an interest has passed to, or is vested in, a charitable organization on the date of the gift and the interest would be defeated by the performance of some act or the happening of some event, the possibility of occurrence of which appeared on that date to be so remote as to be negligible, the gift tax charitable deduction is allowable.[117]

NOTE: These rules are the same as those used for determining whether the estate tax charitable deduction (Q 17:35) is allowable under similar circumstances (and, for that matter, whether the income tax charitable deduction is available under similar circumstances).

Endnotes

CHAPTER 1

1 That is, an organization described in Internal Revenue Code of 1986, as amended, section ("IRC §") 501(c)(3).
2 That is, it is an entity described in IRC § 501(c)(3).
3 IRC § 509(a).
4 IRC § 4946(a).
5 IRC § 4958(f)(1).
6 The *private inurement doctrine* is a body of federal tax law applicable to all tax-exempt charitable organizations; it prohibits the inurement of the organization's net earnings to persons who are insiders with respect to the organization. The doctrine is intended to prevent payment of unreasonable compensation and other transactions that provide unwarranted benefits to insiders. Usually, the self-dealing rules (Chapter 3) apply to private foundations rather than the private inurement doctrine (Q 1:39). In general, see Hopkins, *The Law of Tax-Exempt Organizations, Seventh Edition* (John Wiley & Sons: New York, 1998; annual supp.), Chapter 19.
7 The most controversial court opinion on the point is *United Cancer Council, Inc. v. Commissioner,* 165 F.3d 1173 (7th Cir. 1999).
8 IRC §§ 4941(a), 4942(a), 4943(a), 4944(a), 4945(a).
9 IRC §§ 4941(b), 4942(b), 4943(b), 4944(b), 4945(b).
10 IRC § 507(b)(2).
11 IRC § 4941.
12 Federal Tax Regulations ("Reg.") § 53.4941(d)-1(b).
13 IRC § 4941(d)(1)(A); Reg. § 53.4941(d)-2(a)(1).
14 IRC § 4941(d)(2)(A); Reg. § 53.4941(d)-2(a)(2).
15 IRC § 4941(d)(1)(A); Reg. § 53.4941(d)-2(b)(1).
16 IRC § 4941(d)(1)(B); Reg. § 53.4941(d)-2(c)(1).
17 IRC § 4941(d)(1)(C); Reg. § 53.4941(d)-2(d)(1).
18 IRC § 4941(d)(1)(D); Reg. § 53.4941(d)-2(e).

19 IRC § 4941(d)(1)(E); Reg. § 53.4941(d)-2(f)(1).
20 IRS General Counsel Memorandum ("Gen. Coun. Mem.") 39107.
21 Gen. Coun. Mem. 39632.
22 IRS Private Letter Ruling ("Priv. Ltr. Rul.") 9726006.
23 IRC § 4958(c)(1).
24 IRC § 4941(d)(1)(F); Reg. § 53.4941(d)-2(g).
25 Reg. § 53.4941(d)-2(b)(2).
26 IRC § 4941(d)(2)(B); Reg. § 53.4941(d)-2(c)(2).
27 IRC § 4941(d)(2)(C); Reg. § 53.4941(d)-2(d)(3).
28 IRC § 4941(d)(2)(D); Reg. § 53.4941(d)-3(b).
29 IRC § 4941(d)(2)(E); Reg. § 53.4941(d)-3(c).
30 *Madden v. Commissioner,* 74 T.C.M. 440, 449 (1997).
31 Reg. § 53.4941(d)-2(f)(d).
32 IRC § 4941(d)(2)(G); Reg. § 53.4941(d)-3(e).
33 IRC § 4941(d)(2)(F); Reg. § 53.4941(d)-3(d).
34 Reg. § 53.4941(d)-3(d)(1).
35 Reg. § 53.4941(e)-1(a)(2).
36 IRC § 4941(e)(2); Reg. § 53.4941(e)-1(b)(1).
37 IRC § 4941(e)(3); Reg. § 53.4941(e)-1(c).
38 IRC § 4963(d)(2)(A).
39 IRC § 4963(d)(2)(B).
40 IRC § 4963(d)(2)(C).
41 IRC § 4941(a)(1); Reg. § 53.4941(a)-1(a)(1).
42 Priv. Ltr. Rul. 9530032, revoking 9343033.
43 IRC § 4941(a)(2); Reg. § 53.4941(a)-1(b).
44 *Id.*
45 IRC § 4941(c)(2); Reg. § 53.4941(c)-1(b).
46 IRC § 4941(b)(1); Reg. § 53.4941(b)-1(a).
47 IRC § 4941(a)(1); Reg. § 53.4941(a)-1(a)(1).
48 IRC § 4941(b)(2); Reg. § 53.4941(b)-1(b).
49 IRC § 4941(c)(1); Reg. § 53.4941(c)-1(a).
50 IRC § 507(a)(2).
51 IRC § 4942.
52 IRC § 4942(d).
53 IRC § 4942(g)(1); Reg. § 53.4942(a)-3(a), (c).
54 Reg. § 53.4942(a)-2(c)(1), (5).
55 IRC § 4942(d)(1), (e)(1)(A); Reg. § 53.4942(a)-2(b)(1).
56 IRC § 4942(d)(1), (f)(2)(C).
57 Reg. § 53.4942(a)-2(c)(3).
58 IRC § 4942(e)(1)(A).
59 Reg. § 53.4942(a)-2(c)(3).
60 Reg. § 53.4942(a)-3(b)(1).
61 Reg. § 53.4942(a)-3(b)(2), (7)(i).
62 IRC § 4942(g)(2).
63 IRC § 4942(a); Reg. § 53.4942(a)-1(a)(1).
64 IRC § 4942(b); Reg. § 53.4942(a)-1(a)(2).
65 *Id.*
66 Reg. § 53.4942(a)-1(a)(3).
67 IRC § 507(d)(2).

68   IRC § 4943.
69   IRC § 4943(c)(2)(A), (3).
70   IRC § 4943(c)(2)(B); Reg. § 53.4943-3(b)(3).
71   IRC § 4943(c)(2)(C); Reg. § 53.4943-3(b)(4).
72   IRC § 4943(d)(3)(B).
73   Reg. § 53.4943-10(c).
74   IRC § 4943(d)(3)(A).
75   IRC § 4942(j)(4); Reg. § 53.4943-10(b).
76   Reg. § 53.4943-10(b).
77   IRC § 4943(c)(6); Reg. § 53.4943-6(a).
78   IRC § 4943(c)(7).
79   IRC § 4943(a)(1); Reg. § 53.4943-2(a)(1).
80   *Id.*
81   IRC § 4943(b); Reg. § 53.4943-2(b).
82   IRC § 507(a)(2).
83   IRC § 4944.
84   IRC § 4944(a)(1).
85   Reg. § 53.4944-1(a)(2)(i).
86   *Id.*
87   E.g., Priv. Ltr. Rul. 9451067.
88   Reg. § 53.4944-1(a)(2)(i).
89   IRC § 4944(c); Reg. § 53.4944-3(a).
90   Reg. § 53.4944-3(a)(1)(iii).
91   IRC § 4944(a)(1); Reg. § 53.4944-1(a)(1).
92   IRC § 4944(a)(2); Reg. § 53.4944-1(b)(1).
93   IRC § 4944(d)(2); Reg. § 53.4944-4(b).
94   IRC § 4944(a)(2); Reg. § 53.4944-1(b)(1).
95   IRC § 4944(b)(1); Reg. § 53.4944-2(a).
96   IRC § 4944(b)(2); Reg. § 53.4944-2(b).
97   IRC § 4944(d)(2); Reg. § 53.4944-4(b).
98   IRC § 4944(d)(2); Reg. § 53.4944-4(a).
99   IRC § 507(b)(2).
100   IRC § 4945.
101   IRC § 4945(d)(1).
102   IRC §§ 501(c)(3), 4911, 4912.
103   IRC § 4945(e).
104   Reg. § 53.4945-2(a)(1).
105   IRC § 4945(e); Reg. § 53.4945-2(d)(1).
106   IRC § 4945(e)(2); Reg. § 53.4945-2(d)(2).
107   IRC § 4945(e) (last sentence); Reg. § 53.4945-2(d)(3).
108   Reg. § 53.4945-2(d)(4).
109   IRC § 4945(d)(2); Reg. § 53.4945-3(a)(1).
110   Reg. § 53.4945-3(a)(2).
111   IRC § 4945(f); Reg. § 53.4945-3(b).
112   IRC § 4945(d)(3); Reg. § 53.4945-4(a)(1), (2).
113   IRC § 4945(g); Reg. § 53.4945-4(a)(3)(ii).
114   Reg. § 53.4945-4(b)(2).
115   Reg. § 53.4945-4(b)(4).
116   Reg. § 53.4945-4(c)(2), (3).

117   Reg. § 53.4945-4(c)(4).
118   Reg. § 53.4945-4(c)(5).
119   Reg. § 53.4945-4(c)(6).
120   IRC § 4945(d)(4); Reg. § 53.4945-5(a).
121   IRC § 4945(h); Reg. § 53.4945-5(b), (d).
122   IRC § 4945(d)(5).
123   Reg. § 53.4945-6(a).
124   Reg. § 53.4945-6(b).
125   IRC § 4945(a)(1); Reg. § 53.4945-1(a)(1).
126   IRC § 4945(a)(2).
127   Reg. § 53.4945-1(a)(1).
128   IRC § 4945(b)(1), (i); Reg. § 53.4945-1(b)(1).
129   IRC § 4945(b)(2); Reg. § 53.4945-1(b)(2).
130   IRC § 4945(c)(1); Reg. § 53.4945-1(c)(1).
131   IRC § 4945(c)(2); Reg. § 53.4945-1(c)(2).
132   IRC § 4945(i)(2); Reg. § 53.4945-1(e)(1).
133   IRC § 507(a)(2).
134   IRC § 4962(a).
135   IRC § 4963(a).
136   IRC § 4962(b).
137   *Id.*
138   IRC § 4963(c).
139   IRC § 6212.
140   IRC § 4963(e)(1).
141   IRC § 6213(a).
142   IRC § 4963(e)(1).
143   IRC § 4963(e)(2)(A).
144   IRC § 4963(e)(2)(B).
145   IRC § 4963(e)(2)(C).
146   IRC § 4963(b).
147   IRC § 4961(a).
148   IRC § 4961(b), (c).
149   IRC § 4940(a); Reg. § 53.4940-1(a).
150   IRC § 6655.
151   IRC § 4940(e)(1).
152   That is, entities described in IRC § 4947(a)(1).
153   That is, entities described in IRC § 4947(a)(2).
154   IRC § 4947.
155   IRC § 4948.
156   IRC § 4942(j)(3)(A); Reg. § 53.4943(b)-1(a), (b)(1).
157   IRC § 4942(j)(3)(A); Reg. § 53.4942(b)-1(b).
158   Reg. § 53.4942(b)-1(c)
159   IRC § 4942(j)(3)(B)(ii); Reg. § 53.4942(b)-2(a).
160   IRC § 4942(j)(3)(B)(ii); Reg. § 53.4942(b)-2(b).
161   IRC § 4942(j)(3)(B)(iii); Reg. § 53.4942(b)-2(c).
162   IRC § 4920(d)(2).
163   IRC § 511.
164   IRC § 513(c).
165   IRC § 512(a)(1).

166   IRC § 513.
167   IRC § 512(b)(5).
168   IRC § 6033.
169   Ann. 82-88, 1982-25 I.R.B. 23.
170   IRC § 6104.
171   T.D. 8818.
172   T.D. 8861.
173   IRC § 507(b)(1)(A).
174   IRC § 507(b)(B).
175   IRC § 507(b)(1).
176   That is, organizations described in IRC § 401(c)(3).
177   Priv. Ltr. Rul. 200114040.
178   IRC § 170, 2055, 2522.
179   IRC § 170(b)(1)(A).
180   IRC § 170(d)(1).
181   IRC § 170(b)(1)(B)(i).
182   170(b)(1)(B), last sentence.
183   IRC § 170(b)(1)(C)(i).
184   IRC § 170(b)(1)(C)(iii).
185   IRC § 170(b)(1)(D)(i).
186   IRC § 170(b)(1)(C)(ii), (b)(1)(D)(ii).
187   E.g., *Sheppard v. United States,* 361 F.2d 972 (Ct. Cl. 1966).
188   IRC § 170(e)(1)(B)(ii).
189   IRC § 170(e)(5).
190   This is reflected in the record keeping required to prepare the private foundation annual information return.
191   Abouhalkah, "Foundations Are Flexing Their Muscles," *The Kansas City Star,* June 28, 1998.
192   Johnson, "Foundations of Power," *The Sunday Oregonian,* June 21, 1998.
193   IRC § 4958.

CHAPTER 2

1   IRC § 4946(a)(1)(A); Reg. § 53-4946-1(a)(1)(i).
2   IRC §§ 4946(A)(2), 507(d)(2).
3   IRC § 507(d)(2)(A).
4   Reg. § 1.507-6(a)(1).
5   *Id.*
6   That is, organizations encompassed by IRC § 501(a).
7   That is, entities described in IRC § 170(c)(1).
8   *Rockefeller v. United States,* 572 F. Supp. 9 (E.D. Ark. 1982), *aff'd,* 718 F.2d 290 (8th Cir. 1983), *cert. den.,* 466 U.S. 962 (1984).
9   IRC §§ 170(b)(1)(D)(iii), 507(d)(1), 508(d), 509(a)(1), 509(a)(3), and IRC Chapter 42.
10   Reg. § 1.507-6(a)(2).
11   Reg. § 1.507-6(b)(i).
12   IRC § 507(d)(2)(B)(i)-(iii).
13   IRC § 507(d)(2)(B)(iv).
14   Reg. § 1.507-6(b)(1).

15 IRC § 507(d)(2)(C).
16 IRC § 507(d)(2)(C)(i)(III).
17 IRC § 507(d)(2)(C)(ii).
18 IRC § 4946(a)(1)(B); Reg. § 53.4946-1(f)(1).
19 IRC § 4946(b)(1).
20 E.g., Priv. Ltr. Rul. 9535043.
21 Reg. § 53.4946-1(f)(1)(ii).
22 Reg. § 53.4946-1(f)(1).
23 Form 990 instructions.
24 Reg. § 53.4946-1(f)(2).
25 Rev. Rul. 74-287, 1974-1 C.B. 327.
26 Reg. § 53.4946-1(f)(2).
27 IRC § 4946(a)(1)(C).
28 Reg. § 53.4946-1(a)(6).
29 IRC § 4946(a)(1)(C)(i).
30 IRC § 4946(a)(3).
31 Reg. § 53.4946-1(a)(5).
32 IRC § 4975(e).
33 Rev. Rul. 81-76, 1081-1 C.B. 516.
34 IRC § 4946(a)(1)(C)(ii).
35 IRC §§ 707(b)(3), 4946(a)(4).
36 Reg. § 53.4946-1(a)(6).
37 IRC § 4946(a)(1)(C)(iii).
38 Reg. § 53.4946-1(a)(3).
39 Reg. § 53.4946-1(a)(4).
40 Reg. § 53.4946-1(a)(6).
41 IRC § 267(c)(1); Reg. § 53.4946-1(d)(1).
42 IRC § 4946(a)(1)(E).
43 Reg. § 53.4946-1(d)(1)(ii).
44 IRC § 267(c).
45 Stock constructively owned by an individual by reason of the application of IRC § 267(c)(2) is not treated as owned by him or her if he or she is described in IRC § 4946(a)(1)(A), (B), or (C). Also Reg. § 53.4946-1(d)(1).
46 Reg. § 53.4946-1(e).
47 Priv. Ltr. Rul. 8525075.
48 IRC § 4946(a)(1)(D).
49 IRC § 4946(d).
50 Reg. § 53.4946-1(h).
51 *Id.*
52 IRC § 4958.
53 IRC § 4958(f)(4).
54 Reg. § 53.4946-1(h).
55 IRC § 4946(a)(3).
56 IRC § 4946(a)(1)(E).
57 IRC § 4946(a)(4).
58 IRC § 4946(a)(1)(F).
59 IRC § 4946(a)(4).
60 IRC § 4946(a)(1)(G).
61 IRC § 4946(a)(4).

62   IRC § 4946(a)(1)(G).
63   Gen. Coun. Mem. 39445.
64   IRC § 4946(a)(1)(H).
65   Reg. § 1.482-1(a)(3).
66   Reg. § 53.4946-1(b)(1).
67   Reg. § 53.4946-1(b)(2).
68   IRC §§ 170(b)(1)(D)(iii), 507(d)(1), 508(d), 509(a)(1) and (3), and IRC Chapter 42.
69   Reg. § 53.4946-1(a)(7).
70   Reg. § 53.4946-1(a)(8). A charitable organization, for these purposes, is an organization described in IRC § 501(c)(3), other than an organization that tests for public safety (IRC § 509(a)(4)).
71   Reg. § 1.507-6(a)(2).
72   IRC § 4946(a)(1)(I).
73   IRC § 4946(c).
74   Reg. § 53.4946 1(g)(2).
75   Priv. Ltr. Rul. 8508097.
76   Priv. Ltr. Rul. 8533099.
77   IRC § 4946(c)(5).
78   Rev. Rul. 770473, 1977-2 C.B. 421.
79   Priv. Ltr. Rul. 9804040.
80   Priv. Ltr. Rul. 199943047.
81   Rev. Rul. 80-207, 1980-2 C.B. 193.
82   Rev. Rul. 76-448, 1976-2 C.B. 368.

CHAPTER 3

1   IRC § 4941(d)(1)(A).
2   Reg. § 53.4941(d)-2(a)(1).
3   *Id.*
4   IRC § 4941(d)(2)(A); Reg. § 53.4941(d)-2(a)(2).
5   Rev. Rul. 76-18, 1976-1 C.B. 355.
6   Priv. Ltr. Rul. 9047001.
7   Rev. Rul. 77-259, 1977-2 C.B. 387.
8   Priv. Ltr. Rul. 8234149.
9   IRC § 4941(d)(1); Reg. § 53.4941(d)-2(a)(1).
10   Reg. § 53.4941(d)-2(a)(2).
11   Rev. Rul. 77-379, 1977-2 C.B. 387.
12   Rev. Rul. 81-40, 1981 C.B. 508.
13   Priv. Ltr. Rul. 8723001.
14   IRC § 4941(d)(2)(F); Reg. § 53.4941(d)-2(b)(1).
15   Priv. Ltr. Rul. 8038049.
16   IRC § 4941(d)(1)(A); Reg. § 53.4941(d)-2(b)(1).
17   Rev. Rul. 73-363, 1973-2 C.B. 383.
18   Reg. § 53.4941(d)-2(b)(2).
19   Rev. Rul. 74-600, 1974-2 C.B. 385.
20   IRS Technical Advice Memorandum ("Tech. Adv. Mem.") 9221002.
21   Priv. Ltr. Rul. 9327082.
22   IRC § 4941(d)(1)(B); Reg. § 53.4941(d)-2(c)(1).

23   Reg. § 53.4941(d)-2(c)(1).
24   Priv. Ltr. Rul. 9530032.
25   Rev. Rul. 80-132, 1980-1 C.B. 255.
26   Priv. Ltr. Rul. 9222052.
27   Reg. § 53.4941(d)-2(c)(2).
28   IRC § 4941(d)(2)(B).
29   Reg. § 53.4941(d).
30   Reg. 53.4941(d)-2(c)(4).
31   IRC § 4941(d)(1)(B); Reg. § 53.4941(d)-2(c)(1).
32   Rev. Rul. 78-395, 1978-2 C.B. 270.
33   *Id.*
34   Reg. § 53.4941(d)-2(c)(3).
35   Reg. § 53.4941(d)-2(c)(2).
36   IRC § 4941(d)(1)(C); Reg. § 53.4941(d)-2(d)(1).
37   Reg. § 53.4941(d)-2(d)(1).
38   Reg. § 53.4941(d)-2(d)(2).
39   *Id.*
40   IRC § 119.
41   Priv. Ltr. Rul. 8948034.
42   IRC § 4941(d)(2)(C); Reg. § 53.4941(d)-2(d)(3).
43   Reg. § 53.4941(d)-2(d)(3).
44   *Id.*
45   IRC § 4941(d)(2)(D); Reg. § 53.4941(d)-3(b)(1).
46   Reg. § 53.4941(d)-3(b)(1).
47   Reg. § 53.4941(d)-3(b)(2).
48   Rev. Rul. 76-10, 1976-1 C.B. 355.
49   Rev. Rul. 76-459, 1976-2 C.B. 369.
50   Rev. Rul. 790-374, 1979-2 C.B. 387.
51   Priv. Ltr. Rul. 7751033.
52   Priv. Ltr. Rul. 8842045.
53   Priv. Ltr. Rul. 7751033.
54   Priv. Ltr. Rul. 8038049.
55   Priv. Ltr. Ruls. 9114025 and 7810038.
56   IRC § 4941(d)(1)(D); Reg. § 53.4941(d)-2(e).
57   IRC § 4941(d)(2)(E); Reg. § 53.4941(d)-3(c)(1).
58   Reg. § 53.4941(d)-3(c)(1).
59   *Id.*
60   *Id.*
61   Reg. § 53.4941(d)-3(c)(1), referencing Reg. § 1.162-7.
62   Reg. § 1.162-7(b)(3).
63   Reg. § 53.4941(d)-3(c).
64   Priv. Ltr. Rul. 9325061.
65   *Id.*
66   Priv. Ltr. Rul. 9327082.
67   Priv. Ltr. Rul. 199913040.
68   *Madden v. Commissioner,* 74 T.C.M. 440, 449 (1997).
69   *Id.*
70   Reg. § 53.4941(d)-3(c)(1).
71   IRC § 4941(d)(1)(F); Reg. § 53.4941(d)-(2)(f)(1).

72 Reg. § 53.4941(d)-(2)(f)(1).
73 Tech. Adv. Mem. 8719004.
74 Gen. Coun. Mem. 39107.
75 Reg. § 53.4941(d)-2(f)(2).
76 *Id.*
77 Rev. Rul. 77-331, 1977-2 C.B. 388.
78 Rev. Rul. 75-42, 1975-1 C.B. 359.
79 Rev. Rul. 73-407, 1973-2 C.B. 383.
80 Rev. Rul. 80-310, 1980-2 C.B. 319.
81 Rev. Rul. 85-162, 1985-2 C.B. 275.
82 Priv. Ltr. Rul. 9614002.
83 *Id.*
84 Reg. § 53.4941(d)-2(f)(1).
85 Rev. Rul. 77-160, 1977-1 C.B. 351.
86 Priv. Ltr. Rul. 8128072.
87 See Priv. Ltr. Rul. 9703020.
88 Reg. § 53.4941(d)-2(c)(3).
89 Priv. Ltr. Rul. 9021066.
90 Priv. Ltr. Rul. 8331082.
91 Tech. Adv. Mem. 7734022, Priv. Ltr. Rul. 8824010.
92 Priv. Ltr. Rul. 9226067.
93 E.g., Priv. Ltr. Rul. 9312022.
94 IRC § 4941(d)(2)(F); Reg. § 53.4941(d)-3(d)(1).
95 Reg. § 53.4941(d)-3(d)(1).
96 *Id.*
97 Priv. Ltr. Rul. 9016003.
98 IRC § 4941(d)(1)(F); Reg. § 53.4941(d)-2(g).
99 Reg. § 53.4941(d)-2(g).
100 IRC § 4941(d)(2)(G); Reg. § 53.4941(d)-2(g).
101 IRC § 74(b).
102 IRC § 117(a).
103 IRC § 151(c)(4).
104 Rev. Rul. 74-601, 1974-2 C.B. 385.
105 Reg. § 53.4941(d)-1(b).
106 Reg. § 53.4941(d)-1(b)(3).
107 *Rockefeller v. United States,* 572 F. Supp. 9 (E.D. Ark. 1982), *aff'd,* 718 F.2d 291 (9th Cir. 1983), *cert. den.,* 466 U.S. 962 (1984).
108 *Estate of Bernard J. Reis v. Commissioner,* 87 T.C. 1016, 1022 (1986).
109 E.g., Priv. Ltr. Ruls. 8929087 and 9210040, where the exception was met, and Priv. Ltr. Rul. 9252042, where the exception would not be met and thus the transaction would be self-dealing.
110 Reg. § 53.4941(d)-1(b)(1).
111 Reg. § 53.4941(d)-1(b)(5).
112 *Id.*
113 *Id.*
114 Reg. § 53.4941(d)-2(f)(3)(i).
115 Reg. § 53.4941(d)-2(f)(3)(ii).
116 *Id.*
117 Reg. § 53.4941(d)-2(f)(4)(i).

118   Reg. § 53.4941(d)-2(f)(3)(ii).
119   Reg. § 53.4941(d)-2(f)(5).
120   Reg. § 53.4941(d)-2(f)(6).
121   Reg. § 53.4941(d)-2(f)(7).
122   IRC § 132(a)(4).
123   Reg. § 53.4941(d)-2(f)(8).
124   IRC § 132(d).
125   IRC § 162.
126   IRC § 167.
127   IRC § 132(a).
128   Reg. § 1.132-1(b).
129   IRC § 132(a)(1).
130   IRC § 162.
131   Reg. § 1.132-5(r)(1), (2).
132   Reg. § 1.132-5(r)(3)(ii).
133   Reg. § 1.132-5(r)(3)(ii).
134   IRC § 4941(e)(3); Reg. § 53.4941(e)-1(c)(1).
135   Reg. § 53.4941(e)-1(c)(3).
136   IRC § 4941(e)(2); Reg. § 53.4941(e)-1(b)(1).
137   Reg. § 53.4941(e)-1(b)(2)(ii).
138   Reg. § 53.4941(e)-1(b)(4).
139   Reg. § 53.4941(e)-1(b)(2)(iii).
140   IRC § 4941(e)(2)(A); Reg. § 53.4941(e)-1(b)(3).
141   Reg. § 53.4941(e)-1(a)(2).
142   IRC § 4941(a)(2); Reg. § 53,4941(a)-1(b)(1).
143   IRC § 4941(a)(1); Reg. § 53.4941(a)-1(a)(1).
144   IRC § 4941(a)(1).
145   IRC § 4941(a)(2).
146   Reg. § 53.4941(a)-1(a)(3).
147   Reg. § 53.4941(a)-1(b)(2).
148   Reg. § 53.4941(a)-1(b)(4).
149   Reg. § 53.49411(a)-1(b)(5).
150   *Id.*
151   Reg. § 53.4941(a)-1(b)(3).
152   IRC § 4941(a)(1); Reg. § 53.4941(a)-1(a)(2).
153   Reg. § 53.4941(a)-1(a)(1).
154   Reg. § 53.4941(a)-1(b)(6).
155   IRC § 4941(e)(1); Reg. § 53.4941(e)-1(a).
156   Reg. § 53.4941(3)-1(e)(1).
157   IRC § 4941(b)(1).
158   IRC § 4941(b)(2).
159   IRC § 4941(c)(1).
160   Reg. § 53.4941(e)-1(e).
161   IRC § 4941(c)(2).
162   IRC § 4962(a).
163   IRC § 4962(b).
164   IRC § 7805(b).
165   Tech. Adv. Mem. 9646992.

CHAPTER 4

1 IRC § 4942(f)(2).
2 IRC § 4942(d)(2); Reg. § 53.4942(a)-3(b).
3 Reg. § 53.4942(a)-2(c)(5)(iii).
4 Reg. § 53.4942(a)-2(c)(3)(ii); Rev. Rul. 74-498, 1974-2 C.B. 387; Rev. Rul. 75-207, 1975-1 C.B. 361.
5 Reg. § 53.4942(a)-2(c)(3).
6 Reg. § 53.4942(a)-2(c)(4).
7 IRC § 4942(g)(1)(a); Reg. § 53.4942(a)-3.
8 *Ann Jackson Family Foundation v. Commissioner,* 97 T.C. 534 (1991), *aff'd,* 15 F.3d 917 (9th Cir. 1994).
9 *Passalaigue v. United States,* 224 F. Supp. 682 (D. Ga. 1964).
10 I.T. 3918, 1948-2 C.B. 33.
11 *Passalaigue v. United States, supra* note 9, at 686 (emphasis added).
12 IRC § 170(f)(3)(A); Reg. § 1.170A-7(d), Example (1); Rev. Rul. 70-477, 1970-2 C.B. 62.
13 Rev. Rul. 78-90, 1978-11 C.B. 380.
14 IRC § 4942(g); Reg. § 53.4942(1)-3(c).
15 IRC § 4942(g)(2); Reg. § 53.4942(1)-3(b).
16 Reg. § 53.4942(a)-2(e).
17 IRC § 4942(a)(2); Reg. § 53.4942(a)-1(c).

CHAPTER 5

1 IRC § 4943(c)(4)(B)-(E); Reg. § 53.4943-4.
2 Reg. § 53.4943-10(a)(1).
3 *Id.*
4 Reg. § 53.4943-10(a)(2).
5 *Id.*
6 IRC § 4943(d)(3); Reg. § 53.4943-10(b).
7 IRC § 4942(j)(4); Reg. § 53.4943-10(b).
8 IRC § 4943(d)(3)(A).
9 Reg. § 53.4942(a)-2(c)(3)(iii)(a)(1).
10 Reg. § 53.4942(a)-2(c)(3)(iii)(a)(2).
11 Reg. § 53.4942(a)-2(c)(3)(iii)(b), Example (1).
12 Reg. § 53.4942(a)-2(c)(3)(iii)(b), Example (2).
13 Priv. Ltr. Rul. 8927031.
14 Reg. § 53.4943-10(b).
15 IRC § 4943(d)(3)(B); Reg. § 53.4943-10(c)(1).
16 Reg. § 53.4943-10(c)(1).
17 *Id.*
18 IRC §§ 4943(d)(3), 512(b)(1), (2), (3), and (5).
19 IRC § 4943(d)(3); Reg. § 53.4943-10(c)(2).
20 That is, an organization described in IRC § 501(c)(2).
21 E.g., Priv. Ltr. Rul. 8840055.
22 Reg. § 53.4943-10(c)(2).

23   Priv. Ltr. Rul. 199939046.

24   E.g., S. Rep. No. 91-552, 91st Cong., 1st Sess. 2066-2072 (1969).

25   IRC § 501(f).

26   IRC § 4943(c)(2)(A); Reg. § 53.4943-1, 53.4943-3(b)(1)(i).

27   Reg. § 53.4943-4(b)(1)(ii).

28   IRC § 4943(c)(2)(A).

29   Reg. § 53.4943-3(b)(2)(i).

30   Reg. § 53.4943-3(b)(2)(ii).

31   Priv. Ltr. Rul. 9124061.

32   Reg. § 53.4943-3(b)(2)(ii).

33   Reg. § 53.4943-3(c)(4)(i).

34   IRC § 4943(c)(2)(B); Reg. § 53.4943-3(b)(3)(i).

35   Reg. § 53.4943-3(b)(3)(ii).

36   Rev. Rul. 81-111, 1981-1 C.B. 509.

37   IRC § 4943(c)(2)(c); Reg. § 53.4943-3(b)(4)(i).

38   Reg. § 53.4943-3(b)(4).

39   IRC § 4943(c)(1); Reg. § 53.4943-3(a)(1).

40   Reg. § 53.4943-3(a)(1).

41   IRC § 4943(c)(3); Reg. §§ 53.4943-1, 53.4943-3(c)(1), (2), and (4).

42   IRC § 4943(c)(3)(A).

43   IRC § 704(b).

44   Reg. § 53.4943-3(c)(2).

45   IRC § 4943(c)(3)(C); Reg. §§ 53.4943-3(c)(4)(i)-(ii), 53.4943-8(b).

46   IRC § 4943(c)(3)(B); Reg. §§ 53.4943-1, 53.4943-3(c)(3), 53.4943-10(e).

47   Reg. § 53.4943-10(e).

48   Reg. § 53.4943-3(c)(4)(iii).

49   IRC § 4943(d)(1); Reg. § 53.4943-8(a)(1), (b), (d).

50   Reg. § 53.4943-8(a)(1).

51   *Id.*

52   Reg. § 53.4943-8(a)(2).

53   Reg. § 53.4943-8(a)(3).

54   Reg. § 53.4943-8(a)(4).

55   Reg. § 53.4943-8(a)(5).

56   Reg. § 53.4943-8(b)(3).

57   Reg. § 53.4943-8(b)(4).

58   Reg. § 53.4943-8(b)(1).

59   This is a trust described in IRC § 4947(a)(2), such as a charitable remainder trust (IRC § 664).

60   IRC § 4943(d)(1); Reg. § 53.4943-8(b)(2)(i).

61   Reg. § 53.4943-8(b)(5).

62   Reg. § 53.4943-8(c)(1)-(3).

63   Reg. §§ 53.4943-8(c)(4), 53.4943-10(c)(3).

64   Reg. § 53.4943-2(a)(1)(ii).

65   *Id.*

66   Reg. § 53.4943-2(a)(1)(iii).

67   Reg. § 53.4943-2(a)(1)(iv).

68   Reg. § 1.507-2(a)(8).

69   Reg. § 53.4943-2(a)(1)(iv).
70   Reg. § 53.4943-2(a)(1)(v)(A).
71   IRC § 4943(c)(6); Reg. § 53.4943-6(a)(1).
72   Reg. § 53.4943-6(a)(2).
73   Reg. § 53.4943-6(d).
74   Reg. § 53.4943-7(d)(1).
75   Reg. § 53.4943-6(d)(1).
76   Reg. § 53.4943-6(c)(1).
77   Reg. § 53.4943-6(c)(2).
78   Reg. § 53.4943-6(c)(3).
79   Reg. § 53.4943-6(c)(4).
80   Reg. § 53.4943-10(d)(1).
81   Reg. § 53.4943-10(d)(2)(i).
82   Reg. § 53.4943-10(d)(2)(ii).
83   Reg. § 53.4943-6(d)(4).
84   Reg. § 53.4943-6(d)(5).
85   *Id.*
86   *Id.*
87   *Id.*
88   Reg. § 53.4943-6(e).
89   Reg. § 53.4943-6(b)(1).
90   Reg. § 53.4943-5(b)(1).
91   Reg. § 53.4943-6(b)(1).
92   *Id.*
93   IRC § 4943(c)(7).
94   Priv. Ltr. Rul. 9115061.
95   Priv. Ltr. Rul. 9029067.
96   IRC § 4943(a)(1); Reg. § 53.4943-2(a)(1)(i).
97   IRC § 4943(a)(2)(A).
98   IRC § 4943(a)(1); Reg. § 53.4943-2(a)(1)(i).
99   IRC § 4943(a)(2)(B); Reg. § 53.4943-2(a)(2).
100 Reg. § 53.4943-2(a)(1)(i).
101 IRC § 4943(d)(2)(B); Reg. § 53.4943-1(d)(2)(ii).
102 Reg. § 53.4943-9(c).
103 IRC § 4943(d)(2); Reg. § 53.4943-9(a)(1).
104 IRC § 4943(b).
105 *Id.*; Reg. § 53-4943-2(b).
106 IRC § 4961(a); Reg. § 53.4961-1.
107 IRC § 4963(e)(1); Reg. § 53.4963-1(e)(1).
108 IRC § 4963(c); Reg. § 53.4963-1(c).
109 IRC § 4963(e)(2)(B); Reg. § 53.4963-1(e)(7)(ii).
110 IRC § 507(a)(2)(A).
111 IRC § 507(a)(2)(B).
112 IRC § 507(c).
113 IRC § 507(d)(1)(A), (B).
114 IRC § 507(d)(1)(C).
115 IRC § 4962.
116 TAM 9424004.

CHAPTER 6

1   IRC § 4944(a)(1).
2   American Law Institute, *Restatement of the Law, Trusts—Prudent Investor Rule* (St. Paul, MN: American Law Institute Publishers, 1990).
3   Internal Revenue Manual 7.8.3, *Private Foundation Handbook,* Chapter 16.
4   See Blazek, *Financial Planning for Nonprofit Organizations* (John Wiley & Sons, 1997), Chapter 5, "Asset Management."
5   Reg. § 53.4944-1(a)(2)(ii).
6   Rev. Rul. 80-133, 1980-1 C.B. 258.
7   *Thorne v. Commissioner,* 99 T.C. 67 (1992).
8   Priv. Ltr. Rul. 871806.
9   Priv. Ltr. Rul. 9237035.
10 IRC § 4944(c); Reg. § 53.4944-3(a)(1).
11 Priv. Ltr. Rul. 8807048.
12 Reg. § 53.4944-3(a)(3).
13 Reg. § 53.4944-1(b)(2).
14 Reg. § 53.4944-1(a)(2).
15 Reg. § 53.4944-1(b)(2)(v).
16 Reg. § 53.4944-1(a)(2)(iv).

CHAPTER 7

1   IRC § 501(c)(3).
2   IRC § 4945.
3   Reg. § 53.4945-2 that refers the definition to the rules applicable to electing public charities found in Reg. § 53.4911-2 and 2.
4   Reg. § 53.4945-2(d)(3)(ii), Examples 3 and 4.
5   Reg. § 53.4945-2(d)(l)(vii).
6   IRC § 170(h).
7   Reg. § 53.4945-2(a)(5) and (6).
8   Reg. § 53.4945-2(a)(7).
9   IRC § 4945(d)(2); Reg. § 53.4945-3.
10 IRC § 4945(d)(3); Reg. § 53.4945-4.
11 IRC § 4945(g).
12 Pursuant to IRC § 117(a), as it was in effect prior to the Tax Reform Act of 1986, to be used at an educational institution described in IRC § 170(b)(1)(A)(ii).
13 The recipients do not apply for the awards as provided under IRC § 74(b).
14 Rev. Rul. 77-380, 1977-2 C.B. 419.
15 Rev. Rul. 76-461, 1976-2 C.B. 371.
16 Reg. § 53.4945-4(a)(2).
17 Priv. Ltr. Rul. 9314058.
18 Rev. Rul. 76-460, 1972-2 C.B. 371.
19 Rev. Rul. 75-393, 1975-2 C.B. 451.
20 Rev. Rul. 74-125, 1974-1 C.B. 327.
21 IRC § 4945(g); Reg. § 53.4945-2(b) and (c).
22 Reg. § 53.4945-4(b)(5), Example 2; Priv. Ltr. Rul. 7851096; Rev. Rul. 85-175, 1985-2 C.B. 276.
23 Reg. § 53.4945-4(b)(5), Example 1; Priv. Ltr. Rul. 9115061.

24 Priv. Ltr. Rul. 8542004; Rev. Rul. 73-564, 1973-2 C.B. 28; Reg. § 53.4945-4(a)(4)(iv).

25 IRC § 4945(d)(4)(A).

26 Reg. § 53.4945-5(a)(4).

27 Reg. §§ 1.170A-9(e)(4)(v)(b), 1.509(a)-3(c)(1)(iii)(a).

28 The printed version of Publication 78 can be ordered from the IRS Reading Room, 1111 Constitution Avenue, Washington, D.C. 20044.

29 Rev. Proc. 89-23, 1989-1 C.B. 844.

30 Priv. Ltr. Rul. 8542004; Rev. Proc. 81-6, 1981-1 C.B. 620.

31 Hopkins and Blazek, *Private Foundations: Tax Law and Compliance* (New York: John Wiley & Sons, 1998), Chapter 9, contains checklists and sample documents to aid in the process.

32 Reg. § 53.4945-5(a)(5).

33 See Colvin, *Fiscal Sponsorships, 6 Ways to Do It Right* (San Francisco: San Francisco Study Center, 1993).

34 Reg. § 53.4945-5(a)(4)(iii). The international organizations are designated by executive order under 22 U.S.C. § 299.

35 Reg. § 53.4945-5(a)(5); see Rev. Proc. 92-94, 1992-2 C.B. 507 for contents of a "currently qualified" affidavit from the grantee.

36 IRC § 508(a) notice is required from such organizations to prove their public status.

37 Priv. Ltr. Ruls. 8030104 and 8515070 indicate the extent to which some private foundations go in assuring that their grants to foreign organizations meet the expenditure responsibility test.

38 IRC § 170.

39 The rules were adopted in 1994. Milton Cerny outlined the rules pertaining to nonprofit organizations in the February 1995 issue of *The Exempt Organization Tax Review,* in an article titled "The Americas: An Expanding Nonprofit Sector."

40 Priv. Ltr. Rul. 9129040.

41 Reg. § 53.4945-5(b)(1).

42 IRC § 501(c)(2).

43 Priv. Ltr. Ruls. 9050030, 9219033, and 9306034.

44 Priv. Ltr. Rul. 9310044.

45 Reg. § 53.4945-5(b)(2).

46 Reg. § 53.4945-5(c)(1); examples of grantee reports are in Chapter 9 of Hopkins and Blazek, *Private Foundations: Tax Law and Compliance, supra* note 31.

47 *Charles Stewart Mott Foundation v. U.S.,* 938 F.2d 58 (6th Cir. 1991).

48 Reg. §§ 53.4945-5(b)(7), 1.507-3(a)(7) and (8); see Chapter 13.

49 IRC § 4945(d)(5); Reg. § 53.4945-6(b).

50 *Underwood v. U.S.,* 461 F. Supp. 1382 (N.D. Tex. 1978).

51 *Kermit Fischer Foundation v. Commissioner,* 59 T.C.M. 898 (1990).

52 Rev. Rul. 82-223, 1982-2 C.B. 301.

53 Rev. Rul. 80-97, 1980-1 C.B. 257.

54 Reg. § 53.4945-6(b).

55 IRC § 4945(I)(2).

56 Rev. Rul. 77-213, 1977-1 C.B. 357; *Hans S. Mannheimer Charitable Trust v. Commissioner,* 93 T.C. 5 (1989).

57 Reg. § 53.4945-1(d).

CHAPTER 8

1   IRC § 4940(c) and Reg. § 53.4940-1(d).
2   Reg. § 53.4940-1(d)(1).
3   Rev. Rul. 64-104, 1964-1 (Part 1) C.B. 223.
4   IRC § 302(b)(1).
5   Rev. Rul. 75-336, 1975-2 C.B. 110.
6   Priv. Ltr. Rul. 7847049.
7   Instructions to Form 990-PF, Part I, column (b), at p. 6.
8   IRC §§ 514(a)(1) and 4940(a)(2).
9   Reg. § 53.4940-1(d)(2).
10 Priv. Ltr. Rul. 8909066.
11 IRC §§ 642(c) and 663(a)(2); Reg. § 53.4940-1(f); Priv. Ltr. Rul. 9724005.
12 IRC § 4940(c)(4)(A).
13 Rev. Rul. 73-320, 1973-2 C.B. 385.
14 Priv. Ltr. Rul. 9320054.
15 Reg. § 53.4940-1(f)(1); Priv. Ltr. Rul. 8425114.
16 Reg. § 53.4940-1(d)(3); Priv. Ltr. Rul. 8214023.
17 E.g., IRC § 368; Priv. Ltr. Ruls. 8906013 and 8730061.
18 Priv. Ltr. Ruls. 8852001, 88462001, 8846005, 8752033, and 8650049.
19 Reg. § 53.4940-1(f)(2), which refers to IRC § 1015.
20 IRC § 4940(c)(3); Reg. § 53.4940-1(e)(1)(i).
21 *Lettie Pate Whiehead Foundation, Inc. v. U.S.,* 606 F.2d 523 (5th Cir. 1979), *aff'g* 77-1 U.S.T.C. ¶ 9157 (N.D. Ga. 1977).
22 *Indiana University Retirement Community, Inc. v. Commissioner,* 92 T.C. 891 (1989).
23 Reg. § 53.4940-1(e)(1)(ii).
24 Priv. Ltr. Rul. 8802008; Rev. Rul. 74-579, 1974-2 C.B. 383; *Indiana University Retirement Community, Inc. v. Commissioner,* 92 T.C. 891 (1989).
25 Rev. Rul. 74-579, 1974-2 C.B. 383.
26 Essentially grants and other disbursements for charitable purposes, adjusted for amounts set aside unrecovered from past years, as discussed in Chapter 4.
27 IRC § 4940(e); Reg. § 53.4940-1(d)(1).
28 *Foundation Management Report,* 7th ed. (Washington, D.C., Council on Foundations, 1993).
29 Reg. § 53.4940-1(f)(1).The regulations specifically say: "For purposes of this paragraph, a distribution of property for purposes described in section 170(c)(1) or (2)(B) which is a qualifying distribution under section 4942 shall not be treated as a sale or other disposition of property."
30 Shares of a corporation for which "market quotations were readily available on an established securities market."
31 IRC § 170(b)(1)(E)(ii).
32 IRC § 170(e)(1)(A)(ii).
33 IRC § 4942(g) as discussed in Chapter 4.
34 Reg. 53.4942(a)-3(c)(2)(iv); see Greif, "Achieving Maximum Use of Excess Qualifying Distributions," *Journal of Taxation of Exempt Organizations* 11, no. 3 (November/December 1999).
35 IRC § 4948.

CHAPTER 9

1   IRC § 501(c)(3).
2   E.g., *The Nationalist Movement v. Commissioner,* 37 F.3d 216 (5th Cir. 1994).
3   Tech. Adv. Mem. 9711003.
4   In general, see Hopkins, *The Law of Tax-Exempt Organizations,* 7th ed. (New York: John Wiley & Sons, 1998).
5   IRC §§ 501(c)(2) (last sentence, 501(c)(25)(G).
6   Reg. § 1.513-1(b).
7   IRC § 513(c).
8   *American Academy of Family Physicians v. United States,* 91 F.3d 1155 (8th Cir. 1996).
9   IRC § 513(c).
10 *Commissioner v. Groetzinger,* 480 U.S. 23 (1987).
11 E.g., *National Water Well Association, Inc. v. Commissioner,* 92 T.C. 75 (1989); *West Virginia State Medical Association v. Commissioner,* 91 T.C. 651 (1988), *aff'd,* 882 F.2d 123 (4th Cir. 1989).
12 Reg. § 1.513-1(b).
13 E.g., *Clarence LaBelle Post No. 217 v. United States,* 580 F.2d 270 (8th Cir. 1978).
14 E.g., *Carolinas Farm & Power Equipment Dealers Ass'n, Inc. v. United States,* 699 F.2d 167 (4th Cir. 1983).
15 Cf. *Consumer Credit Counseling Service of Alabama, Inc. v. United States,* 78 U.S.T.C. ¶ 9660 (D.D.C. 1978).
16 *Living Faith, Inc. v. Commissioner,* 950 F.2d 365 (7th Cir. 1991).
17 IRC § 501(m).
18 E.g., *Florida Hospital Trust Fund et al. v. Commissioner,* 103 T.C. 140 (1994), *aff'd,* 71 F.3d 808 (11th Cir. 1996); *Paratransit Insurance Corporation v. Commissioner,* 102 T.C. 745 (1994); *Nonprofits' Insurance Alliance of California v. United States,* 94-2 U.S.T.C. ¶ 50,593 (U.S. Ct. Fed. Cl. 1994). See, however, IRC § 501(n).
19 Reg. § 1.513-1(c)(1).
20 Reg. § 1.513-1(c).
21 Rev. Rul. 60-228, 1960-1 C.B. 200.
22 Reg. § 1.513-1(c)(2).
23 Reg. § 1.513-1(c)(2)(i).
24 E.g., Tech. Adv. Mem. 9147007; Priv. Ltr. Rul. 9137002.
25 E.g., Gen. Coun. Mem. 39860.
26 *National Collegiate Athletic Association v. Commissioner,* 914 F.2d 1417 (10th Cir. 1990).
27 IRS Action on Decision 1991-015.
28 IRC § 513(a); Reg. § 1.513-1(a).
29 Reg. § 1.513-1(d)(1)(2).
30 Rev. Rul. 78-51, 1978-1 C.B. 165.
31 *San Antonio Bar Association v. United States,* 80-2 U.S.T.C. ¶ 9594 (W.D. Tex. 1980).
32 *Texas Apartment Association v. United States,* 869 F.2d 884 (5th Cir. 1989).
33 Rev. Rul. 78-52, 1978-1 C.B. 166.
34 Rev. Rul. 66-338, 1966-2 C.B. 226.

35   Rev. Rul. 61-170, 1961-2 C.B. 112.

36   Priv. Ltr. Rul. 8503103.

37   *Id.*

38   E.g., *National League of Postmasters v. Commissioner*, 69 T.C.M. 2569 (1955), *aff'd*, 86 F.3d 59 (4th Cir. 1996).

39   E.g., *Oklahoma Cattlemen's Association, Inc. v. United States*, 310 F. Supp. 320 (W.D. Okla. 1969).

40   E.g., *Louisiana Credit Union League v. United States*, 501 F. Supp. 934 (E.D. La. 1980, *aff'd*, 693 F.2d 525 (5th Cir. 1982)).

41   Priv. Ltr. Rul. 7902006.

42   Priv. Ltr. Rul. 9023081

43   Reg. § 1.513-1(d)(3).

44   Rev. Rul. 73-386, 1973-2 C.B. 191, 192.

45   Rev. Rul. 76-94, 1976-1 C.B. 171.

46   Reg. § 1.513-1(d)(4)(ii).

47   E.g., Rev. Rul. 78-98, 1978-1 C.B. 167.

48   Reg. § 1.513-1(d)(ii).

49   IRS Priv. Ltr. Rul. 9320042.

50   Reg. § 1.513-1(d)(4)(iii).

51   Reg. § 1.513-1(d)(4)(iv).

52   IRC § 513(b).

53   IRC § 512(b)(7), (8), and (9).

54   IRC § 512(a)(5).

55   IRC § 513(a)(1).

56   *Executive Network Club v. Commissioner*, 69 T.C.M. 1680 (1995).

57   IRC § 513(a)(2).

58   IRC § 513(a)(3).

59   Rev. Rul. 710581, 1971-2 C.B. 236.

60   IRC § 513(a)(2).

61   IRC § 513(d)(2).

62   IRC § 513(d)(3).

63   IRC § 513(e).

64   IRC § 513(f).

65   IRC § 531(g).

66   IRC § 513(h)(1)(A).

67   IRC § 513(h)(1)(B).

68   IRC § 512(b)(1)-(3), (5).

69   Reg. § 1.513-1(b).

70   Reg. § 1.513-1(b)-1(c)(5).

71   E.g., *Harlan E. Moore Charitable Trust v. United States*, 9 F.3d 623 (7th Cir. 1993).

72   E.g., *Disabled American Veterans v. Commissioner*, 94 T.C. 60 (1990), *rev'd on other grounds*, 942 F.2d 309 (6th Cir. 1991).

73   *Sierra Club, Inc. v. Commissioner*, 65 T.C.M. 2582 (1993), *aff'd*, 86 F.3d 1526 (9th Cir. 1996).

74   *Sierra Club, Inc. v. Commissioner*, 103 T.C. 307 (1994), *rev'd and rem'd*, 86 F.3d 1526 (9th Cir. 1996), 77 T.C.M. 1569 (1999).

75   *Common Cause v. Commissioner*, 112 T.C. 332 (1999); *Planned Parenthood Federation of America, Inc. v. Commissioner*, 77 T.C.M. 2227 (1999); *Oregon*

State University Alumni Association, Inc. v. Commissioner and *Alumni Association of University of Oregon, Inc. v. Commissioner,* 193 F.3d 1098 (9th Cir. 1999), *aff'g* 71 T.C.M. 1935 (1996) and 71 T.C.M. 2093 (1996); *Mississippi State University Alumni, Inc. v. Commissioner,* 74 T.C.M. 458 (1999).

76 Memorandum from Jay H. Rotz, IRS Exempt Organizations Division, National Office, dated December 16, 1999.

77 This approach was tacitly endorsed in *Texas Farm Bureau v. United States,* 53 F.3d 120 (5th Cir. 1995).

78 IRC § 512(b)(13).

79 IRC § 368(c).

80 Reg. § 1.512(b)-1(1)(4).

81 IRC § 514.

82 IRC § 514(b)(4).

83 IRC § 512(b)(13)(C).

84 IRC § 4943(c)(3)(B).

85 IRC § 513(c); Reg. § 53.4943-10(a)(1).

86 *Id.*

87 IRC § 4943(d)(3)(B); Reg. § 53.4943-10(c)(1).

88 Reg. § 53.4943-10(c)(2).

89 Reg. § 54.4943-10(a)(2).

90 *Id.*

91 Reg. § 53.4943-10(c)(2).

92 Reg. § 53.4943-10(c)(1).

93 Reg. § 53.4943-10(c)(2).

94 IRC § 514(b)(1).

95 IRC § 514(c)(1).

96 IRC § 514(c)(2)(A).

97 IRC § 514(c)(2)(B).

98 *Id.*

99 Reg. § 1.514(b)-1(a).

100 IRC § 514(c)(4).

101 IRC § 514(c)(5).

102 IRC § 514(b)(1)(A).

103 IRC § 514(b)(1)(C).

104 IRC § 514(b)(1)(D).

105 *Id.*

106 IRC § 514(b)(1)(D).

107 IRC § 514(b)(1)(B).

108 *Henry E. & Nancy Horton Bartels Trust for the Benefit of the University of New Haven v. United States,* 209 F.3d 147 (2d Cir. 2000).

109 IRC § 514(a).

110 IRC § 11.

111 IRC § 1.

112 IRC § 512(b)(12).

113 IRC § 511(a)(1), (b)(1).

114 IRC § 512(a)(1).

115 IRC § 512(a)(1); Reg. § 1.512(1)-1(a).

116 *Rensselaer Polytechnic Institute v. Commissioner,* 732 F.2d 1058 (2d Cir. 1984), *aff'g,* 79 T.C. 967 (1982).

117 IRC § 512(b)(10), (11).
118 IRC § 6154(h); Form 990-W.
119 Tech. Adv. Mem. 200021056.

CHAPTER 10

1 IRC § 6652(c)(1)(A) as amended by the Taxpayer Bill of Rights 2, § 1314.
2 Expense provisions of IRC §§ 162 and 212.
3 In accordance with IRC § 446(a).
4 IRS Notice 96-30, 1996-1 C.B. 378.

CHAPTER 11

1 IRC § 6113.
2 IRC § 6711(a).
3 IRS Notice 88-120, 1988-2 C.B. 454.
4 IRC § 6711(b).
5 IRC § 170(f)(8)(A).
6 IRC § 170(f)(8)(B); Reg. § 1.170A-13(f)(2).
7 IRC § 170(f)(8)(B).
8 IRC § 6701.
9 Reg. § 1.170A-13(f)(11)(ii).
10 IRC § 170(f)(8)(C).
11 Reg. § 1.170A-13(f)(5).
12 Reg. § 1.170A-13(f)(6).
13 Reg. § 1.170A-13(f)(7).
14 Reg. § 1.170A-13(f)(13).
15 IRC § 170(f)(8)(A).
16 48 *Kiplinger's Personal Finance Magazine* (No. 4, 140 (May 1994).
17 IRC § 6115(b).
18 IRC § 6115(a).
19 Reg. § 1.6115-1(a)(1).
20 Reg. § 1.170A-13(f)(8)(i)(A).
21 *Id.*
22 IRC § 513(h)(2).
23 IRC § 6115(b).
24 Reg. § 1.170A-13(f)(8)(i)(B)(1).
25 Reg. § 1.170A-13(f)(8)(i)(B)(2).
26 Reg. § 1.6115-1(a)(3), Example 3.
27 IRC § 6714.
28 Old (repealed) IRC § 6104(d).
29 IRC § 6104(d).
30 IRC § 6104(d)(1)(B).
31 REG-246250-96.
32 T.D. 8818.
33 REG-121946-98.
34 T.D. 8861.
35 Reg. § 301.6104(d)-3(b).
36 Reg. § 301.6104(d)-3(b)(3)(i).

37   IRC § 6104(d)(3)(A).
38   Reg. § 301.6104(d)-3(d).
39   Reg. § 301.6104(d)-1(g).
40   IRC §§ 6652(c)(1)(C), 6652(c)(1)(D), and 6685.
41   Reg. § 301.6104(d)-2.
42   Reg. § 301.6104(d)-2(b).
43   Reg. § 301.6104(d)-3.
44   Reg. § 301.6104(d)-3(b).
45   Reg. § 301.6104(d)-3(c).
46   Reg. § 301.6104(d)-3(d).
47   *Schuloff v. Queens College Foundation,* 165 F.3d 183 (2d Cir. 1999).
48   Reg. § 301.6104(d)-3(e).

CHAPTER 12

1   IRC § 508(b).
2   IRC § 509(a)(1).
3   IRC §§ 170(b)(1)(A)(vi), 509(a)(1); Reg. § 1.170A-9(e)(1)(ii).
4   Reg. § 1.170A-9(e)(2).
5   Reg. § 1.170A-9(e)(1)(ii).
6   Reg. § 1.170A-9(e)(7)(ii).
7   Reg. § 1.170A-9(e)(4).
8   Reg. § 1.170A-9(e)(6)(v).
9   Reg. § 1.170A-9(e)(6)(i).
10   *Id.*
11   Reg. § 1.170A-9(e)(10)-(14).
12   Reg. § 1.170A-9(e)(3).
13   Reg. § 1.170A-9(e)(7)(i)(a).
14   Reg. § 1.170A-9(e)(8).
15   Reg. § 1.170A-9(e)(7)(iii).
16   Reg. § 1.170A-9(e)(6)(ii).
17   Reg. § 1.509(a)-3(c)(4).
18   IRC § 509(a)(2); Reg. § 1.509(a)-3.
19   IRC § 509(d).
20   Reg. § 1.509(a)-3(c)(3).
21   IRC § 509(a)(2)(A)(ii); Reg. § 1.509(a)-3(a)(3).
22   IRC § 509(a)(2)(A)(ii).
23   *Id.*
24   IRC § 509(a)(2)(B).
25   Reg. § 1.509(a)-5.
26   Form 1023, instructions as to line 1.
27   IRC § 508(b).
28   Form 1023, instructions as to line 11.
29   *State Department of Assessments and Taxation v. North Baltimore Center, Inc.,* 743 A.2d 759 (Md. Ct. of Spec. App. (2000)).
30   Reg. § 1.642(c)(5)-5(a)(5)(iv).
31   IRC § 508(b).
32   IRC § 508(e)(1).
33   IRC § 508(a)(3); Reg. § 1.509(a)-4.

34   Reg. § 1.509(a)-4(c).
35   Reg. § 1.509(a)-4(e).
36   Reg. § 1.509(a)-4(f)(2).
37   Reg. § 1.509(a)-4(g).
38   Reg. § 1.509(a)-4(h).
39   Reg. § 1.509(a)-4(i).
40   Reg. § 1.509(a)-4(i)(2).
41   Reg. § 1.509(a)-4(i)(3).
42   Reg. § 1.509(a)-4(1)(3)(iii); Rev. Rul. 76-208, 1976-1 C.B. 161.
43   Reg. § 1.509(a)-4(e)(2).
44   E.g., Priv. Ltr. Rul. 8825116.
45   There are tens of IRS private letter rulings on this point. The practice has become so common that Congress once considered creation of a separate category of public charity status just for them—a new IRC § 509(a)(4).
46   Priv. Ltr. Rul. 9442025.
47   Priv. Ltr. Rul. 9438013.
48   Tech. Adv. Mem. 9847002.
49   Reg. § 1.509(a)-4(e)(2).
50   Reg. § 1.509(a)-4(d).
51   *William F., Mable E., and Margaret K. Quarrie Charitable Fund v. Commissioner,* 70 T.C. 182, 187 (1978), *aff'd,* 603 F.2d 1274 (7th Cir. 1979).
52   Reg. § 1.509(a)-4(e)(1).
53   IRC § 509(a)(3)(A).
54   Reg. § 1.509(a)-4(e)(1).
55   That is, an entity described in IRC § 501(c)(4).
56   That is, an entity described in IRC § 501(c)(5).
57   That is, an entity described in IRC § 501 (c)(6).
58   IRC § 509(a), last sentence; Reg. § 1.509(a)-4(k).
59   IRC § 509(a)(3)(C); Reg. § 1.509(a)-4(j).
60   Rev. Rul. 80-207, 1980-2 C.B. 193.
61   Rev. Rul. 80-305, 1980-2 C.B. 71.
62   Reg. § 1.509(a)-4(j)(1).
63   See, e.g., Hopkins, *Starting and Managing a Nonprofit Organization: A Legal Guide,* 3rd ed. (New York: John Wiley & Sons, 2000), Chapter 19.

CHAPTER 13

1   IRC § 507(a).
2   Reg. § 1.507(a)(8).
3   IRC § 507(b)(1)(B); Reg. § 1.507-2(b) and (d).
4   IRC § 507(a)(2).
5   Reg. § 1.507-3.
6   Begin with Priv. Ltr. Ruls. 9033054 and 9033044 and go forward to find countless examples.
7   Priv. Ltr. Rul. 9121036; also see Priv. Ltr. Ruls. 9814047 and 9805020.
8   Priv. Ltr. Rul. 9342057.
9   Priv. Ltr. Rul. 9052025.
10   Priv. Ltr. Rul. 9101020.
11   Priv. Ltr. Rul. 9103035.

12   Priv. Ltr. Rul. 9204016.
13   Priv. Ltr. Rul. 9132052.
14   Priv. Ltr. Rul. 9115057.
15   Reg. § 1.507-1(b)(6) and (7).
16   Priv. Ltr. Rul. 8619047.
17   Reg. § 1.507-3(a)(8)(ii)(b); Rev. Rul. 78-387, 1987-2 C.B. 270.
18   Reg. § 1.507-3(a)(8)(ii)(a).
19   Reg. § 1.507-3(a)(6).
20   Fiscal Year 1999 CPE Text for Exempt Organizations and Priv. Ltr. Rul. 9802037.
21   Reg. § 1.507-3(a)(9)(iii), Example 1.
22   Reg. § 1.507-3(a)(9)(iii), Example 2.
23   IRC § 507(a).
24   IRC § 507(g)(3); Reg. § 1.508-9(a)(2).
25   IRC § 6104(c).
26   Reg. § 1.507-1(c)(1).
27   Reg. § 1.507-1(b)(3).

CHAPTER 14

1   Reg. § 53.4942(b)-2(a)(4).
2   Priv. Ltr. Rul. 9509042.
3   Reg. § 53.4942(b)-1(b).
4   Reg. § 53.4942(b)-1(a)(1)(i).
5   Reg. § 53.4942(b)-1(a)(2)(i).
6   See also *The Elizabeth D. Leckie Scholarship Fund v. Commissioner,* 87 T.C. 251 (1987).
7   IRC § 170(e)(5).
8   Reg. § 53.4942(b)-3(a).
9   IRC § 4940(d)(1).
10   IRC §§ 4942(h) and 170(b)(1)(E); Reg. § 1.170A-9(g)(1).
11   Reg. § 53.4942(a)-3(c)(2)(iv).

CHAPTER 15

1   This tax exemption is available under IRC § 501(a) as an organization described in IRC § 501(c)(3).
2   IRC § 170(c)(2).
3   In general, see Hopkins, *The Law of Fund-Raising,* 3rd ed. (New York: John Wiley & Sons, 2001).
4   In general, see Hopkins, *Starting & Managing a Nonprofit Organization: A Legal Guide,* 3rd ed.(New York: John Wiley & Sons, 2000).
5   In general, see Hopkins, *The Second Legal Answer Book for Fund-Raisers* (New York: John Wiley & Sons, 2000), Chapters 8 and 9.
6   IRC § 4958.
7   It is possible that some investment income of public charities is subject to the tax on unrelated business income, such as where the revenue involved is derived from a controlled organization or is unrelated debt-financed income (Chapter 9).
8   IRC § 4947(a)(2).

9 Reg. § 1.170A-9(e)(10).

10 IRC § 170(b)(1)(A)(vii).

11 Reg. §§ 1.170A-9(e)(11)(B), 1.507-2(a)(8)(iii)(B).

12 Cf. Reg. § 1.507-2(a)(8)(iv)(A)(1).

13 Tech. Adv. Mem. 8836033.

14 E.g., Priv. Ltr. Rul. 9807030.

15 Reg. § 1.507-2(a)(8)(iii).

16 *Supra* note 13.

17 Also Priv. Ltr. Rul. 9807030.

18 *National Foundation, Inc. v. United States,* 87-2 U.S.T.C. ¶ 9602 (Ct. Cl. 1987).

19 *The Fund for Anonymous Gifts v. Internal Revenue Service,* 97-2 U.S.T.C. ¶ 50,710 (D.D.C. 1997).

20 *The Fund for Anonymous Gifts v. Internal Revenue Service,* 99-1 U.S.T.C. ¶ 50,440 (D.C. Cir. 1999).

21 IRS Exempt Organizations Continuing Professional Education Text for Fiscal Year 2000, Technical Topic P 2 B (2).

22 E.g., *New Dynamics Foundation v. United States,* No. 90-197T (U.S. Ct. Fed. Cl.).

23 Reg. § 1.170A-1(c)(5).

24 *Commissioner v. Duberstein,* 363 U.S. 278, 285 (1960), quoting from *Commissioner v. LoBue,* 351 U.S. 243, 246 (1956).

25 Reg. § 25.2511-2(b).

26 *United States v. American Bar Endowment,* 477 U.S. 105, 116-117 (1986).

27 *Hernandez v. Commissioner,* 490 U.S. 680, 692 (1989).

28 E.g., Rev. Rul. 81-307, 1981-2 C.B. 78.

29 *Darling v. Commissioner,* 43 T.C. 520 (1965).

30 Rev. Rul. 77-225, 1977-2 C.B. 73.

31 *Lawrence v. United States,* 75-1 U.S.T.C. ¶ 9165 (C.D. Cal. 1974).

32 IRC § 507(b)(1)(A).

33 Reg. § 1.507-2(a)(8)(i).

34 *Id.*

35 A donor-advised fund established within a community trust must be administered in or as a component part of the trust (Reg. § 1.170A-9(e)(1)).

36 Reg. § 1.507-2(a)(8)(iii).

37 Reg. § 1.507-2(a)(8)(iv).

38 Reg. § 1.507-2(a)(8)(iv)(A)(1).

39 *Id.*

40 Reg. § 1.507-2(a)(8)(iv)(A)(2).

41 Reg. § 1.507-2(a)(8)(iv)(A)(3).

42 Reg. § 1.507-2(a)(8)(iv)(F).

43 *Id.*

44 Reg. § 1.507-2(a)(8)(iv)(B)-(E), (G).

45 Reg. § 1.507-2(a)(8)(i).

46 *Id.*

47 *Id.*

48 Reg. § 1.507-2(a)(8)(ii).

49 *Id.*

50 Priv. Ltr. Rul. 9014004.

51 Gen. Coun. Mem. 39748.

52 Gen. Coun. Mem. 39875.
53 Exempt Organizations Continuing Professional Education Technical Instruction Program Textbook for Fiscal Year 1995.
54 IRC § 509(d).
55 Priv. Ltr. Rul. 2000370053.

CHAPTER 16

1 See Hopkins, *The Law of Tax-Exempt Organizations,* 7th ed. (New York: John Wiley & Sons, 1998), Appendix C.
2 IRC § 508(a).
3 That is, organizations described in IRC § 501(c)(4).
4 That is, organizations described in IRC § 501(c)(5).
5 That is, organizations described in IRC § 501(c)(6).
6 That is, organizations described in IRC § 501(c)(7).
7 That is, organizations described in IRC § 501(c)(19).
8 IRC § 508(c)(1)(B).
9 That is, an organization described in IRC § 501(c)(3).
10 Reg. § 1.501(c)(3)-1(b).
11 Reg. § 1.508-3(a)-(c).
12 Reg. § 1.508-3(d).
13 Reg. § 1.509(a)-4(c).
14 Reg. § 1.501(c)(3)-1(c).
15 Reg. § 1.509(a)-4(e).
16 Reg. § 601.201(a)(3).
17 Reg. § 601.201(a)(2).
18 Reg. § 1.508-1(a)(2)(i).
19 That is, an organization described in IRC § 501(c)(4).
20 Rev. Proc. 92-85, 1992-2 C.B. 490.
21 Form 1023, Part II, question 1.
22 *Pius XII Academy, Inc. v. Commissioner,* 43 T.C.M. 634, 636 (1982).
23 *Id.*
24 *Public Industries, Inc. v. Commissioner,* 61 T.C.M. 1626, 1629 (1991).
25 *National Association of American Churches v. Commissioner,* 82 T.C. 18, 32 (1984).
26 *The Nationalist Foundation v. Commissioner,* 80 T.C.M. 507 (2001).
27 *The Church of the Visible Intelligence That Governs the Universe v. United States,* 1983-2 U.S.T.C. ¶ 9726 (Ct. Cl. 1983).
28 *American Science Foundation v.Commissioner,* 52 T.C.M. 1049, 1051 (1986).
29 Rev. Proc. 90-27, 1990-1 C.B. 514.
30 Reg. § 601.201(n)(2)(ii).
31 Rev. Proc. 90-27, *supra* note 29 § 6.03.
32 Reg. § 601.201(n)(1)(iv).

CHAPTER 17

1 IRC § 170(a).
2 IRC § 2522(a), (b).

3   IRC § 2055(a). In general, see Hopkins, *The Tax Law of Charitable Giving*, 2nd ed. (New York: John Wiley & Sons, 2000).

4   IRC § 501(c)(3).

5   *Id.*

6   IRC § 170(c).

7   These are organizations described in IRC § 501(c)(6).

8   These are organizations described in IRC § 501(c)(4).

9   IRC § 62.

10 IRC § 170(b)(1)(F).

11 IRC § 68.

12 IRC § 170(b)(1)(B).

13 *Id.*

14 IRC § 170(b)(1)(A).

15 IRC § 170(d)(1).

16 IRC § 170(b)(1)(A), (B)(ii).

17 Reg. § 1.170A-8(a)(1).

18 IRC § 170(b)(1)(D)(i).

19 IRC § 170(b)(1)(D)(ii).

20 IRC § 170(e)(1)(B)(ii).

21 IRC § 170(3)(5)(B), (C).

22 IRC § 170(e)(5)(A).

23 IRC § 170(b)(1)(C)(i).

24 IRC § 170(b)(1)(C)(ii).

25 E.g., *Greene v. United States,* 13 F.3d 577, 584 (2d Cir. 1994); *Sheppard v. United States,* 361 F.2d 972, 977-978 (Ct. Cl. 1966).

26 IRC § 170(b)(1)(C)(iv).

27 IRC §§ 1221, 1222(3)

28 IRC § 170(e)(1)(A).

29 IRC § 179(b)(1)(C)(iii); Reg. § 1.170A-8(d)(2).

30 Reg. § 1.170A-8(d)(2)(i)(a).

31 *Woodbury v. Commissioner,* 900 F.2d 1457 (10th Cir. 1990).

32 Reg. § 1.170A-1(b).

33 Rev. Rul. 78-38, 1978-1 C.B. 67.

34 E.g., *Ferguson v. Commissioner,* 99-1 U.S.T.C. ¶ 50,412 (9th Cir. 1999), *aff'g* 108 T.C. 244 (1997).

35 E.g., *Dyer v. Commissioner,* 58 T.C.M. 1321 (1990).

36 IRC § 301 *et seq.*; IRC § 1361(a)(2).

37 IRC § 1361(a)(1).

38 IRC §§ 1363, 1366.

39 IRC § 170(b)(2).

40 IRC § 170(d)(2).

41 IRC § 170(e)(3).

42 IRC § 170(e)(4).

43 IRC § 170(e)(6).

44 IRC § 170(e)(6)(F).

45 IRC § 703(a)(2)(C).

46 IRC § 702(a)(4); Reg. §§ 1.702-1(a)(4), 1.703-1(a)(2)(iv).

47 Reg. § 1.170A-1(h)(7).

48 Rev. Rul. 96-11, 1996-1 C.B. 140.

49 IRC § 705(a)(1).
50 IRC § 705(a)(2).
51 IRC § 705(a)(1)(B), (a)(2)(B).
52 IRC § 705(a)(1)(B).
53 IRC § 705(a)(2)(B).
54 That is, a limited liability company is classified as a partnership for federal income tax purposes; it is a pass-through entity, with its income and losses taxed at the membership level.
55 IRC § 170(a)(2).
56 Reg. § 1.170A-11(b)(2).
57 Priv. Ltr. Rul. 7802001.
58 IRC § 170(e)(1)(B)(i).
59 E.g., *Losch v. Commissioner,* 55 T.C.M. 909 (1988).
60 *Orth v. Commissioner,* 813 F.2d 837, 843 (7th Cir. 1987).
61 IRC § 2503(g).
62 IRC § 170(h).
63 *Satullo v. Commissioner,* 66 T.C.M. 1697 (1994).
64 IRC § 1221(3).
65 IRC § 401(a)(9)(c).
66 IRC § 72(f).
67 Reg. § 1.170A-1(g).
68 *Grant v. Commissioner,* 84 T.C. 809 (1985), *aff'd,* 800 F.2d 260 (4th Cir. 1986).
69 IRC §§ 170(e)(1)(A), 1221(3).
70 Reg. § 1.170A-1(g).
71 IRC § 170(j).
72 Reg. § 1.170A-7(a)(1).
73 *Logan v. Commissioner,* 68 T.C.M. 658 (1994).
74 Rev. Rul. 89-51, 1989-1 C.B. 89.
75 *Id.* See IRC § 208A(d)(C).
76 An IRC § 501(c)(6) organization.
77 Reg. § 1.170A-4(c)(2)(ii).
78 E.g., *Stark v. Commissioner,* 86 T.C. 243 (1986).
79 IRC § 1011(b); Reg. § 1.1011-2(a)(1).
80 IRC § 170(f)(3)(A).
81 IRC § 170(f)(2)(D).
82 IRC § 664.
83 IRC §§ 671-679.
84 IRC § 664(c).
85 IRC § 664(d)(1).
86 IRC § 664(g)(4).
87 IRC § 4975(e)(7).
88 IRC § 664(g)(1).
89 IRC § 664(d)(2).
90 Reg. § 1.664-3(a)(1)(i)(a).
91 IRC § 664(d)(3)(A).
92 Reg. § 1.664-3(a)(1)(i)(b)(1).
93 IRC § 664(d)(3)(B).
94 Reg. § 1.664-3(a)(1)(i)(b)(2).
95 Reg. § 1.664-3(a)(1)(i)(c).

96   Reg. § 1.664-3(a)(1)(i)(c)(1).
97   Reg. § 1.664-3(a)(1)(i)(d).
98   Reg. § 1.664-3(a)(1)(i)(c)(2).
99   Reg. § 1.664-1(a)(7)(ii).
100   IRC § 642(c)(5).
101   IRC § 642(c)(5)(A).
102   IRC § 170(f)(2)(B).
103   Reg. §§ 1.170A-6(c)(2)(i)(A), (ii)(A); 20.2055-2(e)(2)(vi)(a), (vii)(a); 25.2522(c)-3(c)(2)(vi)(a), (vii)(a).
104   For details, see Hopkins, *The Second Legal Answer Book for Fund-Raisers* (New York: John Wiley & Sons, 2000), Chapter 9.
105   IRC § 514(c)(5).
106   IRC § 501(m)(5).
107   IRC § 170(f)(3)(B)(i).
108   IRC § 170(f)(3)(B)(iii).
109   IRC § 170(f)(3)(B)(ii).
110   IRC § 2033.
111   IRC § 501(c)(3).
112   IRC § 2055(a).
113   IRC § 2055(e)(4).
114   IRC § 2522.
115   IRC § 501(c)(3).
116   Reg. § 25.2511-1(c).
117   Reg. § 25.2522(c)-3(b)(1).

Index

INDEX

INDEX

2X

Made in the USA
Lexington, KY
24 August 2010